Quarry

FICTION • POETRY • ESSAYS

HELWIG • METCALF • SHIELDS

A stripe of tiger, curled
And sleeping on the ribs of reason
Prints as clear
As Eve and Adam, pearled
With sweat, staring at an apple core

— Anne Wilkinson (1910–1961)

Quarry Magazine

VOLUME 41 NUMBER 1 WINTER 1992

GENERAL ISSUE

Editor	Steven Heighton
Managing Editor	Melanie Dugan
Book Review Editor	Carolyn Bond

Associate Editors

Tim Andison	Sharon Hunt
Allan Brown	Tara Kainer
Carlene Bryant	Joanne Page
Eric Folsom	Lorinda Peterson
Cheryl Sutherland	A. Colin Wright

ISSN 0033–5266 ISBN 1–55082–032–X

This issue of *Quarry Magazine* was published with the financial assistance of The Canada Council and the Ontario Arts Council. *Quarry* is listed in the Canadian Periodical Index, Canadian Literature Index, Canadian Magazine Index, Canadian Business and Current Affairs Database, American Humanities Index, and Index of American Periodical Verse. Back issues are available in the original from the editor and in microform from Micromedia Limited, 20 Victoria Street, Toronto, Ontario M5C 2N8.

Manuscript submissions and subscription requests should be mailed to:

Quarry Magazine
P.O. Box 1061
Kingston, Ontario
K7L 4Y5

Manuscripts must include a SASE with Canadian postage or International Reply Coupons. Subscription rates are $20.33 for 1 year (4 issues) or $36.38 for 2 years (8 issues), GST included.

Distributed by the Canadian Magazine Publishers Association, 2 Stewart Street, Toronto, Ontario M5V 1H6.

Cover art: Judith J. Leidl, "Dog", reproduced by permission of the artist.
Typesetting by Susan Hannah, Quarry Press.
Published by Quarry Press, Inc., P.O. Box 1061, Kingston, Ontario K7L 4Y5.

Publications Mail Registration Number 7293. Issued March 1992.

Contents

POETRY

INTERVIEW

ESSAY

Anna Akhmatova

REQUIEM 1935-1940

No, I was not sheltered by foreign powers.
I was with my own sad people then.
The skies that spread over me were ours.
I have always been where my people have been.

In the terrible years of the Yezhov purges, I spent seventeen months lining up in front of a prison in Leningrad. Once someone recognized me. Then a woman with blue lips, standing behind me, who had, of course, never known who I was, came awake from the stupor that held us all and asked in a whisper (everyone spoke in a whisper there);

"Can you write about this?"

And I said, "Yes."

Then something like a smile touched what had once been her face.

A NEW TRANSLATION FROM THE RUSSIAN
by David Helwig

The mountains bow themselves before this sorrow.
No movement in the great river.
Bolts and bars: the prisons are very thorough.
Inside, prisoners burrowed inside their narrow
cells. And a deathly shiver.
For someone, somewhere, there's a cooling breeze,
sunset luxuriant and sweet.
We know of no such thing. For us there is
only the hateful grinding of the keys,
the tread of soldiers' feet.
We woke as if for early mass and walked
through streets of city wilderness.
We met those who were deader than the dead.
The sun grew small, the Neva thickly fogged,
and yet — more hope than hopelessness.
A verdict . . . and then tears, a sudden flood.
Now she's cut off. She's on her own.
As if the others had knocked her to one side.
As if they'd drained her sore heart of blood.
She walks a step . . . staggers one . . . alone.
The unchosen friends from those two years possessed,
where have they got to now, where are they all?
What do they see behind the blowing snow?
What do they dream they see in the moondog's glow?
I sent them this as a farewell.

PROLOGUE

That was when only the peaceful dead
were seen to smile. And that was when dim
Leningrad hung there beside
its prisons like a useless limb.
That was when, senseless from pain,
the regiments of convicts came
and went, and when train whistles sang
goodbye — and that was the only song.
Over us stood deathly stars
as Russia, a guiltless victim, writhed
under the boots, and writhed in blood
under the Black Marias' tires.

1

They came to take you away at dawn.
I followed as if at a funeral.
Children cried in a darkened room.
On your lips an icon's chill.
Remember the mortal sweat on your brow,
the holy candle dripping, guttering.
I am like the Streltsy wives now —
at the Kremlin towers, wailing, muttering.

2

It flows so quietly, the quiet Don.
A yellow moon enters the room,

cap on one side, comes in the window,
the yellow moon, and sees a shadow.

It is a woman whose health is gone.
It is a woman who is alone.

Husband dead and son away
in prison. Pray for me when you pray.

9

3

No, not me, but someone else in pain.
I could not, could not — not what happened.
Cover it in hangings of smooth black.
Take away the lanterns...
    Night!

4

You should have been told how it would end,
the aftermath of wit and laughter
and easy affection of all your friends,
Tsarskoe Selo's naughtiest daughter.
How you would celebrate the new year,
parcel in hand, the three hundredth person
in line, melting ice with your tears
under the crosses on the prison.
Watch the jailhouse poplar bending.
There isn't a single sound — inside
how many innocent lives are ending...

5

Seventeen months, and still I cry
your name. Your name's the one
I call to the hangman from my knees.
My terror, my son.
All confusion, now and ever.
Animal or person?
That's a difference I can't decipher.
And when's the execution?

Dust on a flower,
the sound of a censer,
meaningless tracks.
Star-bright enormity
shines in my eyes, I see
death in its looks.

6

The weightless weeks in flight.
I won't really have known
how it was — you in prison, my son,
watched by the white nights.

And once again, watching, spying,
with a hawk's burning eye,
they are talking about your high
cross, and death, and dying.

7

SENTENCE

And the stone word crushed
my still living breast.
I was ready. Never mind.
I'll manage. I'll go on.

I have a lot to do today.
I have to murder memory.
I have to turn my soul to stone.
I have to learn to live again —

or else ... A rustle of fire,
of summer, outside my door.
I had long foreseen it, this
bright day, deserted house.

8

TO DEATH

Sooner or later you'll come. Why not now?
I've opened up the door, put out the light.
Your coming's easy, magical, and so
it's very difficult for me to wait.
But come to me in any shape at all.
Come as a thief, a lead pipe in his fist.
Or poison gas out of a falling shell.
Or typhus drifting in a sickly mist.
Or come as that old tale, your favourite trick,
one so familiar it makes us sick —
I catch sight of the secret policeman's hat;
the pale house manager leads him to where I wait.
It's all the same to me now. The Yenisei flows
swirling across Siberia. The pole star shines.
And now the final horror hides from view
the blue-grey light of the beloved eyes.

9

Madness has spread its wing
and covered half my soul,
and gives me fiery wine,
and its black valleys call.

Now it's all come clear,
how I am the one vanquished.
Inside me all I hear
is someone else's gibberish.

And what am I to take
with me? Nothing. Nothing.
(No matter how I pray
and in spite of all my pleading.)

Not the terrible eyes of my son,
gone stone-hard with suffering.
Nor the day the terror came.
Nor the hour of our prison meeting.

Not the coolness of his hands
not the linden's shadow trembling,
nor that tiny, far-off sound —
the words of a last consoling.

10

THE CRUCIFIXION

*"Do not weep for me, Mother,
when I am in the grave."*

I

Skies of fire, the heavens shaken.
Angel choirs praise the great day.
To his father, "Why hast thou forsaken?"
To his mother, "Do not weep for me . . ."

II

The Magdalen beat herself and cried.
John the beloved hard as rock.
But where the silent Mother stood,
no-one looked or dared to look.

EPILOGUE

1

I learned how faces fall apart.
Fear blinked from every eyelid,
cheeks deeply inscribed by the heart's
pain, in cuneiform, blank and rigid.
How ash-blonde locks of hair, or black,
turn to silver suddenly
and fright makes the dry laughter shake.
The smile subsides resignedly.
It's not just for myself I pray,
but for all those who were with me, all
who stood there freezing and in July's
heat, under that blind red wall.

2

The hour of remembrance once again draws near.
I feel you with me: I can see and hear

the one they had to drag up to the door,
and one who'll tramp her native earth no more,

another one who'd shake her lovely head —
"Coming here is like coming home," she said.

Call them all out by name: you know I would,
but they took away the list — it's gone for good.

But it's for these I've woven this wide shroud
out of the meagre words they spoke aloud.

Everywhere, always, I'll remember them,
will not forget, no matter what may come.
And if they silence my exhausted mouth,
from which a hundred million souls cry out —

my people — let them still remember me
upon the eve of my remembrance day.

And if the country sees a time when they
want to build a memorial to me,

I will agree, I will accept it, but
only on one condition. Let it not

stand by the seaside town where I was born —
my last link with that sea is long since gone —

nor by the sacred pine in the tasr's old
wood, where a shadow seeks me, unconsoled,

but right here, where I stood three hundred hours,
waited day after day at a bolted door.

Because I am afraid that blessed by death
I might forget — the street rumbling beneath

the Black Marias, how a cruel door closed
and an old woman became a wounded beast.

And slowly from my motionless bronze eyes,
let it run down like tears, the melting snow.

And may the pigeons coo by the distant stone
walls of the prison, as the ships sail on.

Paul Mutton

ADJECTIVES

the guest's absence no one thinking
the bloody corpse in the alley
wondering what god made this

the soporific of mortgages
no one to butcher the tyrants
with a gun and then a sword

then a knife and then
then my friend with a rock
nothing succumbing

to beauty as beauty is
a lonely room
the small price of freedom

Christopher McPherson

ICE FOG

The Storymonger is having the time of his life, sitting at a table for one, with his pouch full of words and his pen full of people, folding his hands together and eating his own flesh. He has his eye on the redhead in the corner, a true Celtic beauty with a heart of stone. He knows her by the cruel turn of her perfect shoulder, the swelling sensuality of her thighs. He can't *see* her thighs, under the table, but he knows they are there, heavy, strong, jouncing gently to the murky druid music in her head. He has to know these things; it's his job. Somebody has to do it.

The trouble is, she's not going to look at him with those green eyes as soft as warm butter. Robin Hood has just come in at the street door, dressed in a Lincoln green trenchcoat, carrying his bow and arrows in a plush lined Samsonite leather case. He is smirking about something. He has brought a little of the ice fog in with him; it cringes and turns to drizzle.

The redhead is nursing her white rum like a grudge. Her thighs are warm through, but it is raining into her drink. Robin picks her out of the crowd, strolls over and asks her if she can lend him a grand.

No, she says, but that's a cool raincoat.

It's a trenchcoat.

Sorry.

Want some pearls? He has a pocket full of them, pulls out a handful, silksmooth and perfect as her thighs, still salty from the tears of oysters.

Are they hot?

Well, maybe a little. I never learned to swim. Buy me a drink?

Here, have mine. It's full of drizzle.

He pulls up a chair and fondles her thighs; she hardens her heart and softens her eyes. She doesn't tell him she works days on the telephone, torturing the privacy of the public with her strident ring and her well-oiled words. He doesn't tell her he wears the trenchcoat because it is good for flashing elderly ladies on the subway.

She tells him she is a designer. He tells her he has had to give up

17

stealing from the rich and giving to the poor. No skin off the rich; they're all insured. As for the poor, they're a bunch of bloody ingrates. He's thinking about going into real estate.

He puts both his lips in the glass and snorfles at her diluted rum like a horse in a bucket of beer.

Later they will drift out into the night, and the ice fog will make halos around them. They will go to her place and he will shoot her microwave with a silver arrow, and eat granola in bed, and disappoint her. She won't be able to get rid of him; her heart will sink down into her gall bladder; her thighs will shrivel to sticks; in the end she will have to move out and live in her car, a Japanese hatchback. She will sell her fingernails on the street.

The Storymonger unfolds his hands; his bones are showing. There are no more people in his pen; they have leaked out in his shirt pocket. There are no more words in his pouch, only pregnant pauses. He goes home to his hungry room and paints pictures of pigs till dawn intrudes.

OUR COW

The day my lover brought home the cow, our lives changed.

A warm cow on a cold morning. Break open another bale to make her happy. Sweet memories of summer live within the strings. Lean your cheek against her flank and feel the unborn hoof kick you in the head.

We went from poverty to wealth in a single day, and were bound fast. Every luxury comes with chains. But no lifeless lump of margarine would pass our door again. No milk, skimmed to within an inch of its life, then spray-desiccated to a bag of latent pumps.

The gallon jars and plastic buckets gathered in our spring. Bright cream rising, yellow as buttercups, thick as custard. We ran our car on milk: a gallon of skimmed for Hiram and Brenda, a gallon of whole for Heather and Phillip, some butter for Marie. Paid the gas and then some.

We bought the mare to keep the cow happy. They both had daughters and soon the barn was full of female energy. Our garden grew rich on shit. We fenced the bush, tying the rails to trees with baling twine. Cassidy, the cat, would sit on Clover's back as I milked her. Rich stream of golden milk, thrubbing into the pail. We developed a good relationship with the artificial inseminator.

I place another carton of two percent in the shopping cart. The voices never shut up, but all I hear is the quiet mooing of mornings gone.

Olivia Byard

GIRLS ON THE GOWER 1955

The coarse ground leant us rough rest
until a blind calf stumbled into our crude tent
laying it flat with a single blow. We emerged;
citizens after war: soaked, bedraggled,
to watch breath rise from the herd
into a grey dawn like smoke from crowds
of coal-fired chimneys. In the low barn
animals warmed us. Shifting uneasily
at out attempts to milk them, cattle were ladies
dancing slowly to entice the reluctant sun.
Collies lounged in the doorway, laughing;
sardonic timekeepers of this gymnastic event,
their quick wits worked the cows like clockwork,
striking time, place, in each slow day
with tiny nudges, wide grins. Their ancestry
was doubtful, but they, supreme; confident
of an elite carved from ability, not pedigree.
Afternoon; donkeys struck across the sands
to Llanelli laden with cockles; women after:
bare feet prodding the beach with long sticks
and toes. Sweaters clung damply with grim affection
but little success; goose-pimples grew strong
and ambitious. We dreamed of body hair.
Farmers, like our forebears, for this one week,
we followed the blind calf and hungry puppies
doggedly down to the night's dry stabling.

Robert Hilles

SMALLNESS

My father is small.
My words are small as they
try to reach him as he sleeps.
Later, I watch his fingers play
in his pants pocket as he stands
across from me and smiles.
He only has two teeth left
the rest rotting and falling out.
He laughs when I say something silly
and I like that.
My life is small.
When I ask my father a question
he writes something down
and I turn away knowing how small
his writing will be.

Cities are small so are countries.
Planets are small so are gods.
Death is small the way it
opens inside of someone
like the smallest bloom
of the season.
My memory is small it contains
only the voices you have used
when you sing to me at night.
Each space we cross is small
and as you touch me I feel how
beautiful small is.

Nothing is large. Everything is small
even what a god prepares for us
when he has the time.
And when I think about that
I am happy because being small

is the most important thing there is.
Without that we would all wait
too long to escape.
So when I touch you or come
to you with a flower in my mouth
think of smallness.
Those who are always trying to be large
to hold in their hands something
big and powerful are fools
because all that they will find is that
that is the smallest thing of all.

APPLES

Apples fall to the ground
and the boy fills a sack with them
and drags it to where his father
stands smiling as if life
held only mysteries like this.
Someday the boy will be a soldier
and will die a great distance
from this apple tree.
The man will already be dead
and will never know how his son
falls. Each takes a bite from
a different apple and watches
the other chewing as if
the apples sweetness could be
seen in another's face.

The boy would rather be playing
with his friends or in his room,

but he likes to feel
the apple's flesh swell in his mouth.
When he is a soldier, he will think
about this day many times
remembering the shape of the apple
as it filled his hand.
Even when he hoists his gun
in the heat of battle and squeezes the
trigger he will imagine that he is
holding an apple.
But when he dies he will be thinking
of something different as the apple
in his throat swells until no more air
can get around it.

The boy took the sack of apples
into his mother who would can some
and make pies with others.
Later in the kitchen, the boy
watched his father wash his hands
and turn with his still damp
hands to his wife and kiss her neck.
The boy put one of his hands
in his mouth and it tasted of dirt
and apples. As he stood there sucking
his fingers, his throat began to lose its
dryness and his life continued around
him and he felt like an apple on a giant
tree waiting to ripen.
As his father passed him he carried
the empty sack back to the yard outside.
The father stood below the empty tree
asking himself something that the
boy would never hear.

Michael Penny

AMPERSAND (SUMMER) (#1)

Ampersand crouches in the hollow
that is the centre of a seed.

He counts the layers of cells
to the outside,

but himself knows
no way out,

until the seed shoulders aside soil
for shoot

& light & water,
&, for one moment,

it looks like it's joined sky
to earth by its ambition.

Ampersand watches the sun
extract leaves, then flowers,

(Ampersand pauses a step,
empetalled & langourous,)

then fruit,
& Ampersand finds

more seeds, soft & green,
which harden their skin

about the hollow
in which Ampersand now crouches,

waiting for shoot & leaf
& flower &

AMPERSAND (SPRING) (#1)

Ampersand was comfortable
in the middle of his sentence,

but sap learned winter
was about to edge into leaf

& single blades of grass,
joined not to earth or sky but root,

were unacceptably
outward-looking.

Ampersand, normally cosy
between the beginning & the end,

was scared of what might grow
from these extremities.

A part.
They might grow apart.

Ampersand was comfortable
& in the middle of his sentence,

determined to fuck-up
his next parole hearing

so as not to be dropped
by the cancellation of his after

into a world
about to discontinue

snow & ice & paralysis.
Sentenced to start again.

Ampersand was comfortable
in the middle. . . .

AMPERSAND (AUTUMN) (#1)

Ampersand joins the cold that is
to the cold that will be,

as each night
brings new frost

to edge the leaf
in all the earth colours but green.

This death at the extremities
travels down the stem

to reach the roots
which are still confident in the warm earth.

But cold air must make cold ground,
& Ampersand who joins them

finally conveys cold to cold
to root & tree & sky,

& leaf falls
from the cold that is

to the cold that has become
Ampersand.

Stan Rogal

BLUE ROSE

(for Baudelaire)

Calling for an aesthetic of the unexpected.
Wearing the Fool's coat to be other than.
Coughs up toads &
        shits flocks of starlings
Singing from his asshole
        to conjure amuse.
Body layers boxed with rats & further dragons
Defies decoration.
As crystal burns an icy flame &
        refuses to break but shatters
                on lines & by laws of its own.
This heart.
So far from any home
No absinthe could make fonder
Operates within a fracture.
The image appearing for its mere effect
        & giving rise to other.
Images.
As this rose
Arose thru violence so purple
        the petals slashed the eyes of any passing glance.
Ecstatic red visions no saint
        shot full of Eros could hope to blossom
Or arouse. Only B.
Grinding sparks between his knees & the concrete
        flickered a thorny blue instant &
                unbreaking
Shattered.

Peter Goodchild

NIGHT IS GRADUALLY ENCROACHING

The church was nearly empty, because I was early for the morning service. A woman walked in and sat down right next to me. We had a few seconds of whispered conversation.

At the end of the service she said, "How long have you been coming here?"

"Nearly three months. Why?"

"Just wondering."

I was also just wondering. But people gathered into small groups for chit-chat or drifted away, and Ginette also drifted away, or at least away from me.

The week finally passed, and it was Sunday again. I got downtown about an hour early, so I went to a doughnut shop for a coffee. And there she was, standing near the cash register. I said hello.

"Hi! Are you having a coffee here, or to go?" she asked.

"Umm — to go. Would you like a ride over?"

"Sure."

We drove to the church, but then we sat in the car for a long time, drinking our coffee and talking about the colours of the autumn leaves. When we finally went inside, she whispered, "Would you like to go out for lunch afterwards? Or are you busy?"

I nodded. "Sure, I'd love to."

After the service, she asked me where I'd like to go for lunch, so I suggested a favorite restaurant of mine.

We sat there and talked. Smiling, she said: "So is church a good place to meet women?"

"I don't know. I'd never really thought about it that way."

"Well, who knows. Maybe it's better than supermarkets."

"Supermarkets?"

"Yeah. I heard a couple of women talking yesterday. One of them was saying that supermarkets are much better places for meeting people than bars, for instance."

"Hmm, could be. I never had any luck with supermarkets."

I finally asked her for her phone number. She gave it to me, and I

28

gave her mine. She put her head in her hands, laughed, and said, "Oh, God."

"What's the matter? Are you upset? Tired?"

"No."

On the third Sunday morning there was a sudden violent storm, and I wasn't sure if she'd be going to church. I wasn't even sure if I wanted to go myself. But it gave me a perfect excuse for calling her — and I was shy enough to think I needed one. She said she would go if I would. I asked her if I could give her a ride, and she said okay and gave me her address. I picked her up in front of her apartment building. The rain stopped before we got to church.

Part of the reason she had wanted to go to church that day, in spite of the storm, was that she had promised someone named Jeff that she'd talk to him after church. After the service we stood with several people for a while. I didn't have much chance to talk to her, and we weren't even standing very close to each other. She spent a lot of her time talking to Jeff.

Eventually I heard her say she was going home. Jeff asked if she'd like a lift, and she said yes. She said goodbye to me. There was a question in her eyes.

She called me that evening and apologized for not being able to talk to me because of Jeff. I said it was okay. I didn't intend to, but I blurted out, "You know, you're really very nice. It would be so easy to fall in love with you."

"Well," she said, "I don't recommend it."

"Why not?"

"I'm not the loveable type."

We were both silent for a few seconds, and then I said, "Listen — can I come over?"

"No."

"Why not?"

"I should tell you, I have a boyfriend."

"Jeff?"

"No, no."

"You live together?"

"Yes."

"I had a feeling there was something like that going on," I said. But we kept on talking. "Who was that Jeff guy?" I asked, "another lover?"

"No."

29

"Oh, come on, you weren't just discussing your stamp collections."

"Listen, if you can't trust me then you shouldn't be talking to me. . . . He likes me a little more than I like him. And now he. . . . Okay?"

Ten minutes later I asked her if I could meet her somewhere.

I picked her up and we drove around. She remembered a restaurant she liked, so we went there. We talked for hours. She made me swear not to repeat the stories she was telling me, she said she was telling me things she had never told anybody else. She said she wasn't going to leave Mark, her boyfriend. She also told me he didn't want to marry her. He was already married; if he got a divorce, he'd have to pay his present wife a lot of money, because too many of his business interests were in her name.

"But he's a saint, he lets me do whatever I want."

"Why won't you leave him?"

"Because."

"Because why?"

"Because of everything."

Ginette was a lawyer, and she made a lot of money. Her boyfriend's income was about twice hers. I was poor.

After consuming pie and coffee for several hours, we left. As we walked to the parking lot, she took my arm, sighed, and said, "I think we'll be friends for life."

"I hope so."

I drove her home. I gave her a kiss on the cheek.

The next day, Monday, she called at lunch. "Thanks for a lovely day yesterday," she said, "I almost called you last night and told you I was coming over to spend the night."

I asked if I could see her later. We met at a downtown bar at five o'clock for a drink.

We saw a magazine lying on a seat. She said she used to read it all the time. "I can see a bit of that streak in you," I said. "How a good-looking woman can fuck her way to the top, that's the theme of any article in that magazine."

"Listen, asshole, if I was that type, I wouldn't be hanging out with you."

Late that night we walked to her apartment building. In the lobby we said goodnight. I gave her a hug.

"At least you get hugs and kisses whenever you want them," I said.

"No, I don't."

I went home. I spent the rest of the week telling myself not to call her, but every time the phone rang I hoped it was her.

She called again five days later, on Saturday night. "Can you give me a ride tomorrow?" she asked. "Mark doesn't like lending me his car. He thinks I'm a bad driver."

After church we went to a restaurant. As we were driving there, she said, "I've decided to be nicer to Mark from now on. After all, it isn't his fault he's living with a neurotic." I didn't reply, I just gave her a dirty look.

I tried to stop myself from calling her, but five days later, on Friday, I suddenly changed my mind and called her at work. I asked her if I could take her out to dinner, and she said yes.

That evening we held hands and got into some fairly graphic descriptions of our sexual pasts. "I've been to bed with over three hundred men," she said. "Once a girlfriend and I added up how many men we'd had."

I squeezed her hands. "God," I said, "all this talk about. . . . Why don't we go somewhere where we can discuss this in more detail?"

She laughed. "I think we're in lust with each other. But . . . I don't think it would be a good idea for us to go to bed. . . . I don't know. Let's do something. Do you feel like going out dancing?"

So we went out and drowned ourselves in loud music for a few hours. Then I drove her home. I finally gave her a real kiss. "I'm going home," I said, "but if you don't feel like staying home you could get a cab and come on over to my place. Or drop in any time and tell me to shove over."

The next day, Saturday, I kept staring at the phone, but I didn't pick it up. I didn't want to keep drifting into something that would never work. And she didn't call me.

So the next day we arrived at church separately. We treated each other like strangers. We were both in the same mood: needing to be free from each other.

Several times during the afternoon and evening of that Sunday, I picked up the phone, but then put it down again.

I even disconnected the phone at one point, I was so sick of waiting for it to ring. But an hour later I plugged it in again and called my sister. I mentioned my affair, but only cryptically. I think I used less than a dozen words, but she apparently read my mind, and she began a long lecture: "Tell this woman she should make up her mind who she wants. . . ."

Ginette called again one morning. She said she was just calling to say hello, but I could tell she was upset. I asked her why.

"Well, if you must know, because Mark insisted on jumping on me first thing in the morning."

"He's never heard of foreplay?"

"No."

She even called me at two o'clock one morning. She was crying. She said she was scared. She said she was lonely. I asked her if Mark was there, but I knew he was, and I knew that his presence or absence had nothing to do with it. I asked her if she wanted to meet me somewhere. "No," she said, "just talk to me."

But over the next few weeks, I felt that I couldn't go on with it. One night I swore — again — that I was going to tell her that the relationship had to end. But I couldn't say anything that night, because the next day was her birthday.

The next morning I told myself I wasn't going to call her to wish her happy birthday: perhaps the insult would do enough damage to separate us. But at about ten to five I suddenly changed my mind and called her at her office. She said she had just been on the phone trying to reach me, but that my line had been busy, and it was obviously because I had been dialing her at the same second. I suggested we meet after work, and I bought her a small present.

She introduced me to her own sister that evening, and the three of us went out to dinner and had a great time. Mark was out of town for the day on a business trip. Ginette said he had had the opportunity to come back early but that he didn't believe in celebrating birthdays.

Soon after dinner, her sister insisted on grabbing a cab and going home alone, but she was smiling as she left, as if she wanted to leave the two of us alone for a while.

That night Ginette came over to my place for the first time. We played some new cassette tapes I'd bought. I showed her some plants I was growing.

"I should have made love to you before," I suddenly found myself saying. "I counted three other occasions when I could have done — maybe. And I was thinking: Three strikes and you're out."

"Nice fantasy."

I gave her a hug. I kissed her. I raised the back of her dress and put my left hand into the back of her panties and ran my hand over

32

her bum. She wasn't protesting yet, so I ran my hand around to the front and down to her pubic hairs. Her pussy was surprisingly wet.

I whispered, "Just a minute." I pulled her into the bedroom and onto the bed. I pulled her underwear off and took off her shoes and buried my face between her legs. I got undressed. I asked her to take off her dress, but she said no.

"Just hold me for a minute," I said.

She not only held me but began to run her hands over my back as I kissed her. I took the rest of her clothes off. I finally knew what lay beyond that hitherto well-guarded border, the neckline of her dress. She had a body like a swimmer's, and breasts like a sixteen-year-old's. Her nipples were small bright buttons. Her pussy was shaved to a narrow band on an otherwise hairless torso. I stroked the dark fur and smiled: "A racing stripe." She raked my hair back over my scalp as we rolled together. But the joy of exploring her clean, perfumed body was too intense, and I came much too quickly, pouring out all my grief and frustration in a great river.

As soon as I fell back onto the bed, she looked at the clock, panicked, and jumped up. She pulled on her clothes and ran into the bathroom to fix her makeup. "I'm late — I'm supposed to be meeting Mark downtown. Shit."

"Wait."

She ran out the door, almost slamming it behind her, after saying, "I don't want to talk right now." After a minute I went outside to find her but she was gone. She called an hour later from downtown. She made me swear that I would never tell Mark what had happened.

Early the next morning she called again. After about ten minutes, she said she wasn't sure we should be seeing each other. I got mad and said, "Listen. You're bored. I'm bored. I have a suggestion. Why don't we call it quits right now? In any case, I don't think you're really interested. I think I'm just a minor form of amusement for you."

She said goodbye and slammed the phone down.

She called back half an hour later and said, "You were wrong about your last remark."

"What last remark?"

"You know."

After several more hours of conversation we both calmed down. The next day, more long talks on the phone. I asked her if I could take her out to dinner again. She said okay. "But I think you should know Mark and I have agreed to start spending more time together."

At dinner she said she was depressed, partly because she wanted to quit her job. We discussed the various options she had, but the essential problem was that she couldn't imagine living on less money, and so she was stuck with a high-stress job. We'd gone over her problem many times and got nowhere.

I told her I was depressed, too, but that my feelings were due to the fact that I always missed her so much when she wasn't around. She became very negative about our relationship.

"I might be marrying Mark one day," she said.

"Are you serious?"

She smiled. "Sure, why not? I've got nothing else to do."

We were silent for a minute. I looked out the window. "Oh, God," I said, "the night."

"What?"

"The endless cycle of night and day. That's what it's like. You're mine, then you're Mark's, you're mine, then you're Mark's."

Over the next few weeks, she simply refused to consider the possibility of leaving Mark, but she told me that our friendship was precious to her.

"I don't understand," I said, "I get the impression you never talk to Mark about any of these things — love, sex, work, anything. You call me in the middle of the night if you're upset about anything. I find that very strange. Most women, when they have some sort of a problem, they talk to their boyfriends. Don't they?"

"I've never talked about intimate things with a lover. A lover and a best friend have always been two different people for me."

"Why?"

"No reason."

"Mark gets your body, and I get your mind, your heart."

"Yes."

"No, it's not even like that. One gets your body, another gets your mind, and nobody gets your heart. One more piece of armour. One more defense. Like your obsession with money."

That same evening, after saying goodnight, she turned to me. "You said something about an endless cycle of night and day. But it isn't an endless cycle, because night is gradually encroaching on the day."

"But which is the night? And which is the day?"

"I don't know."

Once she told me that none of her friends or relatives liked Mark. "But he's completely faithful to me."

"Because he's too much in love with himself to ever love anyone else," I suggested.

"Yes."

Several times she'd said, "You should be careful in asking for something, because you might get what you asked for." And once she elaborated: "I asked for somebody predictable and reliable, and that's what I got."

"Why won't you leave him?" I asked.

"Because."

"Because he's rich and I'm poor. Because money is security. And because three hundred men is enough for any woman."

"Yes."

"What are we going to do?" I sometimes ask.

"I don't know."

Every once in a while we say goodbye forever. We sit in the darkness. Her hand is on the handle of the car door.

Or we go inside. I touch her hair. The elevators in the apartment lobby boom open and closed. "Thank you for being so honest throughout it all," I say. "I think you're wonderful."

"I think you are, too," she whispers.

"We shouldn't really see each other any more. But if you're ever in trouble or upset you must call me," I say.

"And you must call me too if you're ever upset."

Cornelia Hoogland

A WOMAN'S STRENGTH

The moment the cornered rat reared
on its haunches, teeth bared,
was the moment his mother lunged
her spear-body
into the round spear-handle
of the broom and the rat screamed
and blood lept up at her;
it was as if she tore
through the safe crook of her father's arm,
her village on the Wieregen Mere,
her shyness with the Friesan boy
in hiding from the Germans,
her too-accomplishing sister,
the slights and put-downs; as if she
had stalked the Atlantic, cracked the shield,
the prairies, all of Canada beneath
her bloody knees and hands to get here,
into this moment.

She wasn't an unkind mother,
but she didn't comfort the horrified kids
then or ever, as if this way they could better learn
the new country. The eldest child, my husband,
stayed to watch her flick the rat onto newspaper,
then scrub the blood from the chair legs, the walls,
her bare knuckles in the bucket of pink water,
that woman on all fours, her heavy breasts and haunches
gleaming like the purple heart in a bag of skin
when you crack open an egg.

Sometimes when he kneels behind me
lifts my belly so my arms straighten
and my knees bend and he enters
I know he is only as far away as a cougar
is from the deer it tracks,
but just at the moment the animals
skid to a halt he clamps my breasts
into his hands, pushes them up through
my body as if to plaster his own hollow chest;
claiming and fearing
what a cornered woman is capable of.

Andrew Wreggitt

SAFE

I play the guitar like I'm breakin outta jail
— Stevie Ray Vaughn

No one's safe any more, no one's ever been safe. Helicopters fall out of the sky, a man chokes on his lunch, people hurt each other and forgive, or they hurt and don't. It goes on either way.

Robert Johnson singing **Hellhound on My Trail** in 1938. He died on all fours "barking like a dog" after the poison hit his system. His music so pure some believed he sold his soul to the devil.

Now it's Stevie Ray, off the liquor finally, feeling good about playing. A helicopter falls out of the sky with him in it and he's gone. None of it connects to the music, the current of electricity that drove through him, that he played his guitar like he was breaking out of jail, that he was clean this time. It was just a machine breaking down around him, breaking down the machine of the body.

My friend says the whole planet's a slaughterhouse, an abattoir, and we should get used to the idea there are no reasons for any of the things that happen. Nothing follows anything, we just go on, something leaking out of us like light . . .

. . . light at the bottom of a glacier or in the valves of the heart, light the headache brings, bursting in flashes, or the light that a word makes when it goes off in your hand . . . light falling out of all of us, all the time.

Stevie Ray crashed to earth in a ball of fire. Robert Johnson playing at the dance after he'd been poisoned, saying "I'm sick, real sick, but I'm still playin, see?"

watching as they pick up seeds in the yard, or the heart as it skips ahead, following its own dim light. Who can tell any more? Maybe everything.

RAIN

Heavy rain. River lunges against cutbank, then crashes on. Dog up to his belly, laughing in mud and wet leads me down from the path into thickets of alder, willow, checking over his shoulder to make sure I'm following. Where is he taking me?

The river is sad today. No, that's not right. The river is full to the teeth with silt and mud and is busy making something new out of itself. Carving new passages, silting up shopping carts, sculpting the clay bank by the cement plant with its flat, insistent forehead. No. It's me who is sad.

An argument one day and someone leaving in a car. Tail lights blinking goodbye at the cattle guard. Goodbye. For a year I couldn't watch anyone leave in a car. Even when it was me, I couldn't look in the rear view mirror. Couldn't bear certain colours either, faded metallic blue, or the smell of bacon, certain pieces of music, a particular bar . . . Half the world infected. To hell with it. Things are better now.

Wind pushes my hood back and I leave it down. Rain, rain. Plastered down hair. Haze of partial vision, rain drifting in lazy sheets down the river valley. Dog muscles through thick bushes then stands triumphantly in the swollen river, soaking wet, waving a snag of bramble in his tail. He laughs up at me, wanting me to follow him further down the river, past the bridge now . . . okay, okay. What in the world is he laughing at? Past the ducks swimming in the river's elbow, tree branches raking the water's surface, knee deep in the flood and pressing on. Okay . . . okay.

William Knight

"WAITING AT RIVER'S BEND FOR YOU. . . ."

Waiting at river's bend for you
or news of your remains.
It has been five weeks
and the river has dropped,
navigation has ceased.
The lockmasters have drifted
to the taverns below,
but I wait, eddying on the bank,
untangling the abandoned nets of poachers,
salvaging whatever will float.

"THIS WAS YOUR GARDEN. . . ."

This was your garden:
the fat-bottomed plum dropping
to rot in the unmown grass,
a haze of wasps at your feet.

And I was your gardener
a foolish ghost pottering
under the arbour
with rusty shears.

"You don't eat?"
But I knew. You ate
out of sight, your mouth
slick with milk, with pulp.

Peter Bakowski

FIRE, FIRE, IN THE MOUTH OF MANY THINGS

I want your poem to
turn my train ticket into a canary
I want your poem to be
like a gunshot in a convent
I want your poem to take me away
from the forlorn man clawing his Soho pint
I want your poem to
turn his eyebrows into ants
that will bring him a tambourine.

I want your poem to
free those four and twenty blackbirds
from that infernal pie
I want your poem to
play the harp
through my nightmares
I want your poem to
set fire to the mousetrap of
the English class system.

And I will dance with such a poem
beneath a chandelier of fishes.

Gustav A. Richar

WRITERS' WORKSHOP

She said, "You're a writer."

My surprise gave her courage. She blinked quickly before her hazel eyes homed in on me. "Your beard, the short hair, the tall figure are typical."

We turned right at House 14, headed down the cracked walkway to Buildings 23 to 28. The July afternoon brooded between shadows of maple and spruce. Robins crossed the lawn.

I glanced at her. She walked with whipping short steps, her piquant body nearly as tall as mine, though slimmer. It's shocking to say but I thought, if we had children, they'd be beanstalks.

Then she breathed as if revealing a mystery. "The reception clerk said you're Dale Travis Stone." A sheepish grin followed.

I nodded.

"Read your 'Tango for Medusa' in *Periwinkle Magazine*. Your story gripped me."

In those days my publications were meager, and 'Tango for Medusa' was only my second story accepted. The magazine paid lavishly with two free copies, though I had worked a year on the story. How, I wondered, did it grip her?

We arrived at House 23. "Your home for the week," I said. "Mine's 26."

She set her attache case down. The wrinkled olive slacks, baggy around her thighs, were tightly buttoned at her ankles. "Thanks for helping."

"It's not often I meet a reader of mine." She was the first.

Her smile was red lips, white teeth, healthy gums. "Could you show me the campus? In particular the phones. The clerk said the houses don't have any."

"Right," I said glancing again at her body. "Do you take the ballet masterclass?"

She snickered, dry and senile. "I'm a poet." Her words jumped out as if a hiccup would follow.

It's difficult to say what was the deciding factor: her eyes, the short, dark-blonde hair, the fine nose though somewhat too pointed,

42

the mouth or the oval face, but I said, "Come with me to the bus terminal. I must pick up a friend from a previous workshop."

"But I have to phone my sister at three." Sorrow and determination were in her voice as if her well-being depended on that call.

"A beautiful woman like you should *receive* calls." My remark astonished me, left me with a dry mouth.

"Perhaps." Her face was a mask. "She's negotiating with my husband for our separation."

In the car she told me her name (Bobbi Jo Clarke), her age (22 — half of mine), where she used to live (Fields), why she didn't want to have children, what clothes and make-up colours suited her, and that she would enter university in the fall to study for a B.A., majoring in East Germanic languages (all dead for centuries). These facts made me wonder if Bobbi Jo had dreams.

While we waited for the bus she phoned her sister. It was long distance and Bobbi Jo required a handful of coins. I stood politely outside the reach of her conversation but watched her with growing interest. A week at a writers' workshop necessitates togetherness with other students. Friendships grow rapidly.

In the terminal's main room other people waited too. Beside the lockers, a teenage couple practised a steamy good-bye. At the window, overlooking the oil-stained yard, a young woman, staring at her window reflection, chewed on one of her hair locks. A muscular man rushed by in sleeveless black T-shirt, torn jeans, unlaced construction boots and a greasy, red baseball cap. With him the smell of stale beer.

Suddenly Bobbi Jo shouted, "Never."

The muscular man twitched around, squinted. At the window the woman turned. Other people craned their necks. The teenage couple's rehearsal continued.

Bobbi Jo waved frantically at me, requiring more coins. Now everyone stared at me; even the teenage couple — annoyance in the young woman's face, pride in the man's, his hand still under her blouse. "Serves you right," I said to myself. "The price of young flesh is to be embarrassed."

"He wants to keep the house," Bobbi Jo said moments later, still agitated. "Since he doesn't have the money to buy me out he's offering long-term monthly payments equivalent to half the house value."

Never having had such dealings, I was confused and asked innocently, "Are you separating or divorcing?"

"He thinks I'll change my mind in a year. Come back to him. Oh, he would love that. The little wife returning with tears in her eyes begging for another chance." She sucked in her cheeks, made fists. "Never."

The PA-system quacked something about a late bus. I swore silently.

"Did you come by bus or train?" I had to calm her. The friend we were waiting for disliked such commotion.

"He drove me up."

"Who?"

"My husband."

Complications lengthen a novel, sour relationships, but they are other people's problems. My world, particularly on Sunday afternoon, didn't require disturbances.

"You're wondering," she said close to me. "It's simple. We spent a few days at his parents' cottage to see if I would reconsider. No talk about financial aspects of the separation. We negotiate that through my sister. She's a stockbroker."

My losses on the market flashed up. "Where is he now?"

"Drove home. He has to work tomorrow."

I was relieved.

"He's a policeman," she added thoughtfully, "and that contributed to our problems."

I excused myself. In the washroom before a dirty mirror I ran cold water over my hands. "Policeman," I said to my opposite self, "and you dolt want to have her." (Dabbed water on my forehead.) "Policeman! — Well."

For the rest of the wait we leaned against a wall. Without being asked, she gave me a condensed version of the three days at the cottage.

"He wanted me to lie on the dock, canoe, fish. But I had to write an important paper."

"Do you write for a magazine?"

"It's my university correspondence course, English Literature. Next Thursday is the deadline."

I closed my eyes. The heat was oppressive. Bobbi Jo babbled on. "He never accepted my wish for a higher education. Thought it was just a fancy. I showed him. At the cottage I studied every day, wrote a stack of notes, lived on sandwiches. He cooked for himself and got irritated." Her hellish chuckles reminded me of a fracas in a henhouse raided by a weasel. Slightly flushed and angry she looked better than ever.

"And how about the nights?" I asked calmly, amazed at my shameless curiosity.

Her voice was angry, sounded as if coming from a crevasse. "It was all his plan. The outhouse is far back in the bush. Really! And how dark July nights can be. Spooky. Everywhere creeping, crawling, jumping noises. And the wolves!"

I removed my sunglasses, looked into her eyes.

"He took advantage," she said meekly. "I should never have gone to the cottage but I wanted to show him my independence." She hit the wall with one fist.

"Tell me about the wolves." I admire their rousing howls on moonlit winter nights, though couldn't remember hearing them around my cottage in the summer.

She told me of tormented cries across the water, of low grunts from the swamp, and of the occasional screech in the bush behind the bedroom window. These unknown, encroaching noises fattened her fear to terror, panic, forced her into the husband's arms.

"He liked that," she said, still upset, not knowing if she should smile or look stern or put up a compassionate expression.

Courageously I inquired, 'Sex dispelled your fear?"

She nodded. "My weakness," she said with a sigh, "but that's over. Never again will I sleep in a house surrounded by wolves."

When I explained the source of the noises she had feared, she seemed genuinely surprised, didn't laugh. Just said, "The animal."

The usual evening breeze never developed. Sultry heat crouched over trees and residences. Moths and mosquitoes crazed around lights. I walked Bobbi Jo to 23, kissed her greedily, left for my house. There were other peoples' manuscripts to be read, suggestions to be made, improvements to be proposed. Now, on Tuesday, with Bobbi Jo on my mind and her peach-fragrant body always close by, it became difficult for me to be constructive in the workshop. It's beyond any doubt that writing and sex are intimately related. But even after attending several workshops, I had not found the balance between flesh and pen.

Before I reached my house, friends from previous literary meetings taking part in this workshop called through the open windows of House 25. Sitting in the living room, they offered a nightcap. I entered and had the definite feeling that we humans are regularly regurgitated in time. Thank God, I don't remember previous existences with their many possibilities — my friends could have been my wives or sisters, or, God forbid, my nurses in a mental home — and I pity every person who is seeking counsel in past reincarnations.

The three women — writers in the mid-bloom of fifty — held court around a low table. They held their glowing cigarettes at eye level, obviously afraid of snuffing them out if lowered. In plastic cups gin and tonic with ice.

"What d'you think of the workshop so far?" asked Belinda. She smoked a cigarillo dipped in cherry wine.

I talked about the educational quality of the workshop leader, his linguistic richness, and the quality of the students, particularly the life experience shown in poems of a few younger ones.

"Did you have a pleasant evening?" asked Charlotte, her pale blue eyes waiting for a straight answer. She had four children.

First I apologized again for having had to pass on a proposed joint dinner, then told them about the urgent trip downtown, not forgetting to mention the extravagant price of women's swim-wear. This whetted their inquisitiveness.

"And how is Bobbi Jo." Viviane put on her English smile, blew smoke through her nose, plucked an invisible tobacco flake off her lip.

"We just returned from the Emergency Ward of the hospital," I said slowly to create tension.

The three mothers were concerned.

"Bobbi Jo had run out of pills, forgot the new package at home."

"What's wrong with her?" Belinda inhaled more cherry-flavoured smoke.

"Dislikes pregnancy."

The ladies exchanged glances, raised their brows.

Viviane wondered, "And she told you why she had to see a doctor?"

"Why not?" I tried to be reassuring. "Today's youth are free about their bodies."

Unconvinced they asked for details, hungered for gossip.

"Well," I said sitting back in my chair, "I'll give you an account of this afternoon. Perhaps it'll stimulate your creativity:

Bobbi Jo returned to the classroom some time after three. She sat down at her place beside me, wrote a note and pushed it on my pad.

I read: *Will have to phone again at five. It's complicated. Help me. Please.*

She touched my hand.

We had just worked on a poem of another member where the fictional 'I' (or so we all hoped) made love on top of a desk.

'Sure,' I whispered.

She relaxed without participating in the next round of criticism. An elderly poetess lyrically lamented the loon, a lake, and the night.

The workshop leader was polite.

'He wants to split the personal belongings in my presence only,' said Bobbi Jo quietly to me.

The teacher talked about the danger of oversentimentality in nature poems.

'Never,' Bobbi Jo daydreamed aloud and blushed when everyone looked at her. 'Sorry,' she said, 'I'm under stress.'

The women in the classroom strafed me with looks. Somehow they held me responsible for her actions. I cursed myself. I get involved with another man's wife; she sees me as her confidant, not her lover. Maybe it's my face, eyes, high forehead which make me trustworthy, a priest listening to confession. How unwanted.

A quarter to five in the college's entrance hall. Muteness swathed the building now almost deserted. Bobbi Jo and I sat on a bench opposite a phone that received calls. She insisted on that. We discussed the workshop, other members, their fiction and poetry. As we talked she began to move her arms and legs as if insects swarmed over them. Nervously she glanced at the phone, the floor, finally at me.

'Don't laugh,' she said. 'Whatever I say, don't laugh.'

I took her hand, said, 'I won't,' and blew her a kiss.

'For months I've dreamed of a man like you. Gentle, caring, and a writer.'

I thought it a good line for a romance novel but couldn't write it down. Hence it mingled with other important lines, became obscured, vanished. 'When did you get married?' Now I was her priest.

As she told me her face relaxed. 'I thought happiness would rise forever. On Wednesday I graduated from high school, on Saturday we married.'

'Rather romantic. Congratulations.'

'For the first two years, yes. The last two — poison and fire.'

'I'm sorry,' I murmured and without knowing why and without wanting to, added, 'But these years didn't damage your charm.'

How she laughed. And for how long. A young hen having discovered her first laid egg. As a good sport crazed by peach fragrance, I chuckled with her, though I had missed my own funny line.

She recovered, patted my shoulder, said, 'You're a riot. Like my father. Charm is ancient.'

I decided to colour my hair, have a face lift, update my vocabulary. Then she said, 'I'll phone my sis to see what the bastard's up to.' I recovered, relieved to be ancient and without any of her disasters.

On the phone Bobbi Jo's voice increased in volume. I walked to the far end of the hall, still heard scraps of questions, denials, accusations. No escape. To my relief I found a bulletin board and read: *Robert offers a ride from vicinity of Brooke and Landstale for split gas. Have condoms, seek sex. Pat the Potter. Sassy has room for rent. The Church of the Holy Grail welcomes you to an hour of dance, meditation, and love.* Scribbled underneath: *Knights sheathed, Dames willing, Pairs —*

'Absolutely not,' Bobbi Jo screamed, then, talking rapidly, slammed her flat hand several times on top of the phone box.

It's sad to say but I was as concerned about her as any collector of tropical birds who has stalked his game, even knows when to set the trap and now has to be afraid the bird will succumb before being caught. No doubt self-interest, maybe even self-preservation was on my mind.

Twice she gave her sister the number of the pay phone. Hung up. When she turned toward me she showed no sign of the heated debate.

'It's complicated,' she said. 'I'll miss the house.'

I sat down beside her, waited.

'Sis or her husband will phone back in 15 minutes.' She leaned back, breathing defiantly.

Since Sunday I had been unable to write anything of substance. My diary entries were only catchwords, phrases. The distance to fame increased. Bobbi Jo's slacks were tight.

'In June,' she said and clasped her hands behind her head, 'a neighbour gave us baskets of strawberries. I made my first jam. He came home, complained I was wasting my time. It was complicated. An hour later he got the message, fried eggs for his dinner. The jam was beautiful but it took hours until it became thick. Around 10 he stood at the bedroom door and asked me to come to bed. That's how he is. Eat, screw, sleep. I added water to the jam.

'He came to the kitchen every so often but admitted the jam was still too thin. At midnight he demanded I come to bed. Demanded! I threw the ladle at him but missed.' She giggled, glanced at me.

'I slept on the sofa. Never heard him leave the house in the morning. You can't believe the pleasure I had scraping jam off the kitchen wall.'

'Did the jam gel?'

'Oh, it was beautiful and delicious. Made sure he didn't get a spoonful.' She jumped up with an urgency. 'Excuse me,' she said, hurried to the washroom.

How refreshing the silence. I leaned back. Why not escape, quit the workshop, stay sane.

The phone rang. I ignored it. The phone screamed. Another emergency, I thought, and picked up the receiver.

A man said, 'Could I speak to Bobbi Jo Clarke?'

'She's in the washroom.'

There was a pause, then he cleared his throat and said with authority, 'I'm Wesley Clarke, her husband. Would you be so kind as—'

I interrupted, having no desire to invade a women's washroom. 'When your wife comes back she'll speak to you. I've no idea when —'

He cut me short. 'It's her old trick. She knew I'd call. You, sir, are probably a writer.'

Astonished, I said, 'How did you know?'

There was a pause when only his breathing gave signs of his presence and then, as if sharing a secret, he said, 'Writers are her latest craze. Please don't think I want to defame her, but she needs psychiatric care which she refuses. The past two years have been unbearable.' His voice softened. 'I've lost a promotion because of her. Should you ever get involved with her, though I pray it doesn't happen, you'll be in mental danger. First, your creativity will be sapped. No writing with her around. Then your money will evaporate. Soon, after a short happiness, you'll find that whatever you hope to get from her becomes more difficult to obtain. Finally it's impossible.'

He took a deep breath, but before I could say anything, he droned on, 'This afternoon I found an oboe and a bassoon in a closet. Expensive instruments. She doesn't even read music and there isn't a soul in our town who could —'

'Hold on,' I shouted, 'here she comes.' I waved frantically at her to hurry, then said very clearly, 'It's Wes.'

She fled back into the washroom.

I paused in my report, gulped down the rest of my gin and tonic, and was ready to continue when Belinda raised her voice. "Hold it, Dale. Hold it. Is this true?"

To my nod they frowned.

"Impossible," declared Viviane. "Utterly impossible."

The three women argued. I mixed a fresh drink, enjoyed their surprised faces, disturbed voices, knowing glances. Obviously they would dissect my report in hours of discussion.

"Are the men in your house quiet this year?" asked Charlotte abruptly changing the subject.

"There are just two others. Both are taking the conductors' workshop. I only hear them between one and three in the morning when they come in. The wiry one with the curly red hair has the room next to mine."

Belinda said, "He's good looking."

Viviane thought he could be taller but agreed with Charlotte that this hardly diminished his striking appearance.

On my way home I wondered about Bobbi Jo's interest in a bassoon.

"One more day," Bobbi Jo said, "and the workshop is over."

We walked hand in hand along the paths criss-crossing the campus. Away from the residences the night burst with stars. Fireflies beaconed from bushes.

"You're quiet," she said. "Do you also feel sad when happy?"

I searched for an answer, proper and fitting. Found none. Pressed her hand softly. She responded. We hugged, kissed, headed for my place.

The house lay in darkness, the conductors still away. In my second floor room I switched on the desk lamp. Bobbi Jo stayed at the door, her head covered by the shadow of the lamp, legs bathed in the pool of light.

"Sit down," I said moving the only chair to one end of the desk. My unmade bed was opposite.

A love nest without warmth is a closed flower, I thought, and said, "These rooms remind me of a cell in a cloister. Let's have music. What do you like?"

"Anything classical. It's so poetic."

She had no preferences, composer's names meant little to her.

Then I remembered the bottle of wine one of the conductors kept in the fridge. I raced down the stairs. Never would I steal but when I read the price tag on the bottle I was about to change my principle. "Tomorrow I will replace the wine, if . . ."

I found two clean plastic cups, rushed back to my room.

She sat where I left her, reading a manuscript of mine. "I can't resist written material," she said apologetically. "At times it's a curse, this urge to read." She pointed to my manuscript, unfortunately a story of betrayed love. "That's a hell of an opening. Grabbing. I'd like to read on."

"How about real candlelight," I answered, and got half a red candle from my suitcase. After a power failure two years before trapped me with an oversexed, middle-aged woman in a similar room, I travel with a candle.

Bobbi Jo talked about the future. She spoke with determination. In three years she would have a B.A. The settlement could be stretched that far without taking on part-time jobs. I admired her confidence, supported her call for more power to women. Still, she insisted on reading my manuscript.

My neighbour, the red-haired conductor, came home early. I was glad since he would not disturb us later. The walls were poorly soundproofed. He moved the chair, dropped a coat hanger, whistled off tune.

Bobbi Jo winked. "What a conductor," she whispered like a girl.

Beyond the screen of the window the mosquitoes' flights, the repetitive calls of crickets, an owl hooting. I stroked the hand she held across the desk (restraining myself from jerking her across), stammered shameless lies about her beauty, intelligence, and independence, declared devotions I knew would end the day after tomorrow. The candle flickered hellishly. Bobbi Jo read on.

Finally the conductor's bed creaked. He switched off his lamp, cleared his throat twice. Soon he snored.

"Probably conducts an ensemble of beer, ale, stout, and porter," I remarked.

Bobbi Jo laughed, though I didn't know if my remark or the story caused it. To my relief, she put down the manuscript, made no comments but came to the bed. She sat down beside me, her thigh pressed against mine. The scent of fresh peaches. Flesh. She was so close I imagined I heard wolves howl.

Suddenly she hugged me, kissed me, and said, eyes closed, "Please, forgive me. Please. Forgive me."

I was perplexed. What should I forgive?

For a while we clutched each other, kissing noses, ears, eyes; sucking lips, licking throats, probing each other's body.

As casually as possible I suggested, "Let's undress."

She made certain her blouse was hung up properly, that paper tissues were on hand. Acting like a long married couple we seemed to celebrate an anniversary whose significance we had forgotten. Yet when I felt her nakedness, carried her to the bed, the urgency, the lust returned like a rising sun over fields of red peppers.

"Forgive me," she whispered. "You are kind. Gentle. You'll understand. I don't want you inside. Please. I'll show you marvelous things. Please. You'll be surprised. I promise. But not inside."

"Why?"

"I'm still married. I couldn't face Wes when I have to see him."

"Aren't you separated now?"

"Of course."

"So?"

"The vows. It's only over when we're legally released from them."

God, I thought, why do You send me half-moral women? Because I'm a non-believer? We lay quietly for a while, then her hands and head and lips began to move.

Well, well, well, well — well.

A demanding knock on the door. My neighbour's door. The night froze us in.

"It's an omen," muttered Bobbi Jo. "An omen."

How ominous a sound at night. Unbearable the wait between knocks. Finally the conductor woke, staggered through the room, opened his door.

I heard clearly his "Oh."

"Barnie," sighed a woman, and after a while, "I'm leaving my husband."

Gently I rubbed Bobbi Jo's back, urged her to continue but she lay rigidly across my chest.

The conductor moved back to his bed. The woman stayed outside the door.

"I can only offer you friendship." The voice from the bed.

Bobbi Jo's breasts were cold. She wriggled herself free, got out of bed.

"But you . . ." stammered the voice from the door. "I thought . . ."

"Think of my position. What would I do with my wife, my son?"

Once more I got hold of Bobbi Jo's thigh but she pushed my hand away.

From the door, "You were comfort, understanding. Hope. Don't leave me alone." Her voice rose momentarily. "You promised."

He babbled on about friendship. She wanted more.

Bobbi Jo finished dressing. I was uncomfortable standing naked beside her.

"You can't go," I whispered and then — the devil put the words in my mouth — added, "Why doesn't she go inside the room? Why is he in his bed?"

"Holy Grandmother," said Bobbi Jo. "She could have a revolver in her hand and he's cowering behind the bedspread. Wes once investigated a crime like that. I've got to get out."

She went to the window. I groped for my underpants.

"Take out the screen, I'll climb out, hold on to the rain gutter, cross to the house corner and shimmy down the pipe."

Calm words were no help. Invaded by fear, she wouldn't stop for anything.

"If something really terrible happens," she was hysterical by now, "we'd be witnesses. Wes would find out. Oh, my God, Dale, my B.A.!"

These dreams of being with a young woman. A curse in every man's mind. Twenty years ago I would never have got involved with a married woman. Now, removing the screen, feeling the mosquitoes in my face, I hoped she and the pipe would tumble into the wild roses below.

Bobbi Jo climbed out the window. Her hand held on to the plastic guttering. It bent, cracked. I grabbed Bobbi Jo around the hips, helped her back into the room.

She sat down and began to cry. I gave her paper tissues which she ignored. The screen replaced, I realized our commotion had alarmed the conductor and his visitor.

We had missed the end of their tragedy but could hear the woman move slowly down the stairs. The house door snapped shut. The darkness around us relaxed.

We waited half an hour. Bobbi Jo sobbing and hiccupping, I stroking her hair and arm.

"Before her death, my grandmother promised to protect me whenever she could. That was her omen tonight. Do you believe in such things?"

People's minds before sex are not where they should be, I thought. "If you believe in para-psychology you should express it poetically," I said, now thoroughly annoyed.

Again she hugged and kissed me, murmuring, "Please, forgive me."

I shrugged.

Down the dark stairs and through the living room I guided her to the house door, stepped outside with her, watched the tall figure until she disappeared into her house.

The night smothered lawn, trees, buildings. No stars. Only moths and mosquitoes around the lamps along the walkway.

"Where do all the loves, all the dreams, all the desires go?" I asked myself looking into the darkness. "Perhaps there is some-where a fog-shrouded archive where bored librarians store our mishaps, from where we are urged to act out new foolishness."

Suddenly a seated figure on the bench below the nearest maple moved, sighed loudly, then sobbed heartrendingly.

Well, well, well, well.

A.F. Mortiz

IMAGINATIVE PURITY

Now
no thing is pure
but the senses
still
create and taste
of all things
the purity.

The eye in bright poisoned air, the tongue
drowning itself for joy in water white
from gleaming faucets,
        pure silver
        reflecting in miniature spring windows,
        a vase of forsythia on a sill . . .

the tongue and eye
taste purity.

Then memory brings its knowledge
and the words of trustworthy witnesses,
the ones who have delved, who have gone there
where nothing is seen:
        cancerous infusions, intangible as spirit,
        from waving fields, mighty mills,
        sublime images of peace and power,
and unknowable
chemicals sent to eat chemicals
by the guardians, desperately tired.

Till all the being abhors and savors
the pure world it creates, the pure delight
the senses take in ignorance,

and wonders at itself:
I walk in a death I do not know.
I revel in the body of this death.

Eric Folsom

DESPERATE MANNERS

despite efforts at thinking
the icefields remain
like pins in a graph
a testament to cynicism
and fatigue of the metal kind
that blows the top off
men's and women's lives
sentient sardines
in a roofless airplane

surprisingly I remain
happy as a lark
and twice as guilty
surrounded by enormous lies
predatory in the darkness
on either hand a steep gorge
rises to the occasion
in my throat
but I have allies
who are negotiating my release

WHITE DIVA

white diva
every rescuing woman
and witch of the westmoreland
be with you
use the phone in the birthing room
reverse the charges
to the men who love women
who love men who love
don't listen to the voices
that say you deserve
whatever you get
tell them politely
but firmly
to fuck off
listen to the white light
that emanates from your uterus
shines out through your eyes
you are the heroine
the one who redeems
her great-grandmother
from her life of assembly lines and beatings

ON EMBRACING

Just holding
and being held,
a simple radiance
with the eyes closed,
forgiveness finally
like a drink of water
or like sleep
that makes you forget
about solitary pain
how it drills a hole
through your raw
and abscessed skin,
through your flesh,
and draws out
your heart,
your liver, your tongue,
pulls out every organ
until your true friend
blocks the opening,
makes a tourniquet
of his arms,
and dresses the wound
with his body.

"INHABITING THE WORLD"
AN INTERVIEW WITH CAROL SHIELDS

by Laurie Kruk

Carol Shields, winner of the 1990 Marian Engel Award for her body of work, is the author of eleven books, the most recent being a novel, *Republic of Love*.

KRUK: *Various Miracles* was the book that caused people to label you a postmodernist. And then you had *Swann's* experiments with narrative voice and point of view. How well do you feel the postmodern label applies to those works?

SHIELDS: Well, I certainly think the stories are more adventurous. I really thought of them as experiments when I started out; just trying out different things. So just the fact that they were experiments was a kind of liberating influence. I didn't really know if they'd ever form a book; I'd hoped, I guess, that they would. Some of them seemed more like narrative ideas than stories. And, of course, I have certainly read postmodernist fiction, and even though I have as much trouble as anyone else *defining* it, I have a sense of what it is, a feel for what it is, and I expect that some of those stories, certainly not all of them, fall into that general category.

K: I think you said somewhere that you wrote those stories to help you loosen up the narrative point of view so that you could write *Swann*, which you were having trouble with.

S: Yes, that's absolutely true.

K: So you wrote the stories for *Various Miracles* more or less around the same time?

S: Yes. I had already started *Swann*, and had got stuck, so I just put it aside. I spent about a year [on *Various Miracles*]. One of the stories I had written earlier, but the rest I hadn't, the rest I wrote during that one year.

K: So you saw them as going together, as a book of experiments.

S: Yes — and of course, after a while, I saw that there was another kind of theme that seemed to be running through them. But that just happened; I didn't sit down and think, "Oh well, I'm going to be writing about language." I was just writing about a number of different things that I was thinking about. But I very consciously — in writing those stories — decided that I would let the stories have their way, in a sense, which is something I hadn't done much before.

K: I just want to get at how much you're interested in the postmodern experiment — in terms of what you like to read, and what you like to write. . . .

S: I'm very interested in it, but I'm only interested in it when the language that underpins it has a kind of animation and felicity about it. . . . I'm trying to think who else's stories I've liked, in that mode. . . . I love William Gass; he's a writer I like very much. I've liked some of a man called Guy Davenport, he's an American too. There don't seem to be very many *women* postmodern writers, do there?

K: I think you said something about wanting to combine the two literary modes: combining the postmodern language play with a realist's sense of character and story.

S: Yes. And I don't know why we *can't*. And this is another thing: a newly converted postmodernist is the most elitist of critics. Unwilling, really, even to consider notions of character. And I wonder why . . . and I can't help thinking that we will bring the best that postmodernism offers [into fiction], because it offers a lot to a writer.

K: Like the freeing up, which you've noted, in your later books.

S: Yes!

K: I wonder if there is a kind of qualitative difference, as well as a quantitative difference, between a novel and a short story. A short story is of course much smaller, but is there a different feel to it, or can it do different things, as compared with the novel?

S: I have thought about that, but I haven't resolved it very well. Sometimes I think of short fiction as being more closely allied to poetry than novels. I don't think of the short story in that old Hemingway sense, of being exceedingly spare, so that every detail in it must add up to the statement of the story. I like a kind of *novelistic* density in short fiction. . . . I suppose I resist some of the myths; like, people say "it's harder to write a good short story than a novel." I just think that's total nonsense. It's harder to write a novel, every time, than a short story.

K: Because it's just — bigger?

S: Yes, it's just bigger. And it's a tremendously complex balancing act.

K:You told me why you started writing the stories of *Various Miracles* — it was to help you with *Swann* — but a lot of women have said that writing short stories is just a practical choice for them, because, especially when they have children, they don't have the time to write a novel. And you once said you're primarily interested in novels. Is that still true?

S: I think so. When I finished *Swann*, I wasn't ready to start a novel again, so it made perfect sense for me [to work on short stories] and I thought, "Oh, this is rather a nice rhythm, actually: not to do novel after novel."

[When you write] there's the rather abstract reward of actually just finishing something; and then there's the *real* reward of placing it somewhere. Because as I was writing *Various Miracles*, I was selling them [the stories]. And I can see why people would like this. With a novel, you go two or three years without any reinforcement at all. But I don't think it makes much sense to be writing short stories, if that's not your form . . . just because it happens to fit in with raising children, or whatever. I feel sometimes, when people show me their short stories, that they should be writing a novel. It's a different way of thinking, it's a larger way of thinking, they're thinking out a larger design — so that the actual writing seems out of proportion to the story that they're telling. It doesn't fit.

But I don't think of the short story as 'filler' and unimportant. Writing *The Orange Fish* stories gave me a great deal of happiness. I loved writing those stories. I didn't feel I was working in an inferior form — that's what I wanted to say. Because, funnily enough, most of my favourite writers — like Mavis Gallant, and Alice Munro — are short story writers. And short stories that are memorable do have a wonderful power about them. I'm an enormous fan of Alice Munro, and her stories often have for me that novelistic feel to them. And I think she's wonderful at shaping the *ends* of her stories; I don't know anyone who writes better endings than she does.

K: When you are contemplating putting out a collection of short stories, you must look at the book and see how it works, with all the stories together. There are stories written around the same time as those included, for example, which were left out of *The Orange Fish*, so you must have had a sense of what its shape would be.

S: Yes. Well, I didn't leave them out, my editor did, and so he was maybe more conscious of the shape. He also spent a lot of time with both those books [*Various Miracles* and *The Orange Fish*]—he was the editor for both.
K: Who was the editor?

S: Ed Carson. He spent a lot of time on the arrangement of those stories; he felt they had to be arranged in a certain way. And as soon as the book came out here in Winnipeg, I ran into a friend of mine — the day after she bought the book. And she said, "Oh, I read — whatever it was, the last story in the book ["Milk Bread Beer Ice"] — first." And I said, "Oh, if you only knew how much effort this man put into organizing them!" [laughs] And then I thought, well that's the way I do it; I always read the shortest story first. I look through the table of contents and pick the shortest one, and then I might start at the back — I certainly don't read front to back. . . . I heard Alice Munro say something, in a radio interview, about why she hasn't written a novel. And her belief is, that isn't the way life *is*, life is much closer to the structure of a short story: life is anecdotal.

K: I think you said you had trouble with the artificial nature of plot.

S: Yes, I do. I see it more and more as a set-up. The novel I'm writing now, there is some of this kind of set-up. But I hope I'm approaching it somewhat parodically; I think I am. Well, I hope so. . . . I sort of feel I'm using the conventions, instead of being used by them.

K: You also said, in *The West Coast Review*, "I like to think that these categories of reader response are breaking down as rapidly as the boundaries between genres, and that this process has been accelerated by feminist writing."

S: Well, I guess most of the writers I know, where I see this breaking down, have been women — starting with Susanna Moodie. And certainly with Alice Munro's *Lives of Girls and Women*: I think crosses that boundary. *A Bird in the House*, which is my favourite

Laurence book, feels very much like a novel to me. Maybe there are men who are doing this too — but why can't I think of any at the moment? And I think people like Daphne Marlatt and my friend Sandy Duncan, who's using fable and novel — women seem to be doing a lot of this. And maybe there are real reasons for it; maybe women's writing comes out of different forms — it comes out of diaries and journals and letters, and it comes from . . . different places.

I suppose there's nothing about existence that interests me more than language does. I think it's what makes us human, and it embodies us in a way that physicality doesn't . . . for me. I guess I'm interested in the transcendent moment where people do sense something spiritual, or are somehow enabled to. I'm not talking about people who are connected to religions, or other forms of spirituality — but just sort of a human spirituality. And what creates those moments? We don't know; I think it's a kind of chemistry, but I think language has to be a very large part of it. Chemistry, but I think language has to be a very large part of it.

. . . .

K: Were you thinking of the question of art when you were writing *The Orange Fish*, and its title story?

S: Well, I guess I'm always thinking about the question of art in a way. The making of art, and who makes it, and *how* it's made. Because it always seems to me that it really comes from common clay. And it's extraordinary to think of that, that people are capable of doing, making something larger than they are. So the mystery of art is something I suppose I'm always thinking about.

But no, with "The Orange Fish" I wasn't thinking about that particularly. I was thinking about — death, of getting old. And of how one thinks of going toward death in this linear way, of simply going through birthdays, and going through years. But the other way of arriving at death is through . . . multiple images. Which is what happens to the painting of the orange fish. So that death arrives . . . in another direction. It's a kind of space-time thing. That was what I was going after. The orange fish isn't dying because it's getting older and older; it's dying because there are suddenly millions of them. So that death simply comes on a different time line. I don't think many people *did* understand that . . . but it's all there, if you read it!

K: Did you write *A Fairly Conventional Woman* with the issue of the artist in mind?

S: I thought of Brenda Bowman as a woman who discovers that she is an artist, and nothing in her life has prepared her for that acceptance. And she's someone who thinks of art in a kind of mystical sense, but of course how can it be mystical when she herself has not thought of herself as having [an] entrée to that world of mysticism? I try to talk about the way the images for the quilts arrive in her head. So I suppose that was a way of demystifying [the artist], too.

K: You said *A Fairly Conventional Woman* was your favourite book. Why?

S: I loved writing it. Structurally it's certainly the most daring of those four early novels, with its going backward and forward in time. And I loved dealing with the fifties, as a period, and just thinking about that time again, talking about it. And you've probably noticed in all my fictions that I love the idea of the randomly assembled group of people — for whatever reason they are assembled. And so this is why I loved this — writing about the convention. It gave me a lot of pleasure to write. And it gave me a lot of pleasure to fit it in with the other novel, *Happenstance*. It was like a game, playing it, and getting everything just right. In fact there are two chapters in each book on their [Brenda and Jack Bowman's] meeting, because I think that is the great narrative that married people share.

K: How they first meet, and become interested in each other . . .

S: Yes. The other thing I wanted to do was write a novel about an intelligent woman who hadn't necessarily had a lot of formal education. I wanted her to be reflective. I almost never find reflective women in novels. And I think everyone has this reflective side, why doesn't it get into our novels?

K: What do you think about the argument that women write differently than men?

S: I think there are certain things about the tone of a woman's voice that differ. It tends to be much more intimate . . . more personal. It has a 'present-tense' feel about it, to me. . . . I guess the thing that worries me when you start to talk about women's voices is that you get into this idea of a 'miniaturist' voice . . . which I think is diminishing to women. That precious, Katherine Mansfield-ish kind of voice. So that worries me a little bit, but I certainly think that women deal very differently with [similar] kinds of experiences.

K: Would you say there's more interest in people's daily lives?

S: Yes, although I understand that men are now starting to write domestic novels and they're thought of as being very sensitive and revolutionary. [laughter]

K: It does seem that, by virtue of their socialization, women particularly emphasize personal relationships in their writing. Joan Clark told me she wasn't interested in 'reinventing the world'; I believe she meant that a lot of male writers like to create a world. Whereas it seems that a lot of women are more interested in going down, deep. . . .

S: Inhabiting the world, I think: that's what I would say.

K: Do you feel your fiction is in any way an expression of your feminism?

S: I think, inevitably, it is, but it's not something I sit and think about as I write.

One time I asked a friend of mine, who's Jewish, how much time she spends thinking about being Jewish. And she said, "About as much time as I do thinking about being a woman." Which I thought was a good response; it's absolutely *part* of her. And I feel being a feminist is part of me. And I'll always express myself as a feminist, simply because — it's the only language I know.

K: You said before that you write for yourself. You don't particularly write for a female audience, or think about that?

S: No, I don't think about audience very much when I'm writing. I think about *making* something, that's how it feels to me. That I'm making something.

K: Even in the sense of sewing . . . or quilting?

S: Yes — very much so.

K: How conscious are you of your style, when you're writing?

S: I'm very conscious; maybe too conscious.

K: Do you still write a few pages and then rewrite them the next day, so that you're going over the sentences 'with a fine-tooth comb'?

s: Yes; I love sentences.

k: Do you ever feel restrained by conventional punctuation?

s: Actually, I love punctuation, too. . . . I'm quite happy with conventional punctuation. I guess I do see certain changes [in my sentences] and part of it comes from editorial direction. Ed Carson does not like semicolons. And I do, because I really like British novels — they use a lot of semicolons. There was a time when I didn't use many dashes, and now I'm using them more. I find that sometimes it functions like a semicolon, but it also gives — when you set something in dashes — that marvellous thought, just beneath the thought before.

I love long, complicated sentences. But they have to work. They have to come in on this wonderful landing — I always feel they're like airplanes. [laughter] They've got to come in right, and they've got to make absolute grammatical sense. I'm not very interested in — reading or writing — short, declarative, Hemingway sentences.

k: You're another one of our *claimed* Canadian authors, though you grew up in the States. Do you think about the differences between Canadian and American literature?

s: Well, I think the first Canadian book I ever read was Marian Engel's *The Honeyman Festival*. And I thought, "Why am I loving this so much?", because nothing much was happening. But I loved it because I was in that woman's mind. Then I always like to say I 'discovered' Alice Munro — because she hadn't published a book yet. But I was in bed one night, this must have been in the late sixties — maybe she had published *Dance of the Happy Shades*, although I hadn't read it and hadn't heard of her — and I was reading in the *Montrealer* magazine her story "The Red Dress" which is still one of my favourite stories. And I thought, "Oh! This is amazing. And she's Canadian." So I felt I'd discovered her, this wonderful writer. And she is, I think, our best writer. I'm delighted at the acclaim she's had with this last book.

k: Other Canadian writers?

s: Well, I always read Atwood's books. And I think it's marvellous too . . . what she's done for Canadian literature and for women internationally. I always read them with interest. I'm very interested in her work.

K: What do you think about the change between *The Handmaid's Tale*, her last novel, and *Cat's Eye*?

S: I love *Cat's Eye*. Much more [than *Tale*]. I read it on the plane, on the way to my thirty-fifth high school reunion. So I was really ready to read about memory, and how it works.

I also thought it had wonderful writing in it, very careful writing — the most careful I've ever seen in a book of hers. The wonderful thing about Margaret Atwood is, she always seems to know, two or three years ahead of everyone else, what we're going to be talking about. She's prophetic. And I'm full of admiration for her.

K: Do you like Mavis Gallant?

S: I love *much* of Mavis Gallant, not all of it. *From the Fifteenth District* I think is my favourite book. It's *full* of *compassion*. I thought she was very close sometimes to being almost sentimental, but never, *ever* overstepped. It's a beautiful, a beautiful book.

I remember once driving in a car, and turning on the radio in the middle of a reading of a short story. And I could tell that it was a Mavis Gallant story, even though I had missed the introduction. The same thing happened to me once at the cottage, listening to the radio and I tuned in to the middle of a Marian Engel story: I just knew. And I thought, "Isn't that amazing, and wonderful, and enviable, that these people have a voice so personal that you can pick it up, like a voiceprint."

I love Margaret Laurence, too. I guess I love *The Stone Angel* the most. *The Diviners* left problems for me, but still I can remember finishing it, and I couldn't sleep that night . . . I was just so much caught up in that narrative, that sense of it all. . . .

Oh, and I love Beth Harvor's stories, too. I've always admired her.

· · · ·

K: Do you feel, as you're working on your new novel, that there's a pressure on you to write in ways you've written before?

S: No, I don't feel any pressure. And I don't think that writers should ever feel that they have to top their last book. That's a false challenge; that isn't the way the creative life works at all. We're all trying to write the best books we can. I don't think people try and write less than that.

I was worried just before *Swann* came out: I had pre-publication jitters because I thought it was such a different book. And that people would say, "Why doesn't she write the way she used to?" Because actually there were a couple of reviews of *Various Miracles* which said just that. I expected that. If readers are on to a certain thing, they really don't want you to change too much.

This may be very arrogant of me, but this is one of the nice things about getting older: you really don't care that much — everyone is just going to have so many books that they're going to be able to write in their lifetime. You know it's a finite number. And I guess I do feel the pressure of that. I don't know how many more books I'll write. And I'm trying to do something different in this new novel, which is to get away from the set-up of the isolated character in their situation. And get in some of the noise and confusion of the world around them. I've put much more of that in — that's the different thing — and it's made the book quite long. But I hope it's got a kind of texture that my other books haven't.

K: Bringing in more background, more 'ground' for the 'figures'?

S: Yes . . . I really mean the noise of the world around people. Because I think that's been part of the problem with realistic fiction: that it hasn't been realistic. I just read Anita Brookner's new novel, which I liked, but this is what she was doing: if you read the novel you'd think the character went from year to year without being invited to a party, or having any discussions with his colleagues. It's a kind of false isolation, and she's done it for a special effect. But I want to make it *more* realistic, in a way that realistic novels haven't done.

John Metcalf

PICKING WINNERS

In 1988 I was interviewed at the Eighth International Conference of Canadian Studies at the University of Catania in Sicily. The following quotation formed part of the published interview. Giovanna Capone of the University of Bologna asked me:

> In addition to your writing, you also have a very important and dedicated commitment to you activity as editor. Dealing with the contemporary is always a difficult task. Do you ever get the feeling of being somewhat critically arrogant?

To this question I responded:

> A writer *has* to have a degree of arrogance to survive and to keep producing in the face of the general indifference and an editor needs something of the same resolution. I'm very aware, though, that I have blind spots and prejudices and that's why I've always chosen to co-edit — first with Clark Blaise and then with Leon Rooke and Kent Thompson.
>
> I'm also very aware that one shouldn't go on doing this job too long. I've been doing it for thirteen years now — thirteen years of annual anthologies, that is. I've been editing texts for schools and universities for over twenty years. Within the next five years I think I'll be withdrawing from all this entirely.
>
> In many ways, of course, I shouldn't have been doing this job at all. My work *has* been arrogant and partisan in that it's tried to promote certain writers and sorts of writing and has tried to limit and demote others. In other words, I've been editing *as a writer* and as a front-line fighter in the literary wars. Ideally, editors should be above the fray but Canada has a sore lack of commentators whose literary judgement can be respected. And an abundance of literary pundits with sawdust for brains. Our periodicals and magazines don't encourage intelligent literary debate or review so we're forced to eat the dry bread of *Saturday Night* and *Books in Canada*. We just

don't seem to produce Edmund Wilsons or Cyril Connollys. We're forced to make do with poor Bobby Fulford. And during most of the time I've been editing, the academic fraternity, far from supporting what I would have thought was *obviously* the best, doggedly upheld as excellent, writing that was, by any standard, verging on the rank. Mazo de la Roche, Callaghan, Buckler — that sort of stuff. So the universities, by manning the nationalist barricades, declared themselves as enemies of good writing. But the enemy is legion — complacency, a resolute love of the mediocre, literary nationalism, astonishing levels of illiteracy, the general anti-intellectual tenor of Canadian life, a school system destroyed by fad and soft-centered populist politics. It is always salutary to remember that despite the untold millions poured into literary subsidy and despite the almost incessant blathering about 'Canadian culture' by ministers and bureaucrats, a novel or collection of stories sells, if well-reviewed, an average of 500 to 1000 copies and that figure *includes* sales to libraries. There seems to be some evidence in the last few years that those figures are now too high.

But the main enemy of art in Canada has been narrow Canadian nationalism. Here's an anecdote which might suggest — although inadequately — the bitter nature of the struggles over the last fifteen years. When Clark Blaise once went to read at York University in Toronto, Dave Godfrey who was teaching there at the time told his students that they would incur his displeasure if any of them attended a reading *given by an American* . . .

And this kind of small viciousness hasn't ended yet. Blaise's work is still excluded from some allegedly representative anthologies. As is Leon Rooke's. As is mine. The "official" reputations of Normal Levine and Mavis Gallant are only just recovering from the stigma of expatriation.

So, yes, I've been *monumentally* arrogant. By anthologizing what I consider the best in short fiction I've tried deliberately to *create* a taste in Canada which wasn't here when I emigrated. I've tried to create a taste which goes very much against the Canadian literary grain. "Journalism," as Louis Dudek has bitterly said, "is the *literature* of Canada." I've tried quite deliberately to create a readership and I've tried to coach that readership in the art of reading. I've *failed*, of course, but I've *tried*. I've tried to stress technique, language, and rhetoric. If you look back over the last twenty or twenty-five years, you'll see in school and university textbooks I've edited that these concerns have been consistently taught — and promoted. The editing, the anthologizing, the teaching, the readings by *Montreal Story Teller* and the *ECW Road Show*, the correspondence with younger writers — it's all been an attempt to build a literary sophistication, to tie us more firmly to the best writing in English. I've tried to promote Canadian writing but within the context of writing-in-English.

For weeks after an interview or an important conversation we find ourselves thinking at odd moments: What I *should* have said was . . . This essay gives me the opportunity to revisit Professor Capone's question — or charge, rather — of critical arrogance. In a period when the traditional verities are under fierce assault and when the very ideas of evaluation and hierarchy are to many university teachers of English intellectually embarrassing and when the only critical constants seem to be indeterminacy and flux, how can I feel confident in my ability to select the best writers for the anthologies I edit? How can I even continue to use expressions like "the best writers"? Isn't the age of such anthologies over, played out? How can such anthologies speak to the concerns of a pluralistic society, to the concerns of women, visible minorities, native peoples, the differently abled, and the aged?

All good questions. All worthy of an answer.

All literary judgements are subjective and the best the anthologist can hope for is to have been right more times than wrong. I can hear voices asking, What does 'right' mean? but let me return to that question a little later. Literature and our reactions to it are constantly changing and over the years there is a continuous shaking-down and winnowing-out. If I have gleaned one piece of wisdom from watching the evolution of Canadian writing over the last thirty years it is that the one constant is diminution.

Even in the last ten years Canada's literary landscape has dramatically changed its face. Ten to fifteen years ago there was one Canadian canon — a canon hastily cobbled together by nationalistic academics. Now, as Ray Smith has observed, there are two, an Eastern canon and a Western canon.

(As an aside, future historians should explore the role of David Arnason in the creation of both.)

Reputations that once hung over the literary battlefield like searing flares are now burned down to ash and cinder. When I first came to Canada, Hugh Garner was considered a story writer to reckon with. Morley Callaghan's reputation was high and inviolable. He was hailed as the Father of the Canadian Short Story. Watch for slippage. Margaret Laurence once seemed to dominate our literary world but now seems a transitional writer, a writer more at the end of a tradition, less our contemporary than we had thought. Rudy Wiebe is more celebrated in the western canon than in the eastern. And where now is Dave Godfrey?

All, you will notice, winners of the Governor-General's Award for Literature.

Dave Godfrey, founder of presses, vociferous anti-imperialist, cultural spokesperson, *animateur* of nationalist brouhaha, won the Governor-General'sAward for his 1970 novel *The New Ancestors*. In the same year, Norman Levine published *From a Seaside Town*. The one drifts down towards history's footnotes, the other stands more and more clearly revealed as at the centre of our literature.

Any takers for the view that *Canada Made Me* will come to be seen as one of the core Canadian books?

And what is Time doing to the reputations of our poets? We find that we have bestowed ludicrous accolades on E.J. Pratt; that much of Earle Birney will be jettisoned; that F.R. Scott is hopelessly imitative; that A.J.M. Smith is too consciously clever; that Ralph Gustafson is costively cultured and Purdy more than a mite garrulous . . .

The British-Scottish-Irish-Empire Loyalist canon celebrated in Margaret Atwood's *Survival* — a book rumoured to have sold eighty thousand copies — is now, only nineteen years after the book's publication, no canon at all but simply a curiosity in our literary history, a dead, closed little world of wretchedly bad writers to whom nationalist fervour gave a brief semblance of life.

I was born in England in 1938 into a middle class family. The writers I grew up on — say until the age of twelve or thirteen — were mainly the middlebrow writers of the first third of the century. Where are the looming figures of that period now? Where are H.G. Wells, Arnold Bennett, John Masefield, John Drinkwater, Alfred Noyes, Robert Bridges, Hillaire Belloc, Michael Arlen, Hugh Walpole, Rupert Brooke, J.B. Priestly . . .

It is all rather like a fading sepia photograph one peers at attempting to make out the features of a scarcely remembered relative.

And what happened to the critical reputations of their contemporary modernist opponents? Those reputations are still high but they have suffered a diminution: D.H. Lawrence, Ford Maddox Ford, Virginia Woolf, Ezra Pound, T.S. Eliot . . . Still very much *there* but more admired than *read*, I'd venture.

One single anecdote can suggest the ephemeral nature of literary reputation and serve as a memento to the complacent pundit.

In 1924 Michael Arlen published a novel called *The Green Hat*. It was the talk of literary England and was one of the very first monumental block-busters. Who has heard of it now? Who remembers Michael Arlen? In the same year but to no fanfare whatsoever and to almost total critical neglect, a pathetically shy, slightly mad, flamboyantly homosexual writer called Ronald Firbank paid to have published a most peculiar slim volume entitled *Prancing Nigger*. Here are its opening sentences:

> Looking gloriously bored, Miss Miami Mouth gaped up into the boughs of a giant silk-cotton-tree. In the lethargic noontide nothing stirred: all was so still, indeed, that the sound of something snoring was clearly audible among the canefields far away.
>
> 'After dose yams an' pods an' de white falernum, I dats way sleepy too,' she murmured, fixing heavy, somnolent eyes upon the prospect that lay before her.
>
> Through the sun-tinged greenery shone the sea, like a floor of silver glass strewn with white sails.
>
> Somewhere out there, fishing, must be her boy, Bamboo!

In 1926 he published, again at his own expense, a book some would judge one of the masterpieces of twentieth century writing, a slim volume entitled *Concerning the Eccentricities of Cardinal Pirelli*. Firbank's reputation has been kept alive by other writers and by a tiny but always-growing readership. What pundit or anthologist in 1924 could have predicted such strange turns and twists of literary fate?

Fully aware, then, of the subjectivity of judgement and of what a damn fool history can prove one to be, let me try to answer the question: How can you be so arrogant as to presume to judge contemporary work?

The beginning of my answer must be: How can I *not* judge? Academic opinion may currently dislike such words as "better" and "best" no longer believing them to be useful or even meaningful but artists will always feel different. Most writers, pronounced "dead" by literary theorists in the universities, look upon university theorists as obscurantists busily spilling their seed on the ground. Artists have no problems whatsoever with "better" and "best." The jazz pianist Paul Bley once said, "You go to where the heat is and you *become* the heat." There is a hunger in all good young artists for 'the heat'; they need to measure and sharpen themselves against it. Unlike theorists, they have no problems knowing what 'the heat' is or where to find it.

The whole of the artistic life is concerned with evaluation. When an artist puts down a line on a piece of paper, he is comparing that line consciously or unconsciously with the line he's seen in the work of others and with every other line he himself has previously drawn. Every stroke is made against the accumulated knowledge and taste of his entire life as an artist.

It is this kind of knowledge — a carpenter's knowledge of wood, a smith's of steel, a potter's knowledge of clay and fire — that I bring to reading and anthologizing. I feel comfortable as an anthologist because I know why and how the writers are doing what they are doing. To be somewhat paradoxical, I *recognize* new writers. I intend the word 'recognize' in its sense of 'identify something or someone *as being known before*'. That doesn't and does make sense. I regard my editing and anthologizing as an extension of my own writing and look upon short story writing in Canada as in some senses an almost co-operative activity. It's as if we've all got our arms in the same huge mixing bowl though in the Baked Goods section at the annual fair there's stiff competition for first, second, and third.

First, second, and third? This business of evaluation and hierarchy is not an *absolute* matter. It is not so much a question of having to decide if Mavis Gallant is a better writer than Alice Munro but is more a matter of understanding that both are in a different class from Margaret Atwood.

And as to those earlier questions about whether anthologies can speak to the concerns of a pluralistic society, to the concerns of women, visible minorities, native peoples, the aged, etc., there is a simple answer; they're the wrong questions to ask. Such concerns are the business of bureaucrats, politicians, the politically correct in universities, and self-censoring editors in textbook publishing. Writers do not sit down to address 'society', pluralistic or otherwise; they sit down to wrestle with language. The anthologist must understand that struggle and concern himself solely with the quality of the words on the page, with the depth and quality of the experience the story affords. There are, of course, 'special interest' anthologies — collections of stories or poems by women, blacks, gays, black women, gay natives, ex-nuns — but, not surprisingly, they are often of a wavering quality and it is hard to avoid the conclusion that the anthologizer is interested less in art than in, say, gayness or ex-nunness.

The anthologizer does art a disservice to select stories and writers to serve or bolster political ends or to mirror fashionable orthodoxies. I was disturbed by Robert Weaver's latest Oxford University Press anthology *Canadian Short Stories: Fifth Series*. The aim of the anthology was to present the best story writers of the second half of the eighties. One of the selling points of the book in the catalogue advertising was: "New Canadian and native Canadian writers included." How horribly revealing is that word 'included'. Examination of the contents further revealed that 'New Canadians' meant of 'West Indian origin'. Being 'new' or 'native' seems a less than adequate qualification for being selected for an anthology of the best writing of the second half of the eighties. And it was doubly unfortunate that the three stories in question were among the weakest in the book. It is hard to avoid the conclusion that Weaver was deliberately indulging in the lunacy of literary affirmative action.

Earlier, I promised to return to the question of what the word 'right' meant when I said that the best the anthologist could hope for was to have been right more times than wrong. 'Right' means a general consensus amongst readers, critics, teachers, anthologizers, bibliographers, and literary historians that a writer is of lasting importance. It is a consensus which takes a long time to evolve. I would suggest that there is a first stage which takes about twenty-five years and then a second stage which takes about another twenty-five wherein the judgements of the first stage are reconsidered. Those writers I have claimed as being our best are approaching the end of the first stage. So far — and I stress *so far* — I seem to have been more right than wrong. But what about the *next* twenty-five years?

Morley Callaghan's reputation as a story writer was high in his first twenty-five year period and the consensus was strong. A few years ago, close to the fifty year mark, it began to weaken. Consensus is now crumbling. In a few more years perhaps only half a dozen stories will survive and even those mainly in the context of school books and literary history. How could this have happened? Why did it take so long? The answers must take into account the lack of literary sophistication in the country, the Canadian capacity for nationalist self-delusion, the lack of any domestic competition, the dreadful lapse from attention in *O Canada* of Edmund Wilson, Callaghan's famous friendships with Hemingway and Fitzgerald, Weaver's cossetting and promotion of his reputation on CBC, sheer longevity . . . But as the years rolled by none of this could disguise the formulaic constructions, the vitiating sentimentality, the numb plod of the language.

I have stood against the consensus on Callaghan for years. I still stand against the prevailing consensus on Margaret Atwood's short fiction and on W.D. Valgardson. In a recent critical overview of Canadian short fiction Michelle Gadpaille of the University of Toronto claims Alice Munro, Mavis Gallant, and Margaret Atwood are the three greatest story writers in Canada. I share her admiration for the first two but predict that Margaret Atwood's fiction will suffer the same fate as Callaghan's; it limits itself too seriously by its didactic and moralizing qualities. Valgardson's work is shallow, his language lax and lacking any fierce edge, yet he is represented in nearly all anthologies and George Woodcock has pronounced him to be one of the three best story writers in the country. Or was it one of the best two? He also wins CBC Literary Competitions — an ominous sign, I would have thought. So I remain serene. We shall see what the next twenty-five years will bring.

To survive the first twenty-five years, a writer must have talent. To survive the second twenty-five, a writer must have had something more. I would suggest that the survivors are going to be those whose work was difficult and demanding, even off-putting, when it was written; to caricature the point, it's the grit of Mavis Gallant we'll be reading in fifty years and not the Brautigan-inspired milk-chocolate-soft-centres of W.P. Kinsella. It is a commonplace that strange and demanding work becomes easier over time; we grow into it. That which is easy when written usually rots down to become literature's invisible leafmold. Any story to which we have to give now the benefit of the doubt is doomed to oblivion. Any story which we now suspect of flaws, soft spots, imprecisions, exaggerations . . . time will more clearly reveal it all.

We most certainly *have* classic stories; our problem might be our inability to recognize them. Just as an exercise in provoking the gods, I'd suggest that Norman Levine's story "A Small Piece of

Blue" is one of them. It was one of the very few stories omitted by the Penguin Books editors from *Champagne Barn*, Levine's selected stories.

Sometimes it takes nudging and shoving and championing before a writer gets slotted into his or her deserved and proper place and the anthologist thereby plays a part in creating consensus and establishing the canon. Geoff Hancock's *Canadian Fiction Magazine* special issue on Mavis Gallant, for example, must be credited with bringing her more centrally to our parochial attention. Similarly, in anthologies and essays I have urged on readers and critics the pleasures and accomplishments of Norman Levine and Clark Blaise. There will doubtless be shifts and adjustments in the rankings of those story writers I've selected in my anthologies as 'best' but I don't think that I've failed to recognize important contenders or esteemed the untalented. Despite the present general disregard, I remain steadfast in the belief that Hugh Hood's *Around the Mountain* and Clark Blaise's *A North American Education* — along with other slighted volumes — will come to be seen as classics of our literature. I remain content with what I've done.

Really?

Doubt should always nag the anthologist. It is a necessary anxiety. Surely posterity . . . This is one of my horrors. One of the 4 a.m. rehearsals when sleep won't come. Is it possible — surely not? — that posterity might view me much as I view such silly old buggers as Sir Arthur Quiller-Couch and A.L. Rowse?

It is entirely possible.

But, for me, the die is cast.

How, then, do I set about making choices?

In the year that I was born, 1938, Cyril Connolly published a book about literary style called *Enemies of Promise*. When I read this book years later it changed and deepened my understanding of literature to such an extent that I can say absolutely seriously that the book changed my life. Connolly's career as writer, reviewer, editor, publisher, book-collector, cultural impresario and *arbiter elegantiae* also suggested to me the possibility of a literary life lived passionately. Here from the book's opening chapter is the passage which had such a profound impact on me so many years ago:

> What kills a literary reputation is inflation. The advertising, publicity and enthusiasm which a book generates — in a word its success — imply a reaction against it. The element of inflation

in a writer's success, the extent to which it has been forced, is something that has to be written off. One can fool the public about a book but the public will store up resentment in proportion to its folly. The public can be fooled deliberately by advertising and publicity or it can be fooled by accident, by the writer fooling himself. If we look at the boom pages of the Sunday papers we can see the fooling of the public going on, inflation at work. A word like genius is used so many times that eventually the sentence 'Jenkins has genius. *Cauliflower Ear* is immense!' becomes true because he has as much genius and is as immense as are the other writers who have been praised there. It is the words that suffer for in the inflation they have lost their meaning. The public at first suffers too but in the end it ceases to care and so new words have to be dragged out of retirement and forced to suggest merit. Often the public is taken in by a book because, although bad, it is topical, its up-to-dateness passes as originality, its ideas seem important because they are 'in the air'. *The Bridge of San Luis Rey, Dusty Answer, Decline and Fall, Brave New World, The Postman Always Rings Twice, The Fountain, Good-by Mr. Chips* are examples of books which had a success quite out of proportion to their undoubted merit and which now reacts unfavourably on their authors, because the overexcitable public who read those books have been fooled. None of the authors expected their books to become best-sellers but, without knowing it, they had hit upon the contemporary chemical combination of illusion with disillusion which makes books sell.

But it is also possible to write a good book and for it to be imitated and for those imitations to have more success than the original so that when the vogue which they have created and surfeited is past, they drag the good book down with them. This is what happened to Hemingway who made certain pointillist discoveries in style which have almost led to his undoing. So much depends on style, this factor of which we are growing more and more suspicious, that although the tendency of criticism is to explain a writer either in terms of his sexual experience or his economic background, I still believe his technique remains the soundest base for a diagnosis, that it should be possible to learn as much about an author's income and sex-life from one paragraph of his writing as from his cheque stubs and his love-letters, and that one should also be able to learn how well he writes, and who are his influences. Critics who ignore style are liable to lump good and bad writers together in support of preconceived theories.

An expert should be able to tell a carpet by one skein of it; a vintage by rinsing a glassful round his mouth. Applied to prose there is one advantage attached to this method — a passage taken from its context is isolated from the rest of a book, and cannot depend on the goodwill which the author has cleverly established with his reader. This is important, for in all the books which become best-sellers and then flop, this salesmanship exists. The author has fooled the reader by winning him over at the beginning, and so establishing a favourable atmosphere for putting across his inferior article — for making him accept false sentiment, bad writing, or unreal situations. To write a best-seller is to set oneself a problem in seduction. A book of this kind is a confidence trick. The reader is given a cigar and a glass of brandy and asked to put his feet up and listen. The author then tells him the tale. The most favourable atmosphere is a stall at a theatre, and consequently of all things which enjoy contemporary success that which obtains it with least merit is the average play.

A great writer creates a world of his own and his readers are proud to live in it. A lesser writer may entice them in for a moment, but soon he will watch them filing out.

One sentence from these paragraphs was the Damascus Road experience for me: "An expert should be able to tell a carpet by one skein of it; a vintage by rinsing a glassful round his mouth." (I don't think 'skein' was the word he wanted; oddly enough, Connolly can often be a clumsy writer.)

This sentence changed the way I thought and felt about prose. As the sentence grew in my mind, the implications and ramifications continued to amaze me. The sentence forced me first of all to stop thinking about plot or context. It forced me to think about *how* a writer writes; it forced me to think about verbs and nouns, adjectives and adverbs, the nature and level of diction, the placement of words, the rhythms of sentences, the functions of punctuation. In brief, it forced me to consider writing as *technical performance*, as rhetoric organized to achieve certain emotional effects.

The sentence also implies, of course, that the entire story, the entire book, must be written with an intensity that will live up to and survive the sort of scrutiny given to the one paragraph. Connolly is implying a prose written with the deliberation usually given to poetry.

The sentence further implies that form and content are indivisible, that the *way* something is being said *is* what is being said.

The sentence also suggests that a piece of writing should be a refined pleasure — as is wine, as are the old Persian carpets made before the introduction of aniline dyes. This in turn implies that good prose is not something we read through for comprehension, for information, as a medium for getting us from A to B. Connolly suggest we *taste* the prose, fondle it, explore and experience it. What a radical way of looking at prose this is! For when we have explored it, we have not finished with it; we cannot then dismiss it as "understood". We can come back to it again and again as we do with paintings or music. "Understanding" in the utilitarian high school or university sense is a barrier to understanding; if we have read properly, we have not "understood" the prose — an intellectual activity — rather, we have *experienced* the prose by entering into a relationship with it. Prose which is brilliantly performed offers inexhaustible pleasures.

Connolly is a harsh taskmaster. He will not tolerate a single sour note. He is urging the writer to aim for nothing less than perfection. This is imposing an almost unendurable burden but on the other hand what really is the point in aiming lower?

Evelyn Waugh reviewed *Enemies of Promise* on its appearance and offered these criticisms:

> . . . he recommends the habit of examining isolated passages, as a wine taster judges a vintage by rinsing a spoonful round his mouth; thus, says Mr. Connolly, the style may be separated from the impure considerations of subject matter. But the style is the whole. Wine is a homogeneous substance: a spoonful and a Jeraboam have identical properties; writing is an art which exists in a time sequence; each sentence and each page is dependent on its predecessors and successors; a sentence which he admires may owe its significance to another fifty pages distant. I beg Mr. Connolly to believe that even quite popular writers take great trouble sometimes in this matter.

Waugh is here applying a sensible brake to what some might regard as Connolly's extremism. Waugh is quite correct in saying that "the style is the whole" and correct also to point out that prose "exists in a time sequence." One might also point out other possible dangers in choosing paragraphs purely at random; the writer might be affecting an awkwardness of voice or syntax to describe indirectly the character and circumstances of the narrator; the reader might accidentally happen upon a passage where the writer is employing a deliberate flatness or is deliberately indulging in purple prose for comic purposes the reader of an isolated paragraph is not privy to. All this is true but it's been my experience that, making allowances for the fact that writing "exists in a time sequence," Connolly's emphasis and prescription is always revealing, always rewarding.

(Connolly's basic attitudes towards writing are in the tradition of the aesthete and the dandy and readers should be aware that some gifted writers and sensible critics are repelled by them. Waugh spoke of "Mr. Connolly's preference for the epicene" and in the same review I quoted from earlier he wrote, "in all he admires and all that strikes him as significant, whether for praise or blame, there is a single common quality — the lack of masculinity. Petronius, Gide, Firbank, Wilde . . . the names succeed one another of living and dead writers, all, or almost all, simpering and sidling across the stage . . .")

Choosing stories, then.

I am likely to enter a story in an arbitrary manner. I might read the first sentence first but am just as likely to read a paragraph at random. All that concerns me is to get a feel for the quality of the language — the Connolly prescription. When I start reading, I'm waiting for the writing to plug me into its current. I am more excited by a single spark of language than I am by reams of solid competence. A hash of a story, a veritable dog's dinner, can interest me more than quires of competence if it's touched by the fire of language.

I was reading a story the other day by a beginning writer, perhaps the second story she has published. Within four sentences I knew she was a writer I wanted to read and keep an eye on. What will happen to her writing in the future I have no idea; I can find good writing but I can't predict careers. I will preserve her anonymity but here are the story's first four sentences:

They call it a state of emergency. White dervishes scour Stephen-ville, the blue arm of the plough impotently slashes through the snow. In St. John's where my mother is, the wires are frozen with sleet and the electricity is out. She's in the plaid chair, I know, one emergency candle and a flashing drink of rye.

The spark?
Well, yes, of course — *flashing*.
Good writing has a tension in it. To read it is rather like putting your hand on a rope or cable which is stretched taut; the cable is alive under your hand. Slack writing *feels* slack. When I use the word 'tension' I don't necessarily mean writing which is flashy, vibrating, giving off sparks; the writing could equally well be calm and majestically slow-moving. It isn't possible to lay down rules for the creation of tension nor is it really possible to describe it. The best I can offer is that I can feel it when I put my hand on the prose. Not much help, I know, but here are some examples:

Priests called on us, though not for the sake of our dodging souls. They came to the camp to relax, to release their eccentricities like dogs that needed a good run in the country. They kept a respectful distance from the unholy water, crossing themselves against it, while at the same time dealing fearlessly with the other fluid elements my parents had on hand. Our hospitality was reciprocated by their own brand of generosity. Almost any spiritual perk could be ours for the asking. If they drank too much, they got reckless and would dispense blessings like pie-eyed fairy godmothers. Trigger-happy, they sanctified the toaster, the shot glasses, the Crest Hardware calendar — once Father Donelly winged a fly in midair — on and on until our kitchen grew hazy and numinous with grace, more sacred than the Vatican itself.

(Terry Griggs from "Quickening" in her collection *Quickening*.)

With only minutes to go before his train's departure, the barmaid in the Great North-Western Bar and Buffet set before him a double scotch, a half of best bitter, and a packet of Balkan Sobranie cigarettes. Flipping open his new wallet, he riffled the crisp notes with the ball of his thumb. The notes were parchment stiff, the wallet so new it creaked. Smiling, he dismissed the considerable change.

The scotch made him shudder. The aroma of the Sobranie cigarettes as he broke the seal and raised the lid was dark, strange, and rich. He was aware of the shape and weight of the wallet in his jacket's side pocket. Stamped in gold inside the wallet were the words which gave him obscure pleasure: *Genuine Bombay Goat.* With a deft flick of his wrist, he extinguished the match and let it fall from a height into the ashtray; the cigarette was stronger than he could have imagined. He raised the half of bitter in surreptitious toast to his reflection behind the bar's bottles. Smoke curling from his nostrils, he eyed the Cypriot barmaid whose upper front teeth were edged in gold.

(John Metcalf from "Single Gents Only" in his collection *Adult Entertainment.*)

His mother had come of age in a war and then seemed to live a long greyness like a spun-out November. "Are you all right?" she used to ask him at breakfast. What she really meant was: Ask me how I am, but she was his mother and so he would not. He leaned two fists against his temples and read a book about photography, waiting for her to cut bread and put it on a plate for him. He seldom looked up, never truly saw her — a stately, careless widow with unbrushed red hair, wearing an old fur coat over her nightgown . . .

(Mavis Gallant from "His Mother" in *From the Fifteenth District.*)

The woman who opened the door was small. She had a dressing-gown on over a nightdress. Her hair was grey, fuzzy, and held in place by a net. Though it was early afternoon the fact that she had obviously just come out of bed did not seem as startling as her face. The eyes were there. So was the mouth. But where her nose should have been there was a flat surface of scarred flesh with two small holes.

'You caught me undressed.'

I told her I wanted a room for one night. She led me upstairs to a bedroom. A square room with a window and a large four-poster bed. 'It's a feather bed,' she said. 'They are much better than spring or rubber. The feathers they sleep with you like another person.'

My first impulse was to make some excuse, leave, and find another place.

'The clever doctors, to them I ought to be dead.'

She said this without sadness or humour. Then she showed me the bathroom, the light switch, asked me if I liked music, if $1.50 was not too much for the room, and placed on the kitchen table some cold chicken with sliced cucumber that she had taken from the ice-box.

(Norman Levine from "A Small Piece of Blue" in *One Way Ticket*.)

In those days I was spending a lot of time out at the Montrose Record Center on Bélanger, west of Montée Saint-Michel. As you come over from the centre of town, east on Jean Talon or Bélanger, you'll be struck by the flatness and lack of charm of this neighbourhood. What is it, northern Rosemount or eastern City of Montréal? I've forgotten the boundary sheets, if in fact I ever knew them. It's *calme, plat, terne*, though you might be interested by the Italian neighbourhood between Papineau and D'Iberville, lots of *gelata* parlors and *sartorie*. On Papineau near Bélanger there are two dozen brand-new multiple dwellings, quadruplexes and octoplexes inhabited by Italians who have made a few bucks since they got here; they may own a store, or four dump-trucks, or a gardening business — the city is full of Italian gardeners — in which they employ relatives, more recent arrivals.

These enormous new places they're living in, along Papineau, are built exactly like all others all over the island, but the Italian ones somehow or other have an unmistakably Mediterranean air, very curious to discover in Montréal in the pale watery haze of early March, the snow melting, evaporating, obscuring the weak sun. It's the paint. They've all been painted in the most cheerful colours. Instead of brown brick and fake-modern light fixtures, you get yellow or white stucco or pink or electric blue, with plenty of enormous lamps in the wide windows.

This is certainly gay and distinctive, but when you are past the Italian strip, you're past the charm; the streets north and south no longer have names but numbers, First Avenue, Seventh Avenue, all the way out to the extreme east end, where Forty-fifth Avenue winds off into fields. In a city with a rue Mozart, rue Guizot, rue Danté, this dull system seems regrettable.

(Hugh Hood from "Bicultural Angela" in *Around the Mountain: Scenes from Montreal Life*.)

My father has a job, selling for Walker Brothers. This is a firm that sells almost entirely in the country, the back country. Sunshine, Boylesbridge, Turnaround — that is all his territory. Not Dungannon where we used to live, Dungannon is too near town and my mother is grateful for that. He sells cough medicine, iron tonic, corn plasters, laxatives, pills for female disorders, mouthwash, shampoo, liniment, salves, lemon and orange and raspberry concentrate for making refreshing drinks, vanilla, food colouring, black and green tea, ginger, cloves and other spices, rat poison. He has a song about it, with these two lines:

And have all liniments and oils,
For everything from corns to boils . . .

Not a very funny song, in my mother's opinion. A pedlar's song, and that is what he is, a pedlar knocking at backwoods kitchens. Up until last winter we had our own business, a fox farm. My father raised silver foxes and sold their pelts to the people who make them into capes and coats and muffs. Prices fell, my father hung on hoping they would get better next year, and they fell again, and he hung on one more year and one more and finally it was not possible to hang on any more, we owed everything to the feed company. I have heard my mother explain this, several times, to Mrs. Oliphant who is the only neighbour she talks to. (Mrs. Oliphant also has come down in the world, being a schoolteacher who married the janitor.) We poured all we had into it, my mother says, and we came out with nothing. Many people could say the same thing, these days, but my mother has no time for the national calamity, only ours. Fate has flung us onto a street of poor people (it does not matter that we were poor before, that was a different sort of poverty), and the only way to take this, as she sees it, is with dignity, with bitterness, with no reconciliation. No bathroom with a claw-footed tub and a flush toilet is going to comfort her, nor water on tap and sidewalks past the house and milk in bottles, not even the two movie theatres and the Venus Restaurant and Woolworths so marvellous it has live birds singing in its fan-cooled corners and fish as tiny as fingernails, as bright as moons, swimming in its green tanks. My mother does not care.

(Alice Munro from "Walker Brothers Cowboy", in *Dance of the Happy Shades*.)

Thibidault and son: he was a fisherman and I always fished at his side. Fished for what? I wonder now — he was too short and vain a man to really be a fisherman. He dressed too well, couldn't swim, despised the taste of fish, shunned the cold, the heat, the bugs, the rain. And yet we fished every Sunday, wherever we lived. Canada, Florida, the Middle West, heedless as deer of crossing borders. The tackle box (oily childhood smell) creaked at our feet. The fir-lined shores and pink granite beaches of Ontario gleamed behind us. Every cast became a fresh hope, a trout or *doré* or even a muskie. But we never caught a muskie or a trout, just the snake-like fork-boned pike that we let go by cutting the line when the plug was swallowed deep. And in Florida, with my father in his Harry Truman shirts and sharkskin pants, the warm bait-well sloshing with half-dead shiners, we waited for bass and channel cat in Okeechobee, Kissimmee and a dozen other bug-beclouded lakes. Gar fish, those tropical pike, drifted by the boat. Gators churned in a narrow channel and dragonflies lit on my cane pole tip. And as I grew older and we came back North (but not all the way), I remember our Sundays in Cincinnati, standing shoulder-to-shoulder with a few hundred others around a clay-banked tub lit with arc-lamps. Scummy pay-lakes with a hot dog stand behind, a vision of hell for a Canadian or a Floridian, but we paid and we fished and we never caught a thing. Ten hours every Sunday from Memorial Day to Labour Day, an unquestioning ritual that would see me dress in my fishing khakis, race out early and buy the Sunday paper before we left (so I could check the baseball averages — what a normal kid I might have been!) then pack the tackle box and portable radio (for the Cincinnati double-header) in the trunk. Then I would get my father up. He'd have his coffee and a few cigarettes then shout, 'Mildred, Frankie and I are going fishing!' She would be upstairs reading or sewing. We were still living in a duplex; a few months later my parents were to start their furniture store and we would never fish again. We walked out, my father and I, nodding to the neighbours (a few kids, younger than I, asked if they could go, a few young fathers would squint and ask, 'Not again, Gene?'); and silently we drove, and later, silently, we fished.

(Clark Blaise from "A North American Education", in *A North American Education*.)

Each of these excerpts has an originality, an authority, a power which marks it off from the general run of writing. Have these very different pieces anything in common? There is in all of them a concentration of the world's observable details but not all the pieces are concerned with description and evocation. Alice Munro, for example, is creating modulations of voice, suggesting the child the narrator once was, echoing other voices the child has heard. (For a detailed discussion of these techniques in this story see my essay "Casting Sad Spells".) In my own piece, I am using observed external detail to describe character. Terry Griggs is building comic rhetoric. How I love the word 'sanctified' in her sentence about the inebriated priests: "Trigger-happy, they sanctified the toaster, the shot glasses, the Crest hardware calendar . . ." Hugh Hood is working on the evolution of that very distinctive tone of his — that informal formality, that heightened vernacular which seems so easy but is so singular.

But the extracts do have one thing in common. Each is marked by an individual sense of rhythm, by an individual sensitivity to sound. Of course, different stories by the same writer will employ different rhythms, different rhetorics according to the story's demands but even so every mature writer has, if I may put it like this, a different way of walking. Eventually we can recognize a writer's characteristic constructions and sounds much in the way we can recognize at a distance through familiarity and love the special gait, that unique way of walking, of a wife or husband. Sounds and constructions, rhythms, silences, cadences carved by punctuation — all the subtle technicalities which together add up to a writer's voice — I'm urging you to pay to prose, then, the courtesies you pay to poetry.

I've been reading stories for so long now both published and in manila envelopes that my own response has become professional and possibly even eccentric. At a quick count, I've edited twenty-two anthologies so far and I'm working on two more at the moment. In addition, I've edited or generally readied for publication collections by Isabel Huggan, Ann Copeland, Robert Gibbs, Leon Rooke, Hugh Hood, Dayv James-French, Don Dickinson, Diane Schoemperlen, Keath Fraser, Terry Griggs and Steven Heighton and as I'm working now for the Porcupine's Quill Press new manuscripts threaten me weekly.

I laughed in delighted recognition a few months ago when I was reading Humphrey Carpenter's new biography of Ezra Pound, a life entitled *A Serious Character*. The sentences that made me laugh concerned the writer and editor Ford Maddox Ford:

> He [Pound] delighted in Ford's brisk off-the-cuff literary judgements, which were nearly always right, and in his ability as an editor to detect the quality of a manuscript almost by its smell. ('I don't read manuscripts,' Ford would say, 'I know what's in 'em.')

These lines put me in mind of a passage I'd written years before in a novella called "Travelling Northward":

> Yet another thick manila envelope. He knew what it would contain. He sighed and tossed it onto the counter to open and read later in the day.
> It would contain a manuscript by a young writer who realized how busy he was but dared to hope that he wouldn't mind just jotting down several pages of single-spaced constructive criticism of the enclosed which had been written under considerable personal difficulties.

But as for being "nearly always right" . . . I hope I am. And I certainly *claim* I am. But the truth is, as we have seen, that time often treats anthologizers and literary pundits harshly. Time has certainly not been kind to Ford Maddox Ford. The literary kaleidoscope slips and shifts. What once seemed certainties soon become problematic, then forgettable, then forgotten.

Some of our anthologies — even famous ones — are disasters. Raymond Knister's *Canadian Short Stories* published in 1928 is a sad, lumpy embarrassment of a book. Here are its contributors: Duncan Campbell Scott, Frederick William Wallace, Edward William Thomson, Sir Gilbert Parker, Charles G.D. Roberts, Marjorie Pickthall, Merrill Denison, Morley Callaghan, Stephen Leacock, Norman Duncan, Alan Sullivan, McLaren Imrie, Will E. Ingersoll, Mazo De La Roche, Harvey O'Higgins, Thomas Murtha, and Leslie McFarlane. What barren fields poor Knister had to graze. From the vantage point of 1991 — 63 years later — I'd give him 2 out of 17. Yet these undistinguished stories are now being touted by our nationalist critics as forming the tradition to which we all belong.

These critics claim that Knister's anthology is somehow the herald of 'modernity' and looks forward to the 'modern' story. Actually the reverse is true. It was a collection of largely hack work by journalistic workhorses, a display of the end of a tradition of popular magazine writing by a group of industrious and amiable old frauds. It led nowhere. In my library I have a photograph of Bliss Carman and Sir Charles G.D. Roberts, both in evening dress, Roberts with fixed monocle, Carman with his typical, slightly bewildered Stan Laurel expression, Roberts somehow suggesting Ollie or W.C. Fields, sanctimonious public rectitude with two extra aces up its sleeve. Surely it's no accident that this pair and others of that period remind me of vaudeville and silent comedies, of the fruity bombast of a Sir Donald Wolfit touring *Macbeth* in the provinces. Does this literary past *really* speak to us? Or are we lending ourselves, rather, to an academic invention?

In 1968 Dennis Lee, poet and editor, really tempted the gods when he edited an anthology for the House of Anansi entitled *T.O. Now: The Young Toronto Poets.* But then he added another subtitle: *Preview of a New Generation.* These were his choices in 1968 for the future: Greg Hollingshead, Doug Fetherling, Barry Charles, Andre Scheinman, Ian Young, Peter Skilling, Robert Read, Peter Anson, Charles Douglas, Ted Plantos, Kenneth Yukich, Eldon Garnet, and Wayne Clifford.

Despite these predictions, Lee later went on to become poetry editor at McClelland and Stewart.

All anthologists are putting their literary taste on the line; all would like to look back from the vantage point of fifty years on and pat themselves on the back for the depth and validity of their taste and judgement. But there are endless pitfalls for the anthologist. He can pick out a talented newcomer and encourage and publish that writer only to find that he or she immediately and inexplicably dries up and is never heard from again. Drying up is the absolute opposite of what happens with some writers; alcohol has silenced more than one for whose work I've had high hopes. Some have committed suicide. Domesticity smothers some; divorce rends others. Some succumb to the quick returns of journalism, the pleasure of a daily byline. Some, talented, simply have no stomach for the hardships of the writing life; they find themselves unwilling to forego income, pension, security; unwilling to offer up their eyesight and unwilling to ruin their digestive systems by years of Brunswick sardines and cheese sandwiches in return for the indifference of what audience exists and the offhand insults of critics.

Some simply have bad luck.

All those who wither on the vine complicate the anthologist's task.

The anthologist likes to claim — indeed, does claim — that he sees more clearly than most the shape and outline of a decade or a generation but the anthologist is probably as much molded by the times as is the next man. Who could now ignore gender and colour and, in Canada particularly, native people and regions? They *should* be ignored, of course, but we are all susceptible to the pressures and assumptions of the *Zeitgeist*.

The percipient anthologist — usually a kindly person — is also at danger from that very kindness; it is easy to persuade oneself that work is better than it is simply because the writer is young and trying hard and has managed a certain success. It would probably be beneficial for writers and anthologists and for the literature to fix on a rule that a writer not be anthologized until he or she has published two books. How awkwardly immature work is going to stick out in anthologies as time reveals it more harshly.

All anthologists are liable to lapses of taste and exhibitions of bad judgement. The anthologist who puts together annual collections is particularly prone to errors of judgement because the constraints of an annual tend to mean that he cannot watch a promising newcomer over a period of time and form considered options about the writing and the writer's staying power. It is easy to be momentarily dazzled by flashy work which turns out to be a flash in the pan — as I was by the first few stories of Patrick Roscoe.

The first story of his I read was charming. It was *faux-naif* but well-handled. The second story I read was also charming. By the time I'd read five, the charm and the sweetness had become cloying and that which had at first seemed lyric began to sound more like a monotonous and deliberately naughty incantation, the expression of an extravagant, if not hysterical, sensibility.

Most of my anthologies have been annuals — selections of 'the best' stories of the year. The word 'best' is allowed a little leeway in the circumstances of an annual selection. We tend to be a little less forgiving in anthologies which set out to survey and represent a decade or, indeed, the entire history of the short story in Canada. I have never put together an historical anthology — partly because I feel so doubtful about the quality of our earlier writers. I *have* done several anthologies which claim to represent our best writers and these are inevitably controversial because of the writers they omit. I have never included among our best story writers, for example, Margaret Atwood. She has returned the favour and excluded my work from her recent historical anthology, co-edited with Robert Weaver, *The Oxford Book of Canadian Short Stories in English.* As did Robert Weaver from his last two anthologies *Canadian Short Stories: Fourth Series* and *Fifth Series.* As did Wayne Grady from *The Penguin Book of Canadian Short Stories* and from *The Penguin Book of Modern Canadian Stories.* As did Michael Ondaatje from his recent anthology *From Ink Lake.* In fact, my work has been excluded from every trade anthology of national scope for the last fourteen years. This would suggest either that my work is by common agreement very bad indeed or that the anthologists in question are possibly allowing extra-literary concerns to colour their judgement.

Anthologizing will always be partial and imperfect but it is an important activity. Anthologies, taken together, form a rough consensus about what is happening within the genres. Anthologies are part of the shaping and forming and framing of a literature. Different editors have different biases and literary debate and partisanship are inevitable and healthy. Some editors will operate as feminists, some as nationalists, some as opportunists, some will celebrate regional writing, others will favour mainstream realist writing while some will wish to promote the postmodern and the experimental.

The anthologist, simply by selecting, exercises considerable influence over the direction of the literature and over the canon. Selecting has, of course, two aspects: the elevation of what is selected and the suppression of what isn't.

Let us consider the elevation of what is selected.

Twenty years or so ago in Canada what was necessary was to break out of the time-warp and drag the short story into the mainstream of the twentieth century. My generation of story writers straddled two artistic worlds neither of which had much to do with the Canada we actually lived in. We came out of the preceding generation of American writers but we were aware that the stuff of our inheritance from then had ossified, had become, in Kent Thompson's words, 'Academy Stuff'. Knowing and feeling this, we were all engaged, variously, in working out new forms, new strategies. The worlds we straddled, then, were the world of American past mastery and the new, as-yet-uncreated world of our own invention. The literary actuality in Canada was that audience and critics were so hidebound that they had not really begun to grapple with the work of those writers whose influence we were trying to escape. Naturally, there was little understanding at first of what we were trying to do. Canada still clasped to its bosom the warty crudities of Hugh Garner and the slick heartwarming hayseedery of W.O. Mitchell.

We forged new shapes and I understood my job as writer-editor as the establishing of those shapes. This meant that in addition to writing the stories themselves it was also necessary to teach people how to read them. It was necessary to teach people that new shapes are not simply a technical concern of interest only to writers; new shapes enable us to see and feel anew. It was necessary to teach technique, the nuts and bolts of writing, to enable people to approach the evolving aesthetic.

Editing became for me a crusade.

While I was hammering away on the educational front striving to drive home the importance of diction, punctuation, rhythm, cadence — all that which makes up style — the entire academy trundled its big guns around in entirely the opposite direction and spent a decade or more firing thematic and nationalistic blanks. The acrid clouds of smoke obscured the view for years.

It has all been somewhat frustrating though I do see signs now of encouraging change. Perhaps the most encouraging sign of all is that a new generation of writers is asserting itself and is creating necessarily new shapes. Certain names — among them Keath Fraser, Douglas Glover, Linda Svendsen, Diane Schoemperlen, Dayv James-French, Terry Griggs — already seem to be dominating the contemporary scene.

It was, perhaps, not simply coincidental that the three editors with whom I have chosen to co-edit were all brought up and educated in the USA. My first co-editor was Clark Blaise, my second, Leon Rooke, my third Kent Thompson. Between 1976 and 1990 we have together been responsible for *New Canadian Stories*, *Best Canadian Stories*, the *New Press Anthologies* and the *Macmillan Anthologies*. All three co-editors brought to the process of selection tastes which had been formed by and in the American tradition. (They knew quite intimately the work of the younger and emerging writers in the States, writers who were in many instances acquaintances or friends. They brought to the selection of stories a richer and more rigorous judgement than would have been possible for one brought up on and restricted to a purely Canadian experience — if a purely Canadian experience is, indeed, even a possibility.)

I was not making a conscious decision to work with people versed in the American tradition. It was more a case of working with friends whose own work I admired. It is not perhaps surprising, however, that I was drawn to work which was energized by contact with the source.

(It surely cannot be *too* much longer before the academic inventors of an indigenous tradition which descends, allegedly, from Duncan Campbell Scott — a "tradition" which runs counter to the *obvious* truth — are laughed out of the encyclopedias and literary guides.)

I've always thought that the ability to recognize talent must be widespread, that talent must be fairly obvious to anyone capable of reading, but lately, and particularly during the writing of this essay, I've been recalling anecdotes and incidents which might suggest that to many other people talent is not blindingly obvious.

I remember sending Clark Blaise's story collection *A North American Education* to Anna Porter at McClelland and Stewart in 1972 with a covering letter urging its virtues. I had recently published with McClelland and Stewart a novel called *Going Down Slow* and was thought (mistakenly) to have some influence. Clark's collection was sent back almost by return mail with a letter saying that Anna Porter had found the stories "boring." The book was subsequently published by Doubleday and remains one of the most dazzling Canadian collections ever published. It also remains vastly undervalued.

In the mid-seventies, I became aware in the literary magazines of Leon Rooke's work. Some of the stories seemed more than a little strange to me but I was in no doubt about their power and importance. I *expected* new talent to be challenging, uncomfortable, even off-putting. It usually is. I gathered a few stories together as a sample and took them to Michael Macklem, the publisher at Oberon Press. I urged them upon him. He tried to read one or two but was defeated. Eventually, he said he'd publish a collection because I assured him it was important but only on condition that *I* would make the selection and that *he* wouldn't be required to read it. That book was *The Love Parlour*, Leon's second book and first in Canada. I also put together his third collection *Cry Evil*. Macklem tried to read some of the stories but was again baffled. He asked me to write out for him a few explanatory sentences about each story but later admitted that the stories remained incomprehensible. His bafflement seemingly persists because he is currently compiling an anthology for Harper-Collins of the best short stories Oberon has published over the years; Rooke's work has been excluded.

When Leon and I left Oberon, I moved immediately to ECW Press. I persuaded the publishers, Jack David and Robert Lecker, to publish Leon too. I remember Jack phoning me after he'd read *Death Suite*, the manuscript Leon and I had put together, to ask if I were *sure* that Leon was the right stuff. I assured him. Some little time after this, Leon went to Toronto to do a reading and Jack went to hear him. He phoned me the next day and said, "*Now* I get it. I just couldn't hear the voices on the page until I heard *him* reading the stuff."

Nor was Jack David the only one who couldn't hear. One Canadian reviewer of the deeply Southern novel *Fat Woman* stated that it was set in Nova Scotia.

Keath Fraser, too, had to struggle against literary deafness. A thick manila envelope plopped through the mail-slot one morning and I weighed it in my hand gloomily while drinking breakfast coffee. Feeling oppressed, I ripped the envelope open and glanced at the first paragraph. An hour later I was still in the kitchen almost slack-jawed with admiration. And re-reading. The story was "Le Mal de l'Air." Leon concurred. I phoned Keath Fraser accepting the story for *Best Canadian Stories 1982* and asking to see other work. He said that my call had come just in time to preserve his resolve to go on writing. His stories had, apparently, been rejected by literary magazines all over the country. It still seems inexplicable. A few phone calls and letters soon rectified that most peculiar situation.

So possibly I do have some odd ability to hear things on the page earlier than most other readers. I'm still not totally persuaded that's true. But the point of these anecdotes is to suggest that sometimes the anthologist can invigorate the literature by giving early recognition and emphasis to new writers and new forms.

The reverse is also true. An established anthologist past his prime can fail to recognize important new voices and can continue to promote fading talents he had fostered decades earlier. As I said in the extract from the interview which begins this essay, I'm aware that one should not go on anthologizing too long. My 'retirement' has been set for 1993 when I will be 55.

I was in part prompted to this decision by one of Waugh's letters to an editor who had asked for a contribution to his literary magazine. What Waugh wrote of himself as a writer applies also to the anthologist. Waugh wrote:

> ... in studying your own pages I find that the great majority of the names which are quoted as those of important young writers are wholly unfamiliar to me. That will demonstrate how ignorant I am of recent literary movements. I don't think this is a particularly unhealthy condition for an elderly writer. There are flibbertigibbets who in middle age attend international cultural congresses and busy themselves with the latest fashions. Few of these are notable for their literary production. A writer should have found his *métier* before he is 50. After that he reads only for pleasure; not for curiosity about what others are doing. Please do not interpret this as scorn or jealousy of the young. It is simply that their tastes and achievements are irrelevant to his work ... In middle age a writer knows his capacities and limitations and he has a general conspectus of his future work ...

In essence, then, I have tried to elevate in my anthologizing work which is stylish and elegant, which is taut and quick to the touch. I have promoted the idea of writing as something to be experienced rather than understood, of writing as performance. I have stressed always the centrality of language and rhetoric. By my early championing of Clark Blaise and Leon Rooke and by my co-opting them as editors, I ensured that sophistication and originality were being demanded of the form.

Let us look now at the other side of the coin.

What has my anthologizing tried to restrain or suppress?

There is a strain in Canadian writing which seems to pride itself on being, well, Canadian. And what 'Canadian' seems to mean in this context is utilitarian, lumpy, old-fashioned, innocent of stylistic sophistication of any kind — sophistication of technique being seen as typical of decadent centres like New York and London. This kind of writing prides itself on appearing in long johns and gumboots. *Jake and the Kid* could stand for its 'rural' expression, Hugh Garner and W.D. Valgardson for its urban counterpart. It is nationalist, populist and anti-American, difficult to define further but easy to recognize. Here is Terrence Heath, author of *The*

Truth and Other Stories, talking about its prairie manifestation:

> . . . one stream of prairie writing angered and still angers me.
> For want of a better designation, I would call it the Aw Shucks
> School of Prairie Literature. Wedded to the prevailing oral tra-
> dition of North American writing and some second-hand
> black mountainism, the Aw Shucks School has given birth to
> an interminable number of grandmother poems, pub poems,
> and just plain corn, which make even the Germanisms of
> Grove and Wiebe worth the effort. Aw Shucksism may have
> its roots in the book *Who Has Seen the Wind* and the CBC
> radio series *Jake and the Kid.* The hillbilly narrator, who cer-
> tainly never lived on the Prairies, was, I think, created for an
> Eastern audience in about the same way and for the same rea-
> sons as Amos and Andy were created for white, middle-class
> listeners in the United States. W.O. Mitchell's work was rela-
> tively harmless and amusing. When it was wed to Academe, it
> became cornball and, in my opinion then and now, dangerous.

And here from Academe is the same dumb beast seen from a
slightly different angle, Professor T.D. MacLulich from his
Between Europe and America: The Canadian Tradition in Fiction:

> . . . Canadian literature, especially Canadian fiction, has never
> been notable for its innovations of form. Indeed, its conser-
> vatism has contributed to its distinctiveness from American lit-
> erature. Until very recently, much of the best Canadian fiction
> has sought to occupy a middle ground, using the conventions
> of the bourgeois novel to make significant statements about
> life in particular parts of our country, at particular times. As a
> result, the central tradition in our fiction is found in the work
> of writers such as Grove, Callaghan, MacLennan, Buckler,
> Ross, Mitchell, Wilson, Laurence, Richler, Davies, and Munro.
> These authors do not produce 'popular' literature in the vul-
> garly commercial sense; yet neither do they rely on superficial
> treatments of trendy subjects nor on clever tricks played with
> narrative point of view. They write books that are accessible to
> a wide readership, and they do so without sacrificing their pri-
> vate vision to commercial demands. We should be encouraging
> such writing (and some of us are), rather than calling for exper-
> imental or language-centred fiction. After all, what will we get

if Canadian fiction joins our poetry in adopting the international style? At best, another incarnation of *The Studhorse Man*. At worst, and a more likely result, more works like Bowering's *A Short Sad Book* and *Burning Water*. The games these works play with Canadian themes do not announce the health of a national tradition, but seem to predict its death, crushed by the weight of excessive self-consciousness.

There is much in what MacLulich writes with which I sympathize — of which more in a moment — but I find it hard to think of this passage as being about literature. It seems to me it is about nationalism. MacLulich values the writers he lists not for their literary accomplishments but for their Canadianness, for the conservatism which differentiates them from American writing.

However deep my feelings for Canada, I cannot bring myself to express that passion by embracing the prose of F.P. Grove.

MacLulich's positions are largely shared by Professor David Jackel who wrote the chapter on the short story in the *Literary History of Canada Volume IV*. Here is Professor Jackel's conclusion, the shaggy herbivore heaving itself out of the pre-*glasnost* slough and lumbering into full view:

> The recognition given [to the short story] within Canada was accompanied by serious international attention to the work of Gallant, Munro, Atwood, and others. Less encouraging was the tendency to find the short story a ground on which to battle over the merits of experimental and self-reflexive fiction at the expense of more traditional forms. As well, the promotion of a vague and rootless cosmopolitanism which would somehow accord with 'international standards' invoked but never defined, seemed to deny the Canadian-ness of Canadian short fiction. Such a quality does not require the blatant parading of Canadian settings and issues; it can, as many writers have shown, be made apparent in the ways various themes are presented and considered. Hood, Atwood, Munro, Gallant, Vanderhaege, and others, know their country, its regions, its concerns, its peculiar points of view, even when their stories use non-Canadian settings or deal with human issues that transcend the local or the national. T.D. MacLulich has properly observed that Canada's continued existence, as George Grant claimed, has traditionally been based on an assertion of

particularity against the homogenizing claims of continental-ism and universalism. 'Canadian fiction,' MacLulich asserts, 'has provided some of the most eloquent expressions of our devotion to such particularity'. Writers who seek to attune themselves with currently fashionable theories of art, and neglect the realities of their time and place, add to the risk that literature will become merely source material for social scientists and cultural historians. Fortunately, the variety, the substance, and the quality of many short stories published between 1972 and 1984 give some reason to hope that dogmatic, doctrinaire, and ill-grounded 'international' views will not in the end prevail.

That is the official, Establishment view of the short story in Canada in 1990 — Nanny Has Spoken — and THAT is what I have been anthologizing against for twenty years or more.

It is not only the view of Academe but also the view of many writers and readers and, unfortunately, and inevitably, the view of many students in colleges and universities.

One of the responsibilities of the anthologist in Canada is to attempt to counter the hidebound conservatism and rabid nationalism of such influential sparklers as MacLulich and Jackel. Only in the old Soviet Union and in a variety of Third World hell-holes — and in Canada — would literary historians presume to prescribe rather than describe and castigate any non-toeing of the line. They are calling quite openly for a State Literature.

How long will it be before they move from prescribing to proscribing? Why has no one in a Canadian university commented on this intellectual shabbiness? Why has no one . . .?

But let's not ask silly questions.

I reviewed the *Literary History of Canada Volume IV* in *Saturday Night*. Much of Professor Jackel's chapter on the story is devoted to countering critical positions I had advanced in earlier essays and in *Kicking Against the Pricks* and *What Is a Canadian Literature?* The following brief extract from my review will have to stand as rebuttal to the above; thinking about Professor Jackel's opinions makes me glum:

It is difficult, if not unseemly, for me to comment on the views of Professor David Jackel because much of his chapter is spent countering opinions and arguments I advanced in earlier criticism. I must also note that he describes my own fiction as uneven and, in general, a bit too *arty*. That noted, I must confess to finding his criticism too meat-and-potatoes; he prefers the traditional to the innovative, seems not averse to a firm dollop of moral, and sees stories as a weapon in the armoury of Canadian nationalism.

Although this is not the place to continue our debate, I think Professor Jackel has entirely misunderstood me when he implies that I have urged writers to 'neglect the realities of their time and place' in favour of internationalism. Quite the reverse is true. What I've been saying for twenty years is that to write well about Livelong, Saskatchewan, one must draw on the entire range of technique and sensibility world literature affords. Canadian writing should not pride itself on toiling onward with the rusted tool kit of an Edward McCourt.

Professors MacLulich and Jackel don't seem to have grasped that all good writing is to some extent "experimental or language centered." The style a writer spends a lifetime to create — that special way of walking — is created with language and all good writing is in that sense "language-centered." Language perfectly forged for the task at hand is literature's central and enduring pleasure. We do not return again and again, for example, to Shakespeare's history plays for their themes; we do not return to them to muse over his views on hierarchy or the divine right of kings; we return to them to savour again and again the almost unbearable pleasures of language performing at high voltage. What lies behind the strictures of the good professors with their denigrations of style and innovation and their calls for writing about doughty "themes" is a stunted understanding of literature's possibilities.

Are we not yet mature enough as readers to question the very idea of 'aboutness'?

Too many of the writers in MacLulich's 'central tradition', who should have approached language as if they were cabinet makers, banged and hammered it like rough carpenters on a construction site. Or, just as bad, indulged themselves in faded period gentilities, purple ornament, and flabby periphrasis. Despite the bizarre professional claims for its importance, such writing will not last.

All good writing is, to some extent, experimental. Writers have to push at the conventions, have to experiment to discover their own voices within the tradition or in opposition to it. They cannot keep working in the dominant manner of a great predecessor; they cannot write in someone else's voice. There is no point in my trying to write Hemingway stories; there is no point in writers half my age trying to write Alice Munro stories. The search for new forms is not some mere 'technical' preoccupation of writers; the new forms *are* the new voices, the new sensibilities, *are* the stories.

It follows, then, that traditions themselves do not stand still. The 'traditional forms' to which Professor Jackel would have us hold allegiance are in fact fossil moments in an endless process of change, a process without which literature cannot remain alive. When he calls for loyalty to these forms, he reveals a profound lack of thought about literary history and an amazing insensitivity to the pulse of creation going on about him. Who exactly is Professor Jackel to instruct Diane Schoemperlen, say, or Terry Griggs, that they ought to be writing like Duncan Campbell Scott or Sinclair Ross? He would have been one of those who, on the discovery of cooking, would have insisted on warming gobbets of meat in the time-honoured way between one's thighs. His pronouncements in the *Literary History of Canada* are not the sensitive and percipient judgements of a finely-honed literary mind; they're simply Old Fartism writ large.

The 'mainstream' of writing is not a straight concrete-lined canal but is rather a river which meanders, which flows into backwaters, which sometimes breaks its banks and changes course entirely. It also happens from time to time that the river silts up and sits a stagnant marsh and when that happens some strong talent will emerge to blast the channel clear — often using dynamite manufactured elsewhere.

During this time I've been anthologizing, the 'mainstream' has changed course and has widened itself to include writing that couldn't have been imagined in Canada thirty years ago. Leon Rooke's work, for example, seemed at first mildly crazy; he is now one of the pillars of the establishment. Some critics describe Rooke's work as 'post-modern' but it seems to me that he is far more a traditional writer than might appear, a writer using some 'post-modern' devices for traditional ends. Nearly everything he writes is — thank God! — charged with moral passion. Not for him self-reflexive noodling. His is the voice of the preacher. If criticisms can be brought against his work, they surely must be not that he is aridly experimental but that he is, at times, sentimentally moralistic.

The shift in the 'mainstream' channel has been away from naturalism and realism — and, one might add, ineptitude — towards a variety of concerns some of which could be described as 'post-modern'. But it is important to think carefully about what we mean by 'post-modern'. It is a simplification to think that up to this or that year 'modernism' prevailed and then subsequently that 'post-modernism' became the orthodoxy. Critical labels are sometimes little more than a convenience for critics. All writing is on a continuum. We could perfectly justly say, for example, that Ray Smith was writing 'post-modern' stories in 1969 with his collection *Cape Breton Is the Thought-Control Centre of Canada* years before the 'post-modern' designation was in common use. Nor would it be unreasonable to say that Alice Munro and I were toying with certain 'post-modern' problems as early as 1971. We were both writing stories which commented on themselves or which quoted other texts. In 1973 Alice dedicated to me as a birthday present a story called "Home". In the same or the next year I dedicated to her a story called "The Teeth of My Father". Both stories arose, in part, out of our discussions of theoretical problems. In an essay called "What Is Real?" that Alice wrote years later for my anthology *Making It New* she again touches on similar concerns.

Sometimes we can see a writer writing in a 'modernist' and almost 'pre-modern' style within the covers of one book. Consider Margaret Laurence's *A Bird in the House*; the book contains 'modernist' stories such as "To Set Our House in Order" but also contains stories such as "The Half-Husky" which could have been written at a much earlier period by Garner or Sinclair Ross on a bad day.

All this is to suggest that there are no neat divisions in literary history; styles and techniques flow and eddy in ways no doubt annoying to historians. Writers don't set out to be 'post' or 'pre' anything; they are working hard to find ways of delivering the goods. And by 'the goods' I mean the aesthetic and emotional engagement which I believe all good writing must engender. Some ways work; others do not. If they don't, the writing is 'experimental'.

And here is where I share some of Professor MacLulich's anxieties. If I have concerns about the general bag of tricks called 'post-modernism' they are that the writing can all too easily trickle away into the sands of cleverness, self-consciousness, pastiche, and parody. Far too much of 'post-modernist' writing seems to me to represent a flight from emotion.

The last time I was talking to George Bowering of matters 'postmodern' he said pityingly of another writer, "The poor bugger still believes in all that humanist crap."

So, I find, do I.

Anthologies probably seem to readers to be outside the flow and flux of the business of writing going on. They stand apart from petty and bewildering detail and direct our attention to what is significant. Or that perhaps is how it seems at the time. But anthologies, too, are subject to time passing and fall into disfavour and become fixtures on the shelves of used-book stores. The real judges of our literature are its readers. What survives is what readers want over a long period of time. What survives is what people come to love and hold in their hearts. Anthologies play a part in this process of winnowing but it is surely a very much smaller part than their editors would like to believe.

How deflationary for pundits, aesthetes, embattled theorists, for those with the temerity to believe that they have been influencing the course of the nation's literature, how deflationary to learn that in 1992 one of the most sought-after books in second-hand and antiquarian book stores from coast to coast is *Anne of Green Gables* (1908).

Reviews

Sam Solecki, John Metcalf, and W.J. Keith, *Volleys.*
The Porcupine's Quill, 1990

This is the first volume in the Critical Directions series, which the publisher declares will "explore directions through which criticism can uphold its most urgent responsibilities: to the honouring of literature and language, to the cultivation of a more profound, more valuable experience of art and life, and to the building of a more enlightened society." Although it remains to be seen whether the series can live up to these lofty ambitions, the authors of this three-sided debate do at least address these questions. Criticism is not, for them, a sterile exercise.

An earlier version of Sam Solecki's essay, "Some Kicks Against the Prick", appeared in *The Bumper Book*, edited by John Metcalf, in 1986. It is an affectionate reply to Metcalf's stylish and curmudgeonly attacks on virtually all of Canadian literature and society. Solecki doesn't defy Metcalf's assertions that the essential content of any fiction is its style, that most Canadian literature before 1950 is "rubbish" and that cultural nationalism is misguided folly. Instead, Solecki attempts to show that Metcalf advances these views for reasons of self-interest, namely: "to argue the case for his own work, to squeeze it into the canon ... to teach his readers how to read him, and, finally, to offer a tacit evaluation of his own work." Thus, Metcalf's critical emphasis on rhetorical style plays to the strength of his own fiction, and his rejection of the notion of a Canadian literary tradition leaves the field open for writers with roots elsewhere, like himself and Leon Rooke, and Canadians whose allegiance is to the international modernist style, like Mavis Gallant and Norman Levine.

Solecki refers in passing to another distinctive quality of John Metcalf's criticism: its sheer delight in the cut and thrust of polemic. This quality is obvious in Metcalf's "Dear Sam," presented as an address to a 1988 conference at the University of Guelph. It is in fact the second instalment of his rebuttal of Solecki, the first being *What is a Canadian Literature?* Having, in that book, dismissed Solecki's notion of a distinctively Canadian tradition, Metcalf turns here to two other points: the idea that the short story is a minor genre compared with the novel, and Solecki's apparent distinction between style and content in fiction.

They are closely related points, and Metcalf deftly relates them to the ambitious goals of the Critical Directions series when he picks on Solecki's contention that only the novel is "an adequate vehicle" for "a world view." Not only is the very notion of "a world view" a joke, Metcalf asserts, but to regard literature as a "vehicle" for "something to say" is to create a dichotomy between medium and message that every writer knows to be false. Aligning himself with such supreme stylists as Flaubert, Oscar Wilde and Evelyn Waugh, Metcalf maintains that " 'style is not a seductive decoration added to a functional structure' but is rather 'the essence of a work of art'."

In reaction to Solecki's valuation of "moral" novelists, he dissects selected passages to show that Rudy Wiebe has "a tin ear" and D.H. Lawrence wrote "gibberish." "Are you able to ignore such questions in your enthusiasm for Lawrence's 'world view'?" Metcalf demands of Solecki. "How can you believe that Lawrence's 'world view' exists independently of the words and sentences in which it is couched?"

Both Solecki and critic W.J. Keith suffer rhetorical blows in the course of Metcalf's extended attack on Rudy Wiebe's well-meaning but "ponderous and inept" novels. So to round out the volume, Keith is given a chance to reply, with the essay "A Dream of Laocoön." In the main, it's a fence-sitting exercise, an attempt to agree with both Solecki and Metcalf. But when Keith defends Rudy Wiebe, he partly succeeds in turning Metcalf's own arguments against him, showing that the flawed passages Metcalf ridicules play a formal role in Wiebe's large and complex novels. "Style," then, is more than merely elegant prose; even "barbarous" prose can, as in Faulkner, be an integral part of a work of art.

Volleys is hardly at the cutting edge of critical discourse, but is a stimulating launch for the publisher's Critical Directions series. My chief complaint is that it is a slight book, which rehashes an already familiar debate. I couldn't help thinking, as I read, that for the price I could have bought two or three issues of *Brick*, each of which would have more, probably better, essays on a wider variety of equally important subjects.

Colin Morton

Patrick O'Connell, *Hoping for Angels*.
Turnstone Press, 1990

Hoping for Angels falls into four sections. It opens with two suites of poems, "The Blue Man is Drowning Again" and "Hoping for Angels," followed by a loosely collected sequence of prose poems, "A Memory of Winter," and ending with the suite of prose poems, "A Thousand Swallows." The heart of the book beats in the first two suites, though there are some striking poems elsewhere.

The "blue man" personifies a view of a world imbued with despair that struggles to accept and be delivered from itself into a rapturous and visionary hope. Various sources of despair are explored: the destruction of a sense of divinity and mystery; a sense of insignificance and cheapness of self, and of an impending annihilation of that self; the very landscape as taking on the aspect of one's sorrow; and the poetic speaker as victim of the unthinking self-hatred of others. O'Connell earns the right to hope despite this despair, by poetically probing and transforming rather than denying it. The arena of action is interior, rather than communal; but he speaks to all who are troubled by the ubiquitous polarity of disappointment and faith.

What hope can help balance sadness? There is the ancient hope of deliverance, nourished in a fierce clarity of yearning. There is a visionary acceptance of life's outcasts as welcoming and elevating companions, offering the healing solidarity of tramps: "The last shall come first." And there is a way of looking at the small particulars of the world that sacramentalizes them with a revelatory and jewel-like significance: "one silver wheel cover/wobbles its way/down the road."

The suite "Hoping for Angels" balances the blue man's despair with beatitudes of the imagination. Blessings come in surrendering to beauty in the particularity of things. This beauty can make Eden of earth, and is the only true preparation for love and dying. It reveals itself to those who notice hidden resemblances between things: a cauliflower is like a tree. Seeing creatively, by a great pattern of analogies, bestows a deep sense of personhood on one. These are "Inner Riches," better known to the poor than the rich, who are distracted by power and possessions from seeing things ever fresh and anew.

There are some difficulties for O'Connell to resolve, lying at the centre of his craft. On occasion, abstract, metaphysical words are parachuted into the texture of his verse: words like "eternity" and "transcends." These work against the concreteness of his imagery, and his emphasis on the particular. But the poem "One raindrop on a long stick" mediates a sense of transcendence with more poetic honesty. This links with the significance of O'Connell's "hoping" for angels, rather than seeing and naming them directly. As with Simone Weil, divinity is present only indirectly "here below." We wait on it, but, like waiting for Godot, life's significance lies in *how* we wait, not in the arrival of Godot: "But to ask what I am waiting for would miss the point. I simply wait."

At his best, O'Connell's images have a sense of "coming" to him with forceful surprise, and being shaped into poetry, rather than being selected to fit some pre-conceived intellectual plan, or conjured up by an effort of will. Like his acrobat, O'Connell recognizes that his craft "is no mere exhibition/or sentiment of desire/this is where the intellect surrenders/to vulnerability and grace." Yet, at times, a poem reads like a somewhat glib assemblage of images willed up to satisfy the desire to complete another poem, and thus lacks its intended revelatory impact. There is an inconsistency in O'Connell's poetics that encourages this. For he speaks, sometimes, of poetic vision as something one can conduct and control precisely; "I, maestro/of celestial events"; and "this vision is simply a matter/of control/by walking at precise angles." If heaven is present only indirectly, in analogies that come to us among particulars, then it is not something we can see by a deliberate act of will. It is more like what surprises us at the corner of an eye: "I always could see heaven/out of the corner of an eye."

Despite these difficulties, a distinctive voice speaks strongly in this first collection of poems. O'Connell's second collection should be even stronger.

Roger Nash

Contributors

Anna Akhmatova (1889-1966) was one of the major Russian poets of her time. Her international reputation continues to grow.

Peter Bakowski lives and writes in St. Kilda, Victoria, Australia.

Olivia Byard has published poetry in many British magazines, including *Lines Review* and *Iron*.

Eric Folsom has published his poetry in many Canadian journals. He edits the Kingston magazine *Next Exit*.

Peter Goodchild has published poetry in *The Fiddlehead* and *Canadian Forum*. His next book, a study of Northwest Coast native mythology entitled "The Raven Tales and Their Origins", will be published by Chicago Review Press.

David Helwig's recent work includes a translation, *The Last Stories of Anton Chekhov*, published last summer by Oberon, and *The Beloved*, a long poem to be published, also by Oberon, this spring.

Robert Hilles has published four collections of poetry, most recently *A Breath at a Time*. The poems in this issue of *Quarry* are from a new work tentatively called "Raising of Voices." He lives in Calgary.

Cornelia Hoogland writes poetry and studies the Grimms' fairy tales in Coquitlam, B.C.

William Knight is a writer based in Winnipeg.

Laurie Kruk, a Ph.D. candidate at the University of Western Ontario, is specializing in Canadian literature and female fictions. She is also working on a manuscript of poetry.

Christopher McPherson is currently at work on a collection of short fiction, "Pictures of Pigs: Twenty Stories About Love, Death, Sex and Food." He lives in Victoria, B.C.

John Metcalf has been involved in Canadian Literature for almost thirty years as a writer of fiction, essays, and reviews, and as an editor and anthologist. His most recent collection of short stories is *Adult Entertainment* (Macmillan, 1988).

A.F. Moritz has published poetry in *Canadian Literature*, *Yale Review*, and *Partisan Review*. In 1990-91 he was a Guggenheim Fellow in poetry.

Colin Morton's second book of poetry, *How To Be Born Again*, is forthcoming from Quarry Press. He lives in Ottawa.

Paul Mutton writes and produces radio programs and literary arts specials while working nine to five at the Dr. Sun Yat-Sen Classical Garden in Chinatown, Vancouver.

Roger Nash teaches in the Philosophy Department at Laurentian University in Sudbury.

Michael Penny was born in Australia and educated at the Universities of Alberta and New Mexico. His poetry has appeared in many magazines, including *Dandelion* and *The Malahat Review*.

Gustav A. Richar, a graduated Mechanical Engineer, is living on a lake north of Pointe au Baril, Ontario. His short stories have appeared in many magazines, including *Dandelion* and *Zymergy*.

Stan Rogal has published his poetry in many magazines, including *Poetry Canada*, *The New Quarterly*, *The Antigonish Review*, *Conspiracy of Silence*, and *The West Coast Review*.

Andrew Wreggitt is the author of four books of poetry, most recently *Making Movies* (Thistledown), which won the Writers' Guild of Alberta Poetry Award.

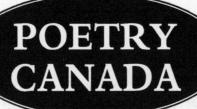

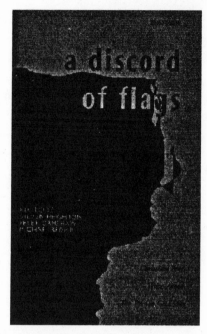

17002

01

7 72006 17002 4

Quarry

FICTION • POETRY • ESSAYS

LILBURN • MOURÉ • YOUNG

... where syllables hang, undone
in the air
vibrating: blades in the hands of a host
of fathers, lost
in thought and body, here ...

— John Takamura (1961–1991)
from "Still Lives"

Quarry Magazine

VOLUME 41 NUMBER 2 SPRING 1992

GENERAL ISSUE

Editor   Steven Heighton

Managing Editor   Melanie Dugan

Book Review Editor   Carolyn Bond

Associate Editors

Tim Andison   Sharon Hunt

Allan Brown   Tara Kainer

Carlene Bryant   Joanne Page

Mary Cameron   Eric Folsom

Cheryl Sutherland   A. Colin Wright

ISSN 0033–5266 ISBN 1–55082–032–X

This issue of *Quarry Magazine* was published with the financial assistance of The Canada Council and the Ontario Arts Council. *Quarry* is listed in the Canadian Periodical Index, Canadian Literature Index, Canadian Magazine Index, Canadian Business and Current Affairs Database, American Humanities Index, and Index of American Periodical Verse. Back issues are available in the original from the editor and in microform from Micromedia Limited, 20 Victoria Street, Toronto, Ontario M5C 2N8.

Manuscript submissions and subscription requests should be mailed to:

Quarry Magazine
P.O. Box 1061
Kingston, Ontario
K7L 4Y5

Manuscripts must include a SASE with Canadian postage or International Reply Coupons. Subscription rates are $20.33 for 1 year (4 issues) or $36.38 for 2 years (8 issues), GST included.

Distributed by the Canadian Magazine Publishers Association, 2 Stewart Street, Toronto, Ontario M5V 1H6.

Cover art: Simon Andrew, *Knife of Damocles* (oil on paper, 1992).
Typesetting by Susan Hannah, Quarry Press.
Published by Quarry Press, Inc., P.O. Box 1061, Kingston, Ontario K7L 4Y5.

Publications Mail Registration Number 7293. Issued June 1992.

Contents

ESSAY

Paul Dutton

DANGER

He is watching him watch his wife with eyes he cannot see behind
which lie dangerous thoughts he watches him watch the eyes fixed
on bare foot, lean and delicately formed, long toes pressed into
carpet, smooth round heel below slender ankle disclosing the
structure of articulated bones, joint bending to let outer edge of
foot caress broadloom, showing a sole tinged reddish-orange at
heel and ball, pale white of arch crinkling as her foot curls in and
shifts to press bent toes into plush nap he sits a bit away on watching while eyes he doesn't know are watching him watch him
thinking dangerous thoughts he imagines being acted on, acting
on impulse arising from bare foot on plush nap he sits on in
stockinged feet that are wide and flat, stubby toes in wool socks,
smooth flesh of heel below plump ankle obscuring the structure of
articulated bones, joint bending as he rises and walks to the
kitchen where she stands at the cupboard and takes down a glass
he watches her hold in a hand that is lean and delicately formed,
long fingers pressed against smooth transparent surface, faint blue
veins running over slender wrist disclosing the structure of articulated bones, joint bending to let hand extend glass towards him,
showing a pale white palm pressed against the glass's far side, the
creases in the palm flattened by the glass that is then filled with
liquid he sips while eyes he cannot see are watching him watch
eyes behind which form dangerous thoughts he imagines being
acted on in the other room where a plump hand folds into a fist,
short fingers pressed into a palm that creases deepen in, a tracery
of blue veins running over thick wrist obscuring the structure of
articulated bones, joint bending back and forth, as if to flex the
muscles there or perhaps as a gesture of impatience, the fist slowly
unfolding, the fingers spread and extended, anticipating the glass
that is to be brought to them, reaching out for it and closing
around it, lifting it to sip liquid from, and over its brim, to watch
him watching his wife with eyes behind which lurk dangerous
thoughts as white feet pad on kitchen linoleum, flesh on the feet's

outer edges spreading in small bulges against the hard surface, flesh of her left foot squeaking slightly when she pivots to face the refrigerator door she opens and bends down beside, her face illuminated by the light emanating from the refrigerator in the darkened room in which dangerous thoughts form into a glass extended towards him, over the brim of which he watches her eyes with eyes he cannot see watching the slow unfolding of fingers from a fist into a flattened hand impatient for the vessel holding liquid that is lifted to lip and sipped at, eyes over brim watching hand place glass on carpet toes press into nap in early afternoon of sun slanting into the room he watches in with eyes that brim with inarticulate thoughts.

Michael Holmes

TRANSLATING NERUDA

if my name was jesus
could you clutch with me
at burning noon?
allow my tongue and night
to brush the copper sky
from your white skin?

we inhale spanish:
    our feet almost touch
the scorpions and sand of tangier,
    the pulsing green
of the amazon floor —

we exhale slavic and stand
    for Christ's sake
in moscow or helsinki spring;

it is cold in line
    and we stamp our feet
like leaden horses.

last night we embraced
tentacles of orchids
and nearly dreamt
our lives away.

i forgive the truth whispered:
you will write jesus in pencil
on a yellow slip of paper.
the curse will be sharp and bloody
when the rusting blade
and Pablo's ghost
close fast on that name.

please love, bury me
beneath the willow,

do not throw the knife
to the chaotic waterfall:

the poor men shall not
pray or find it there.

Erin Mouré

---

4 DREAMS OF THE ADRIATIC SEA

Adriatic Sea 1

A few women in shirts & bare legs scoop water out of the boats
with rusted cans. "O wide Adriatic wonder".
A few women with orange singlets & t-shirts lay down in the sun
in front of the president's maison-blanche, playing be-bop on their
walkmans.
Or old '60s music. Surf references by The Beach Boys for
instance. That idiotic, the head as usual
northern
trying to conjure up the Adriatic Sea.

Which none of us has ever seen, though we know
the term, "Adriatic shipping"
& whisper it to each other as we walk
the darkened city, the boys in front of their houses,
six layers of paint on the doorframes,
one for each layer of immigration,
the fifth one
just under the surface
the soft paint of the Adriatic.

"Two sweethearts" the boys say of us passing,
meaning "women" or "candy", not knowing our shared sweetness.
A few women scoop out the Adriatic Sea, it fills up, they scoop it
    out again.
The president's soldiers run out across the lawn,
tell us to stop kissing.
The shoreline of Albania, perhaps, or
the coast of Yugoslavia.
A body of water we long for, having never seen it,

having only dreamed it with these women who persist
in moving water,
scooping water,
having believed it is out there. Waiting. Like a fish, waiting.

Adriatic Sea 2

Or, the coast of Italy. Blue water at the coast of Italy, the smell of
coffee just now steamed on the stove, the red ring of the burner,
glow. Horse noise on the street now. Horse noise stumbling over
the cobbles in her former drunkenness, now invoked splendifer-
ous with no grain of alcohol whatsoever. The iron balconies &
women scolding her she is leaning up a building, four floors with
balconies & wood grey shutters on the coast of Italy. Having
thought of Italian wine made out of blue water desaltified
Adriatic can you imagine what this wine would taste like? she
asked. The women black skirts & immense flowers scolded & told
her to shut up. But can you imagine this wine? she shouted on the
cobbles. A blue wine, of blue water?

Adriatic Sea 3

They say they are horses in the Adriatic & the women are scooping out the water to free them, their rusted cans fill up & empty
behind their legs, running in a trickle back into the sea. Water
finds its own level they say, the boys standing in the basement
using a hose to measure the sagging floor, so much can be mea-
sured with water, water displaces water, water finds its own level,
people crawl in the window at night as if robbery is a motive. Still
there are these horses, their chests lunged outward in the sea,
drinking the grain in with their eyes, the grain of the water,
tremendous blue depth of the water, the nets & fishes & industrial
dumping, they drink it in with the eyes, knowing the women try
but cannot free them they must free themselves, dream for themselves a shore with balconies dock cobbles & Italian bicycles
instead of cars, then lunge up & outward, their swift backs wet,
startling the bystanders.

Adriatic Sea 4

O wide Adriatic wonder, wide sea she cried out, standing in the
doorway, the horse hurting, shaken at the edge of water, making
sense of these grainy letters, the wash of memory, the cobbles we
remember seeing as we raised our chests & shoulders, our pale
skin stuttered with bluest water, out of the sea. Till we looked
like trapped fish in the pictures, the sea dug out behind us with
pails, leaving marks of our passage, the water in our mouths &
membranes, our throats struggling open, as if this is the loss we
came to, craving, *it so scared us, finally*

*"How the most sacred, in her infant handwriting, became the most
scared. The truest things, if spoken here, would sound like nonsense."*

What could she have said, then?
Her words, or was it a faint melody,
the burr of her voice you were so used to,
you had already loved.
Explosives, fuel-air, barred by the Geneva Conventions,
used on the ones who fled.
The road charred litter of this.
Empty sacks of cars.
Jerk, asshole, arrogant, mocking,
incapable!
The roasted ones, still raw meat on the inside,
their skin, that organ
incinerated.

You can scarcely pick your way around it.

What could she have said, then?

"Northern people," they say, "flee north."

2

Their rooms doused with gasoline &
torched. The black smudge on the telephone,
sound of her voice uttering
"manipulator, liar, treacherous fool!"

Skyward. Clustered rain on civilian peoples,
face of war. The voice she longed for, the sound of
a sofa thrown into the back of a truck.
"Being" thrown.

That's it. Fire rained down from the sky on the survivors
of the first clashes. Some of them were seen leaping from the trucks,
hurling their gaseous bodies outward, haloed with orange light.

History of angelic order. Piece of cake.
"You're reprehensible," she shouted.
"Even this is reprehensible!"

Get these words out of my mouth, she said.
My name is not Geneva.
There are no conventions.

3

Or nothing, probably.
We stood with the shadows of the leaves
on our mouths, the door open
to the garden. Or that other
time, the slipstream of coffee splattered
in a halo across the door.
"Smartass, cold, emotional cripple!"

Our arms hung at our sides.
The bus marked with the Red Crescent
completely blackened, silent, suddenly
a door opens & the prisoners step out, alive.
No one would have believed it.
As if the Geneva Conventions covered only
"swiss watches."

Time pieces. Duty free
on the plane back from Lisbon.

Probably none of us spoke, that moment.
The small coins of the leaves
pressed onto us, & us stuporously silent,
singular, our bodies ticking,
fully clothed.

4

The end of the trip-wire, visible over
several miles on the infrared screen.
In the market, women go about their business,
the flat baskets of bread.

There are so few words for what we have done.

"Trees with their new leaves, aphidic."
"Remonstrative, castigatory, perfidious, cruel."

5

In essence, a hair trigger precision of the voice,
the muscle bursting into guttural flame, thru the exact
preposterous window of the skin.
The heart brushing the leaves of grass
before take-off.

Humiliated & mocking. Her careful hands
holding a time-bomb of the alphabet. AB.
Later, the voices as gutted as a truck shot by news
cameras, littered among other trucks, empty,
the dazed drivers in their identity kits of skin
gone into spasmodic flutters.
Playing tissue & comb music.

In essence, swan song. O turn your head now,
the oily sunlight beams somewhere
above the fires, & the birds
preen themselves

of oil. Liking the music. Ingesting
their own destiny. Wanting to sing.

Kim Carter

CHEWING GUM

My mother always said
ladies do not chew gum in public
unless they charge by the hour.

Chewing gum leads to big hair,
ankle bracelets,
and secrets thin as lingerie.

I have her Catholic quilt.
I'm afraid I'll be a cow in my next life,
or a pewter-haired hausfrau with a sticky purse.

In Rome for refinement,
I wear a safe pink dress.
But I am tested at the Spanish Steps.
A boy with big olive eyes
pesters me with offers:
marriage, his vespa, then gum.

The click of his Chiclets
sounds like a loaded gun:
somewhere inside me
the lady starts dying.

I am shy
until the purples tickle my tongue.
Then my jaws suddenly kick:
an unladylike assault.

We go for a long, long ride.
The wind gives me big hair.
He asks me if I'd like an ankle bracelet.
I tell him let's have secrets.
We speak the language of gum.

We chew across the Tiber,
snap our way to the Roman Baths.
Hours pass. Our mouths still move in rhythm
when the shadows spread their arms
along the cool, ancient tiles.

Now I know
it isn't gum my mother was worried about:
it was the oasis of water, the fruit
waiting inside my mouth.

WALKING ALONE AT NIGHT

Night
tumbles with moonlight, ochre leaves.
Magic of a ferris wheel.
I want to stop, watch it revolve,
but I remember too many headlines;
too many women buried in ravines.

Night is no friend
with its slow-moving cars,
devious pubs,
hunger of the wolf pack.

Streetlamps shiver into life.
I try to look assertive,
wrong shoes, wrong skirt.
Clench keys between fingers,
willing to maim or blind.

A man flashes by.
He has no idea
why a scream bubbles at my lip,
why I want to yank up the darkness
like a windowblind.

Scott Boyce

"A GUEST! A GUEST!"

We thought at first the hippo meant harm —
when he surfaced suddenly, right
against our stern — but he was only greeting us
playfully; he went under again,
and reappeared behind us. Our terror
subsided too quickly
to leave a mark, and laughter brought
the purple hills closer
as we rowed our large rowboat on.
It had been a long afternoon, but Ntoroko's
thatch had at last
withdrawn into the yellow landscape left
behind, and looking
over the side I could see weeds
waving up at us, harbingers
of fresh shore. Soon too I was
able to make out figures on the beach ahead . . .
Men were pulling the day's catch
from boats, a child was stalking a tolerant stork,
and women were standing calf-
deep in the water; they had seen me
and their cries to each other
carried out to us like tiny birds flying out from shore:

"Mgeni! Mgeni!"

CUPS FILLED BY GOD AND BY MAN

In a hushed
world by the Zaire
River one night I hear
a melody of grief sung by
a woman and a man in the
darkness of a hut I cannot
see, their cries resonating
through the sky the forest the
river and my blood, in symmetry
with the daylit sounds of joy,
their grief a clean blade
slicing along the grain of
soft wood, universal,
timeless, and ritual,
their pain the pain
of loss, the hurt
of living

At the Ugandan border post
one day I hear a man and
a woman crying out in
pain from inside a
concrete building,
their cries harsh
full of fear
alien

I remember when I was lost in
forest how I forgot
the mosses on the trees.
I missed the trail
and came back to the maple split by storm.
Magellan, they say,
proved beyond a shadow
the world is globe.
But the Spaniards could have been right
when they were wrong and
called the New World
India. In the forge of science
we have lain the heated ball
upon the iron
and hammered it flat. And flag-
tattered we now return
in the panicked ark
of Christopher. Brave the ropes
to the crow's-nest and
see that home has disappeared.
We can hear what sounds like surf
but the wings of mutant birds are darkening the decks.

The selection:

The large and small Ojibways that everyone would recognize; J.B.'s pairs with green gut that bend to a point in front like Arabian slippers; the bearpaws that Richard says are good for turning around — having no tail to catch on pickets or alders or get imbedded under snow; and the magnesium alloy army snowshoes, light and fast, but snapping if you so much as tap them against a tree to get rid of slush (we stick the broken ones tail-first in the airtight till they glow blue and hiss, then take them out into the night like torches).

I get paired with some big Ojibways at first, huge boats stuck on my feet, learn fast that if I don't lift straight up with each step I'll take on a ton of snow, like a tramp steamer crashing through waves in a typhoon, and come home with my crotch muscles screaming. And going down trail that's already been broken I trip many times over the shoes as they spar like twins for position, and sometimes lie leg-twisted in the snow for minutes, glaring at the clouds as they drift across the sky.

But the lighter Ojibways I later put my mitts on become an extension of my body and carry me fast down cutline and trail. By this time, too, the snow has stopped falling and the cold and wind have hardened the lake's surface to a crust I skim over feeling like Christ on the Sea of Galilee. Ten K of magnetometer a day becomes the easy norm. And the campward treks shift from merely promising relief: the steady rhythm of my scuffing snowshoes breaks me into song. *KC Lovin'*, *King of the Road* billow into the winter air.

McInnes Lake, 1990

Caroline Adderson

OIL AND DREAD

A jolt. Wide-open eyes. Every day now Des wakes like this, disoriented, a man who has been moved in his sleep. A whisper, his mother's name for him, disturbs like a finger traced around his ear. Finally, Ita's rolling over in the bed delivers him, brings time and place. Her waxy face surfaces and inhales. She is swimming in sleep. Des slides out of bed and picks from the clothes horse his big trousers, a shirt the size of a sail. He dresses as he moves through the small rooms, leaving the house before both arms are in his jacket.

In this treeless place the wind reveals itself in the unceasing transport of clouds, the swelling of crows on the power lines to larger, more ragged forms. Reeled in again to the water, he follows a dry-stone fence that disappears where its parts have been returned to the ground. Past *Feely's*, Ita's store, the dirty windows and milk boxes and lottery tickets that make them their living. Near the beach stands an abandoned cottage. Its rotten thatch, shiny like threads of mica, sags and stops the door. Des wades thigh-deep through nettles, leans in the paneless window. Inside, all is as it was left when years ago the vanished occupant made his break with Ireland. The blankets, drawn back on the bed, are marbled now with mildew. On a table soft with dust, a tin mug from that last breakfast.

A stone falls from the fence behind him. Des starts, smashing his head on the sill, then stands rubbing the spot: where Ita claims God touched him with His Mighty Finger when Des became a Catholic to marry her and a perfect circle of bald appeared. He is bleeding.

The dog cowers by the fence, ears flat against its black head. Its eyes roll upward as in pictures of the martyred saints.

"Fuck you."

Its tongue fawns. What Des cannot stand, even in his own dog: anything like submissiveness. With his foot, he raises the muzzle up, up until he can grab it and feel the throat block with straining.

When he lets go, the dog pauses on its haunches licking around its mouth, then bounds away toward the water.

A flock of crows blows in like paper ash. The frustrated beat of the ocean. Weekends, he brings his daughters here, makes them say, as he points to the blurred false-front of Ireland's own distant coast, "Mayo" and "Sligo" and, for a joke, "Newfoundland." Now this shore is home to his dread. Whatever threatens him, he feels for certain from here it will come, from the water, doom or a boat-load of judges.

The dog is barking. Its tail flails as it shuttles in the surf. Tug-of-war: dog and bird.

"Hey! Leave off!" Des crosses the beach to where they are battling. At his feet, the dog is jawing a live wing. The bird, black throat open in soundless rage, twists and thrashes and rocks the dog's obstinate head. It hisses at Des, panicked bravado. Des grins. With the side of his boot he kicks the dog away.

Des needs all the strength of his big hands to clutch the bird to his chest. "I-i-i-ta!" He hammers the bed with his boot. Finally she sits up, blonde hair sticking to the sides of her face as she groans at the ceiling. In Des's arms the bird convulses and, loosening a wing, flaps wildly, hisses. Ita gapes. "What are you after bringing home, you fucking crazy Des!"

"Give me a hand." He goes into the kitchen and from there can hear her fall out of bed and stumble around the room. "You're an eejit, Desmond Martin. What time is it? Didn't you hear me up half the night with Old Man and his pissing and moaning? Jesus! Some of us have a funeral to go to today! You and your creeping around at all godless hours. It's a sin."

She appears in her bare feet, nightdress, a green housecoat. Cigarette between her lips, she heads to the gas range for a light.

"Ita!"

"What? Can't I have a fag?"

"Will you look what I've got in my arms!"

She faces the bird and softens. The cigarette goes in her pocket. "What happened?"

"Oil."

"Poor thing." She begins taking the dirty dishes out of the sink. "Des, you are a saint and a lover of the wee animals."

When the sink is filled with soapy water, Des, so he can take off his jacket, has Ita hold the bird. It wrenches free immediately, smashing its wings against the counter, sloshing water on Ita and the floor. It stabs at Des's eye with the lance of its beak.

"Jesus, Ita!"

"Jesus, you!" she shrieks.

He wrestles with its beating wings. The bird collides with the window, jettisons a spray of liquid shit that just misses Ita. She screams: "The devil's in it! Fuck off! Fuck off!" When at last he recaptures it, beak in his fist, wings in the vice of his huge hand, she is laughing. "A hell of a way to get up in the morning!"

She takes a brillo pad and begins scrubbing the bird. "Was there oil on the beach?"

"None."

Hers is not to question mystery. She changes the subject. "You didn't hear Old Man last night crying for his dead brother? Course not or you wouldn't have been up at the crack of day! I had to lay out all his gear in the middle of the godless night." She pauses and sniffs. "Do you think we should have brought the girls up?"

"A funeral's no place for kids."

"At Mary's age I loved a funeral." She squints at him. "You'd be happy to leave our poor babes in Letterkenny all the year, wouldn't you? You don't love your daughters."

He sees where she is leading him. Her regular accusation. The girls come home every weekend.

"You don't. Not like I do. Every day's misery without them. I mean it when I say I'd have ten more if you'd only get a job."

She drains the soapy water, refills the sink. Next, Des knows, she will remind him he is Canadian.

Under her breath: "Sure there's more work in Canada . . ."

The bird twists in his hands.

"This is the only thing I have to say: when Old Man dies — God forgive me for mentioning such a thing on the very day we put his brother in the ground — when he dies we're all going to Canada."

"*We are not going to Canada*!" Des roars.

"Why not? Sure you've never shown any kind of love for this country!"

He scoops the bird out of the sink, trailing a watery skirt. With its head suddenly free, it screeches, snakes a long neck toward Ita.

"Jesus!" She ducks.

Des leaves her standing in chaos. The dog has been waiting outside and is eager at his heel, but he shuts it out of the shed. He kicks clear an area on the dirt floor then shifts the spasming bird under his arm, stoops to lay down a bed of old newspapers.

Back in the house, Ita leans into the mop, dragging long on her cigarette. Her housecoat is drenched.

"What do you want?" Des asks from the door. "Sausages? I'll run over to the store."

She won't look at him. "I want you out of this hairy mood."

"What mood?"

"So tight-lipped and always sneaking down to the beach. It has to do with that Canadian boy you wouldn't bring home the other night, doesn't it?"

"Will you get off that?"

"Then it's your not drinking any more. It's the Total Abstinence Society of the Sacred Heart around here. Cutting yourself off altogether isn't healthy." She glances at him, then doubles full-face. "Did you take that off the clothes horse?"

He looks down at himself, shirt-front ruined with the molasses-stain of oil.

"Is that your pressed white shirt for the funeral?" She takes the mop in her hands, a weapon, and comes raging after him.

Old Man is sitting on the edge of the bed cleaning his nose with his little finger. He seems to be looking across the room where the red Christmas bulb burns continuously under the picture of the Sacred Heart. Des coughs and Old Man looks up, frowning. He wipes his finger on the front of his undershirt and crosses himself.

"We're putting my brother in the ground today," he says. "Pray for Peter Feely."

"He was a good man." It occurs to Des as he says this that he hasn't thought of his own brother in years.

"No, he wasn't. He was just too old to be bad."

"I'm going to dress you. Have you washed?"

"I don't wash."

"Don't tell Ita that."

"*You* don't tell her."

Des gets Old Man's underwear from the bureau. Slowly, Old Man raises his arms, thin, stained in patches the colour of tea. Des peels the undershirt off this trunk, over his head, then is startled to

26

see he has left him completely naked.

"Jesus," says Old Man. He waves his wormy hands in the air. A fumbling with the fresh shirt, an attempt to guide shaking hands into arm holes, but Old Man is tangled in his own underwear. To hide what shames him, he draws up the round bulbs of his knees. Finally, his flushed face appears, glaring indignantly, showing the raw gums behind his lip. Des offers his forearm. Old Man clutches it without meeting his eye, hoists himself onto bare bowed legs.

"Did Ita hammer you on the head?"

"What?"

"There's blood where your poll is bare."

Des bends and takes an ankle, pushes a horny foot through the leg-hole of the briefs. Scrotum long on the thigh, translucent and fine as waxed paper. Old Man smells of tobacco and urine.

"Has there ever been an oil slick around here?" Des asks.

"When I was a lad, there was a fellow away in the head. He wouldn't take communion. Used to do his business down by the beach, what I don't know. Knocking stones together. One day doesn't a big wave roll up and snatch him away? We all went down and waited for the body to be spat back up. And when it came . . . What d'you think?"

"I don't know." Des straightens and tucks the undershirt into the briefs, lowers Old Man back onto the bed.

"Guess."

"I don't know."

"Well, what are we talking about, man!"

"I don't know what *you're* talking about."

"Oil! He was blackened all over with oil. Black like his very own soul!"

"You're full of it," says Des.

They struggle into the shirt, Des's great fingers grappling with the small buttons. Then he crosses the room and lifts the kilt that Ita has left spread over the back of a chair. A grey and blue plaid, it makes Old Man look thin and white as a stick of chalk.

"Bonnet on his chest, Peter Feely will be buried in the costume of the Blue Raven Pipe Band."

He gives Old Man his arm again so he can stand and step into the kilt. "You'll look great yourself."

Old Man sniffs loudly. "I suppose Ita thinks that since I'll be decked out same as the corpse, I'll follow quick to the grave."

"She doesn't."

"You can tell her I don't intend to die."

Des laughs. With the diaper pins Ita left on the bureau, he fixes the kilt through Old Man's shirt to his underwear.

"Then again, oh Jesus, if I never die Ita'll get tired of waiting and go off to Canada anyway without me."

"Listen. No one's going to Canada. All this bloody talk about Canada."

"It'd be a terrible thing to be left behind, a whole ocean of water between us. Who in the world'd fix my tea?"

Almost a month ago Des met that boy in the pub. Ita introduced him to Des as his "wee countryman". Afterward, neither could recall his name. They knew his face though: fresh and amazed. Later Ita would describe the dimple in his chin as the place where God's Mighty Finger had touched him when he was in the womb.

He was touring Europe on his break from university. "At last I hit Ireland, an English-speaking country. I head straight for the pub where I can get some conversation. This old guy accosts me. He yaks for hours. Finally, I tell him I can't understand a word he's saying. He's totally surprised. *You're* very clear, he says!"

"It's not *how* they talk that gets me," said Des. "It's how bloody long it takes them to get to the point!"

The boy leaned forward and looked at Des earnestly. "Talk to me, man. I love the boring, flat sound of your voice."

When Ita left with a pint for Old Man waiting at home, they were all drunk. She whispered in Des's ear: "Bring that poor little fucking Canadian home. He can sleep on the sofa."

"Whiskey?" Des asked. He went to the bar and bought a bottle. "Sorry it's not CC."

"S'okay," said the boy. "I can get that anytime."

The publican roared for everyone to clear out, but they were only half-finished the bottle. Outside the moon shone on the backs of the men talking in the yard. Des cradled the whiskey in one arm, took the boy on the other and led him around the pub to where the mountain's silhouette was a crouching animal. A rutted road ran straight up the slope, a track for driving sheep and the turf-cutters' donkey carts.

They had climbed for a few minutes when Des started to laugh. "Ita says bring that poor little fucking Canadian home." Then he sang it: "Brr-ing that poooor little fuck-ing Can-ay-dian hooome!"

"Ita's great," said the boy. "Ita's wild."

"First time I slept with Ita . . . ." From both sides of the track the panicked drumming of fleeing sheep. "She got . . . she brought out her account book from the store. Wrote: I solemnly swear . . . I will marry Ita Mary Feely!"

"And you had to sign!"

"That's not all! Had to swear and sign on the line I'd convert!"

The boy whistled. "She's tough all right."

"In here, man." They had come to a half-ruined shed, three stone walls, a roof of corrugated metal. They fell inside, righting themselves to a view from high above the houses, pub, Ita's store. Des unscrewed the cap and drank, passed the whiskey to the boy who could barely find his own mouth with the bottle.

"How 'bout them Blue Jays?" said Des.

They began to snicker again, Des first, the boy catching it. They were both buckled over and howling before Des could put in words the rest of his story. Finally: "I had a laugh on Ita." Heart pumping wildly, leaning into the boy, he slurred. "Ita's account book? I didn't write my name. Wrote a different name so she wouldn't have anything on me. Desmond Martin. She was howling mad, not because she knew it wasn't my name, but because she'd been calling me Martin all along, see? I said everyone called me Martin, but she wouldn't have any such fucking coarseness, people calling each other by their surnames."

"What's your name then?"

"Martin Sinclair! Desmond was the name of my dog."

Now they were in agony, hysteria. Des could not breathe. He pounded his foot on the earth floor, whiskey overturning, both scrambling to save it, then lying in silence, aching. Eventually, Des dragged himself out to urinate. The boy called after him, "Lucky your dog wasn't named Spot!"

"Still . . . there's more!" Des staggered up the slope so he could urinate on the metal roof of the shed. "Already married, kid on the way" — then his voice drowned in the rush of liquid drumming.

When he crawled back into the shed, the boy hooted. "How'd you get out of it?"

"Didn't. Ita doesn't know. Church don't know. Priest was a fossil. I think he died the day after. He'd married Ita's old man, too, for Christ's sake!"

"Jesus. There's a word for that . . . "

"Lots of words. Fucking-against-the-law are some of them." He could see the boy's amazement. To Des it was clear what the joke had turned into: this was how much he had come to love Ita.

"She was pregnant?"

"Not Ita! Back in T.O. *Shit . . . Did I say that*?" Des laughed and felt around for the bottle. The boy did not reply.

"It's fourteen years dead. I was your age, for Christ's sake. I never told anyone before."

More silence. Des hoped the boy had passed out. He took another swig of whiskey, the after-taste caustic.

"Asshole," said the boy.

Des shoved him hard against the wall, then let him go. The boy struggled to his feet, groaning. He lurched forward and out of the shed while Des poured the remaining whiskey over his own head. Cold down the contours of his face, it seeped in and burned his eyes.

He thought the boy had gone out to urinate. "Oh, Canada!" A minute later: "Fucking little Can-ay-dian!" Now Des stumbled out of the hiding place, into the wide open side of the mountain, white light, cold face of the moon. The boy was gone.

Ita sets the teapot in the middle of the table. Old Man, still in his piper's costume, bonnet askew, sucks on his gums and stares straight ahead. After a long silence, he sniffs. "Aye, we buried him well."

With a long even-toned cry, Ita collapses onto the table. Her back begins to tremble and her hands open wide like fans. Soon she is shaking the table, sobbing, the teapot lid rattling.

Old Man sneers. "Shut up, Ita. It's too late for the banshee."

She straightens, face red, smeared with tears and mascara. She forces out her jaw and her fist hammers the table with such force that Old Man quivers. "Fuck you!" Ita roars. "Who was up all night listening to your pissing and moaning? I was, you bastard!" Back of her hand over her forehead, she rolls her eyes, imitating Old Man. "Me God, me brother's dead and I'm the last of the true Blue Ravens! Me God, I never liked him and in heaven he'll know it, too! I'm afraid to die meself!"

Old Man turns red and sniffs.

"Lay off him Ita," says Des.

"Don't you tell me what to do!" Suddenly she springs from her chair and lunges for Des, grabs a handful of hair in one hand, smacks him again and again with the other.

"I-i-i-ta!" He sinks into her breasts, trying to push her away. Old Man claps his hands, cackling. Then Ita falls forward with her arms around Des's neck, sobbing again, shuddering.

"Oh, Jesus!" she cries. "Oh, Jesus! My uncle is dead and my children are in Letterkenny!"

Both men give up a roar of laughter. Ita, tears suspended, rises on her knees. "That's funny?"

"Shhh." Des pulls her close.

"With that eejit's carrying on, I didn't get my sleep last night. I'm exhausted. I don't know what I'm doing."

"Ach," says Old Man. "If you don't know, Ita, then we're really lost."

"What's the matter with you, Des? Why won't you tell me? Don't you love me any more?"

"More than ever."

Old Man mutters as they kiss. He clears his throat. Now that Ita is off her guard, he takes the opportunity to expectorate into his saucer.

"Des, something bad is going to happen. I feel it."

"Shhh." He kisses her again.

Old Man looks up, crossing himself alarmedly.

Des pours a cup of tea and puts it in Ita's hands. She takes her chair. For a long time they sit in silence, then Old Man begins a long recounting of the funeral's events.

"I'll go and have a look at that bird then," says Des.

It is not where he left it on the newspaper. He finds it behind some paint cans, wings half-spread, head lowered. Reaching down, he wags his fingers, expecting assault. The bird does not move. It has stiffened in the corner trying to extend wide its wings where there is no space, trying to stretch out its life. The black eye is still a shiny bead. Des carries it out of the shed and throws it over the fence into the neighbour's field.

Ita is undressing in the bedroom. In a half-slip and brassiere, she is hanging her black dress in the wardrobe.

"The bird's dead."

"Not another body to bury. I've had enough."

"I'm going up the mountain to see if a slick's coming in."

"You're away in the head! I thought you were going to open the store!"

31

He is already in the car when she appears at the front door clutching closed her blouse and waving to him. He unrolls the window.

"Leave something at the holy well for my uncle!"

Earlier that afternoon he drove in the funeral cortege, Old Man beside him, Ita in back leaning over the seat to brush her father's shoulders or straighten his baldric. Old Man stared ahead at the pipers marching on either side of the hearse. Finally, he passed comment. "That's a god-awful noise they're making." When Des turned around to look at Ita, he saw how the procession trailed, mourners in black fighting the wind.

Later at the grave site, Des was one of the men lowering the coffin into the earth. The rope did not burn or harm his hands. The coffin was as light as if they were burying Peter Feely's soul without his body. As they worked, hand-over-hand, Old Man stood at the top of the grave with the big drum. Head high, dried bloom on the long neck of a plant gone to seed, jaw set, staring fiercely.

Coffin in place, they drew the ropes out of the grave and waited in silence, mourners' feet apart to brace against the wind, priest's robes swollen and rippling. They were watching Old Man as he slowly raised the baton. He poised, a salute, mourners suspended. From a distance, the falling broken voice of a crow. When the arm dropped, the drum sounded relief — a hollow bottomless beat stronger than the wind's hoarse breathing. Then, as if in retaliation, the wind snatched Old Man's bonnet from his head and set it sailing through the tombstones.

And the power of Old Man's sacrifice for his dead brother, all his strength in a sound, rocked Des and gave him the vision of his own brother. He saw him at age thirteen or fourteen, bird-cage bare-chested, hair raised on his head and mouth torn open, a scream of indignation, some long-forgotten injustice. The first time Des had thought of his brother in years was earlier that day, dressing Old Man. He was puzzled why he remembered him yet again, in childhood now instead of as he had seen him last, in his twenties, grown to manhood. Drum sounded again. Scream persisted. Peter Feely's daughter was keening for him.

Driving through the village, Des does a double-take. A boy on a bicycle waves at him and for a second Des thinks it is the Canadian. He sees one almost every day now, these look-alike, pretend Canadians, and wonders where they have suddenly come from.

Passing the pub, he continues up the mountain until he meets a herd of sheep chewing cud in the middle of the road. They do not start or move when he sounds the horn. Only when he opens the door and steps onto the road do they heave and bolt. Minutes later, the road runs out. He has driven most of the way up the mountain and will now follow on foot the ridge of its naked back.

The first part of the ascent is steep, a muddy sheep track around broken faces of stone. The heather, past its prime, is a cover of papery blossoms faded brown and coral. His big boot misses the track, sinks into the peat and sometimes scrapes away the green skin of the mountain, exposing bare bone rock. When he comes over the top of the first plateau, sweating and breathing heavily, the wind strikes him hard. From now on it will be twice the labour, climbing and bending into the wind.

Ocean before him, sky above it an unspoiled blue, though the land is still tamped down with cloud. He rests on a rock, folding to streamline himself in the wind. Turf-cutters have left here long strips of scarring. A nearby ram pauses to look at him, horns ingrown and curling to cage its skull. He thinks again about Ita's ironic hectoring when he turned up in the middle of the night without that Canadian lad. She woke when he was climbing into bed, asked where the boy was, then bashed him around with her pillow for his thoughtlessness. She harped for days.

The wind puts him on his feet. He climbs to the next plateau, the one before the summit, cliffs two thousand feet above the ocean. And now, staring over the grey sea, a mirror of his own foaming agitation, he hears the smash of breakers on the rocks below. The sound is like Old Man's drum. The priest's words at the funeral: every one of us shall give account of himself to God. This is what has been waking him, shivering and nauseous, all along. Why at dawn he finds himself on the beach staring back at where he came from. One way or another, in this world or the next, sooner or later, truth will out.

For fourteen years, when he has thought of his other wife, she has been lying on her back in bed, mound of pregnant belly pushing up under the covers. Fourteen years later, she is sleeping still. She has not even rolled over. The fetus, arrested in the womb, floats patiently in its liquid world. All is as he left it the morning he emptied her purse and, walking out in the sunshine, broke with Canada. The blows he inflicted, her cries. The ocean and a gull wheeling below the cliff. She never told him no. Never said, "Martin! Stop!"

It made him crazy, her passivity. Meaner, his own shame. When he first came to Ireland, he saw a hag in a church yard. He felt her, even at a distance, searching his soul. She spat at him and this was joy — to know he could be resisted and saved from himself. Then he met Ita. He has been loved better than Ita loves him, even excepting her animal ways, but he has never loved more himself. He has been employed by love.

Above the nearly-vertical cliff, the air is condensing on the green peak. It clots, whitens, swells, then is released to cloud over the land. And now, having reached the secret place where clouds are born, he is reminded of another birth. The image he saw at the funeral, his brother as a child, was the image of his own son.

He turns to the ocean. For a long time he stands leaning into the wind, watching the wavering line of horizon. As he stares, his eyes dry and tire and when he finally sees what he has come to see, he cannot be sure that such straining outward has not turned his vision back into himself. Far out in the Atlantic a dark bubble appears. It vanishes easily enough, only a pin-head at this distance. When it surfaces again it is larger, swollen, a blister on the water. He does not actually see it burst. Suddenly slick and black and glittering. It is spreading, moving toward shore, mourning, a funeral cortege. The stickiness of oil and dread.

Running down the mountain, not the way he came, down a spongy slope to the holy well. At the standing stone, he stumbles. Sacred carvings worn to pocked illegibility, he must touch to read. Fingers tremble over depressions, warnings, a child's face, a country. The well itself — a tiny spring trickling into a circle of stones, all around rusted offerings. He digs in his pocket, flings all the coins he has.

John Reibetanz

FROM "GIBRALTAR POINT"

In September of 1791, John Graves Simcoe sailed from England to take up his post as Lieutenant-Governor of the newly created province of Upper Canada. With him came his wife, Elizabeth Posthuma Simcoe, and their two youngest children. The Simcoes spent five years in Canada, a stay shadowed by the death of their year-old daughter Katherine, born at Niagara in 1793, and by the growing acrimony between Simcoe and his immediate superior, Lord Dorchester. Dorchester's niggling antagonism frustrated Simcoe, and contributed to the physical collapse that led to the Simcoes' departure in 1796.

The following poems are from a sequence that focuses on some discoveries arising from their stay in what John Simcoe suggestively called "the interior World." "Elizabeth's Ride" is set on her "favourite sands" of Gibraltar — an early name for the peninsula that is now Toronto Island. The phrase "place of meeting" is a possible translation of the Iroquois name "Toronto," the settlement replacing the ancient trading post of Teiaiagon ("the crossing").

Elizabeth's Ride

Am I drummer or drum? My hands
playing the reins, my spurred heels the stirrups,
conduct the hooves' quadrille on packed sand.
Yet, as these footfalls shiver the dank silence

to tatters, the shocks shiver me:
sounding the morning, I am become the morning's
sounding board.
                    So we both thought, at sea,
to fall on this new world as on a feast,

and fell down its long gullet
swallowed in mist, sensing only by heavier
air the land, reluctant at last to trust
the anchor's heft and set foot at Quebec.

Now, not quite at sunrise,
with night's black shell cracking along the cloudbank's
eastern creases, riding this not-quite-island,
I see the Indians were not quite right:

this is no "place of meeting"
but a place of melting. Here the watery earth
lapses to earthy water. Fishing fleets
hailed at a distance loom and dwindle into

hollowing flocks of loons.
Shingles on the beach of this "new world"
split like stage curtains to unveil tableaux
of life that breathed before the Flood. My ride

draws me as hourglass sand
along a track lapped by light and water
towards a black, wakeless pool that takes the land
and gives it back cleansed, sharp-edged, hard

as polished onyx. Locked
in its lidless coffer willows find the arc

they strain and crack for on the surface. Wild
berries ripen to unreachable sweetness;

    ice glosses their blaze.
My velvet riding hood blooms into moss.
Under it I see, one in these waters,
my mother's mothers and my daughter's daughters.

John's Walk

To Detroit, by foot, through the ashes of autumn,
each camp colder than the last,
November a spent sun behind us
and winter a moon towards which we walked.

Clear days broke in vain: our eyes
might have been tricked by blizzards or swathed
in pitch, for all we could chart the woodland
or tell one clearing from another.

They could. The touch of a moccasin
defied the sway of pine and maple
and pathed the forest floor. Their skin
answered to prints our lenses missed:

the lost packhorse drawn through the mesh
of shadows at nightfall; or Smith's compass,
a glimmer of gold dropped in the scrub,
caught by Chippewas angling in moonlight.

We walked one path through two domains,
mine an expanse where the eye cut roads
and flung up scaffolds, theirs a settlement
of branching roofs and river avenues.

The trees provisioned them: beech hollows yielded
larders of nuts and honey, oak
a stock of handtools; elm bark capped
wigwams, and birch bark shod canoes.

This inland sea of wood, to me
uncharted as Mars, or the moon's far side,
whispered to them in familiar tongues;
its trails ran through the thickets of their minds.

They took, as water takes, the shape
of their surroundings — brown skin grained
and toughened, topknots plumed — and grasped
water's way of melting into the earth.

And us? If they were water, we
were ice. The frozen tracts we closed on
mirrored our rigid steps, the grids
imposed on bends and slopes, our brittleness.

So, marching north, we found ourselves
in winter's lair, bedding down nights
like spokes around a hub of fire,
to wake to comb frost from our hair.

On Sunday, two weeks out, we took
the last steep rise in a shiver, gripped
not by cold but wonder at the height
that rose above us at the crest:

pillars of ancient pine, as wide
across as we were tall, as tall
as hills, held up a vault of boughs
over a vast arena, brimming

with mist that seemed to vent the pressure
of a long fermenting silence.
It took me back: the mist incense
bending the stones' chiseled edges,

shaping them to my daydreams; silence
the same across long years and miles
save that, beyond it, like a choir
outside of church, a distant, solemn

descant swept the topmost branches
and set them swimming in the blue,
free of earthbound anchorage —
The wind! I felt none of it — nothing

near me stirred — yet it touched me,
and stirred something as deep within
as the trees' swaying crowns without:

in a white land, an Indian summer.

Elizabeth On Fire

Can't you hear, John? This garden is alive
with snakes, their hissing splits the night's peace. They hiss
    because they are on fire. No, no stove
spits so. They turn to flaming tongues, and sizzle

    until they burst their skins, and from each husk
broods of uncoiling reptiles slide and ignite,
    live brands slithering the paths. Do not ask
again to lay cloths on my forehead: snakebite's

    remedy is to thrust the injury
into cool mud — why won't you fetch some? Rubbish!
    How could the ground be frozen in July?
These roses blaze! I should have been suspicious

    in the beginning, when the sentinel
outside the ballroom said, "There is but a sheet
    of brown paper between this place and hell."
The place, Quebec, thick with winter, yet the heat

    indoors enough to prostrate — devilish,
but worse to come. Remember the oak bower
    tucked above Navy Hall? How we cherished
the coolness of its refuge that first summer

    like Asiatics, sated with noon fruits
under the tuft of shade. Ripped, pillaged by flame
    the evening Captain Shaw spotted rattlers
scaling the hill and — but for a sudden calm —

    the canvas house itself consumed! I found
at most, from that night on, broken rest. They tracked
    me through my dreams, licking along the sand,
snatching, spilling into cups left by the quick

    lift of my horse's hooves. One night, fire
shot at us from a wood; next day, a stray shot

fired by a sentry during his guard tour
just missed your head, and robbed mine of all peace. What

offense of mine lashed these Furies on?
Some trifling slight against the fire god? Surely
   rubbing silk gowns with flannel to summon
crackling sprites of flame can be no crime. Then why

   exact the keenest forfeit yet, stealing
into the temples of a child's head to set
   fires she could not reach to douse, flailing
her arms in desperate fits that only snuffed

   her life's short wick? My Katherine! Did she die
to pay for all the pretty fires I lighted
   on evening walks? I meant no harm. The way
the pale grass and the hooded forest brightened

   and danced reminded me of her, rewarded
my heart as she did, moving so quick and free
   that every flicker burned one of the cords
binding our feet to a world of gravity

   and death. Oh, John, a spume of fire rises
from the blind plunge of life, and rolls its brilliant
   coils through our numbered days. We can ride it
and risk the fanged lick of its spray, or stay pent

   safe in a cage of shadows, growing one,
as darkness thickens, with the rock we cling to.
   Which is the sin? To dive into the sun
and blaze with it, or let the night, sip by sip,

   drain our portion of light?
                              Cool now, my head
and neck. Love, your gift, my rosy talisman —
   carnelians, blooms of fire too quick, too hard
for night to fasten on: love, fasten them on.

The Tongue's Allotment

I

"Come unto these yellow sands." At best
a shifty invitation. Simcoe, playing
Prospero in a family Shakespeare fest
in 1800, four years after failing
to keep the Calibanish Dorchester
from breaking up his cloud-capped Georgian palace
(schemes for "Gibraltar" — his name for the sandbank —
dissolved along with dreams of lofty rank)

could not have dreamt a tempest would sever
the curling tongue of land, its yellow sand
scattered like ashes, sown under the waves
to seed unyielding pastures, lakebed headlands
ploughed by the tide's wrecks and the shore's debris:
Elizabeth's peninsula an island,
John's "Naval Arsenal" of "incomparable" worth
sunk to "the Coney Island of the North,"

even its name suffering a sea-change —
Gibraltar whittled down to Hanlan's Point
in habit's shallow wash. The heritage
slipped with the salmon from their lakeside haunts.
The creeks they named are lost in shunts of sewage
under long-shadowed hulks. Their dream castle
has fallen to the dragon — Castle Frank
a subway stop on a fouled river's bank.

II

What was it like to play Adam and Eve
    and hatch the printless woods with names?
To heft George Yonge's name like a knife, and carve
a furrow up to Holland Landing? Trim
    through glacial fringe to the Grand River
in sheer tribute to Dundas? Baptism
on such a scale demanded nothing less
than lake-sized fonts and squalls of sprinkled blessings.

They poured out hallowed sounds, but as the sand
    loses the water it admits,
the land made little of their baptisms.
Either a muddled earthiness silted
    the banks of memory ("Francis"
sliding into "Grape" Island), or, skull-like,
the names held ground but lost their tongues: the Don
(old word for "water") bedded with concrete.

So the ships' cannon loosed their iron tongues
    and puffed their Gloria Patri
over the bay, igniting the damp morning
when muddy "York" sputtered to life — to die
    soon as the grand old blundering
of that same Duke made his paternity
less prized: the newly fathered Indian
"Toronto" (still mudcovered) rose again.

Alas, poor York — dissolved in '34!
    Didn't its fond godfather see
his castle's keep was sand? Didn't his "dear
Eliza" — noting in her diary
    how gunsmoke, curled along the shore,
"ran with a singular appearance" — see
those cursives as the serpent's calling card
inviting them to scrub their garden party?

III

The names that we compose years decompose.
    Wood-lice tunnel Teiaiagon,
Indian trading post, totem as old
as life on this half of the earth, now one
    with the spent breath of those who spoke
it into life, air over a dead tongue.
Teiaiagon, war-whoop of braves wiped out,
    means no more than its own lament.

This was their place of meeting: Indians,
    John, and Elizabeth pitched camp
on this same ground of sand, one audience
swept by the strains of the same requiem.

Like blood that kept time in their veins,
like death through both the Simcoes' names (Posthuma,
Graves), the black notes ran through the thin fences
    and hammered at the tall, doomed pines.

Natives and strangers staked their settlement
    on names, knowing that names are breath,
and in the play on words we all present,
breath runs and runs, but never outruns death,
    its shadow-rhyme; yet death goes mute
unless breath sings both parts in their duet.
So Shakespeare's namer, mindful of his grave,
    spelled the snake's hiss to tune the waves.

Strangers and natives swapped spells. In exchange
    for labials, the Iroquois
anointed English with their glides: young Frank
took on the name "Tioga," the Colonel
    "Deyonguhokrawen." Prankish
Elizabeth (no Indian name recorded)
stubbing her tongue against his honorific,
    might coolly sip the irony

that "one-whose-door-is-always-open" should
    baffle its callers like a wall.
Her tongue had also tasted the hot need
the Indians felt to keep one brand alive
    from ruins of a lost Eden:
Tioga, once hub of their hunting trails.

She too would turn a burnt end into kindling,
    and name her next girl Katherine.

Postscript:

*The second Katherine was born in 1801. Five years later, John
Graves Simcoe fell ill at sea and died in the port of Exeter soon
after being rushed home. He was buried after a torchlight procession arranged by Elizabeth, who lived on as a widow until 1850.*

Don Kerr

FROM "AUTO DIDACTIC"

32

Dumont rides a bronze horse
by the river where once
or so it was told
he rode a buffalo
down the prairie
that grew the downtown
he shot it   climbed it
knife in hand and it
reared up and rode off
or so it was told
Dumont upon its shaggy back
who has for children of all ages
fifty bullets left for the soldiers
invading the prairie like hail
like rust   like drought
over-running the underdogs
in the shallow rifle pits
shooting nails and dying
Dumont sliding down the river bank
clutching at saskatoons and riding
fifty bullets down the river
reined in on Spadina
riding through the mown grass
of the winners

that man knew Berryman
and this man Yeats
would you be willing to be interviewed?
they say and I say wait
till we've met someone
everyone knows is first rate
and they say who?
well in Montreal there's
someone met Cohen
and the coast thinks the gulf stream's
the main stream but the great plain
is next door to the great plain
and our metropolitan areas
are secondary and tertiary at best
it is the role of the margin
to be marginalized
the role of the hinterland
to hint
        in lower case
        our only caps
are baseball caps
farm machinery caps
or twist off caps

this woman knew Lowell
and that woman Larkin
now I got a list but I'm loyal
I'm taciturn
a plain man
it's the role of the uncanonized
not to provoke the gods
to be the anon of canon
let others be the small bore

but for goodness sake
what of w & r & b & k
well I'd say
it's too early to tell

Tricia McCalham

WHAT GETS LOST

I've been losing things lately. Nothing major, just brooches off jacket lapels and hairclips, that sort of thing. Things that I get mad at myself for losing, mad that I spent money on in the first place. I don't even realize they're missing until something reminds me. Last week I noticed a girl in line at the supermarket wearing a delicate silver pin in the shape of a hummingbird. I suddenly remembered I used to have one almost identical.

My therapist tells me this points to something else. With Dr. Jamieson, nothing can be just what it is. He says my misplacing things is a subconscious attempt to reshape my life. He may have something there. I mean, look at what he's working with — a 28-year-old woman who dropped out of med school halfway through because her hair was falling out in clumps and who now manages a rundown movie theatre on Queen Street.

"Have you ever wondered why you won't allow yourself to succeed, Abby?" he once asked, studying me like I was a smear on a glass slide. I told him I could ask myself questions like that. What I was paying him for were answers.

"Only you have the answers, Abby," he said lightly. "I'm simply here to help you find them."

My friend Lydia recommended that I go to see him. She was worried about me. I'd been spending up to 48 hours at a stretch in bed and living on animal crackers and Coke since I discovered that my boyfriend Jack was married and had a little girl named Emily. I had accidentally run into him two weeks before at the Eaton Centre. I was walking by Collegiate Sports and spotted him browsing. It was a Tuesday afternoon and I was surprised to see him in town during the week. He was a pilot for Air Canada, always flying off somewhere exotic, and I rarely saw him except on weekends.

"Guess who," I squealed, coming up behind him. He wheeled around and at first looked as if he didn't recognize me. "Abby. Aren't you working today?" He sounded accusatory.

"Mental health day. Don't turn me in," I said lightly. "What are you doing in town?"

"Checking up on me?" he asked. He seemed annoyed, not quite himself.

"What's wrong, Jack?" I asked, concerned. "What is it?" Before he could answer a nondescript blond woman carrying a toddler walked toward us. She was motioning impatiently to him.

"Honey, didn't you hear me calling you?" she shouted. "Come and look at these skis. They're a fantastic price."

I stood motionless, numbed. As she approached us Jack reached out to her, quickly took the child from her arms, and turned away from me without a word. As they walked down the aisle, the woman looked back at me and I heard her ask Jack who I was. "Oh, just one of our flight attendants," he said.

There were lots of things I could have done but I didn't do any of them. Detached, I stood there watching them, a family out shopping for the day. I remember thinking that I never even knew Jack was a skier. I left the store, went home and stayed in bed for two days straight. Jack called several times and left messages on my machine, distraught nonsense about giving him a chance to explain, that he had only stayed in the marriage because of Emily, but I never called him back. I couldn't see the point. As I told Lydia, I'm not a complete idiot.

"You're clinically depressed," Lydia shouts from the kitchen, stacking dirty dishes. It is two in the afternoon and I am buried under a mound of covers watching a rerun of "I Dream of Jeannie." Jeannie has just materialized on Major Nelson's lap during a meeting at NASA. Nelson is doing his best to ignore her.

"At least make an appointment, Abby," she says in her motherly tone, stacking up my dirty dishes. "It will help, believe me." Lydia has been seeing Dr. Jamieson since suffering from post-partum depression last year. She swears he saved her life.

It takes me a full two hours to get ready for the appointment. Simple things seem monumental when you're down. Standing waiting for the subway, I remember a story I read once about a depressed man who spent a whole morning trying to decide which shirt to wear. Because he couldn't make up his mind he decided not to go out at all.

Dr. Jamieson's offices are on the 20th floor of a corporate tower at King and Bay. The atmosphere when I step off the elevator is sterile, almost air tight. In the room where the nurse has asked me to wait, one wall is constructed entirely of chunky, pale green glass blocks. I stand in front of them, peering, trying to piece together my milky reflection. A mustard-coloured leather couch lies along another wall. It doesn't strike me as the kind of room where people strip bare their souls, more like a place where business executives strike high-powered deals while holding cellular phones.

When Dr. Jamieson walks through the door, I'm surprised. From the way Lydia talked about him I'd expected him to be the five-piece business suit type. Instead, he seems not much older than me and is dressed casually in a shetland wool sweater and tan cords. He looks expectant.

"You are not seeing me at my best," I tell him unapologetically. I want to establish this up front.

"I'm sure of that, Abby," he says gently, settling into a leather chair across from me, the same colour as the couch. "First, why don't you tell me why you are here."

"Do you mind if I smoke?" I ask. No matter how bad things are, I never forget my manners. He shakes his head strenuously and hands me a cut glass ashtray. I spend the next hour chainsmoking and trying to answer his question. He doesn't interrupt: he just nods from time to time and jots notes in a small bound book on his lap. This could grow on me, I think.

When our time is up, he says, "Abby, you have to choose the life you want and then make that life happen. We'll look at the necessary steps next time." The way he says it, it sounds straightforward and entirely possible. Meanwhile he advises me to take a long walk every day and start eating better. Lydia was right about one thing. He has a soothing effect, like slices of cucumber on tired eyes. At seventy-five dollars a crack, I can barely afford him but he may just be worth it.

I walk out of his office feeling optimistic for the first time in weeks. This is just what I needed, I think, someone to say, Now, This is what we are going to do, the way I had done with my mother. One week she'd be on a manic high, feeling such joy it seemed she could barely contain it. The next week I'd find her in her room, inert and sullen, the shades drawn, the room reeking of rye. The "mean reds" she had called them, dark moods that worsened as she got older. My father was on the road selling most of the time. When he was at home, he was distant and complacent, the kind of man who said things like "You make your bed, you lie in it." I guess that's why he never left her, even though I sometimes prayed he would.

Two weeks have passed since I saw Jamieson. I'm taking it a day at a time, just like he said. We're running a Marx Brothers double bill at the Ritz. My cashier has the flu and I am filling in at the ticket booth. A man who looks a little like Harrison Ford pushes a bill through the slot. I study him through the glass partition. He's wearing a t-shirt which reads: *Make Things Happen*.

"What kinds of things?" I quiz him. I've always been suspicious of people who wear printed slogans on their chests.

He digs his hands into his pockets. "Whatever you want to happen," he says airily. I was soon to learn this man could make the simplest things sound profound.

"My therapist would love you," I whisper, watching him walk toward the candy counter.

After the final credits roll he knocks on the door of my office and peeks his head in. He is polishing off the last of a Crispy Crunch and looks relaxed, as if there is nowhere he has to be. "Do you like expresso?" he asks pointedly, sounding like he cares deeply about how I answer.

"No, I'm strictly a Maxwell House kid," I say, too loud. Ever since Jack I have developed the habit of raising my voice whenever I talk to men.

"That can be arranged," he says, gesturing gallantly toward the front door. "I'm buying."

He helps me lock up and we head down the block to the corner restaurant. We settle into a booth and he orders chocolate cheesecake. His name is Ben, short for Bennett, his mother's maiden name. I like the way he talks to the waitress: one of my arbitrary tests of a man's character is how he addresses the help. When he tells me he is a lumberjack I laugh, not realizing they still existed. He looks the part all right, all chest and shoulders, but there is a softness in him. I had him figured for a landscaper maybe, or a zookeeper. Until the year before, he taught at a community college but finally got so fed up with academia he chucked it and headed up north to a job in a logging camp.

"I love it up there," Ben says, ordering a third round of coffee, "no office politics or hidden agendas. I know exactly what is expected of me."

"You created the life you wanted," I say, studying his eyebrows.

He shrugs. "I just figure life isn't a dress rehearsal." I ask him wasn't that one of Cher's lines and he laughs loudly. "Yeah, but I said it first."

"It's not so much that I don't know what I want but that everyone else seems to," I say wistfully. This is one man who doesn't make me feel I have something to prove.

"Maybe you just never wanted anything enough," he says matter-of-factly. The man gives me credit. I can't help thinking that this is going too well.

Hours later we are sprawled on my couch filling each other in on details of our lives. "It reads like a bad novel," I confide to him, explaining about Jack. "People ask me how I could not possibly have known. He had this whole other life and I was completely clued out."

"You trusted, Abby. Give yourself a break." Paul Bunyan lives, I think, wanting to stroke the hairs on his bulky forearm. I learn that he was married once, until he found out his wife was having an affair with her boss. We agree the parallels between us are startling. I tell him I feel like I'm talking to my brother, if I had one.

Ben works up north five days a week and flies down to see me every other weekend. We sit in downtown clubs talking for hours, share long hot baths while Nat King Cole plays on the turntable, and read to each other from the weekend newspapers. I'm a past master at this part-time stuff.

It's late one Sunday morning and I am still in bed. Ben's been up for hours: he set the alarm because he said he wanted to see Venus in the east. He is sitting on the bed reading aloud from the Globe about some survey on single women. "It says here if women aren't married by the time they're 30, they've only got a ten per cent chance of ever snagging anyone." He knows this will bug the hell out of me and I am already in a foul mood. I've always hated Sundays, a day when nothing seems possible. It reminds me of my childhood and being stuffed into church pews, everything in our small town shut tight and school looming the next day.

"Those interested in that sort of thing best get busy then," I growl, pulling the covers tighter. He slips under the sheets, still with his jeans on, and I can feel the hard cold denim against the back of my legs. He sighs melodramatically and snuggles closer. "Why is it the great women never want what the ordinary ones do?"

"How is Venus?" I ask, casually changing the subject.

"A beacon," he says reverently, and we both drift off to sleep.

"I love him, Doctor. So much my teeth hurt." This is an old Rosalind Russell line and I'm finally getting a chance to use it. It's Monday afternoon and I'm stretched out on Jamieson's couch. Ben flew back to North Bay a few hours ago. "But I feel a show-down coming. How long before he wants to drag me back to his cave by my hair?" That's the great thing about psychiatrists: You don't have to worry how neurotic you sound.

"Ben is not Jack, Abby," he says quietly, wiping his glasses with a special lint-free cloth. "No matter how hard you try and make it so." Stop making sense, I think. Stop it.

Business is slow at the Ritz: our Ingmar Bergman Festival has turned out to be a complete dud. "Does it have to come out of Burbank before people will pay to see it?" I complain to Lydia. We're having hot chocolate and Peak Freans while Hannah, her two-year old, tears fistfuls of pages out of the Sears catalogue.

"Abby, it's February," she declares, fiddling with her French braid. "There's a recession. I mean, really, Bergman? Who needs to be more depressed?"

I detest her logic because I realize she's right. "For God's sake, Lydia, don't you start questioning my judgement. That's what I pay Jamieson for."

Ben wants me to move up north with him. He announces this on a Saturday afternoon while we're in the bath, up to our necks in Mr. Bubble. Nat is crooning "Autumn Leaves" on the stereo. I was afraid of this. I dump a spongeful of soapy water onto my chest before saying anything.

"That's your life I'd be living, Ben, not mine. I'm not the Little House on the Prairie type: I'm the CNN, let's order pizza, sleep till noon type." I try to sound flip but realize this is what Dr. Jamieson will later call a pivotal conversation.

"It could be our life," he says, and the way he looks at me I'm almost convinced. "We could get you a satellite dish." I picture Ben's tiny cabin in the woods dwarfed by a monstrous orb of black wire mesh.

I sit up in the tub and start to shiver. "The outback, or Yonge and Dundas. Why are my choices always worlds apart? Don't make me decide now, Ben."

"Not deciding is deciding," he says flatly, towelling off.

It's March, one of the coldest on record. The streets of Toronto are lined with banks of crusty grey sludge. Lydia is visiting, diapering Hannah on my sofa bed.

"I simply can't imagine my life without my husband and baby," Lydia says. "What did I do with myself before?" She sounds smug and slightly mystified. You did what we all do, I think, picking Hannah up for a cuddle. You looked for something solid, someone you could count on. And when you found it, prayed that you wouldn't let yourself lose it.

I remember the day I got the letter saying I'd been accepted to med school. My mother was sitting at the kitchen table in her nightgown drinking coffee. Her doctor had been trying out different medications in an attempt to lift her melancholy but nothing seemed to be helping.

"Mom, the best news!" I said, pirouetting around the table waving the letter. "I got in." She said nothing, just tapped her cigarette methodically against the ashtray. Then she looked up at me, her face full of the sorrow I'd come to recognize.

"And who's going to be there for me, Abby? They don't need you," she said, making a sweeping motion which took in all of the outdoors. "But I do." Just once I wanted to talk to her about what I needed, the way other daughters must have done with their mothers, but had learned long ago what was possible.

My mother died the following year. She went to bed early one night, complaining that she didn't feel well. The doctor told me she just stopped breathing in her sleep. Sorting through her things afterwards I found a notebook in her bedside table. I read through it expectantly, not knowing what I hoped to find, maybe an answer of some kind, a clue to the dreams she might have once had for her life. Most of the entries were the drunken ramblings I'd heard so many times. But on one page, written on one of her better days, she'd entered the same phrase neatly, over and over again, the way kids were forced to do on blackboards at school as punishment. The four words were: *Try to be happy.*

It's Theme Month at the Ritz: this week it's Island Romance. The lobby is decorated with papier-mâché sand dunes and two fake palm trees I bought from a movie production house. "Blue Lagoon" with Brooke Shields is packing them in. I've given up trying to figure out the buying public. They're lined up for miles it seems, in neon shorts and tank tops. The couple at the front of the line have matching Perrier bottles in cloth satchels hanging from their belt buckles. My cashier is sick again and I punch out ticket after ticket. I'm envisioning my appointment with Dr. Jamieson the next day. I picture it perfectly.

I keep losing things, I'll announce.

He'll weigh this while thoughtfully stroking his perfectly groomed beard. Then he'll ask the big one. "Why won't you allow yourself to be happy, Abby?"

I'll look at him for the longest time, at the degrees on his wall and the designer armchairs flanking his plexiglass desk. I'll wonder why I pay him seventy-five lousy bucks an hour when all he can do is ask questions which have no answers.

Stephen Pender

THE BIRDS OF TARSHISH

Therefore it shall be night to you,
*   without vision,*
and darkness to you, without
*   divination.*
The sun shall go down upon the
*   prophets,*
and the day shall be black over
*   them;*
the seers shall be disgraced,
*   and the diviners put to shame;*
they shall all cover their lips,
*   for there is no answer from God.*
                              Micah 3:6,7

i

the birds of Tarshish are scattered
wire, blood or wine. theirs
are the cries of the Gate

'we have hired a ship for Tarshish
broken with gathering salt. little
know we the will of God. Nineveh
prospers as disease, begetting wrath
and the sinecure of priests. the
temple stands sea-ward'

again the jackals cry.
Jonah sleeps in dust
the air is full, dry. Nineveh
knows the sentience of the moon,
it draws the Tigris
close as the night is sealed

we move with ritual night
to gauge the precedence of owls
my tongue is hot glass or knives
there is no answer from God

it is the time of summer
when the wheat field burns,
when the bulls breed and suffer

   ii

in Tarshish,
the city belies its witness:
the infinite bouquet
death-camas and reeds,
rock, bark and sere skin.
sails widen the horizon
and breathe in the sun.
the land flowers rust
and becomes a chapel
by which mourners encamp.

'if we happen to bleed our sun
(or perhaps ship on the long
journey home) release ravens
to guide us to our eyes'

you who hold flowers,
tainted men, your hair is coarse,
lips the skin of snakes.
I have fled the sea-blood
of the Lord and upon you,
Tarshish, salt-bearer, wisdom,
I lay my guiltless flesh

summer burns and spreads.
pungent rain will come from the north.
O people, build and renew
winter comes lacking faith.

iii

come to the bronze tree,
the trees of coal. burning,
dust settles on our eyes and lips.
O procession to deference,
ships falter in the harbour,
bells ring lorn: *the summer
of pear blossoms*

iv

the ransomed dead have coins
and swollen hands:
God among the skiffs.
we have lost the script,
even so, to death by water,
we shall return to Nineveh.

Tim Lilburn

A Yodel On First Things

I want to chant something.
Give me a beer. All right, thanks, now listen.
The glittering song.
Heavy morning moon over the lake, water's cat muscle flickers
   under ice scab, sun drumming up through birches, snow over
   the lake leans out to meet it.
And hours earlier a DNA twist of light over three billion year rocks.
Everything headlong, written on with cosmology as an African bus.
St. Teresa says the soul is a diamond castle, but I say the mountain's
   waiting is also a mansion and it too diamond.
Behind this bay, the oceanic forest.
There, troll mounds, magma surf, hills
      like huge birds gifted with perfect judgment.
Troll mounds piled round one shining word, greenstone
      jewelled with patience.
The mountains. Through snow fog they dream of us.
Mammothly slow heartline.
Stop thinking. Stop gouging at things.
The world is on a death time, on a carpe diem rush, I'll bark
      a short magic-dream cantata.
Listen, a small band of contemplatives wanders the shore of Lake
   Superior north of Michipicoten.
Poor. With baskets of barks, men, women, greeting the singular
   trees by name. For us.
Politics, the ascesis of wonder. What is required. What I have not
   done.
It's time. Bernard of Clairvaux would do this. Between Michipicoten
   and the Pic River, the humming coast, lake a torque of snake surf.

Here's The Plan

Give up, fall apart, rejoice!
Come into the forest, into the gloom bush.
Walk two days, four days into Noone's Camp, over
    the small nameless lakes behind the first mountains.
Almost everything has been lost. Bring no mirror.
No song. Nothing resembles you.
Spruce gives back no light.
Come up the just-after-the-war logging tracks in winter, a mild
    winter, snowshoes
gumming, streams open under snow, rocks green where water
    shaves crust, up
through invisible brown top-lines, Superior silent below sledging
    surf at ice dunes
past Batchawana Island, ravines narrow as one flute played at
    evening, Jays homicidal,
road closing in with red maple suckers, snow fleas blue in
your tracks.
You know nothing.
Come blessed with injury, come bag-asses, dark with limp.
You're exhausted, right? Plato, Aristotle, the animals to name.
Unscrew, why not, those gold taste buds; they're big as
    cantaloupe, ridiculous, put them in your pocket.
That diesel you've woven into your pectorals, right, hammer it
    free.
Beautiful, now that hydro wire throbbing across your forehead,
    expel the worm.
So much has been lost.
How to look? A tree, a tree, a tree.
Follow skidoo tracks as far as they go, then rise on your own,
    dogging the old cut,
burdock, evening primrose dark above snow, gaps, gaps. Bring a
    ski pole for the
grade. There are stories a stone walked up to a man in northern
    Michigan a hundred
and thirty years ago and bowed to him.
Keep climbing.
Everything must be new. The lakes over the ridges are terrifyingly
    clear.

Citeux, North Of Sault Ste. Marie

We'll live in tin sheet huts on the frozen lake.
Cellophane windows, hide windows, snow shovelled hard round
   floor skids, kerosene heaters with spirating, tendon-blue flames.
Paint what you like
   on the outer walls, x's, aircraft, antlered sturgeon, lizards in
   feathers.
The lake has killed three men this year.
Snowmobiles through the ice.
I'll blow out the road today or the next day.
Come when you want.
Our work here is full hours tending in the garden of looking.
Pink granite nebulae in lava-rock, red pines towering from your
   breastbone, olive-silver cones of scat, blood tips on maple suckers,
   gold lichen, clouds over Superior.
We know nothing.
The eyes ate thugs when you get here, kicking in the door, all
   right, where's the bloody noumenon?
There is no order, the Ojibway say it has a dragon torso.

Bring a loaf of Old Order Mennonite sausage, St. Thomas
   on particularity, leather laces for the broken snowshoes.
Everything else is here.
Perch buffalo under ice in evening,
the bulrushes are edible.
For office, anything, anything, the first verse of Amazing Grace,
   all of the Beverly Hillbillies cawed through to the end, ora et
   labora, and sleep.
Above the afternoon snow, fog, then white mountains clumping
   inland.
Our rule's called How To Be In Contemplation Without
   Rearranging the Furniture By Throwing It Against The Wall?
Nothing there.
Good night, come. The world seems burnt. The bay's full of lamprey
   poison, the shining antidote.

*

*In a bleak time, what to do? There is the desert; it calls, the monastic
home. Going there — the north shore of Lake Superior, the wilderness of northern New Mexico — is an act of ascesis which is also a politics for a time like ours. The Celts did this. The Cistercians did this.
Why not us?*

60

LeRoy Gorman

FROM "DEVOTIONALS"

FAIT𝕳
FEAR

theTVevangelist
· · · · · · · · · · · · · · ·
· · · · · · · · · · · · · · ·
· · · · · · · · · · · · · · ·
· · · · :snow: · · · ·
· · · · :edin: · · · ·
· · · · · · · · · · · · · · ·
· · · · · · · · · · · · · · ·
· · · · · · · · · · · · · · ·
goesonabout sin

world
without
end
world
without

Patricia Young

CHOOSING AN IMAGE TO LIVE WITH

You can find my mother in the graveyard.
It is not death she is drawn to but
the unruffled sky, the place
itself, so sure of its purpose.
We are kind to the dead,

give them a sea-side residence.
a superb view. She walks the labyrinth
of paths scattering long-stemmed
carnations. Today she wears
cashmere blue. Among chestnut

trees and marble tombstones
she is a bright sail, her tartan skirt
flapping. Growing up I rarely saw
my mother outside the dowdy
clothes of household chores.
Once I writhed impatient

in my desk at school — *Visitor's Day*
and where was she? A flash
of lipstick, black curls — a movie star
who'd wandered into the wrong set?
I think I gasped aloud.
Washed up against the world

map my mother obliterated
pale seas, pastel continents.
These days she's drawn to the cemetery.
Every bitter word's been tucked away,
nothing's left but love
abridged, composed on stone.
Again I twist and crane

my neck, again she stops to read
some brief and tragic dates, moves toward,
but never reaches, my father's grave.
On earth we have no choice
but to bend to grief, we must choose
an image we can live with.
If she comes this way I will tell
my mother, I choose you

in a red coat always walking through
that classroom door.

VERBASCUM

The day I dug up a new bed to plant
a row of verbascum
the children were close by
picking blackberries on the shed roof.
Lyle Lovett and his country band
drifted over the fence.

On the hills outside Kamloops verbascum
grows wild; everywhere I looked
spiked flowers rose out of sandy slopes.
When we travelled the interior last
summer I hadn't known them
by name but something in me answered
to their stately, desert beauty
and I wanted for myself
a border of cactus candles.

The day I broke up the sod I didn't hear
the children climb down from the roof,
it must have been hours
since the last berry plunked into
their plastic bowl. I looked up
and saw the sky had turned dark,

it sagged in the centre —
a sheet held at four corners.

I lifted those small leafy plants
out of clay pots and kneeled
in the dirt, an ache
running through the ground
and up into my body like a slow
announcement of death, or
had my digging released some nameless
sorrow locked in the earth?
How long since the children ambled
away, since the neighbour's
tape deck fell silent as a threshing
machine in the deep snows
of winter?

Beverley Daurio

A SCATTERING OF OBSERVATIONS ON CANADIAN PUBLISHING,
NATIONALISM, AND THE WRITER AS ARTIST

Ann Wallace recently returned from the Frankfurt Book Fair, the
most important Rights Trade Fair in the world. Held annually in
Frankfurt, Germany, for more than two centuries, the Fair plays
host to deal-making publishers from almost every language group
and country on earth. Frankfurt is a great source of gossip about
world publishing trends.

My husband and I are having coffee in Bentley's, a Stratford bar,
with Ann, whose Canadian literary publishing company, Williams-
Wallace International, does a great deal of business in rights sales
and co-publishing arrangements at Frankfurt.

Ann has been telling us what the former East German presses
have been doing in order to survive after the devastating funding
cuts that came with Germany's reunification. East German publishers who want to stay afloat are publishing non-fiction: a feminist examination of witchcraft, the history of tomatoes. Poetry lists
have been reduced or chopped completely. Short fiction and literary novels are suffering. I sit and sip my coffee, wondering if
Canadian literary writers realize how dependent they are on the
grants publishers receive to help offset the deficits their books create, and if they understand why those subsidies are necessary.

Murder mysteries, Ann says. To save her neck, a British feminist
literary publisher has turned to murder mysteries. And no more
poetry.

John Metcalf has made something of an ancillary career for himself
in Canadian letters by repeatedly calling for an end to subsidies for
Canadian writers and publishers. The idea seems to be that subsidies
make writers bad, that too many books are published, and that if
only Canadians allowed publishing activity to return to the grand
crucible of the scarcity/market-driven model, without government
support, then things would be swell. In a recent article in *Books in
Canada*, Metcalf describes the practical results if his program were
implemented:

. . . magazines will be xeroxed on cheap paper . . . editors will not agonize over the size of the print run. One hundred copies will probably cover it . . . The costs of publication will be borne by their authors . . . spartan books . . . would be bought . . . by a tiny audience interested enough to write in and ask for them . . . Distribution would be mainly by mail . . . Most of this activity would be ignored . . ." ("*Trial by Jury*," John Metcalf, *Books in Canada*, October 1991.)

Interestingly, as Clint Burnham, 1991 co-director of the Toronto Small Press Book Fair, and a small press publisher, points out in a letter to *Books in Canada* in a subsequent issue, the lively underground literary activity which Metcalf says will be reawakened if subsidies are ended is already alive and well, and has been since the early '60s. There are hundreds of underground presses and magazines in Canada performing in precisely this manner in the literary community. And as I said in another letter to *Books in Canada*, nearly every Canadian press and magazine which has published Metcalf's work, and nearly every Canadian press with which he has been affiliated as an editor, is subsidized.

Yet Metcalf is more or less correct in his description of what would happen. But he is terribly wrong when he intimates that "good" Canadian writers would somehow rise to the top out of this underground of exchange. He uses the example of Contact Press, an important Canadian small literary house of the 1950s that published, among others, Gwendolyn MacEwen and Al Purdy. But the Contact writers, including Margaret Atwood and Raymond Souster, all became known through publication by subsidized presses, and would very likely have languished in obscurity without subsidies. Where, in Metcalf's model, do the books get out of the incestuous literary community and out to Canadian readers? Grants have, in fact, enabled Canadians to build an indigenous publishing industry, in an amazingly short period, which is now garnering Booker Prize nominations and international raves.

John Metcalf is not the only person who complains about subsidies; he simply does it more publicly and bravely than most. Although the general population supports subsidies to Canadian culture by a wide margin (and I agree that the 97 cents per capita per annum which Canadians donate through their taxes to support Canadian writing and publishing is a very small price to pay for the value they receive), people do still wonder about subsidies. One *Globe and Mail* critic wondered why literary houses don't simply publish a best seller or two and get themselves out of the fix they seem to be in. Now, why didn't the publishers think of that? There is a complementary story for writers, originally told by Crad Kilodney:

> An extremely wealthy publisher invites his old friend, a writer, to his daughter's wedding. At the reception, the publisher, resplendent in top hat and tails, takes the scruffy-sweatered, inappropriately-trousered writer aside.
>
> "Why don't you write me a pot-boiler I can sell?" the publisher asks. "It'd be easy for you. Just sit down and knock the thing off, get yourself some money so you can afford to do the stuff you like."
>
> "I don't know," says the writer slowly. "Did you ask your daughter to turn a few tricks to help pay for the wedding?"

The only way to make real sense of the present publishing and writing environment in Canada is by having a look at a brief comparative history of American, British, and Canadian publishing.

We live, because of our close and long-term ties with Britain and the United States, not in a hermetically sealed culture, or even in a culture which is keenly aware of the necessity of self-preservation, as Quebec is, but in the English-speaking world. The current Canadian writing and publishing climate is a direct result of historical, economic, and geographical realities. To understand this, we have to go all the way back to the first printing presses, which became widespread in Europe during the 16th century, the beginning of the age of book publishing.

Early British printers produced books in Latin, which were exclusively religious in nature, and were written and read by an elite made up of educated clergy, lay philosophers like Erasmus and Sir Thomas More, the aristocracy, and more rarely, by members of the public. The first bible in English was not printed in England, and was suppressed there. Many of its disseminators were burned at the stake. But by Shakespeare's time there was widespread publishing in English, and the printers, who also sold their own books directly, prospered. By the late 19th century, with the advent of near-universal public education, thousands of books were printed annually in editions ranging from penny pamphlets to leather-bound volumes. By the 20th century, British publishing was an established and important industry, comprising a wide range of publishers with a variety of publishing specialties — from books replete with colour pictures for children, to cookbooks, religious and philosophical treatises. There were also trade literary publishers, including The Hogarth Press, run by Virginia and Leonard Woolf out of their Bloomsbury basement, which produced the first English editions of works by Sigmund Freud, as well as many other substantial contributions to contemporary thought. Soon there were also multinational corporations like Penguin, whose classy but inexpensive editions are available in almost every English language bookstore in the world.

The development of publishing in the United States began when the first printing presses were imported into Boston in the early 17th century. The English tradition of printers selling their own books was continued there as well. A book shop was inevitably attached to the printer's shop, and, occasionally, door to door salesmen were employed. Early American publishing was concentrated in the northeast, where the denser population could support such activity. American publishing began before stringent international copyright agreements, and the printers, rather than purchase and re-sell expensive British editions of works already printed across the ocean, would bring over one or two copies of the latest British works by boat, reset the type, and shamelessly pirate British books. These pirate editions were relatively inexpensive to produce, and were popular in the colonies whose people were still, despite the revolution, looking a bit toward home. At the same time, though, the public's growing appetite for books in the 1800s created a good market for homegrown books by writers like Edgar Allan Poe, James Fenimore Cooper, Herman Melville, and Nathaniel Hawthorne, which were issued beside and in the same kinds of editions as the pirated British works by popular writers like Sir Walter Scott. As time wore on, copyright laws were agreed to by the English speaking governments of England, Canada, and the U.S.A., but the printer/publishers of the United States had already benefitted enough from their pirating to become prosperous, as had American writers. These early American presses evolved into the major houses we know today, like Random House and Farrar Straus and Giroux.

Strong, indigenous publishing industries in England and the United States grew almost naturally out of a conjunction of timing and population density which supported those nations' writing and publishing for a long time before greater ease in communication and travel made international competition simple.

The situation in Canada was quite different. Although the first printing press arrived in Halifax in the mid 1700s, the population density enjoyed in the American northeast was not available here, and the imported presses were of a kind which produced newspapers and broadsides, their owners being less oriented to books out of economic necessity and more political, like the early Toronto printer William Lyon Mackenzie. It was already very inexpensive for established American or British publishers to run off a couple of hundred extra copies of their books and to export these books into Canada; some of them even lied and said the books had been printed in Canada, a situation which was the subject of some of Mackenzie's broadsides. Although there has always been book publishing in Canada, since confederation, to lesser and greater degrees, this situation still holds today; once all of the initial costs (including cover design, editing, advertising, printing, overhead, and more) are covered by the large print runs supported by larger populations in England and especially the United States, it is very cheap for them to keep the presses running a little longer, and to ship these overrun books into Canada at prices it is very difficult for Canadian publishers, with their smaller print runs and higher unit and initial costs, to compete with. The same holds true for Canadian bookstand or newsstand bookselling, over which American publishers have more or less a stranglehold. Multinational companies have incredibly lower unit costs and higher profit margins than Canadian presses, as well as much larger promotion and advertising budgets, and so the books that come from Penguin, Bantam, Dell, Scholastic, and Doubleday, for instance, much more easily reach the Canadian reading public than books which are written and printed here.

Canada's population — around 28 million — is spread across thousands of miles, and nearly 7 million of these people speak French as a first language, leaving perhaps 12 million potential adult English-language book buyers . . . this is a small and hard to reach market.

The situation of the Canadian writer was extremely marginal until about 25 years ago. Most Canadian writers had to find publishers in Britain and the United States, and found little or no sympathy, during the country's early and formative years, for works with a distinctive Canadian flavour, unless their foreign publishers were reasonably certain their books would be avidly purchased by foreign English-speaking markets, like Susanna Moodie's *Roughing It in the Bush*, which seemed exotic to English readers and confirmed their ideas about an uncivilized Canadian wilderness. With the exception of anomalies like this book, American and British publishers did not expect the English or Americans to be interested in Canada. The same has held true for branch plants of these publishing companies in Canada, who, until recently, produced hardly any Canadian-authored books at all. These branch plant companies were little more than warehousing and distribution centres for books written and sometimes printed in the United States or in England, and as the recession and the FTA have taken serious bites out of their Canadian offices' profitability, retrenchment to their former behaviour is being seen. In tough times, the multinationals' Canadian editorial departments are cut first. Owned outside the country, branch plant publishers had and have little interest in Canadian writing, and no reasons except financial ones to produce any — they can sell their cheaper, foreign, books easily here, find no or little market in their own countries for Canadian writing, and can make more money with little risk and less trouble simply by ignoring Canadian writing.

About 25 years ago, during the nationalist fervour which surrounded the Canadian centennial, many studies were done which delineated this situation clearly, and the Canada Council was set up to try and help Canadian artists, including writers, to compete in their own market, by providing them with money for time to work on their art. A couple of years later, this aid was extended to Canadian publishers producing the work of writers of cultural merit, to help them overcome the disadvantages of competing with cheaper foreign books. What this means is that widespread, national publishing in Canada is only about 25 years old — and that is very young indeed. In this short time, Canada has produced not only viable publishing companies in every region from coast to coast, but international superstars like Margaret Atwood, Mavis Gallant, Mordecai Richler, Rohinton Mistry, and Alice Munro, and a burgeoning domestic and international awareness of the high quality of Canadian writing. There are already Canadian Studies departments at universities in countries around the world, including Germany, Denmark, and the United States, and Canadian literature is finally being taught at most Canadian universities.

With very few exceptions, Canadian literature is still published by Canadian companies. This makes sense to foreign publishers who have branch plants in Canada, as we have already seen. They rarely take chances with Canadian writers. Before a Canadian edition of Nino Ricci's bestselling *Lives of the Saints* was eventually published by the Canadian literary house, Cormorant, the manuscript was shopped to many of them, without success. Branch plants mainly want books which can easily be sold in other markets, because the Canadian market is so small. The multinationals are interested in making money, and not in finding, defining, and refining a Canadian literature — yet their books, just as in the 1800s, from Danielle Steel to *The Joy of Sex*, still dominate our market on newsstands and on bookstore shelves, and, sadly, even in our publicly funded libraries.

Eighty per cent of Canadian authored books are published by Canadian publishers, and the percentage is much higher for fiction (nearly 100% for first, most risky books) and poetry (almost 100% for all books) — and most of these are published by the Canadian literary presses. It should be noted, however, that large, mainstream majority-Canadian-owned houses are also subsidized, and not only through the arts councils; they are also eligible for varying amounts of Department of Communications Industrial Development Funding which is not available to presses with sales below a certain level.

When I was growing up in Pickering, Ontario, Canadian literature was not taught in our schools, with odd exceptions like Robert Service's "The Cremation of Sam McGee." Entertaining though it was, this poem was very distant from my experience; and at any rate, no-one told me it had been written in Canada. When I was eight years old I had already decided to write; it was all I ever wanted to do. But I must say it was a difficult thing to imagine, because there seemed to be no Canadian writers; it was beyond imagination to expect to ever meet one in the flesh.

Television is, of course, one of the greatest dissuaders from literacy— not just literacy as the ability to read at an adequate level, but cultural literacy. We, and our children and adolescents, are surrounded by an endless stream of American imagery, thinking, and cultural artifacts which bear little real relevance to our actual lives, and which can only alienate us from our actual experience, rather than make us feel securely part of the Canadian community and cultural fabric.

I am not a nationalist in the sense that I think we should shut the doors and ban or restrict other influences — in fact, I think that Canadian openness and curiosity about other cultures is a very healthy opposition to, for instance, American xenophobia. But I think we are all disturbed and concerned when those other cultural influences are allowed to dominate our own culture, are allowed to fill every cultural opening; not only does that do a grave disservice to our own writers and artists, by not supporting their work, but we are missing out on that pleasant recognition and confirmation of our own real lives which is to be found in Canadian writing.

There is, of course, a more serious side to this need for attention to our own culture. It is a received wisdom that those who forget history are doomed to repeat it, and it is in our writing that we will find that history, those memories, as well as the complexities and present day problems and issues preserved, expanded, interpreted and explained. And that history and that present is unique to Canada, no matter how much American TV we watch or how many American books we read: the urban strangeness of St. John's, Newfoundland, mixed with a fishing based culture and older English, Scots, and Irish accents; the long history of oppression of the blacks of Halifax and the destruction of Africville; native cultures, whose expression has been muted in the predominant cultures; the experience of present day New Brunswick Acadians, of Anglo-Quebeckers; the multitude of experiences of urban Ontarians, and their contrast and similarities with our long Ontario roots in farming; green Christmases in British Columbia. Our culture is fascinating and complex, and our country huge and hard to reach; it is our writers who make connections, understanding, and elucidation of these myriad experiences possible.

Somehow, and I think largely because we have always been awash in the words and images of other countries, Canadians' historical memory is generally both short and narrow. We must be one of the most amnesiac countries in the world, as far as our own cultural realities are concerned. The nature of our forgetting is social, experiential, cultural and political; our own history is taught, not as a long series of political struggles, between first nations and imperialists, between Métis and white family compact, between prairie interests and Bay Street money, for instance, but as a series of smoothing over troubles by backroom politicians who

73

smile when it's over and tell us that everything is fine, the railroad will go through (or be cut off). In public contemporary consciousness, there is not an awareness of the difficulties and complexities which make up our country: there never was a general strike in Winnipeg, there is no discrimination against people of colour, the rebellions of 1837 were innocuous and inexplicable individual acts; there never were *No Jews* signs publicly displayed on resort buildings in Ontario; pioneers were never driven to suicide by black flies; women have never been treated like chattel under the law and have always had the vote; men have never died in northern mines and lost limbs hauling logs out of the bush with horses. Central Canadians may imagine Saskatoon as a tiny backward outpost, rather than a large, beautiful city; the list could go on and on, but it is our writing, reflecting this diversity, beauty, and different realities, which can link us.

About a year ago, a friend who had just temporarily quit literary publishing wrote to tell me that he was working on a commercial science fiction novel about giant carnivorous bats. *Hibernaculum*, set in Toronto, touches very seriously on issues of development in the Toronto city core, nuclear power, genetic experimentation, and Toronto culture, in a format that has elements of both the thriller and traditional science fiction. (For more about *Hibernaculum* and its author, see, "I Enter the Unearthly Cathedral," David Lee, *paragraph*, Volume 13, Number 2, 1991. Lee is the former co-publisher of Nightwood Editions, which specialized in jazz and other music histories, as well as social theory and avant garde fiction and poetry.) In many ways, and more than any literary novel I've read in years, it eloquently describes many aspects of Toronto culture, good and bad. It's the first book I've read that actually made me homesick for Toronto.

During part of our correspondence, he brought home to me something I had been too busy or obsessed with our national "literature" to notice: that what now seems to be missing from our culture is the linking material, the popular culture writing which is created to be read, not as deeply unsettling (for instance) to one's traditional existence or one's concept of aesthetics — but as entertainment.

It's true, I think, that writers, to some extent, always create for publication. This is very true after a certain point in a writer's career: it is a rare writer who will write a twentieth novel after the nineteenth (and all the others) have been rejected by every possible publisher. Indeed, this is one of the strongest arguments made by publishers to arts councils and arts councils to their governments in favour of continued subsidies for publishing: that without places to publish, writers will be effectively silenced in Canada, unless they write American or British sorts of books and sell them to publishers in those countries, as, for instance, Joy Fielding does.

When Canadian readers are tired and want to curl up with something unthreatening but delightful, they tend to go to the classics, like Jane Austen, or a psychological narrative book that has been highly recommended, like the latest Robertson Davies or Alice Munro, or a genre book, like science fiction, thrillers, or the murder mysteries being published by the British feminist publisher Ann Wallace spoke about.

Genre writing, meant primarily for the entertainment of the reader, has a bad name among Canadian writers, as the usual response to the joke near the beginning of this essay, about the derelict writer at the wedding, shows.

There are probably many reasons for this, among them that American and British publishers and writers have tended to do our popular culture work for us, so that it seems, perhaps, almost treasonous to think sometimes of writing as work, as many an American or British writer does. What we have needed in Canada, we thought, was much more in the vein of Virginia Woolf or William Faulkner, in a Canadian version.

Furthermore, there are psycho-social reasons for avoiding midrange writing which are linked very closely to the view of writing we tend to hold here, and the view that creative writing instruction, even in its secondary school incarnations, tends to emphasize: that is, that writing a novel, for instance, is a confessional activity, an ego-expression, a vast explosion of the genius self over several hundred pages. Genre and populist writing is not primarily a forum for self-expression, except in a very roundabout way. Genre writing, at bottom, first expresses societal norms and wishes in a safe, anxiety-alleviating manner. Taboos are broken only to be fixed again. Women aren't beaten by their husbands in bodice rippers — the men always turn out to be misunderstood wealthy gentlemen; evil killers are inexorably brought to justice in murder mysteries by agents of goodness.

There is something generous about providing one's fellow citizens with intelligent entertainment, isn't there?

If one makes a list of popular literary works in Canada (that is, books read by thousands of people), it is likely to include: books by Margaret Atwood, *Two Solitudes*, by Hugh MacLennan, *Lives of the Saints*, by Nino Ricci, *The Apprenticeship of Duddy Kravitz*, by Mordecai Richler.

Many of these writers end up being vilified by literary writers, if only privately (though it's gone much farther in the case of Margaret Atwood, who has been publicly criticized for everything from alleged coldness in her reading style to the way she does her hair — in my opinion, totally unfairly and in a peculiarly destructive way. Atwood works hard, gives of herself politically, which she doesn't have to do by any means, and has published something like thirty well-received books). The ostensible reason for this nasty chatter is that these are not works of aesthetic genius; they don't blow up the boat and leave you paddling through a dark, post-modern lake of the soul in your pyjamas.

Now, I have to confess that the brilliant soul-pond sort of experiment is what I tend to prefer — when things are good and I want to be challenged, which is often. But the fact is that when I get tired, perhaps after a stressful night of writing, or a long dull day of reading unsolicited manuscripts, I turn to those kinder works: to the classics (which of course Canadians can't now produce) or a murder mystery.

Most people I know will admit to the same behaviour. And I, for one, would rather read about a Black detective in Halifax, a First Nations detective in Toronto, or a WASP detective in downtown Regina . . .

I think that there is a difference between an artist who happens to be a writer — Nicole Brossard comes to mind as a clear example — and a writer, who, comfortable or not with the surrounding world, is happiest crafting stories. By stories, I mean novels and fictions which are narratival and psychological — composed of writing which is reasonably straightforward, probably dependent on image and metaphor for its beauty — and which emphasize the primacy of the individual protagonist in his or her struggle for acceptance, redemption, justice, or whatever.

There are grey areas, and levels of artistic subversion in writing, which range from Steve McCaffery's occasional hatred of the page to the delicate upheavals in bourgeois lives in a singing work by Mavis Gallant.

But there are also thousands of Canadian writers who would probably be happy ranging back and forth between the kind of art writing that Brossard and Woolf would agree is very taxing (and that is usually very hard for publishers to sell), and the sort of entertaining books Canadians lack in their own vernacular that readers tend to buy by the thousands. Even here.

In between writing her more stylistically adventurous and psychologically costly novels, Virginia Woolf turned to populist and simple forms of writing. These books — including *Orlando* (a cross-dressing feminist fantasy) and *Flush* (the biography of a favourite spaniel) — sold much better during her lifetime than her serious works.

People's biggest complaint about subsidies has always been that they don't support books that sell — and the truth is that in most cases, even selling 2000 copies of a literary book would not create a profit for the publisher (believe it or not, 2000 is an incredible number of copies to sell in Canada of any literary title from a literary press). Or they say there are too many books being published. Or, there are too many bad books. Etcetera. The claim is that the supposed "hothouse atmosphere" of Canadian subsidized publishing has led to a frenzy of unthinking book production which somehow diminishes our literature. For some reason, the same complaints are not made here about American junk. Even though, if you walk into any Canadian variety store, what you will see is the result of precisely such a frenzy of unthinking book production.

I've thought about these issues a lot. I'm totally in favour of subsidies. But I can't help but be somewhat affected by the complaints, and I've often wondered why the many amazingly good novels (for instance) Canadians have produced in the past twenty years, including:

Ana Historic, by Daphne Marlatt; *Beautiful Losers*, by Leonard Cohen; *Heroine*, by Gail Scott; *A Dream Like Mine*, by M.T. Kelly; *News from a Foreign Country Came*, by Alberto Manguel; *Canadian Sunset*, by David McFadden; *The Prowler*, by Kristjana Gunnars; *In Search of the Perfect Lawn*, by Michael Dean; *Midnight Twilight Tourist Zone* and *The True Story of Ida Johnson*, by Sharon Riis; *Mauve Desert*, by Nicole Brossard; and a hundred others

have not gone farther in impelling people toward a greater fondness for indigenous literature. Apart from some terrible and intractable practical problems for Canadian publishers (bookstore and library resistance to Canadian work, and tiny promotion budgets, among them), I think the answer may lie, oddly enough, in the lack of a greater number of simple, entertaining books. Canadian writers and publishers haven't been there, providing entertainment and comfort when readers were tired, and so Canadian books are less sought after when readers are ready to be challenged.

I'd like to remind the reader that Canadian publishing is very young. It is, I believe, silly and petulant to demand that in a mere twenty-five years Canadian writers and publishers ought to have been able to churn out a fully formed and mature literature, representing not only the multitudinous origins of writers here but also the full range of writing useful to a society, from Canadian romance to serious literature. Yet our serious literature is, in my opinion, quite mature and exceptional. I believe that in this area Canadian writing is as good or better than that found in any other English-speaking country.

What we still lack is commercial fiction writing and publishing.

The last time we spoke about it, my friend with the science fiction manuscript still didn't quite know what to do with it. He quite wisely expects resistance to a Canadian setting from American publishers, and there is no Canadian publisher that specializes in Canadian science fiction and is capable of getting fat, embossed mass market paper SF books on airport newsstands in Canada. (Canadian publishers who publish genre work usually do so occasionally, and their books tend to be distributed in the same manner, and with the same limitations, as their literary titles. This is not the fault of the publishers: it has more to do with the stranglehold American houses have over newsstand distribution.)

It is my contention, however, that without intending to, Canadian publishers have skewed the market toward literary books. Maybe this is what the people who complain about subsidies are really trying to say: that the literary community is only satisfying high culture demands, and ignoring the legitimate needs and desires of a large percentage of the population in the process. When a Canadian writer sits down to write, it is probably great literature that he or she sets out to produce, because that is what we tend to want to publish here.

When I teach creative writing, I tell my students to read and read and read. I tell them that there are no rules. I want them to concentrate on what they believe, first of all, and secondly on the mechanics of working in words.

I still think it's essential for all writers to read, to understand grammar and the mechanics of writing, but I may be wrong when I insist that there are never any rules.

In most creative writing classes, students who ask for rules about what-to-write and how-to-write (as opposed to asking for good grammar and style resource books, self-editing techniques, feedback on particular work, and other things useful to artists as well as craft writers) are still exhorted to poetic self-expression, even when that is not really appropriate to their needs. These students claim to be there in class because they want to learn how to do something properly. They think there is a methodology to writing, and that this methodology ought to be known to the instructor. It's possible that more effort should be made to accommodate such students. Rather than sending so many of them off to a future of occasional publication in workshop newsletters, perhaps they ought to be tutored in the subject that interests them: written entertainment in the form of stories.

When a good, competent story teller sits down to write a novel, what is often produced is a good, competent story. Reasonably comforting, probably, and trailing the ribbons of acceptance of the society in which the writer lives. Not, however, great literature; and if the book is fraught with that annoying explosion of confession and self-indulgence which my slush pile tells me is endemic, then who does it serve? There is a plethora of barely competent Canadian work, published and unpublished, that tries to be literature, and it is possible that there is something off-balance about a culture that produces only writers who believe themselves to be always, and restrictedly, artists. What is wrong with writers learning to also value their craft, and to turn their hands more often toward work which serves their society and makes them a living, even in the guise of entertainment? Who wants to read work that is merely derivative of Gertrude Stein?

On the other hand, millions want to read work that is derivative of P.D. James.

I have to admit I am somewhat uneasy with this thesis. I never would have thought this way about Canadian writing fifteen years ago, when I was more worried about the possibilities of literature in Canada, and had had less access to thousands of unpublished manuscripts. But the need is there, not only in terms of a greater range of cultural material, but also for the financial health of writers and publishers. It seems uncharitable to separate writers into artists and non-artists, as if one were more valuable than another. I do believe that readers will finally make those decisions for us, and know the difference whether we, as publishers or writers, ever do ourselves.

On the other hand, Canadians, and I among them, like to bandy about solutions to problems, even when, sometimes, as with the current "constitutional" debate (sic), there isn't necessarily a problem at all. Over the past five years, Canadian literary presses have increased their sales dramatically through specific, practical improvements in distribution, and sales efforts, made possible by co-operative ventures and the work of some tireless individuals. Having said this, however, it is very clear to me that the time of relatively easy (it has never been *easy*) literary publication is nearing an end. Writers will find it more and more difficult to place first books, and especially poetry books. The arts councils are demanding more from publishers in terms of sales; at the same time, the atmosphere of frugality emanating with real chill from Ottawa, and the threatened FTA with Mexico (which increases the likelihood of more damage, particularly to the legislative infrastructures supporting culture) mean that even literary publishers are being forced to think seriously about saleability when they sign an agreement to publish.

In other words, I think I am being rather more predictive than prescriptive here. As publishers' literary lists become tighter, more writers will turn naturally to more populist kinds of writing, and with excellent results, both financially and in terms of the works' popularity with readers. I suspect that many literary publishers will begin to produce split lists, as has already happened with Talonbooks' spotty incursions into science fiction, Beach Holme's

Tesseracts series, and Douglas & McIntyre's adventures with mysteries. Canadian genre and popular writing is a necessary element of our cultural evolution.

And I think many of us will be happy when we walk into a variety store and finally see some Canadian books there.

XXX: POEMS by Frank Manley, Claude Paradox,
James Whittall.
Jaw Bone Press, 1990

Light Like a Summons, edited by J. Michael Yates.
Cacanadadada Press, 1990

These two short anthologies set out to accomplish for eight
Canadian poets what Oberon's *Coming Attractions* series does for
short story writers — to provide enough material from each of the
authors to give a good sampling, rather than merely a hint, of their
work. *XXX* (yes, that's the title) includes three male poets from
the Montreal area; *Light Like a Summons* brings together five
women from British Columbia: Mary Choo, Margaret Fridel,
Eileen Kernaghan, Sue Nevill, and Laurel Wade.

The gender difference may be more apparent than real in these
collections in terms of a particular social point of view. (The
women are better writers than the men, but that has nothing to do
with their politics.) The men certainly attempt to speak with one
voice, and provide a militant, seven-part "Manifesto" to make sure
that the voice is recognizable. However, they are concerned more
with formal than with personal issues, with a loosely conservative
attempt to "remake poetry from the scraps of form left . . . by the
pre-Sixties poets," and with an indiscriminate attack on
Postmodernists and Deconstructivists, female and male alike.

Frank Manley and James Whittall are both strongly attracted to
satire, particularly parody, and handle the genre well. Manley's
selections include the neatly turned "The Shell Game" (after
Margaret Atwood) and the heavier, less successful "Susan Musgrave,
This Is for You"; Whittall evens the gender balance with his
superbly incomprehensible "The Immaculate Deception, *for
Christopher Dewdney*" and also provides a competent satiric piece,
in the manner of F.R. Scott, called "Portrait of the Canadian Poet as
Domestic Fowl":

Here is a strange and exotic bird.
To the rich he is a precious thing:
he'll mimic their speech for a single grape,
for a handful of bread crumbs he will sing.

O do not ask to set him free!
He's happiest caged and on display,
and cannot recall how to work his wings
so he'd never think to fly away.

Claude Paradox favours direct broadsides over the subtler word play of the other Xs, such as his anti-establishment rants "The God Game" and "Billions and Billions Served." He often presents himself with a Milton Acorn *redivivus* persona, as in the rough-hewn love poem "Husbandry":

I was only there to find
for myself and believe in the strength
of the bones
that lie beneath
all the beauty you appear to me.

All three voices continue, for the most part, with this kind of stridency, though Claude Paradox can pause briefly to acknowledge his human uncertainties — "Sometimes, you know . . . my eyes don't see / everything I hear" (*"When It Come"*); and Frank Manley, who exhibits the most broadly based talent of the group, can produce a simple, poignant description that doesn't require, and passes easily beyond, his official militant position:

Within the darkening shadows, on wood,
the rain clings in perfect, harmless drops . . . .

J. Michael Yates begins his "Afterward" to *Light Like a Summons* with a quotation from the mythographer Joseph Campbell: "Art should bring myth and the cosmology together." Campbell's dictum makes a good epigraph for the collection, suggesting both the breadth of concern and degree of commitment shown by these five poets. Though Yates goes on to remark, with an uncharacteristically modest gesture, that "In this project . . . I am not an impresario", the book he has organized is both substantial and well varied.

Mary Choo moves directly into mythical narrative with a four-poem sequence exploring the symbolism of the pelican. The verse is simple and evocative in "Moonpiper", for instance, where "a white pelican / walked in my garden last night / assessing the moonlight" and is finally seen with "his feathers blown / right as a rose." Margaret Fridel experiments with a number of forms here, including the closed couplets of "Alberta: Aunt Mary's Farm" and "Painting of Lady Playing Violin", and a kind of abstract *haiku* (similar to Douglas Fetherling's work in *Rites of Alienation*):

> The striations of the tiger
> Could be shadow cast by bars
> But are not. And are.

The poetry of Sue Nevill and Laurel Wade is closest in general effect to that of the three men considered above. Nevill exhibits a strong social consciousness and a preference for poetry of statement: "let the private parts / of public streets / hang out / on rotten walls / and dying fences" (*"Increase Your Word Power"*). Wade is the more naturalistic of the two, producing fine genre pieces with "Nearing Porteau Cove" and "Deer Lake", and exhibits a soft-spoken sense of humour with the "Dance of Drink":

> He lives between
> the empty
> and the full
> neither undrunk
> nor
> drained
> Nor
> in panic
> because of this.

The work of Eileen Kernaghan effectively brings together the individual strengths of the other four writers with its sensitivity, wit, large vision, and command of verse technique. These qualities are well exemplified in "Dune Woman" —

> Sleeping
> on cool sand

the dune woman
draws slow warmth upward
from the earth's core

— a piece which justifies Michael Yates' statement that "Each poet
is an accomplished artist, sage, inflector of myth."

Allan Brown

Don Dickinson, *Blue Husbands*.
The Porcupine's Quill, 1991

Blue Husbands is a good title. It seems to speak to a time when
many husbands say they're feeling glum. The title of Don
Dickinson's first book, *Fighting the Upstream* (1987), was equally
suggestive, but of a more traditional masculine posture, variously
perceived as courageous or damnfoolhardy.

That first collection of stories was well received (and *Blue
Husbands* was itself shortlisted in 1991 for the Governor General's
Award). In these pages (*Quarry* 37/4), I remarked on Dickinson's
artistic tact in evoking and, what is more rare, respecting "the mystery of inarticulacy." True, in a few places, he spelled out for us
what the central character couldn't say, but he never came near
pushing the story aside for the sake of promoting an Idea or Big
Theme. In his second book he is less inclined to let things be, and
the stories suffer for it.

Not all of them. "The Sample Case" recalls the oblique graces of
Fighting the Upstream. The spring of the action is a shameless gim-
mick: Grandfather's will leaves $100 to his grandson on condition
that he and Grandmother distribute the contents of his sample case
to customers on his old sales route. The opening scene, the reading
of the will, is pitched in an uncomfortable key — full of concrete
detail yet appearing to be funny about Grandfather, with his youthful weightlifting prowess (lifting a Percheron!) and the two silly
aunts and down-to-earth old Grandmother. The trip itself is not
played for laughs, however. Its dullness and mysterious inconse-

quence harmonize with the late-fall landscape of tree, field and small town, all economically and vividly evoked. The story here develops its own rhythm and leads into a poignant, understated conclusion.

Unfortunately, other stories are marred (in two cases, ruined) by authorial interference. Two linked stories, "Flying" and "Per Ardua ad Astra", concern the rescue of a suicide and the consequences for the rescuer, one of many blue ex-husbands in the book. The would-be suicide is a tediously chattering nutcase who quotes G.M. Hopkins ("The Windhover") while the narrator holds him by the collar as he dangles from a train trestle. No reader could be so insensitive as to miss the message in the suicide's name — Darwood — but in case we do, Dickinson also loads every other rift with ore. It turns out that the rescuer's son was injured in an absurd (i.e. meaninglessly meaningful) accident *at the same time* his dad was saving Darwood, and is now paralysed. When Darwood is later released from the asylum, he arranges to meet his savior *at the very same spot* on the trestle. And so on, including ruminations on fate, heroism, mortality, randomness, etc.

Some of these ideas also get in the way of "The Accident Business", the story of two old people who conspire to escape the rest home — in itself an interesting though not unhackneyed subject. The seriocomic possibilities are not developed, and we are not allowed to see them onto the bus. Why does the reader have to suffer this fate?

In "Thirty-three Thousand Push-ups", we also have the beginning of a story, and part of its middle. The blue husband performs his record-breaking stunt in order to win back his wife; he does, but the story ends without showing us their reconciliation — which is where the real story lies waiting. I understood, I think, why the man 'worked out' his unhappiness this way, but I wanted to know what sort of woman would be wowed by it.

These stories too often have just that air of false determination about them — as if the author decided to do calisthenics before our very eyes and win us by sheer perverse stamina. He tosses up a handful of tightly-assembled quirks (as characters, they are elusive in reality but populous in fiction), puts them into a left-handed spin, and makes a Point.

I hope this is all a passing fancy and that on the next round Dickinson will give up calisthenics and exercise his talents freely.

Carolyn Bond

Pierre Morency, *A Season for Birds*, translated by
Alexandre L. Amprimoz.
Exile Editions, 1990

In this gradually infuriating book, the pen-and-ink lithograph of a
scruffy and blotched crow recurs, expanding in six repetitions,
from average colophon size to its full-page final appearance that
also carries a cryptic and unpunctuated multiple pun, to wit IDEN-
TITY SIN NO SECRET.

The voices of the poems thus darkly interrupted sometimes posture, or bluntly assert, or drift into sing-song, all presumably striving to isolate sense in "the corroding indifference of crass con-
sumer life", as Morency's short biographic note hints. There is no
quarrel with such a purpose, which is helped along most ably by
Alexandre Amprimoz's clear translation from the original French.
The work is presented collaterally with confidence and with no
sense of effort, as though the two minds flowed one into another.
Good translation, the near-matching of words as close as breath
with others usually far less native, always merits praise. IDENTITY
SIN NO SECRET, perhaps. Amprimoz himself may have been reflect-
ing on the hazards of the translator in poems recently published in
The Canadian Forum when he observed

> If you've got your grammar
> And your accent just where you want them
> You will not understand.

Though scarcely a heartening remark for readers of Morency,
the hint may obliquely point to some rewarding sense which carries through these selections made from 1967 to almost the present.
The text assumes a kind of post-mortal stance reflected in six
untranslated headings (from *"poèmes de la froide merveille de
vivre"* through *"éffets personnels"*) toward a coda, an apotheosis
called "twelve days in a night". The planned ambiguity survives
easily throughout. What English structuring, for example, could
bring across the tricky adverb of *"au nord constamment de
l'amour"*? Human sexuality as an implicit principle of both liberation and enslavement pervades many of the poems in enclosed and
smothering atmospheres where the bravura male potential seems
to exist solely for its own definition:

it is inside my breast that i write
lost   dripping in my own blood
between flower vases and women's faces

i seldom go out
i spend my days within my ribs
and when i travel i go down to my belly
down to the deepest voices
to meet with the swimmer of light
who spreads herself in the wells

This egocentric turn of imagery characterizes most of the volume, and, in league with flickers of surrealism, rather spuriously
raises the expectation that something really thoughtful is about to
be said. A growing isolation of voice and reader, of poet from subject, often results, as in "'night harms us" ("la nuit nous nuit"):

why are we so far from ourselves
as soon as the windows turn black
and crack amidst the bones of the room
why are we so far from ourselves

And who knows? All this may be intentional and cleverly done in
ways to which Amprimoz is privy — a limb of the deconstructionist revolt. Is the hint of Rimbaud's *Une Saison en Enfer* in the title
a set-up for those who might enjoy the vitality and risk of *"Je est
un autre"*? No key to the fantastic parade is forthcoming. The
parade itself turns a distant corner from the droning edge of the
text. The symbolic moment quickly fades.

Despite the steady movement from death to a resolution in light,
there is no corresponding sense of innocence lost and regained, no
real energy of hope. The performance throughout is carefully man-
nered; its voices declaim at an unruffled pace:

i will have hands to get back up in the swamp
i will have hands to pelt my mount of flames
i will have hands to rebuild the compass
i will have hands to break down the walls that restrain you

Morency believes "The poet will avoid speaking of peace", a biographic note explains, "preferring to work with the words of knowledge, nature, tribe, power, blindness, light, crowd, shelter, fog." In all this homogenizing of feelings and imagery, which gives the last poem of the collection the same beige tones as the first, Morency nowhere acknowledges the *cause célebre* which Yves Bonnefoy, one of the French language's master poets, has been spearheading for decades, in recent years from a chair at the Collège de France. Bonnefoy would restore the poet to bardic status. Reviewing five newly-published translations of Bonnefoy's poetry and essays on prosody in the *Times Literary Supplement* last year, the poet Stephen Romer praises Bonnefoy's vision of poets and critics working together to "open by a few more doors the mind's relationship to itself" and "a lucidity, a short time ago still prohibited, except in moments of extreme tension . . ." The antithesis of bardic speech for Bonnefoy is what Romer calls the language of the mediatized world with its mirages of writing.

Some few poems in this volume seem aimed toward this elevation of the poet to ancient respect and responsibility, and the poet's speech too. In its final images, the last poem, "twelve days in a night", offers a tree, possibly a survivor, left from extinction and a bird of restricted habitat:

> it is a day
> made for writing
> the word   *housefinch*
> it sang a while ago
> in an elm in the park
> and the snow all around
> became salt riddled with holes
> the sun broke through
> the walkers' broken bodies

Is this deconstructionist optimism, a *fin de siècle* springtime echo of Blake's garden in the city?

In "furious night," dated 14 May 1974, best of all the book for its bardic *élan*, Morency reaches a vatic height to which everything else appears a long approach. The entire construction over four pages is of subordinate adverb clauses and phrases thrusting fierce images of brutality and illness at the reader:

when the shadow of the walker
when the black earth under the nails

when the dazed charge
when the night people freeze in their tracks
when the old uncle is ridiculed

when the pipes in the canal
when the soft leather strips

when the clots of blood
when we bulge

With its wide disparities of attitude to the denizens of "crass con-
sumer life" and a consistent refusal to spell out cures for its troubles, *A Season for Birds* nags irreconcilably at the reader. The
crow's enigma remains.

J.W.H. Bell

Karen Connelly, *The Small Words In My Body*.
Kalamalka Press, 1990

The Small Words In My Body, Karen Connelly's first book, is the
latest recipient of the Pat Lowther prize for poetry awarded by the
League of Canadian Poets. Connelly is a young writer, just 22
years old, but the originality and formality of her poems suggest a
maturity beyond her years. These are carefully crafted works, constructed with exact detail and acumen.

The book is divided into three sections. The first is organized
into four suites which deal with the poet's relationship to her
father ("The Remarkable Cheapness of Blood"); her sister's death
("Grave Digging"); heterosexual relations ("Why People Have
Lovers Now") and her struggle to claim her own space as a poet
("Languages I Have Failed to Learn").

This first section, by far the longest in the book, describes a long
period of imprisonment, hibernation or gestation. The poet writes
as though she were a tiny animal trapped underground, and she
describes her primordial world as from a small, dark space situated
on the edge of terror. The atmosphere is cloying, the landscape is
colourless and cruel. Life is predatory and violent, treacherous and
bleak. Because "[b]lindness is a way of life", people come together
but never touch. As in the following passage, Connelly's depic-
tions of human relations are sardonic and macabre:

I am gathered like new grass cuttings
    in your arms, almost alive.
There is bribery with the hands,
        washing skin raw.
Nerves jump and shudder like live wires in rain.
This touching is safety, is love, is forgiveness.
Then you sleep.
            "A Moth in a Glass"

The poems in the first section are disturbing, full as they are of
slaughter, dissections, and disembodied limbs. Her images — a
splinter slipped under a fingernail, fish-hooks in human flesh, a
poisoned dog, a cat's "neck cracked/like a thin twist of copper" —
are like guts spilled out to be augured, and they become oracles for
divining what is dream or memory, where knowledge lies, whether
anything at all is real.

At the heart of Connelly's book lies an investigation into language as the essential tool of the poet, and here in Part One the word is made flesh. Language is not only tactile but visceral: thoughts, emotions, and the abstract are embodied in skin and blood, bone and sinew. She carves and cuts "the small words from [her] body"; she speaks about the "skin" of words. And yet, although she is a "believer", "words will not cure everything":

> Breathless unless in the mouth,
> on a page, they are flat and black
> and have little to do with the details
> that make a life.

"The Small Words in My Body"

Words, it seems, cannot mediate reality, and in Suite Four of Part One the poet begins to think of language as something preverbal. Poetry, she proclaimed in "The Fifth Season" (from Suite One), "is the song of those people/who did not learn words." In "Languages I Have Failed to Learn" she names what belongs to her, describes her poetical landscape as that which exists apart from language already known.

Connelly surfaces in Part Two of her book, "Learning Colour and Demons, Northern Thailand"; it is a relief almost physical. We emerge into the openness, sunlight and colour of this foreign land and escape the claustrophobia of home. Her images are richer, softer, delicate but enduring, and although here she encounters a language she is unable to speak, "For the first time, she understands the words."

The Small Words in My Body gathers momentum until it spills over with orgasmic intensity in its final section, "She Arrives in a Loose Blue Skirt, Spain." It is a tribute to Nancy Holmes, a poet through whom Connelly has discovered the other side of love. Here is light and joy and music; the poem is a tangled garden of metaphor: vibrant, brilliant, alive. Holmes can speak all the languages; she is whole, "has the grace of grass lengthening green." And she can love with an innocence Connelly has previously never known:

You think, my God, I must have dreamt it,
     that people hurt each other,
     it was a nightmare
     never true.
The lovers have been this gentle
     since the first morning.

In Part Three the landscape plays Connelly like an aeolian harp; there are, actually, glimpses of the Romantics throughout this book of poems: in the correspondent-like breeze that sweeps through "The Fifth Season", in Connelly's relationship to the landscape, in the rhymes the poet hears natural forms speak.

There is much in this volume of poems to ponder and enjoy. What Connelly says about the Chinese language of her friend Junwei Qi, "the tongue is wind-touched/the words . . . danced from the lips", is equally true of her own poems.

Tara Kainer

Northrop Frye, *The Double Vision: Language
and Meaning in Religion.*
University of Toronto Press, 1991

Frye explains in his Preface that the first three chapters of this book
were given as lectures at Emmanuel College in Toronto in May
1990, and he hoped that as a book they would be "something of a
shorter and more accessible version" of *The Great Code* and *Words
with Power.* These chapters are entitled "The Double Vision of
Language", "The Double Vision of Nature", and "The Double
Vision of Time." Seeing that the argument in them was incomplete,
Frye added a fourth chapter, "The Double Vision of God."

The title is once more from Blake — from a poem in a letter to
Thomas Butts (22 November 1802):

> For double the vision my Eyes do see
> And a double vision is always with me:
> With my inward Eye 'tis an old Man grey;
> With my outward, a Thistle across my way.

The same poem ends, "May God us keep/From Single vision &
Newton's sleep!"

Frye's argument, much condensed, seems to run as follows.
With single vision we see language as a literal-descriptive instrument for recording life as history and facts; nature we see (through
the lens by which science has traditionally seen her) as alien and
hostile, to be feared, subdued, and exploited; time is an endless
horizontal line marked by a succession of historical events; and
God is "the reflection of human panic and rage, its love of cruelty
and domination." Single vision is thus self-centred, coldly rational,
inhuman. Bounded by the ego, it turns life into a living hell.

With double vision, on the other hand, we become aware of the
metaphorical-spiritual potentialities in language, its power to tell
of life's possibilities, to imagine many meanings and change; nature
we behold with respect and cherish as our home, where we belong;
time becomes an exhilarating interpenetration of past and future in
the present; and God is the realization of the divine in human
beings. Double vision thus reaches beyond the self, is warmly
responsible, humane. It sees life in its miraculous interrelatedness,
with eyes of love.

It's an inspiring and sobering argument, and clearly there is more from Blake informing Frye's thinking here, perhaps especially the early polemical tractate "There is No Natural Religion" with its "Application" ("He who sees the Infinite in all things sees God. He who sees the Ratio only sees himself only") and the corollary "Therefore" ("God becomes as we are, that we may be as he is").

If this summary is accurate, it was with some difficulty arrived at by this reader. This short book may challenge other readers also. There are several reasons for this — the scope and complexity of Frye's undertaking for one. It's no easy task to discuss and make clear the interrelations between the Bible, literature, history, and myth, through the many kinds and levels and uses of language involved, in 550 pages (the combined space of *The Great Code* and *Words with Power*), much less in 76. There are key terms such as "literal" and "literalism" and many off-shoots — "pseudo-, descriptive-, demonic-, spiritual-, metaphorical-, and imaginative-literal/ism" — to keep track of. Which is hard to do when one is not always sure that Frye is distinguishing between lexical and interpretative definitions of "literal." By the same token, the notion of the Bible as "kerygma" or proclamation, and what Frye means when he says that myth is not anti-historical but rather counter-historical, and metaphor is not anti-logical but counter-logical, are much better understood if we go back to the relevant pages in *Words with Power*.

Secondly, compression doesn't do justice to Frye's encyclopedic reading, or to his habit of generous references and allusion. And his diagrammatical inclinations seem at times to lead away from rather than to clarity. For example, on pages 66 and 67 we read that there are three clearly differentiated, ascending levels in reading the Bible: the metaphorical-literal, the allegorical, and the moral or tropological. Turning to page 68 we encounter another set of three, previously connected with Milton: demonic parody, redemptive power, and apocalyptic vision; and, unless we are in good shape, we may struggle for breath to match or make sense of the two sets of three.

Thirdly, the nature of Frye's undertaking — essentially to distinguish between life-denying and life-affirming perspectives — draws him into a region he has been careful to avoid hitherto: critical evaluation. Consequently, the logic of his argument seems occasionally to run counter to itself and to the meaning and spirit of his book as a whole.

At one point, for instance, Frye says: "Critics have been deluded into thinking that their function is to judge works of art, but their judicial role does not go in this direction at all. They do not judge the writer, except incidentally: they work with the writer in judging the human condition. The writer may let them down: there is as much falsehood in literature as there is in any area of human utterance."

What logical legerdemain here passes the critic from work of art to writer and back to work of art (literature) with the effect of neutralizing critical responsibility?

More puzzlingly, Frye writes: "A superb work of literature is a very precious thing in a literary context, and to the extent that this context is involved, the Gospels are authentic literary treasures. Approaching the Gospels as one would approach works of literature, however, though a correct approach on the literal level, is confined to that level. The Bible is still polysemous, and has many other dimensions of meaning beyond the suspended judgment of the imaginative."

What does "literal" mean here? Are the Gospels works of literature, or not? Are works of literature not polysemous also? (Frye borrows this term from Dante referring to his *Commedia*.) Are superb works of literature not precious in the human context at large? Clearly the author of *The Double Vision* as a whole thinks they are; otherwise he would not have written this book.

As for this reader of *The Double Vision*: he takes note of its puzzles in the context of the whole, salutes the voice of sanity and hope that he hears speaking through it, and concludes that this is what humankind sorely needs to hear as it contemplates the horror of a Gadarene rush to the edge.

P.J.M. Robertson

Contributors

Caroline Adderson's short stories have appeared in *Saturday Night*, *Canadian Fiction Magazine*, and *Ciphers* (Ireland). In 1988 and 1991 she won third prize for fiction in the CBC Literary Competition. She lives in Vancouver.

Simon Andrew, originally from England, now lives in Kingston. He has had solo exhibitions in London, Oxford, and Newcastle.

Carolyn Bond is a Reviews Editor for the Kingston *Whig-Standard* and for *Quarry*.

Scott Boyce is a geologist currently living in Yellowknife, N.W.T. He has worked in camps in various parts of the Canadian North and has lived and travelled in east and central Africa.

John Bell now lives in Temagami, Ontario.

Allan Brown's most recent book of poetry is *The Burden of Jonah ben Amittai* (Quarry Press, 1991).

Kim Carter lives in Toronto. Her poetry has appeared in several magazines, including *Dandelion, PRISM international*, and CV2.

Beverley Daurio edits the fiction magazine *paragraph* in Stratford, Ontario, and is the publisher of The Mercury Press. Currently she is completing a book of her own short fiction.

Paul Dutton's most recent books are AUREALITIES (Coach House Press, 1991) and *Visionary Portraits* (The Mercury Press, 1991).

LeRoy Gorman has published poetry books for children as well as adults. He lives in Napanee, Ontario.

Michael Holmes lives in Toronto where his first book of poetry, "Lupercalia", will be published by ECW Press in the fall of 1992.

Tara Kainer lives and writes in Kingston.

Don Kerr's most recent collection of poetry, *In the City of Our Fathers*, has just been published by Coteau. He lives in Saskatoon.

Tim Lilburn's most recent collection, *Tourist to Ecstasy*, was published in 1990 by Exile Editions. He lives in Saskatoon.

Tricia McCallum is a Toronto writer and poet "currently at work on a collection of her prose and poetry entitled 'Cloudy with Sunny Breaks'."

Erin Mouré lives in Montréal. Her new book *Sheepish Beauty, Civilian Love* will be published by Véhicule Press in autumn 1992.

Stephen Pender has published poetry in *Exile, Descant,* and *Conspiracy of Silence.* He is enrolled in the PhD program at the University of Toronto.

John Reibetanz has published his poetry in many Canadian and American magazines, including *Poetry* (Chicago) and *Quarry* (39/2). His second collection, "Morning Watch", is forthcoming from Véhicule Press.

P.J.M. Robertson, the author of two books (*The Leavises on Fiction: An Historic Partnership* and *Criticism and Creativity: Essays on Literature*), lives in Morrisburg, Ontario.

Patricia Young's most recent book, *Those Were the Mermaid Days*, was published in 1991 by Ragweed Press. She lives in Victoria, B.C.

From the Editor

CONGRATULATIONS

Quarry Magazine congratulates Carolyn Smart — whose long poem "The Sound of the Birds (*for Bronwen Wallace*)", from *Quarry*'s Fortieth Anniversary Issue (40/1&2), was shortlisted for a National Magazine Award — and Judith Cowan and L. Rex Kay, whose stories "By the Big River" and "Travelling", from *Quarry* 40/3, will be reprinted in McClelland & Stewart's 1992 *Journey Prize Anthology*.

APOLOGY

Quarry also apologizes to Andrew Wreggitt for omitting a line from his prose poem, "Safe", in our winter issue (41/1). The missing line should have appeared at the beginning of the final stanza at the top of page 39, and read "What does follow anyway? my friend asks. Maybe the birds I am . . . ."

$5.95

Quarry

ANNUAL FICTION ISSUE

DESOTO • PURDY • SCHOEMPERLEN

He could still hear his voice raised up,
addressing a power that he himself had
long ceased to believe in :"You who have
shown him to me, beautiful and straight;
Mysterious, Merciful, bless him."

–Adele Wiseman (1928–1992),
The Sacrifice

Quarry Magazine

VOLUME 41 NUMBER 3 SUMMER 1992

ANNUAL FICTION ISSUE

Editor	Steven Heighton
Managing Editor	Melanie Dugan
Book Review Editor	Carolyn Bond

Associate Editors

Tim Andison	Tara Kainer
Allan Brown	Janet Madsen
Mary Cameron	Joanne Page
Eric Folsom	Cheryl Sutherland
Sharon Hunt	A. Colin Wright

ISSN 0033–5266 ISBN 1–55082–032–X

This issue of *Quarry Magazine* was published with the financial assistance of The Canada Council and the Ontario Arts Council. *Quarry* is listed in the Canadian Periodical Index, Canadian Literature Index, Canadian Magazine Index, Canadian Business and Current Affairs Database, American Humanities Index, and Index of American Periodical Verse. Back issues are available in the original from the editor and in microform from Micromedia Limited, 20 Victoria Street, Toronto, Ontario M5C 2N8.

Manuscript submissions and subscription requests should be mailed to:

Quarry Magazine
P.O. Box 1061
Kingston, Ontario
K7L 4Y5

Manuscripts must include a SASE with Canadian postage or International Reply Coupons. Subscription rates are $20.33 for 1 year (4 issues) or $36.38 for 2 years (8 issues), GST included.

Distributed by the Canadian Magazine Publishers Association, 2 Stewart Street, Toronto, Ontario M5V 1H6.

Cover art: Don Maynard, *Fire Speaker* (mixed media, 1991).
Typesetting by Susan Hannah, Quarry Press.
Published by Quarry Press, Inc., P.O. Box 1061, Kingston, Ontario K7L 4Y5.

Publications Mail Registration Number 7293. Issued September 1992.

Contents

ZOE IN MARAIS

Eleven months after her father died Zoe ran away from home. She was fifteen. Soon after dawn, carrying her one small suitcase, she walked up the hill from the farm, her new shoes dangling by their straps from her free hand, the sand of the road soft against the soles of her bare feet.

Beside the road the fields were silent in the early morning light but for an ungainly black bird with a long tail, flapping just above the dry grasses.

When she reached the top of the hill and the paved road Zoe sat down on a boulder and brushed the grains of sand from her feet before putting on her white socks and shiny black shoes. A little further along at the solitary yellow post marking the bus stop she set her suitcase down and turned to face the east where the sun was a sliver of red edging over the horizon.

In the valley at the bottom of the hill her mother and stepfather would sleep for another two hours before the sun touched the walls of the shaded farmhouse.

At the Joubert Street terminal Zoe left the bus and with her suitcase in hand she walked out into the city. Shabbily dressed men stood in idle groups in the patches of sunlight on the street corners or lay asleep along the grassy verge that ran down the centre of the boulevard. The Jacaranda trees were pink with blossoms, fragrant in the morning air, growing in a long line down one side of the boulevard. There was little traffic.

Zoe did not like the way the men looked at her and after a few uneasy blocks she returned to the bus terminal and found a bench near the ticket office, sitting with her suitcase tucked close between her feet.

From her vinyl purse she took an address book, the pages mostly bare, and leafed through the few entries: girls at school, the radio station in Lourenco Marques where she sent requests for pop songs, the name of a pen pal in Texas with whom she had exchanged only one letter.

An old postcard slipped from between the back pages and fell to her lap. It was from her friend Bella who had moved away to the town of Marais more than a year ago. Bella and she were not really close friends, it was only because they were rural neighbours and rode the same bus to school that they had met at all. Bella had come to visit at the farm on two occasions. She had never invited Zoe to her own home.

One day during the autumn term Bella was not there when Zoe boarded the bus in the morning and she did not see Bella again. It was not until she received the postcard some months later that Zoe discovered her friend had moved away to another town.

She turned the card over in her hands and studied the picture on the other side, seeing the green and black heights of the Drakensberg mountains outlined against a sky of puffy white clouds.

Slipping the card back into her address book she went across to the ticket office and asked the man behind the wicket if there was a bus to Marais. He told her there was only a bus to Nylstad, which was fifteen miles from Marais, and it left in half an hour. Using one of the crisp banknotes she had taken from her stepfather's wallet that morning Zoe bought a ticket then went outside to wait.

They arrived in Nylstad just after noon. Zoe got down and stood squinting at the unfamiliar landscape as the bus drove away into the glare. From a fruit stand she bought an orange and sat astride her suitcase on the gravel at the side of the road. The fruit was sweet and juicy, leaving her mouth and fingers coated with a sticky residue. Then she picked up her suitcase and began to walk.

The long road stretching out before her shimmered and moved in the heat, pools of water seeming to hover in the distance, always receding as she advanced. They were mirages, she knew, Mr Potgieter had explained it in science class and said it was an illusion, light reflecting in a haze off the road's surface, but they seemed real pools anyway and made her feel very thirsty.

In the shade of a thorn tree she paused and removed her cardigan, folding it neatly before placing it in her suitcase. The air was cooler on her bare arms when she resumed walking. A truck carrying bales of barbed wire passed her, speeding in the opposite direction, and she raised her arm in a wave to the glimpsed driver then stood listening to the sound of the engine slowly fading into the dry silence.

The air was so still that she could hear a humming from the telephone wires on the poles above the highway, conversations endlessly and monotonously receding across the hot plain where the fields were a dry ochre colour broken only by the torn silhouette of a thorn tree wavering in the glare. When she put her hands to the hair at her temples her fingers came away damp with perspiration.

The road seemed endless and her shoes were pinching her feet, the hot sensation of a blister flaming at her heel. She sat down on her suitcase and loosened the shoe buckles a notch and wiped away as best she could the film of dust covering the shiny leather. Behind her in the grass the cicadas buzzed with an increasing insect drone.

In the far distance a blur appeared on the horizon where the road shimmered and merged with the sky. It became a vague shape that held for a moment then broke to merge again with the haze, a moment later appearing again as an approaching shape. By slow degrees it neared and Zoe was at last able to make out that it was a figure on a bicycle. She got up and went to stand at the side of the road.

The cyclist grew nearer and Zoe saw that it was a black man, pedalling hard with his head down, wearing only a pair of faded trousers. He did not look up as he passed her with the soft whirring sound of rubber on tarmac and she only had a glimpse of his face, clenched with effort, his features glistening with sweat. She watched his bent back and pumping legs until his receding form was once more only a smudge in the distance.

A few minutes later a cream coloured van came down the road from the same direction, travelling very fast. Zoe saw the white uniforms of two white policemen sitting in the front as the vehicle whipped by with a crackle of static, the long radio antenna on the roof bent almost double. A hot gust of gasoline fumes blew her hair across her eyes. She picked up her suitcase and began to walk once more.

Sometime later there was the sound of a car approaching but Zoe did not turn around. It slowed as it passed her, a small blue Austin, then came to a gradual stop a few yards further on. As Zoe came abreast of the car the window on the passenger side was rolled down and the weatherbeaten faces of two elderly women peered out at her. "What are you doing out here, girl? Don't you know there's trouble?"

Zoe shook her head. "I have to get to Marais."

The driver leaned across and looked Zoe over carefully. "Are you all alone?"

'Yes. There isn't a bus today."

The woman's eyes moved past Zoe and examined the fields

behind her. "All right," she said at last, satisfied. "You had better get in." She leaned over and unlocked the rear door. "We can give you a lift to Marais."

"Thank you." Zoe pushed her suitcase onto the floor and slid across the seat, feeling the hot leather on the backs of her thighs through the material of her dress. She inched her window down slightly and looked up to meet the eyes of the driver studying her in the rearview mirror.

"Do you live in Marais?" the woman asked as they drove on.

"No. I'm going to visit my brother. He lives there."

"Couldn't he at least come and pick you up?" The woman's tone was sympathetic but her eyes were watchful.

"He was going to but his car broke down this morning." The lie sounded entirely plausible to Zoe and it was almost as if she did have a brother in Marais who at this very moment was bent over the engine of a battered car with a cigarette dangling from his lips as he vainly struggled to get the motor running, knowing that Zoe was somewhere out there waiting for him on the long hot road.

The woman pressed her lips together and moved her eyes back to the road. They drove on in silence.

They passed a sign with the world Teahouse painted on it and ahead a cluster of buildings appeared, the tin roofs glinting silver in the sun.

"Do you think it would be all right to stop for a cup of tea?" the woman in the passenger side said in a low voice to her companion.

"It should be safe out here," the driver answered, slowing the car and bending forward to look at the buildings.

They drove in next to a low farm building with plaster walls and a corrugated tin roof. From behind the house an unseen dog began to bark excitedly.

The interior of the teahouse was cool and shadowy and they sat down near the door, ordering tea from a thin woman with a tired face. There were no other customers.

When the tea came Zoe opened her purse and reached for some coins but the driver put her hand over Zoe's and shook her head, counting out the money herself.

Zoe drank the hot tea quickly then sat and looked through the window at the nearby mountains.

The two women sipped from their cups in a silence broken only by the dull clink of the china. Outside a vehicle pulled up and a door slammed but nobody came in.

After the shade of the tearoom the glare outside was momentarily blinding and Zoe paused for a moment at the top of the steps while her eyes adjusted to the lights. Standing next to the car was the cream police van that had passed her earlier, its rear doors wide open and the motor running. The radio crackled unintelligibly.

The women moved quickly to their car and as Zoe followed two policemen appeared round the side of the building. Between them they supported the cyclist, his hands manacled behind him, his body limp in their arms and his feet dragging ineffectually in the dust. There was a dark splash of blood across his trousers.

As the policemen lifted him to the waiting doors of the van he came to life in a brief resistance, pulling away from the dark interior. One of the policeman slapped him hard on the side of the head, a flat, ugly sound that made Zoe flinch. The man collapsed into the van and the policeman lifted the dangling legs and shoved them into the vehicle before slamming the doors shut. Behind the building the unseen dog was barking furiously with high, frantic yelps.

"Hurry up!" one of the women hissed at Zoe from the car. She got in and they sped out to the main road, the rear wheels sending up a spray of sand and gravel. Zoe turned and saw the man's bicycle lying in the dust at the foot of the stairs and she hoped that someone would remember it was there.

Within fifteen minutes they were on the outskirts of Marais and the driver finally allowed her speed to slacken as they entered the small town at the foot of the mountains.

"Where is your brother's house, girl?" the woman said, watching Zoe again in the mirror.

"He lives just up here." Zoe pointed at random along the tree lined street to her right. The car drove slowly past the houses. "This one, here." She indicated a small house with an apricot tree in the front garden.

"Thank you very much for the lift, and the cup of tea," Zoe said, lifting her suitcase from the floor. Her eyes briefly met those of the woman in the passenger seat.

They nodded curtly to her and watched as she went through the gate and walked to the front door of the house where she set her suitcase down. She turned and raised a hand in a wave as the little blue car drove off slowly, then picked up her suitcase and walked back to the main street.

In the restroom of a service station she stood in front of a grimy mirror and splashed cold water over her face before drinking thirstily from her cupped hands. She took lipstick and eyeliner from her purse and carefully made up her face then ran a comb through her hair.

A block away from the service station she came to the town's hotel, the Kruger, its white box-like shape rising three floors above the quiet street. A limp flag hung over the entrance. Behind the hotel stood a garden, lush with brilliant red flowers. In the near distance the dark mountains towered over hotel and garden, reaching up into the grey clouds that obscured the summit.

Zoe went through the heavy front doors and across the lobby to where a young man sat behind the front desk holding a paperback book close to his face. He looked across at her with an unfocused gaze when she set her bag down and tapped the counter.

"A room for the night, please."

His eyes came into focus. "Single or double?"

"Single, please."

"Just for yourself, is it, Miss?" His mouth with its thin fuzz of adolescent mustache began to form a smirk.

"My brother is meeting me here in the morning. He's a sergeant with the police." She glared at him coldly until he flushed and dropped his eyes.

"Name and address here." He pushed a ledger and pen over the counter.

Zoe wrote down her name, hesitated for a moment, then filled in the address of her school. The boy leaned over and looked at what she had written.

"You have to pay in advance."

She selected two banknotes from her purse and dropped them on the counter.

When he had smoothed out the notes and given her the change he took a key from the wall behind the desk and laid it on the counter. "Second floor," he said, lifting his chin in the direction of the stairs.

As Zoe walked across the lobby he leaned over the counter and watched the motion of her hips.

In her room Zoe sat down on the wide bed and unbuckled her shoes and kicked them off and stretched back on the soft pillows. She heard the sound of running water and closed her eyes, picturing the mountains above the town, the dark volcanic rock rising over the small white hotel far below. She saw green ledges and hidden pools behind a sheer waterfall that tumbled down a precipice in a silent, smoky vapor of cool mist . . . .

It was dark outside when she woke and the room lay in shadow. She quickly got up and turned on all the lamps then went to the bathroom and washed the makeup from her face with hot water and soap. Draping her cardigan over her shoulders she locked the door and went downstairs.

The smell of overcooked roast beef and cabbage rose up to meet her when she looked in at the dining room where only two of the tables were occupied and a bored waiter lounged next to the kitchen door. He looked up expectantly at Zoe but she turned away and went out into the night.

The air was sweet and moist and in the darkness behind the buildings she could hear the sound of a river, broken by the sharp, irregular call of a night bird. The few streetlamps cast weak pools of yellowish light at her feet.

Near the end of the street she saw the movement of figures silhouetted in the glow of light spilling from an open doorway and heard the faint sound of music. Going nearer she smelled the pungent odour of fish frying in the sweet night air.

She soon came to the door of a fish and chips shop, the light and warmth and cooking smell pouring out into the night on a wave of loud African music.

A big radio sat on the counter and next to it stood two men with their backs to her watching the cook drop slabs of battered fish into a cauldron of sizzling oil. Catching sight of her standing in the doorway the cook removed the cigarette from his mouth and turned down the radio. "Yes, lady?"

The two men looked at her, moving aside to make room at the counter. Zoe went forward, catching the sweetish tang of beer on their breaths mingling with the smoky aroma of the hot oil.

"One fish and chips, please." She was intensely hungry.

The cook made up her order first and the two men stood patiently in silence while she paid. Holding the warm newspaper-wrapped parcel in both hands Zoe went outside and sat on the edge of the curb just inside the rectangle of light from the open doorway.

It was her first meal of the day and she ate the greasy food quickly, stuffing the fish into her mouth, her eyes smarting from the vinegar on the chips.

The two men came out with their parcels of food and sat near her on the curb, talking softly in their own language as the music rose again in the shop behind them.

A warmth spread through Zoe's body as she sat there licking the remnants of oil from her fingers, tired but no longer hungry. The night was like a lullaby, the music playing, the men's voices rising and falling in rhythmic cadences, the air sweet and cool. She almost felt happy.

It was late when she awoke to the milky light of midday filling the room. Pulling back the curtains she looked down past the gardens to a wide river. On the bank was a grove of orange trees and a little way beyond them a small white tent was pitched, a campfire sending a thin plume of smoke up to a sky heavy with grey clouds.

Zoe threw back the sheets and opened the window, leaning out on the sill and feeling the touch of a soft drizzle on her shoulders.

She ate breakfast in a café and asked for directions to Bella's house. The waitress told her there was a footbridge behind the hotel that would save her a longer walk through the town. Back in her room Zoe ran hot water into the bath tub and lay there for a long time with the water up to her chin. Only when the water was tepid did she get out and dress, standing by the open window and gazing at the green river.

A well worn path ran through the garden at the back of the hotel down to a field. Zoe went carefully, mindful of her white socks and the clinging blackjack burrs that lined the path, till she was through the orange grove and on the river bank where a narrow footbridge crossed the water.

The wooden planks of the bridge were slippery from the moisture-laden air and she held firmly to the handrail, feeling the structure sway slightly with her weight. The swollen river flowed not far below her feet, opaque and swift.

Over the middle of the river the bridge sagged down, almost touching the water and Zoe paused here, looking back at the distant hotel, white against the dark mountains.

On the bank, near the tent with its lazy campfire, a man stood with a fishing rod. He raised a hand in greeting but she looked away and went on.

A road wound up the opposite bank and by the time Zoe had reached the summit of the hill the drizzle had turned to a steady rain and her hair was damp through, curling at the edges, her cardigan giving off the doggy smell of wet wool.

Bella's house was a plain white bungalow, typical of the town, with orderly beds of red flowers growing alongside the walkway and a small garden with fruit trees next to the house.

After wiping her shoes carefully on the mat and patting her hair into place as best she could, Zoe rang the bell. The door swung open almost immediately.

For an instant Zoe thought this must be Bella's mother. The young woman standing before her bore only a faint resemblance to the girl Zoe has sat with on the bus every morning.

The once demure hair was now swept up into an elegantly styled wave that framed a heavily made-up face. Between fingers with bright red nails she held a cigarette with studied nonchalance. It was only the eyes under the blue shaded lids that Zoe found familiar.

"Hello, Bella."

The girl stared at her blankly. Then a gradual expression of recognition came over her round face, followed by a look of undisguised dismay.

"Zoe! My God. What are you doing here?"

"I came to visit you, Bella."

Bella stared at her with incomprehension, the smoke from her cigarette drifting up like a veil between them.

"You came to visit me?" she said disbelievingly.

"Yes. On the bus to Nylstad, then I got a lift."

"By yourself?"

Zoe nodded.

"On the bus," Bella repeated slowly and Zoe nodded again.

Suddenly aware of the rain Bella stepped back a pace and touched a hand to her hair. "Well. This is a surprise. I suppose you'd better come in."

Zoe wiped her shoes on the mat and followed Bella into the house.

"Actually I though you were someone else when I heard the bell ring," Bella said. "I'm expecting company in a moment."

Zoe hesitated at the edge of the pale carpet that covered the living room floor. The room seemed like a picture in a magazine, everything new and spotless. She glanced admiringly at the long modern couch under the window, the glass coffee table, the tall floor lamps. And Bella standing there in the middle of the carpet, as glamorous as a film star in her white flare skirt with the red leather belt and matching high-heeled shoes.

"You have such a wonderful house," Zoe said, reaching out a hand to touch the smooth leather of an armchair.

"Do you think so?" Bella asked in a pleased voice. "I helped Mother do all the decorating, it's mostly my choices. Everything is new." She stubbed out her cigarette in a wide glass ashtray and smiled at the room.

Zoe still stood at the edge of the carpet. She wished she had worn other clothes and made up her own face.

"It's so wonderful here," she said to Bella.

"Come and see my room." Bella crossed the carpet and took Zoe by the arm. "I'll show you my new dresses. They only arrived this morning." Her voice dropped a tone. "Everything around here is new since Father left."

The bedroom had pink wallpaper and a pink cover on the bed. A mirror in an ornate gilt frame reflected a dazzling array of perfume bottles standing in neat order on the dresser. Zoe counted the bottles, twelve, running her fingers lightly across them, catching the sparkles in her hand.

Bella pulled open a closet and began to lay dresses on the pink cover. "Mother lets me order all the latest styles." She gave Zoe a mock grimace and added, "There isn't anywhere to wear them except to the dances at the hotel on Fridays."

Selecting a dress from the pile on the bed she held it up and inspected herself in the mirror. "What do you think of this one?" Without waiting for an answer she discarded it and selected another. "I don't know which one to wear this weekend."

"They're all so beautiful," Zoe said.

The doorbell rang, two brief chimes, followed by two more.

"That must be Carl!" Bella said, flinging the dress onto the bed. She bent quickly forward to inspect her face in the mirror, baring her teeth once in a wide smile, then ran lightly out of the room. Zoe followed.

A young man in his early twenties with a sunbrowned face and sandy hair stood leaning in the doorway. He wore jeans and a white shirt under a black leather jacket slick with rain.

"Hi, Babe," he said to Bella, clasping her round the waist with one arm and kissing her on the mouth. Bella hung in his embrace a moment with her head thrown back then laughed and pushed him away gently with her red fingernails spread on his chest.

He saw Zoe standing in the hall and winked at her. "Hi." His smile was brilliant against his tanned skin.

Taking off his leather jacket he shook the raindrops away and handed it to Bella. "Who's your friend?"

"Oh that's just Zoe. She dropped in for a few minutes." Bella half turned to her. "This is Carl."

Leaning against the wall he hooked his thumbs in the belt at his waist and stared at her.

"Pleased to meet you," she said and dropped her eyes.

Bella hung the wet jacket on a hook then linked her arm through Carl's and guided him into the living room. They sat down in one corner of the long couch and Zoe slipped into an armchair across the room.

"How about a beer?" Carl said. He flashed a smile across at Zoe. "Want a beer, Zoe?"

"All right," she answered with a glance at Bella.

While Carl was in the kitchen Bella lit a cigarette and patted her hair. Zoe looked out of the big window where the rain streaked across the glass like a curtain.

"He's nice," she said to Bella. "Are you engaged?"

"Oh. I don't know." Bella shrugged and blew a thin stream of cigarette smoke. "Carl is fun to have around." She shrugged again.

Carl returned with three glasses of beer, setting one down on the table in front of Bella then coming across to stand just beyond Zoe's reach so that she had to half rise and lean forward to take the glass. When she looked up at his face he winked at her.

The beer tasted like metal and was too cold but she drank it down in quick swallows, suppressing a belch as she finished. Across the room Bella talked softly to Carl, her hand draped across his shoulders and her fingers toying with the curls at his neck.

A slackness spread through Zoe's limbs and she settled more comfortably in the armchair, clutching the empty glass in her lap. The beads of condensation on the outside of the glass were cool and moist in her palms.

She watched with fascination as Bella leaned forward towards Carl and nuzzled his neck with her red lips, her small pink tongue coming out and flicking at his earlobe, then her pointed white teeth nipping gently at the soft flesh.

Carl groaned audibly and pulled her into his arms, kissing her mouth, his body sprawling over hers.

When they emerged from their embrace Carl retrieved his glass and drained it with a sigh then wiped the back of his hand across his mouth. He looked over at Zoe.

"Finished your beer already, Zoe? You must be a born drinker." He came over and took the glass from her lap. "Come on Bella, drink up. Zoe is way ahead of us."

Bella's face was flushed and she grimaced as she finished her beer in three gulps before handing the glass to Carl. There was a smear of lipstick across her cheek.

Carl winked at Zoe and left the room. Bella lit another cigarette and smoked with quick puffs, blowing the smoke out in little sighs. She did not look at Zoe and they sat in silence until Carl returned with the beer.

When he handed the glass to Zoe she immediately took a deep swallow. "Hey, take it easy," Carl laughed. "That ain't lemonade."

He sat down next to Bella and whispered something in her ear that made them both laugh. Soon they were sprawled across the couch again in a tight embrace.

Zoe sipped her beer and watched the curtain of rain streaming down the outside of the window. Her arms and legs felt weighed down. The afternoon seemed to be flowing past her in the dull grey light with the sound of falling rain, her hands wet around the glass, her mouth sour with the taste of beer, Bella and Carl far away on the other side of the room

She wished it was not raining and that she had her own house and that her hair did not look like a mass of twisted river weeds or her clothes smell like a wet dog.

She felt as if she were sitting under water, the corners of the room filled with aqueous shadows, Carl drifting by to bring her another glass of beer, Bella smoking endless cigarettes. She felt herself almost invisible, sunk in the big armchair, the sound of the rain gurgling past the windows.

Suddenly Bella groaned, a sound like an animal in distress, and pushed Carl away, getting unsteadily to her feet and standing in the centre of the room. Her face was pale and ghostly in the watery light, a faint sheen of perspiration glistening on her forehead and upper lip.

"I must go to the bathroom," she announced, holding her head erect and walking stiffly from the room.

A door slammed and a moment later Zoe heard the spasmodic sound of retching.

Carl grinned at her and lay back on the couch, stretching his legs out and spreading his arms.

"Bella can't take it, can she? Not like you, eh Zoe?"

He watched her for a long while in the dim light and she stared back, seeing only his bright smile and the white of his shirt.

"Why don't you come and sit over here?" he said finally, patting the couch next to him.

Zoe set her glass on the floor and crossed the room, her arms and legs feeling as if they were dragging through water.

Carl sat up and took both her hands in his, slowly running his thumb over the backs of her knuckles. She looked down at his fingers, seeing a dark crescent of grime under the nails.

"Do you have a car?" she asked.

"Yeah, a Chev." Glancing down at his hands he said, "I was working on it today. You can't get that grease out."

"I don't mind the grease. You have nice hands." She liked their shape, the long fingers brown from the sun.

Carl looked up at her face then moved close and kissed her gently on the lips. Zoe shut her eyes and leaned back against the couch, tasting beer and faint tobacco.

A thin shriek pierced the air and Carl released her quickly, as if he'd been burned. Bella stood in the doorway watching them, a spectral presence with a face damp and ashen. She cried out again, a thin and plaintive wail.

"Christ," Carl exclaimed, jumping up and going to her. "Take it easy, Bel. It was just a friendly little kiss."

Bella gave a choked sob and slumped against the wall, gradually sinking to the floor. Her shoulders began to shake convulsively.

"Come on, Bella," Carl said, hovering over her anxiously. "Come on now. It was nothing. Just a kiss. It meant nothing."

Zoe got up and edged past them to the door. "Sorry," she murmured as Carl crouched down, folding Bella in his arms and stroking her face.

Opening the front door Zoe slipped out into the wet afternoon. The rain fell in a dense sheet that plastered her hair against her head and poured over her face as she made her way back down the hill.

At the crossing the water had risen considerably since the morning, overflowing the banks and surging across the boards of the footbridge. Zoe stepped up onto the swaying bridge and began to make her way over the current, feeling the cold water wash over her shoes and up around her ankles.

The handrail had broken loose in one section and hung down in the water, swinging to and fro in the river like a beckoning arm. She stopped and looked down into the swirling eddies where leaves and torn branches spun in rapid circles before being sucked below the surface.

A movement on the opposite shore caught her eye and she looked through the streaming rain to see the fisherman standing near the water's edge and waving his arms at her. Fool, she thought, what's he doing fishing in the rain. She looked away up to the dark shape of the mountain then down again to the black water washing over her feet.

A great weariness seemed to come over her like a sleep. Letting all the muscles in her body go limp she toppled through the broken handrail into the river.

Quickly the water pulled her down, dragging her into the opaque depths, stopping up her eyes and ears. She opened her mouth and let the river draw her into a deep emptiness, turning and turning her away into the vast darkness.

It was night when Zoe opened her eyes. Her chest hurt and she coughed once. The rain had stopped and she could see stars against a clear sky. Each star seemed to flicker with a different colour while a faint music wound between them like a liquid ribbon. Then the music faltered and died away.

Turning her head away from the open sky Zoe became aware of the small campfire next to her and felt the rough texture of a blanket on her hands and chin. The music began again — small, clear notes moving across the fire next to her.

Sitting up she saw on the edge of the glow the figure of the fisherman. He was gazing into the flames while he played a small wooden flute, the thin, questing notes rising above the flames into the night.

Noticing her gaze he removed the flute from his mouth and turned to regard her with dark eyes. Then a smile parted his ruddy lips and he held the flute out to her.

Zoe took it from him, her fingers finding a position over the three holes cut into the soft wood. She held it to her lips and blew, hesitantly at first, then again with a longer breath, removing her fingers from the holes as she exhaled. A brief melody came to her ears and the figure next to her chuckled softly.

She blew another series of notes, varying the position of her fingers this time, and was delighted to hear a simple tune. The fisherman sighed and stretched out next to the fire, hands cradled behind his head, face turned up to the stars.

Zoe played the tune again and a music seemed to come to her unbidden, formed she know not where, flowing out with her breath into the night. In the notes she heard laughter and song, and saw fields green in the sunlight. Next to her the outstretched figure laughed with pleasure.

Zoe played on, letting the music come out of her and swirl through the darkness, the notes dancing with the red sparks of the fire, over the black river and across the sleeping town, past the high mountains and the long road, onward up to the coloured stars, going round and round, flying upward higher and higher and higher.

Diane Schoemperlen

FROM "IN THE LANGUAGE OF LOVE."

The novel from which "Hand" is excerpted is structurally based on the 100 stimulus words of the standard Word Association Test, originally devised by Carl Jung. It is a fascinating list, the first five words, for instance, being: TABLE, DARK, MUSIC, SICKNESS and MAN. The 100 chapters of the novel are arranged in order beginning with TABLE and ending with AFRAID. Using various techniques of "free association," the main character, Joanna, moves through the interlocking maze of her own past, present, and future life. The novel focuses primarily on the important relationships at various stages in her life: with her parents, Clarence and Esther; with her first lover, Henry, a nice but inappropriate man; her second lover, Lewis, an appropriate but married man; and with her husband, Richard, and their young son, Samuel. Also explored are her relationships with other females, such as her childhood friends, Penny and Pamela Nystrom, twins who live across the street, and her adult friend, Margaret. As a collage artist, Joanna's own work mirrors the montage-like structure of the book.

Thematically I am interested in exploring the personal mythologies of language: how even a seemingly simple word can be loaded with different associations and connotations for each individual. What does this imply about the inherent limitations of language and our necessary reliance upon it as a primary means of communication? I am also looking at the selective and associative nature of memory and how we use it (among many other things) as a means of imposing order and meaning on our usually tumultuous lives-in-progress.

Diane Schoemperlen

14. *Hand*

all any of us have perhaps

the shapes a hand makes
when words are no longer enough
and the depth of what can't be said
reaches
to the bone

— Bronwen Wallace
"A Stubborn Grace"

It is the way men hold their hands, Joanna figures, that gives them away. It is the way they hold their hands in unguarded moments that exposes their tenderness, their vulnerability, and gives you a glimpse of all the fragility they've been trying so hard to hide.

The last year of high school there was a rumour going around that you could tell the size of a guy's *thing* by the size of his fingers. There was, so the theory went, a direct correlation between those appendages: short stubby fingers meant a short stubby *thing*, long skinny fingers mean a long skinny *thing* and so on. You just had to decide what you liked the most: length or width. But how could you decide, Joanna wondered, when you'd never even touched one, let alone tried it on for size?

This theory, handy though it might have been, was soon (and then repeatedly) disproved. The first penis Joanna ever touched belonged to a boy named Thomas Hunt. Thomas was a short thin boy with short thin fingers. But when he unzipped his fly and his hard penis sprang out at her, it was long *and* wide. She didn't like to stare so she closed her hand around it, her fingers, it seemed, barely able to encircle it.

They were with another couple at the cottage of the other boy's parents. They were supposed to be at a basketball game but this other boy, Stanley Evans, was wild and bossy in a charming way.

23

He had his mother's car, a bottle of his father's whiskey, and the keys to their cottage slipped secretly into his jacket pocket. Stanley was the kind of boy who could convince you to do things you wouldn't normally do and so off they went.

At the cottage on Buck Lake, they drank all the rye and then Stanley led the other girl, Louisa, into the bedroom. Joanna didn't know Louisa very well but she did know (everybody knew) that Louisa and Stanley had been *doing it* for at least two months.

Joanna and Thomas necked on the couch and she let him put his hands up her blouse and down her shorts. Then she put her hand around his penis and held it carefully. She didn't know what would happen next: would it get even harder, even bigger, would it explode? Slowly, slowly, like a flower folding up for the night, it went soft and Thomas sighed. "Your hands are very cold," he said, but she knew he wasn't blaming her.

He tucked his penis, little and shy-looking now, back into his jeans. He was grinning and shrugging as if it didn't matter but his hands, held palms up before him, those short thin fingers spread, looked frightened and embarrassed.

They turned on the lights and played cribbage, scrupulously ignoring the sounds from the bedroom, till Stanley and Louisa were done and came back into the main room, rumpled and red-faced, holding hands proudly.

Joanna and Thomas went out several more times after that, to basketball games and movies, walking downtown sometimes on Friday night for chips and gravy, milkshakes or pop. They held hands but that was all. High school ended. Stanley and Louisa got married, Thomas went away to university, and they were all relieved to be changing their lives, finding their way to the future.

Joanna, as Thomas had so politely pointed out, always had cold hands.

"Cold hands, warm heart," her father Clarence used to tease her, Joanna having just come inside for supper after building a snow fort in the front yard with Penny and Pamela, rosy-cheeked but disappointed because what she really wanted to build was a snow fort big enough to crawl right inside of, but the roof and the walls were always collapsing around her. Clarence would kneel before her on the braided rug and help her take off her snowboots and mittens. Then he would rub her tingling hands, one by one, between his two big dry palms, blowing on them too. His hands smelled like cigarettes, his warm breath like whiskey, and he said, "Cold hands, warm heart."

Joanne would flex her warming fingers and stare at them, looking for clues to the condition of her own heart. She knew that if you crossed your fingers behind your back when you were telling a little white lie, then somehow the lie didn't count. She also knew that if you kept your fingers crossed when you were hoping and praying for something, you were bound to have good luck. Clearly there was magic in the hands.

If Joanna's right palm was itchy, Esther always said, "Money coming your way, lucky you!" But when she was scratching her left hand, Esther warned, "Watch out, you're going to have to pay and pay."

An itchy nose was also significant. Esther at the stove making supper would scratch her nose and say, "Oh oh, I'm going to kiss a fool," and sometimes Clarence would sneak up behind her, put a hand on each shoulder, whirl her around and kiss her right on the mouth. Sometimes Esther laughed and kissed him back. Sometimes she shrugged him off and pushed him away and then Clarence would make a face at Joanna, rolling his eyes and holding his hands out and open, helplessly.

It is the way men hold their hands, Joanna figures, that gives their secrets away.

Henry putting his fist through the drywall in the bedroom when Joanna said she didn't want to live with him anymore. Then he spread both hands on the wall above the ragged hole and rested his forehead on them. By bedtime his right hand was swollen and purple across the knuckles.

Lewis not washing his hands when he left Joanna's bed to go home to Wanda because he said he liked the smell of her on his fingers. Lewis at the market with Wanda reaching his hand up to wave and then brushing at the air instead.

It is the way men hold their hands, Joanna figures, that can leave you stricken with love.

Her husband Richard holding Samuel after his bath, the moist naked baby curled into his bare shoulder like a kitten. Richard's big brown hand spread across Samuel's neck and shoulders, holding up his wobbly head. Richard nuzzling Samuel's neck, pressing his ear to Samuel's, which looks like a seashell, Richard hoping perhaps to hear the ocean inside. Samuel tucking his feet up and falling asleep in his father's hands.

With children, it is not in the hands, Joanna has discovered, but the feet: those chubby feet so small she wonders how Samuel will ever learn to walk, those baby toes so pink and round like flower buds she is afraid for months to trim his nails for fear of cutting a toe right off.

Even now, the mere sight of Samuel's white-and-yellow plastic thongs abandoned in the doorway of her studio at five o'clock on an early September afternoon can bring her heart to her throat, can rip it right out nearly. It is Labour Day, the end of another summer, and Samuel will start school in the morning.

Joanna leaves the thongs where they are and goes back to the kitchen where Richard and Samuel have the crayons spread all over the table, drawing pictures of buses and dinosaurs, a cow or a dog with horns. Suddenly there is the roar of jet engines right overhead, louder and louder, coming lower and lower as if they will crash right into the house. For a moment Joanna thinks, This is it, this is the end, we are all going to die. But Richard says, happily, "It's the Snow-birds." From the kitchen window they can see front doors opening all up and down Laverty Street, their neighbours on their front steps craning their necks, the women in their aprons holding wooden spoons, a bunch of broccoli, a half-peeled potato, or a big silver pot lid like a shield, the men bare-chested with newspapers or beer in their hands, pointing.

Richard, Joanna and Samuel go out and stand at the end of their driveway, waiting for the planes to come round again. The lady next door waves and calls, "Thank God they're friendly." The elderly couple at the end of the block are rolling their adult son out in his wheelchair, down the wooden ramp, pointing his droopy head in the right direction and holding it there.

They can hear the planes coming up behind the houses and the elm trees, but the sound seems to be coming from all directions at once and Samuel spins around on his bare feet, not knowing which way to look.

They come from behind, right over their house, nine silver planes in perfect formation, swooping with red and white smoke dissolving behind them. Samuel puts his hands over his ears and leaps up and down on the spot, crowing.

Joanna watched the Snowbirds with Clarence and Esther from their front yard thirty years ago. She was Samuel's age then and just as excited. Had she too run outside in her bare feet? Had she too clapped her hands and hollered and spun? Had she too thought the noise and the danger and the fear were half the fun? Did she really remember that day so clearly or was she making it up as she went along?

Richard hoists Samuel onto his shoulders and they are both waving. Joanna has an unmanageable lump in her throat and wonders why it's always the happy memories that make her cry. Richard notices her wet shiny eyes and pats her back gently, grinning.

She gets like this at parades too, especially at the Christmas parade. She can't help herself. The floats, the marching bands, the high-stepping horses, the clowns tossing candy at the children, the Shriners in their funny tasselled hats in their miniature tooting cars, the local car salesmen and the mayor waving from white convertibles, their breath white too in the November morning air.

Last year, by the time Santa Claus came round the corner, Joanna was ready to burst into tears. Santa was laughing and grinning and ho-ho-ho-ing while a dozen green elves and brown reindeer danced and tinkled all around his big red chair. It was the way he waved, Joanna tried to explain to Richard later, back home over hot chocolate and marshmallows. The way he waved, so innocent and yet imaginary, as if he really believed in himself and in the children too, none of them the least bit troubled by the fact that there was a Santa on every corner, in every shopping mall, in every old-time movie. Santa could do anything. Santa could be everywhere at once and all those reindeer too.

It was the way Samuel stood there waving back, stamping his cold little feet in his big blue snowboots on the sidewalk, insisting they stay till Santa was well out of sight. Joanna cried and Samuel said, "Don't cry, Mommy. Everything will be all right. Santa will bring you a nice present too," and Joanna cried even more with Richard's arm around her, his left hand tucked into her parka pocket because he'd forgotten his gloves and Samuel, aged four, was so sure of everything that it broke her fearful motherly heart.

With men it is the hands; with children, the feet. What then, she wonders now as they troop back inside, the Snowbirds safely landed, the sky gone silent again, what then is it with women that gives their secrets away? It is not in their hands or their feet. Women, it seems, are more likely to be aware of these extremities, inordinately conscious of the way they wave them, point them, pamper them and paint them.

Except for Joanna who has bitten her fingernails since she was five, bitten them incorrigibly right down, as they say, to the quick.

quick. n. 1. the living [the *quick* and the dead] 2. the sensitive flesh under a toenail or fingernail 3. the deepest feelings or sensibilities [hurt to the *quick*].

For a time the state of Joanna's fingernails was the bane of her mother's existence. Esther shaking her head and saying, "You'd bite your toenails if you could get them up to your mouth!" Joanna not mentioning that she had tried it once but couldn't manage it. Esther painting Joanna's nails every morning with a foul-tasting brown liquid which made her fingers look as if they were stained with nicotine. Joanna not mentioning that after the first couple of bites you got used to the taste. Esther making Joanna wear a pair of white cotton gloves to bed every night. Joanna not mentioning that the only time she *didn't* bite her nails was when she was asleep.

For a time later on, Joanna too became obsessed with her fingernails and stopped biting them for two whole months, mostly because she wanted to wear red nail polish like Penny and Pamela across the street. But Esther would only let her wear clear because red was for tramps, especially on their toes, and Joanna quickly got tired of stabbing at herself with that little cuticle stick trying to uncover her moons. She bit them all off again one night while watching TV.

She still bites them and once in a while, when Samuel catches her with her fingers in her mouth, he clucks his tongue like Esther used to and says, "Oh Mommy, don't be such a baby!" But other than that, her nails are no longer an issue.

It is not the way women hold their hands or their feet. It is not even in the way they hold their mouths when they're angry or their shoulders when they're frightened. It is, Joanna thinks, in the way they are always holding their breath.

Eric Breddam

SALLY

Sally sat with Harold. He had claimed the Liptik Tower heating vent, the best one west of Knowlton Street. He was a bastard sometimes, big and rough, but he was also the only man who held his place in a fight for that warm space. Little Ned held it before Harold but smack wore him out quick, draining everything until the day Harold — never Harry — came to town, picked up Ned like a rag doll and threw him across the alley-way. "I was being gentle," was all Harold ever said when Sally mentioned it. He liked to sound like he didn't care but she saw the way he puffed up, letting the ragged carpet slide so he could show how tough he was, how winter was not hard on him like it was on her. Sometimes she tried getting close to him for warmth when he did that, putting her hand on his chest. He pushed her away, taking her only when he wanted to, and she would like to cry but she wouldn't do it with him so close. He was big and rough and he was Harold, King Harold, all his own he said, since I was ten. Still, he let Sally stay close enough to at least try and touch him and that was something: she got to share the big warm vent, got a shot of his bottle sometimes, got him on top of her once in a while, scraping her back on the grate and hurting her but loving her too: she called it love when he was not around.

Harold breathed funny when he fucked her. It wasn't ragged, broken, grasping like the other guys — like Ned one time, when he had ten bucks and she needed something on the spot. Harold had heavy breath, sour and solid in her face, his face right over hers, his huge hairy mouth almost swallowing her. With her eyes open she would see his teeth, two rotting on the left, one time pus dripped across her lip, she licked it off and swallowed not thinking, enjoying. And his heavy breath, that could be swallowed too, pulled in, tasted, tasting beer, grease, maybe a little of something else, she didn't know what but she though it might be a flower: she swallowed his breath for that sweet, cloying but delightful *something* she could not identify. One time she breathed it in, swallowing it as he came — she was sure he was coming, sure she could feel him coming he was so magnificently big and she *should* be able to feel it, shouldn't she? Everyone said so.

She swallowed that flower, felt him jerking on her and there was that sudden thrill in her, a sudden light trilling across her belly, a warmth beyond the vent below and Harold above, her toes curling, warm inside, and she arched, thinking *don't stop!*, her shoulder blades wedged between steel, hurting but hurting right: everywhere else she was glowing from nowhere outward, her old flesh suddenly young. It was too quick, Harry — no, Harold, even then she couldn't be too close — Harold rolling away, leaving her wanting more, she tried to grab him, pull him back but he only shoved her down, slamming her head on the steel, saying words she only caught dimly through the pain, "You get pregnant, I'll kill you."

That was a cold day but not like now. It must be November by now, the beginning of the real cold. She still remembered that day — late afternoon, about five or six because she heard the heavy traffic over Harry's breath, the traffic going south, all the people going home, she wondered what their homes were like, sometimes, in the summer she might wander down Knowlton, across the bridge and then along Third going west, to where the best houses were. She walked the streets, watching the kids playing with plastic toys and bikes and on the swings in nice parks, and sometimes they stared at her; sometimes their mother or father or big brother or whatever would growl and watch her carefully and Sally moved on quickly, walking the elm-shaded sidewalk as if dreaming; this was different, so pretty, so much nicer than Knowlton and the concrete and glass. But she never stayed too long, knowing if she tried to bed down the cops would come along, *move along*, and if she didn't move quick they'd put her in the bars, the concrete inside so much colder than it was outside, even in January.

But it was only November and it was okay; she was hoping, had been hoping the two or three times since then, she could never count, since *then*, that Harold would do it again but he didn't; that had been a special time, a special day, one-shot only, like her last two bucks on number two to place, and she always lost. Number two was her lucky number; her only thing, the only thing she could not, would not pawn, was a fake gold #2 pendant, hung around her neck and hidden by her sweater — she never took her sweater off, thank God Harold didn't ask her to be naked, not that he ever asked, only shoved his brutal hands under if he did anything at all. She would not pawn that lucky number two even if #2 never won at the track.

Well, sometimes, one time she remembered it did, won big. She'd bought rounds and rounds at the Oriental, bought for everyone, gloriously drunk with all her friends, bought bottles for afterwards, and rented a room and had a smasher party but in the morning she woke with her foot in puke, her money gone, her sweater still on, her crotch sore. The pendant was still there so she went to Ned and told him all about it and could she bum ten bucks for the track and she'd come back with thousands. He said fuck me first and she did though it hurt and he gave her ten bucks, *this is only a loan*, but she never had to pay him back; Harold came to town and threw Ned out and a week later he was gone, dead someone said, scored somewhere but it was mostly strychnine. Someone asked if Ned had time to scream.

Sally didn't do smack, she didn't do anything except if she had the money she might buy coffee just to stay inside somewhere. Beer was good too. All that other stuff was dangerous, bad, killed people. She didn't want to die. Beer made her strong, invincible, shining like the best ripper in the place, it put her on the stage, gave her presence; people knew she was good when she'd had a few, people came to her when she'd a few down the throat, warm in her belly, growing in her like wildcat courage. She was the best, there was no one better.

But now she didn't have no beer, didn't have anything but Harold, sleeping or dozing or drunk unconscious, she wasn't sure; his eyes were closed, his fur hat, stolen from some stupid cruiser looking for a boyfriend, his beautiful fur hat tilted slightly like a crown, worn casually because Harold was King with or without it. She wanted one too, waited for the day he would find her one. Maybe Christmas, it was only a month to go, she could tell because Liptik had their decorations up and they always only did that late in November, she'd read it somewhere.

It wasn't too bad for November. The air was warm and the snow was wet, melting as it landed on the scrap of carpet covering Sally and Harold. In only a few hours a thick mat had formed over the greasy pattern. Every now and then Harold would knock a little off as he shifted in his sleep. Those were rare moments, though. Harold was a very solid sleeper. Sometimes Sally got scared that he would get caught in his sleep. She wasn't sure who it was that would catch him — the cops or some other, bigger, rougher guy, someone who wouldn't keep her — but she dreamed of it sometimes, waking up scared, reassured when she felt him beside her. She would move closer, sometimes touch him; he would push her away without waking up. Sitting beside him now she thought of touching him. He was

31

asleep. He wouldn't be rough. If she was careful.

She was careful but maybe he wasn't entirely asleep. His eyes opened immediately as her fingers touched his chest. She had been too daring, sliding a finger under his shirt, feeling the thick mat of hair there, like fur almost.

"Fuck off," he said, "Get your hands off me. I don't want you touching me." One big hand swept up, slapping her wrist away. She cried out at the sudden pain.

"And shut up," he added, swatting her face. She cringed.

"Just get away." Harold was fully awake now. He pulled the carpet off her, across himself, leaving her exposed.

"Hey — I'm gonna freeze." She tried to pull the piece back but he hit her again. "I said fuck off."

"But —"

He was standing suddenly, faster than anything, snow falling off the carpet in a thick clump, mostly over her, suddenly cold and shocking. She started to stand and he hit her, knocking her down. "I'm trying to sleep and you start pulling stunts, I said get out of here and I mean it. Get out or I'll kill you." Sally started to stand again; Harold waited until she was on her feet before shoving her with both fists. She remembered Ned as she landed, arms splayed, mouth and eyes wide, then closed hard when her head hit the concrete. She blacked out. When she came to Harold was sitting again, the carpet arranged over him. She started crawling toward him but stopped when he looked at her. He would kill her, she could see it, sense it, feel it. Knew it. She sat back on her haunches, started to plead for the space beside him but he only swore at her again, shaking his fist. "I don't want you here, get out, get out," he was screaming and she knew he was crazy, dangerous, she had to go even if she had nowhere to go to. She reached out one more time and withdrew quickly, stumbling as she turned away. Her ankle hurt, from the fall probably, she didn't care.

She blundered away, the snow becoming sleet and ice, cold now because there was nothing to block the wind. The snow that had been heavy and warm beside the Tower was now being hurled at her, scratching her face and her legs where the holes in her jeans exposed flesh. Like musket shot, thousands of tiny missiles striking, building on each other until she was numb. She stumbled on anyway, up Knowlton to Main, hoping there was another place where there could be just her. Vehicles passed by her intermittently, ghost-lights, unaware or uncaring of her.

Knowlton became a canyon in this weather, the wind and snow a river in full flood; at any time she thought she might be swept away. She had to stop often, hanging on a lamp-post or transit bench, trying to breathe while every breath was tugged away from her.

She hadn't realized she was saying anything — that she was even trying to say anything — only that her mouth was open wide and she was swallowing snow, when a figure stood out nearby. She was at the library, had stumbled a long way despite the wind. Because of it, maybe. If she had stopped she would have died. Now she fell forward, across old, dirty sidewalk-clearings, flapping her arms to stay balanced and failing. Sensation flooded through her legs, starting at the knees, the numbness replaced by pain, her legs breaking ice. Arms grabbed her by the shoulders, dragging her across the drift and into a clear space. She recognized the place as the library steps and the voice as Fearing's, the man who wondered if little Ned had screamed.

Fearing was a freak but he had never hurt her. He had helped her several times, once sharing a find out back of the CPR lines. There had been a hole in the fence, hidden by a bush, and just beyond that, out of sight of security, an abandoned crew car. He had found her on a cold night and told her of it, swearing secrecy; too many people knowing of it would attract the CPR cops and they would be shut down. She never told anyone at all and when others did find it, using it so much the cops could not ignore them, Fearing believed her. He even said he'd let her know if he found another good thing like that.

While they stayed there — about a month in the coldest time of year — he never came close to her. Told her that he was homosexual and asked if she minded that. Oh, no, she didn't mind, couldn't care what he did, it was good to be warm and dry and safe and she didn't have to pay. They even got to storing a little food away from day to day, once about a week's worth of bread they mugged a delivery boy for, once two big chocolate-raspberry cakes they ate so slowly — so careful of how little they had — that when they got to the end the cake was hard as frozen cheese, and still wonderful.

And it was Fearing grabbing her now, dragging her, breaking the numbness and she discovered her eyes were frozen shut — she had been crying without knowing it, mumbling to herself. Fearing was soothing her. He had come from nowhere, it seemed originally. Later, in the crew car, he told her things: told her of walking out of a place called White Rock and into East Hastings one late afternoon, leaving much behind: wife, kids, job. "I don't know why," he said when she asked. "Just had to do it." And then to Calgary and Regina and here and he was saving her. "Maybe I'll surface in Toronto" was what he always said but he had been around for a while now. She didn't want him to leave. "Don't go, don't leave," she was saying, "I'm dying."

"Not yet," he was saying. "Not dying yet. Warm enough here." And pulled her, dragging her flabby, senseless body into the corner, falling over her heavily — she thought suddenly he wasn't gay any more — rubbing her legs through the jeans, putting her hands in his, a scab on her wrist breaking and bleeding, the blood streaking both their hands, warm between them.

When she realized he wasn't trying to fuck her, only warming her, she was abruptly grateful, for once no one demanding Go away, come here, get out, open up, shut up, fuck off, fuck me, fuck you.

"How did you know I was leaving?" Fearing said. It was morning again. The wind and sleet had given way to a bright, cold day. She had slept strongly, dead tired and protected from the wind by the library steps and Fearing. She stared at him blankly.

"I got an old guy day before yesterday," he said. "He was loaded." He sat quiet for a minute. "Now I'm loaded and I'm leaving."

"You said that before," Sally said. "But you never left."

"It's December now," he said. He talked so much, more than anyone she knew. Nobody seemed to have energy to talk except Fearing. And when he talked, which was always, she found herself listening and relaxing. He rolled on and on, rolling words about everything, where he came from, where he was going, what he'd seen, what he wanted to see. He talked about birds: "That's a finch"; flowers: "Roses are difficult everywhere"; people: "Mulroney's not so bad, only it's a shitty world to be in." Fearing was the smartest man Sally had ever met. Everything he said sounded like it made sense.

"You said that before," she said when Fearing started talking about leaving again.

"Except I'm really going this time, and in style. Taking a bus, reserved seat, thirty-six hours to Toronto they say. Getting a new suit today, from Goodwill maybe, throw this thing away." He plucked at the corduroy jacket he was wearing. "Drink coffee all the way, see everything. I've never been east before."

"You're for sure?" she said.

"Yes."

34

"Prove it. Let me see the money."

"Don't be stupid, Sally. I put it away in three different places. Only thing I got is this." He reached into his jacket, pulled out a crumpled paper, smoothed it on his knee and showed it to her. "This ticket will take me all the way and see here" — he pointed to a line on the paper — "this says the seat is reserved. I get to choose. I'm going to take a window and see everything. Never been east before."

"Me neither," Sally said. "Take me with you?"

"Course not. You'd only be in the way. I've been alone since I left and I'm going to stay that way."

"But what about me?" Sally grabbed at him. "Harold threw me away, I got nowhere to go."

"Go back to Harold. He'll take you in. Go naked."

"No he won't."

"Take him something. A bottle or something. He'll let you stay."

"For as long as the bottle lasts, and I'll be lucky to get one drink. Then he'll kick me out again.

"At least give me the money to buy a bottle," she said when he said nothing.

"No way. I need everything I got. I almost got killed for it — the old guy had this big wood cane. Find yourself a guy. Plenty out walking every night, looking for something."

"You know I can't get no guy on my own. I can't get nothing but Harold and he don't want me around no more."

"You'll do all right. I have faith in you."

Sally's rage was sudden. She was hitting him without knowing she was doing it, her fists slamming against his cheek, her mouth opened wide to bite and getting his shoulder. The taste of corduroy and grease sank into her mind quickly, like a laxative, and she was drained as fast as she was angry. Fearing only let her down, stepped away and hesitated before walking away, saying, "You better get going. Library cops or city cops'll notice you soon."

The day could have been worse. Sally managed to sneak past security at the bus depot and into the washroom, taking a stall. It was between rushes. She sat for a long time, bent over, her head on her knees, sleeping. She was wakened a few times when people came in but no one seemed to notice that the one stall was always occupied. No one noticed her feet, one in an Adidas sneaker, white turned grey, the other in a broken man's shoe. It had been new when she got it: she had spotted a kid coming out of one of the doors behind the mall, moving quickly and looking nervous. He was wearing a silly mall uniform and carrying a garbage bag. Before heaving the bag he pulled a box out from the top, placed it high up on a ledge. When he went back in Sally ran up, leaped to knock the box down, found a pair of beautiful shoes. They were tight, hard on her at first, and when she lost the left one she discovered her little toe and the outside of her foot were chafed. She found other shoes for her left foot over time, never willing to give up the salt-worn leather on her right. It was split all along the outside now but held together at the heel and toe, nowhere near good as new but still special.

When she left the depot the final rush was over. She'd been inside all day; it was dark now. She walked back south on Knowlton. Maybe Harold was gone away for a while; maybe she could have the vent to herself. Except Harold almost always came back when it got dark. She expected to find him there, hoped he wouldn't be.

He was. When she approached he stood up fast, yelling. She ran away, heading south. The sidewalks had been cleared. She ran clumsily, her ankle still painful. Her lungs drawing cold air in, burning it and her, expelling pain. She had to have something to take to Harold. Something worthy of a king. The cold surrounded her, the dark pushing it on her. There was no wind, only bitter heavy chill. She continued to run until she came to the bridge, to the point where she would cross into where the people lived, where she would be forced to turn around.

When she stopped her breath caught up, ripping her lungs, ripping so bad she couldn't feel the cold on her legs or face any more; it was all inside. She collapsed on the sidewalk, a greyish heap to any passing motorist, a lump to the cops: *maybe she'll just die and we can clean up the streets a bit*, she imagined them saying.

She could not go on. She'd had a perfect month with Harold but now things were bad, getting worse.

"Are you okay?" A voice above her, deep, masculine. A foot nudged her, digging into her tailbone. "You need some help lady?"

Sally rolled her head off the ground, twisting to see. A tall guy but thin, short hair, a suit on under his overcoat. Black ear-muffs. A respectable man, maybe out cruising. She muttered something.

"What's that?" from above her and another nudge.

"Don't want your help."

The man grunted, bent low. "What do you mean? Do you need help or don't you?"

She though of Fearing. Then of Harold. It wasn't anger but desperation now. Her arm moved faster than she ever thought it could, slamming the man's face, shocking him, knocking his ear-muffs off and sending him sprawling on his back. Pain flashed through her wrist and was forgotten as she scrambled to jump him. He wasn't prepared for her weight, his breath forced out in a thin, steamy cloud. He tried to say something but she was hitting his face; blood appeared at his nose. A rock thrown up by the plows was in her hand and then she was hitting him straight on the side of the head.

She sat back heavily, sitting on his chest, breathing hard. He was still. When she felt like moving again she unbuttoned his coat at the collar, reaching inside for his pocket and wallet. She was pulling it out when she decided she could use his coat. She looked around once, saw no other people, unbuttoned it to the bottom, stripping it off him quickly. He wasn't as big as he had looked from the ground. Hardly any weight. Two or three cars passed. They would not see anything over the snowbanks but her dirty, grey head.

She pulled his shoes and gloves off as well, before running. She was freezing. She chill had grown deeper and the sweat was making it worse. She felt funny in the coat — it was slightly large on her and bulky compared to her own thin jacket and sweater. The hemline around her calf slowed her down. She stopped half-way back to Harold's, hiding behind a garbage bin, to try the shoes. They were slightly large as well but in very good shape. Reluctantly she threw away the old shoe from the mall. The Adidas would not be missed. She walked slowly now, mindful of the ice, conscious that except for her head and face she looked like any other person from one of the offices. Away from the streetlights, in the shadows, people might think she was a late-night worker going home. She tried not to slouch.

She stopped again, near the Tower, to examine the wallet. There was little money but many cards. She pulled out one, green and white, and put the wallet back into the inside pocket. She held the card up when she walked around the corner, so he could see she had something. He didn't start yelling right away, only sat up more and tried to see what she had.

"It's a credit card, Harold. I mugged a guy and got his card. We can stay warm tonight."

"He didn't have no cash?" Harold said.

"No, no," she said. "No cash, just the card. But it'll get us into one of those bank things, and it's warm and dry in them. We can go down behind the mall — nobody there at night. We'll take the carpet, maybe find a blanket. It'll be warm, and there won't be no wind, and we can do what we like."

Harold was standing now; she could see he was shivering. He said, "You sure he didn't have no cash? Where's the wallet? He must have had a wallet — people don't carry these things like a candy bar." He grabbed the card from her hand; her wrist flashed pain. Then he grabbed her. "That's his coat, ain't? Where's the wallet."

"Here, here," she said, reaching in. "There was a little money. I didn't want to tell you, wanted to surprise you, get some rye or something. Bring it to you like a surprise." She pulled the wallet out, gave it to him. He opened it greedily.

"Bitch!" he hit her fully in the face, slamming her back. "Where's the rest? There's only ten bucks here. You fucking hiding it I'll kill you." He was on her suddenly, grabbing at the pockets, tearing the coat, the buttons flying, then her sweater, tearing that, pulling from the neck down. It ripped easily, threadbare to start with. The cold slammed her chest as Harold ripped the pendant, and then was pushing, forgetting the money for a moment, rough, demanding, and she was crying, trying to push him away but it was too late. He kept at her, hurting her, and slapped her when she pushed at him. He slapped her one more time when he finished, more a punch, and heaved off of her, leaving her exposed. She was still crying. He disappeared around the corner, dressing, the card and wallet and pendant in his hands, his fur hat cocked across his head. Sally dragged herself to the vent when the cold was stronger than the pain, pulled the carpet over her body. Her tears mixed with vapour, her body chilled, waiting for Harold to come back with a bottle or maybe some food. She remembered that she hadn't eaten all day.

Bobbie Jean Huff

CELLO MUSIC

In the morning Alice wakes to silence. No children's voices wafting up the stairwell here, no banging of doors or clattering of silverware from down below. Just the hollow, suspended sound of sleepers not quite ready to come to life, the muffled noise of traffic fourteen floors below, and Hugh's alarm clock at eight.

She lies in the narrow bed in her brother's study and looks around the room. It's a tall narrow space, nothing more than an enclosed corridor, really, furnished with the fold-out bed, a low chest of drawers, a bookshelf piled with sheet music, a wooden music stand, and Hugh's cello leaning into the corner by the window.

Two weeks ago Sam had telephoned Vancouver to say that Hugh had been diagnosed.

"He wants you to come," Sam had said. "We have the space. If you could spend a month or so here . . ." His voice drifted away, then back. "Better now, actually, when he's OK."

A child had called out to Alice then, something about a dirty soccer shirt.

"Is he . . . ?" Alice had asked, afraid to complete the sentence.

"He's OK," Sam replied firmly. "He'll be getting out of the hospital Thursday."

Alice gets out of bed and goes into the tiny kitchen. She puts on the coffee and stands by the window looking out over the city. Even at this early hour and from this height she can see that the day's going to be a scorcher. Waves of heat shimmer below, distorting the traffic, trees, people and pavement. The sky is a strange colour for Toronto, a uniform yellowish gray. Alice thinks of tornadoes and of Kansas, then of Dorothy and ToTo on a bicycle heading for Oz.

"Don't jump," Hugh says from the doorway.

He's dressed in khaki pants and a white shirt rolled up at the sleeves. He has always worn white shirts, even as a child. He used to be blond and cherubic, now his hair is straight and dark, almost black. He has long pale fingers and a habit of rarely smiling. And now this new thinness . . .

39

"Coffee's ready," Alice says, getting two mugs out of the cupboard. "Do you want toast? Or English muffins?"

Hugh opens the refrigerator door and takes out fruit juice and butter. "English muffins are OK," he says. He pours out two glasses of juice, reaches under the counter for the muffins and hands the package to Alice. "I'm thinking of going on a special diet. For the immune system."

Alice slices a muffin, puts it in the toaster. "What is it?"

"Rice. Vegetables. Not much else. Herb teas."

"Worth a try," Alice says. But she makes a face. "Do you have a rehearsal today?" Hugh plays in a symphony orchestra. Most afternoons they rehearse. Mornings he practices for a couple of hours in his study. He has a few students that come in the evenings, but he's dropped them for the summer.

"Not today. I thought we'd do something."

"It's really hot."

"We could go to the island."

Sam comes into the room. He's a bear of a man, dark and burly, with a headful of frizzy hair that he ties back with a leather thong. He's wearing white drawstring pants, nothing else.

"So what's the word for the day?" he says, reaching for the juice carton.

Alice hands a muffin to Hugh and sits down to her coffee. "Hugh wants to go to the island," she says.

"It's a good day for it," says Sam, swigging juice directly from the carton. "I wish I could go."

He teaches karate at a fitness centre down on Spadina. He's had his black belt since he was 15; he's been to Japan twice, once for a year. He and Hugh had planned to go over for a month at the end of the summer. Now their plans are up in the air.

"I should call the kids before we go," Alice says. Today is Torey's first day at camp; on the phone the day before, the child was tearful. Torey reminds Alice of Hugh when he was a child: nervous, overly sensitive, apprehensive of anything new.

"If we leave in the next half hour, we can catch the 10 o'clock ferry," says Hugh.

Alice surveys her brother, wonders if he's up to a day in this heat.

"I'm fine," smiles Hugh, reading her mind as usual. "Go and call home. Where they need you."

During their childhood Alice was Hugh's protector. He didn't like sports, but preferred to be indoors, even on sunny days, reading or listening to music. He had few friends, and those he had his father called losers: pale, soft-spoken boys, passive boys who never did anything. Boys on the fringe of life. Mouthbreathers, Mr. Churchill called them. "What did the mouthbreathers do today?" They usually sat in Hugh's bedroom and played cards, practiced magic tricks, or wrote tragic plays, requiring elaborate costumes and the application of heavy make-up.

On Hugh's eleventh birthday Mr. Churchill came home from work early, with a soccer ball wrapped up in shiny blue paper and tied with a silver bow. Come on, he said. We'll go outside and kick it around. I'll show you some techniques.

Fifteen minutes later they were back indoors, Hugh crying, Mr. Churchill furious. Mrs. Churchill, who was icing the cake, disappeared with him into his study, and Alice could hear through the door harsh words flying from her father's mouth: sissy, whiner, crybaby. Fairy.

A while later Mrs. Churchill emerged from the room with red eyes. But Mr. Churchill stayed in his study the whole evening, missing it all: the birthday dinner, the unwrapping of the rest of the presents, the blowing out of the candles. The birthday wish.

Alice and Hugh walk through the city. They've decided not to go to the Island; although it would be cooler, they can't bear the thought of standing in line for the ferry. From Bloor Street they wander into Philosopher's Walk, the coolest place around. As they wind their way through the campus of the University of Toronto, Alice remembers the last time she was here.

"It must have been fifteen years ago," she says. "But everything looks the same."

"Toronto's a lot bigger now," Hugh says, picking up a stick from the path and tossing it into the bushes. "It's not a small town any more. You used to be able to walk anywhere and see people you know, people from your neighbourhood. Now you can go a whole day without recognizing a soul."

They take a seat on a bench under a tree. "I did see Glenda Jackson the other day, though."

"Really?" Alice asks. "What was she like?"

"Tiny. I never realized she was so small. It just doesn't come across on the screen. She was going into Bemmelman's."

Alice takes off her sunglasses. "The last time I was here it was evening, and there was this man. Your typical lecher, I supposed, but he wasn't wearing a trenchcoat. He came over to me and smiled, and then he took out his thing. And you know what, Hugh? It was so tiny, all I could do was laugh. I sat there, I think it was on this same bench, as a matter of fact. I sat here laughing so hard I almost cried."

"What did he do?"

"He zipped himself back up, of course, but the thing was, he looked so embarrassed, so humiliated, I felt terribly sorry for him. I almost asked him to sit down and talk about it."

"You'd never have gotten rid of him. Where was I at the time? You never mentioned it before."

"You were around. I think you were at Rochdale. I'm sure you would have though it perfectly normal."

"Very funny." Hugh stretches his legs out in front of him and closes his eyes. "That must have been the year I met Sam. I was working at that restaurant on the ground floor, what was it called? That health food restaurant?"

"How is Sam?" asks Alice suddenly. It's noon now. The sun is beating directly down on them. She puts her sunglasses back on and stands up.

"He's all right," says Hugh, and smiles. "It's a shock. For both of us. It's probably a death sentence for him, too, after all." He stands up and brushes off his pants. "Hey, I'm thirsty."

They begin to walk again, west towards Bathurst.

One day, not long after Hugh's eleventh birthday, the family was just sitting down to dinner when Hugh, reaching for a napkin, spilled his milk. Mr. Churchill, from the end of the table, said, "Goddammit, Hugh, can't we get through one meal without an incident?" And Hugh burst out crying.

Mr. Churchill stood up then and came around the table to Hugh. "Goddammit," he kept saying. "Goddammit." And Alice watched as her father unbuckled his belt and removed it from his pants.

"Stop crying," he shouted. "Shut up, Hugh."

Mrs. Churchill said quietly, "Calm down, Huey. Stop crying dear." But at the sight of his father towering over him, brandishing his belt, Hugh's whimpering turned into wails.

42

Crack! came the belt across Hugh's shoulders. Crack, crack! and Hugh screamed louder.

Alice looked wildly to her mother to do something, but Mrs. Churchill sat with her hands folded in her lap, as if she were watching a horror film she knew couldn't possibly be true.

Crack, crack! came the belt across Hugh's thin legs, pale in their corduroy shorts. Crack, crack, crack! and Mr. Churchill threw the belt on the floor and strode out of the room and into his study. The door slammed behind him.

Alice pushed back her chair and ran into the room without knocking. She threw herself at her father in a fury, smacking his chest and head with her hands. "How could you?" she cried. "How could you treat my brother like that?"

Alice can't remember what happened after than, if she was punished, or merely sent from the room. What she carried away from the scene, though, was the realization that if she, Alice, didn't take care of Hugh, no one would.

"How's Tom?" asks Hugh. He raises his beer glass, looks at it thoughtfully, puts it back on the table. They're in a German restaurant on Bloor Street. It's cool and dark inside.

"He's OK. The marriage isn't so hot, though."

"I thought not."

A waitress in a white puffed-sleeved blouse and green embroidered skirt materializes out of the dimness with two plates, one of sausage and dumplings, the other Wiener Schnitzel.

"Has he got a girlfriend?"

Alice laughs. "I think so," she says. "Tom usually has a girlfriend. But that's not the problem. It doesn't really bother me. Not the way it used to." She slices off a piece of sausage, chases it down with beer.

They used to meet in this restaurant for lunch, she and Hugh, years ago, before her marriage. Hugh had a thing for German food for a while. He had been to Berlin on tour, had fallen in love with Germany, and with one German in particular, a young oboist whose lover had just returned to his wife.

"The problem is me, I guess," Alice says. "We're so . . . so settled. It makes me uncomfortable. We might be living in the house we die in. We probably are. Our last house. Our last town. I'm almost 42, and it feels as if I'm starting the countdown. Thirty more years, on average, give or take half a decade. That's what? — three more new sofas? Four or five more cars, if we remember to put

43

them in the garage in the winter. Six more TVs." She drops her fork and knife. "God, Hugh. I'm sorry."

He laughs. "What do you mean? You've made my day! I just realized I might never have to shop for another refrigerator again." He reaches over and touches Alice's face. "C'mon, girl. I don't begrudge you a long and happy life."

Alice examines an ashtray with a picture of the Matterhorn in its bottom. "There's this man," she says.

"I thought that might be it."

"That's *not* it. Not all of it, anyhow."

"And are you having an affair?"

"Not really an affair. More of a fantasy. He's just a man I know, a lawyer who lives near us. I see him a couple of times a week, we have coffee. We flirt. I imagine he wants to sleep with me, I don't know for sure. I'm not even sure I want to sleep with him. It's just, he always acts so aware of me. So attentive. I like that. He's someone new, is what it is. I think of him a lot." She smiles. "I wonder how he smells. He has a beard. I'd like to scratch my fingers through it."

"Does Tom know?"

"I imagine he knows something. I must appear preoccupied. And I don't like going to bed with him any more." She tastes her dumplings, reaches for the salt. "Have you ever felt like that, Hugh? You and Sam have been together longer than we have."

Hugh puts down his knife and fork. He hasn't eaten a bite of food, Alice notices. "Well, obviously we haven't been monogamous," he says. "There've been . . . lots of others. Other lovers. But I think both of us would feel that if we had thirty more years ahead of us, we'd want to spend them together."

When they leave it's almost four. Clouds have piled up to the west, the sky has darkened. The first rumble of thunder hits as they cross Brunswick. By the time they reach Spadina the sky has split and opened up. The street smells of hot tar, gasoline, and hamburger grease; lightning flashes all around them.

As they dash into the subway station Hugh grabs hold of Alice's hand.

Sam is in the kitchen when they return, stirring something in a pot. He's wearing black bathing trunks. His hair is wet and loose, it falls to just below his shoulders.

"It's a hot one," he says. He's set up a fan on the counter: it's blowing directly into his face.

Hugh sits down and Alice heads for the refrigerator, pulling out lemons, soda water, ice.

"What are you making?" Hugh asks Sam.

"Something for your immune system." He pours thick yellow liquid from a pot into the ice cube trays he's set out on the counter. "All natural ingredients," he says. "With one exception: the secret ingredient. I picked it up at a photographic supply store."

Hugh wrinkles his nose. "You go first," he says. Alice, handing Hugh a glass of lemonade, sees that he is tired. But so is she. She has forgotten how hot Toronto can get in the summer, how enervating.

Hugh drinks the glass down, then gets up from the table. "I have to work on that new Beethoven."

Sam turns off the fan; the rain has begun to cool things off. For a while he and Alice sit in silence. Then Hugh begins to play, and the room fills with the quiet slow movement of an adagio movement.

"He talks with his music, Hugh does," Sam says. "That piece, it's more Hugh than Beethoven."

"I'm sure Beethoven doesn't mind."

Alice's thoughts drift to her family: whether Torey enjoyed her first day at camp, if Graham got his swimming badge, what Tom is doing this evening without her. Will he play checkers with Graham, watch TV, go to bed early? Or will he call his newest lady-love and arrange a meeting for when the children are in bed?

Sam takes celery, carrots, onions, and fresh ginger from the fridge. He rinses, peels and chops, performing each task neatly, precisely.

And what about Fred, the lawyer in Kitsilano? Will he make love to his wife tonight? If he does, will he close his eyes and think of Alice?

The music from the other room reaches a climax, and without pausing Hugh breaks into a playful dance Alice recognizes from long ago. Sam tips some oil into a pan, turns on the gas.

"We planned on going to Japan this fall," he says.

"Hugh mentioned that."

"We still might go. Hugh has a month off. It's not like Africa, after all. They have medical care there. Want some wine?" He passes Alice a bottle, fishes around for a corkscrew.

"Japan," she says, after pouring herself a glass. "I've always wanted to see Japan."

Sam forks up an onion ring and settles it into the pan. His hands are tan and muscular, Alice notices, his fingers short but graceful as they work. Capable hands, she things, as they transfer the remaining vegetables. Hugh's in capable hands.

"Come with us," says Sam.

"I can't leave the kids and Tom for that long."

Sam nods, stirs. The aroma of onions and ginger fills the room.

"You know what he wants on his gravestone?" he says, without looking up. The dance from the other room soars into double time, and races towards the finish line.

"I'm outta here," Sam says.

For some reason, they both laugh.

Hugh acquired his first cello when he was twelve. He had taken a couple of years of piano, but had never shown much promise for it, and Mr. Churchill, who had never approved, had been so happy when he'd quit.

"We don't have that kind of money," his father said, when Hugh approached him about the cello.

At the supper table a few days later Hugh announced that he had a paper route. Mr. Churchill, slicing a ham apart with an electric knife, smiled over at his son.

"Well, Hugh, good for you. That shows a certain initiative, it does."

A month later Hugh brought home a large brown canvas case. Alice was the only one home at the time. She followed her brother to his room, where he opened the case and removed a cello and bow. For a long moment he held it apart from himself, gazing at it. Then he put it back into its case and put the case under his bed.

"I rented it," he said to Alice. "With the money from my paper route. Now all I have to do is find a teacher."

He didn't mention the cello to his father, but a few weeks later he started lessons. All of his spare time was spent practicing in his room.

Mr. Churchill never said a word about the cello. It seemed to Alice that he never noticed the painful screeches coming from above his head every evening, although he held his newspaper tightly and turned on the television earlier than usual.

The cello marked the first sign of Hugh's independence. In no time at all it seemed to Alice that the noises overhead turned into music, and although Mr. Churchill never complimented Hugh on his increasing expertise or offered to pay for the lessons that consumed every bit of Hugh's newspaper earnings, he seemed to accept, for the first time, where Hugh's interests actually lay.

The house breathed in a sigh of relief.

Hugh and Alice are driving to Kingston in Sam's station wagon. Hugh sticks tapes into the player, listens for a moment and pulls them out again.

The tapes are in a green and white shopping bag between the two front seats. Alice says, "Which one do you want? Let me look."

"I don't think it's here."

Clouds in the east are shielding them from the worst of the sun's rays; it's hazy and humid. The traffic is heavy up until the turn-off for Peterborough.

"Cottage traffic," says Hugh, adjusting the visor.

"On a Tuesday morning?"

"It's like this now until Labour Day."

Alice pulls a tape from the shopping bag and clicks it into the machine. Loud, lilting music fills the car.

"That's Sam's," says Hugh. "The Pogues. The latest rage among our alienated youth."

"It sounds Gaelic, or something. I like it.'

"Irish punk, Sam calls it. The music isn't bad. Just don't listen too closely to the lyrics."

Alice settles back in her seat and looks out the window. A few clouds are moving off towards the south, casting shadows over parts of the lake; elsewhere the water glitters. The Pogues sing out:

> *I could have been someone*
> *So could anyone*
> *You took my dreams from me*
> *When I first found you*

"When did you last see Ma?" Alice asks.

"Not long after Christmas, I think it was. Sam and I drove out for the day. We got caught in a snowstorm on the way back."

"How did she seem?"

"Thin. I don't think she recognized me at first. The nurse had to say, 'This is your son'."

The music speeds up.

> *You scum bag*
> *You maggot*
> *you cheap lousy faggot*

47

Happy Christmas your arse
I pray God it's our last

"She won't know me," says Alice. "Not after six years."

"You look the same."

"The same, except for gray and fat."

"You're not gray."

"Thanks a lot!"

Their father had died of a heart attack six years before. It happened at a supermarket. There was an in-store promotion for the house pizza, shoppers were gathered around a table with their carts. Mr. Churchill took a bite and grabbed his chest. A titter ran through the crowd; people though he was joking about the pizza. When he began to turn purple, a fat woman in a yellow mu-mu stepped forward and caught him as he fell.

Hugh and Alice expected their mother to be devastated. She had been dependent on their father for so long. But within a month of the funeral she had sold the family home in Kingston and moved into a small apartment building overlooking the lake. She joined a bridge club, a musical interest group, she took classes in financial management, flower arranging and upholstery. Whenever Alice and Hugh telephoned, she was either out or on her way out. She had never seemed happier.

Two years ago when Alice was planning a party to celebrate Tom's latest promotion, she called her mother from Vancouver for her recipe for eggplant creole, a family favourite. They talked about the weather and laughed about Mrs. Churchill's friend's husband who used four towels after every shower. Mrs. Churchill had seemed all right. But when Alice finally got around to asking for the recipe, her mother had said, "Eggplant? What's that, dear?"

Alice, thinking her mother wasn't hearing her properly, spelled it out over the phone. "E-g-g-p-l-a-n-t, Mother. Eggplant."

"Why, I've never heard of it, Alice. Is it one of those new fruits you come across these days at the supermarket?"

Alice and Hugh reach the nursing home at noon. They are informed by a nurse that the guests are having lunch. Alice follows Hugh through a maze of bright corridors to the dining room, a bright high-ceilinged room. Some of the residents are eating at tables, many more are in wheelchairs with trays clamped to them. A few, Alice notices, are strapped into their chairs with canvas sashes. The room smells of boiled soup, floor wax and something else, she isn't sure what. She suspects she may be able to identify it in about thirty years.

Mrs. Churchill is sitting at a table with two other women. Alice grabs Hugh's elbow and says, "Stay there." She walks across the room and stands before her mother, who looks up from her bowl of soup and says, "Well, Alice, it's about time you came to get me. I've been here for almost three days now."

Hugh is right, Mrs. Churchill has gotten thin. But something else has happened to her as well, something as elusive as the smell Alice fails to identify. She stoops to kiss her mother and says, "I'm just here for a visit, Ma. The doctor says you're not completely well yet. But look, here's Hugh."

The woman sitting next to her mother says, "Hi, I'm Bertha." She has a yellow kerchief tied around her hair and is so stout the flesh on her arm jiggles as she lifts her soup spoon.

"Hi, Bertha," says Alice.

Hugh kisses Mrs. Churchill. "Would you like us to take you out?" he asks. "For the afternoon? We can buy you cigarettes and have a coke or something. But we'd have to bring you back for dinner."

Mrs. Churchill purses her lips together and looks away from both of them.

"I'll go," says Bertha. "I don't smoke, but I'd sure like a coke."

"Ma," Alice says. "We came all this way, I came from Vancouver to see you."

Mrs. Churchill says nothing.

"I have a cousin in Vancouver," Bertha says. A dribble of soup looses its hold on her lip and rolls down her chin. "Do you know Edna Timco?"

The other woman at the table, who has been staring into her bowl of fruitcup, suddenly comes to life. "Stan and me went to Vancouver on our honeymoon. We're thinking of going back next Christmas."

"My foot you are," says Bertha. She takes up her knife and fork and begins to slice her piece of bread and butter into tiny pieces, chewing each one daintily.

"Come on, Ma," says Hugh. He takes a seat opposite her. "Don't you want to go out? Alice won't be back this way for a while."

"Leave it, Hugh," says Alice. "Besides, it's cool in here." She looks around. Most of the residents are in the serious later stages of mental or physical deterioration. The average age appears to be about 80, or even older. Mrs. Churchill, at 67, is a mere baby here.

49

And apart from her mind and a moderately high blood pressure, there is nothing wrong with her. She may be here for 10 or 20 years. She might be waiting all that time for Hugh and Alice to come and take her home.

"Do you know, Ma," Alice says, "it's so hot outside, you could fry an egg on the pavement. We drove here from Toronto, and the 401 was positively sizzling. Do you remember the 401 highway, Ma? We used to take it to the cottage every summer."

Mrs. Churchill shakes her head slightly. Her eyes still will not meet Alice's. Alice notices Hugh slip from the room. Bertha calls after him, "Don't forget my coke."

Alice takes hold of her mother's hands. They feel cool and dry. "Ma, listen to me," she says. "Hugh's sick, Ma. He's so sick, you just have to be nice to him. He might not be back again to see you. He might never be back."

Mrs. Churchill pushes Alice's hands away and looks at her. "I need to leave here, Alice," she says. "You have to take me home"

Hugh returns carrying his cello. He pulls an empty chair from the table and sits down with the instrument between his legs. Then he begins to play.

The first part of the piece he chooses is bright and swinging; then, reverting to a minor key, it builds into something more ominous. Mrs. Churchill stares out the window. Hugh's brow tightens. Alice thinks he may cry. The music, the atmosphere of the room seems to her to be charged, like a storm about to blow. A moment later the music pauses, while Hugh holds his bow dramatically in the air, and the piece resolves in its former light mood.

A few of the old people clap, including Bertha, who has tears in her eyes. Mrs. Churchill turns back from the window and says, "Why Huey, what a big violin! No wonder you have to put it on the floor to play it!"

As Hugh hugs his mother Alice is struck by a certain similarity between them. What is it? she wonders. Something to do with the skin, perhaps; they're both so pale. And their eyes, their eyes are similar, too. They both share the same look of bewilderment, as if they know there's something coming along down the road for them, and they can't figure out what it is. All they can do is wait.

When Hugh was seventeen and in his final year of high school, he tried to kill himself. It was just before March break; Alice was in her third year the University of Toronto, and when her father called her, she boarded the train for Kingston.

She was met at the station by her two pale parents, and for a moment Alice though that her brother was dead.

Afterwards she realised that to her father it would have been better if Hugh *had* died.

Hugh had fallen in love for the first time. His lover was a boy who had moved to town the previous year. Sandy was in most of Hugh's classes in school.

They began spending all of their spare time together. Hugh told his mother he had a part-time job at a nearby milk store after school. Sandy's parents both worked, and for five months he and Hugh spent long afternoons after school in Sandy's bedroom in Sandy's empty house.

At the beginning of March Sandy broke it off. He had fallen in love with his physics teacher, he told Hugh; they would be sharing an apartment after graduation.

The afternoon Sandy told him, Hugh went home. Neither of his parents was there. He went into the medicine cabinet in his parents' bathroom and swallowed the contents of a whole bottle of aspirin.

Mrs. Churchill found him lying on his bed before dinner. The empty bottle and a glass were on his bedside table. She tried, but couldn't rouse him. The ambulance came and whisked him off to hospital where his stomach was pumped.

Hugh woke that evening. From his hospital bed he told his parents that he was homosexual. Mrs. Churchill burst into tears. Mr. Churchill left the room.

Alice came alone to see him that evening, after she'd arrived home. He was sitting by the window in his hospital-issue dressing gown. There were bars across the window, reminding Alice that this was the psychiatric ward.

Alice said, uncertainly from the door, "Hugh?"

Hugh looked over.

"Hugh," she repeated, coming into the room, and reaching him, wrapped both her arms around him.

When she let him go, Hugh asked quietly, "What do you know?"

"I know it all, I guess. Ma told me."

He turned back towards the window and Alice said, "Oh, Hugh. I've always known. It's not such a tragedy, is it? That you're homosexual?"

A nurse entered the room with his dinner. She put the tray on the table beside his bed, cranked it up. When she left, Hugh said,

"What do you mean, you've always known? I never knew, myself, really, until this year. I was never sure."

"You were always different, Hugh. I always knew that you were different. Remember the mouth-breathers?"

Hugh smiled. They were silent for a while, and then he said, "He'll never forgive me."

The sun was disappearing behind the hospital wall. Someone in the hallway screamed, "No, oh no, oh no, oh no, oh no!"

"Fuck him," said Alice.

It's Alice's last night in Toronto. Tomorrow she will fly home. She and Hugh and Sam decide to go out for a meal. At first she is disappointed; she'd like her brother to herself this last night. But she realizes now that Sam is every bit as much family to Hugh as Alice is herself.

They walk to a small Indian restaurant in a nearby neighbourhood. It's a black rainy night. Sam jokes the whole way in his best mock-Indian accent: "I am waking up this morning and I am rising from my bed and I am looking out the window. Overhead are dark clouds. A gentle breeze is blowing. From the sky are falling tiny drops of water. They are splashing from the windowsill and running down the windowpane and I am thinking to myself, it is fucking raining again."

The restaurant is crowded and smells of jasmine. The tables and chairs are dark and ornate, the walls hung with embossed red wallpaper. Sitar music twangs through a speaker. A waiter in a white turban leads them to a table, takes their drinks orders.

Alice opens a large tasselled menu, looks and says, "None of this means a thing to me. Order for me, would you Hugh?"

"Sam will. He's the food expert of the family."

Hugh and Sam are in a lighthearted, joking mood. They reminisce about their trip to Sweden the previous summer.

"Stockholm is the perfect city for gays," Hugh says, pouring beer into his glass. "The whole place is open-minded, just like everything you've ever heard about it. You walk down the street hand-in-hand, nobody so much as looks at you."

"Except that the place shuts down at seven," says Sam. "A good place to live, but you wouldn't want to visit there."

"We had a great time," Hugh says.

The waiter brings a plate of samosas. Alice reaches for one, she's suddenly starved. "Is Sweden really as clean as they say?" she asks.

"There's no pollution that I saw," Hugh says. "Or litter. It's a very tidy place. I must admit, though, that after a week I'd have given anything to see a couple of beer cans lying on the sidewalk."

"Or a big black buck jiving down the street with a ghetto blaster stuck to the side of his head," puts in Sam.

They laugh. A moment later Hugh says, "You loved it, though, didn't you?"

Sam reaches his hand across the table and grabs hold of Hugh's. "Of course I did, hon."

Alice's thoughts drift to the next day. She thought she wouldn't be able to bear it when the four weeks were up. She's felt all along that her very presence was holding Hugh up, buoying him, keeping him safe. Not the massive does of vitamins he takes twice daily. Not the yellow ice cubes he dissolves into club soda and orange juice, or the brown rice and vegetables Sam makes him faithfully every night.

For that matter, nothing can keep any of them safe.

Alice watches the two men with their fingers still laced together and feels for a moment like an outsider, an onlooker to their happiness, as if she has already left. Sam is saying of a man at a table across the room, "Well, what else can it mean? It's plastered all over his shirt. HSB."

"Hunky succulent buttocks?" Hugh asks.

The waiter appears with plates of food and little bowls of different chutneys. When he has gone Sam says, under his breath, "Tonight we are liking pappadum, Bombay duck and very hot vindaloo on rice. Tomorrow we are having curried asshole."

Hugh finishes, "It is burning going in and it is burning coming out."

Alice wakes early the next morning. It's another sultry day. She packed everything when they returned last night from the restaurant; now she sticks in her nightgown and toilet articles, closes up her case and drags it to the front door. The apartment is quiet. She goes into the kitchen and puts on the coffee. A few minutes later she hears Hugh get up, go into the bathroom.

Alice drinks her coffee standing by the window. Hugh, she remembers, hates to say goodbye; he always has. Alice hears him leave the bathroom, go into his study. A moment later, as she is rinsing out her cup, he starts to play.

He's perfected the Beethoven. She stands listening for a moment as the music builds, then crosses the room, picks up her case and lets herself out of the apartment.

The elevator is already at the 14th floor; she steps inside and presses the button. Descending through the air, she feels for a moment the relief of being suspended between two worlds: Alice, single woman, sister of Hugh; Alice, wife and mother.

On the street she hails a cab. "The airport," she says to the driver, and hoists her case up onto the seat. She gets in and reaches to close the door, then stops. Although Hugh is fourteen floors above her, Alice is absolutely certain that she can hear the final notes of the Beethoven, pure and sweet, floating over the sweltering city.

Vaughan Dickson

CHAPTERS 558 AND 559 IN THE LIFE OF DODGE DRUMMOND

Chapter 558

The Dodge quit work yesterday, a day the sky of which was so full of rain that a few scattered madmen began constructing arks of varying sizes and compositions; a very wet day which caused more than a few people to imagine that the world would have to be tipped and shaken, left upside-down to drain, if the torrent continued. It did, but the world nevertheless remained right side up, brimming. And Dodge quit work and set out, with a jaunty post-employment step, for home and Joan via the Elm Street Diner. Hunched JamesDeanlike against the sky's tantrum, the wet shotgun blasts that met his every upward-glancing eye, he began moving the two blocks westward, obliviously smearing, with each determined bootfall, rain-chased sidewalk serpents: the worms, which cringed and died twice subsequent to his approach. Some, of course, were left to drown or to be not quite similarly crushed by the footwear of other pedestrians. It should be noted, if the full story is to be told, that many others were eaten by birds and a few by children, many drowned in their holes; many were captured, kept in coffee cans until they either died or were extracted from among a wad of newly made friends and impaled repeatedly on a hook — well, we all know that story — and one was actually snatched (by a man wearing a towel) from beneath the downheading stiletto heel of an absolutely dripping hooker named Mandy and dropped into a partially rinsed whiskey bottle destined for C Deck: this particular worm was killed, a day and a half later, by a sunbeam.

As for Dodge, he made it home to Joan but not until fourteen hours after the rain finally stopped. Even on foot, during a knife-stuffed, January snowstorm, it shouldn't have taken Dodge more than six or seven hours to reach his suburban retreat.

What follows, then, prefaces an Odyssey of a type, a sidetrip that was never meant to be, a case history of random ensnarement, of incarceration disguised as ambient world, and of the brain's perception of this prison: a looking out, so to speak, from the jello-encased core of a curiously ignored brunch item. This intersection of fluxes then makes for the interest of the tale: the world that will impinge itself on Dodge vs. the world impinged.

Dodge squinted to read the bar sign through a wall of falling rain: Elm Street Diner. Strange name for a Maple Street bar, though Dodge (again) entering, wiping water and bits of worms on the "Come Again" mat just inside the door. Dark, dry, noiseless: a good sign; a black, blank canvas on which to place the possibilities of my newest presence, thought Dodge.

Dodger! came a voice through the top-and-side-heavy gloom, how be you.

I be fine, answered Dodge, angling for, and eventually gaining, one of the many empty barstools. And how be you, Waldo?

For answer Waldo pulled an expert sleeve of draught and nudged it toward Dodge on a cardboard coaster. Waldo's world was fine, Dodge knew, as long as there was beer to pour and thirsty throats and a place where the two could meet, a place like Waldo's Elm Street Diner on Maple, Dodge thought, a world of spigots and mouths and curtains of smoke that rose and fell on tragic, offbeat shadow ballets; of old men at night and weary students and writers by day, all bent against time and tapped except for beer-money, all close on the heels of an epiphanic transfusion of life awareness, a longer fingernail away from a cut key to the secrets of success or death. All riding Waldo's carousel at $3.50 a spin, around and around like beer mugs through the dishwasher, like beer through the bladder, like dreams through the dreamshredder.

Waldo, the bartender/proprietor/aproned-pudgy-fingered-ana-lyst-of-a-thousand-distresses, punched in.

Joan leave you? he asked. Dodge's head shook negative.

Then she's stayed too long, conjectured Waldo. Negative.

The War? Negative.

Chalk up another *former* job? Yessss.

Ah, said Waldo, well, absolutely nothing I can do about that except give over an on-the-house mug (which he did), which don't help at all really except that it's one you don't have to buy for yourself.

Dodge accepted, as warmly as he could, the pure and good sentiment supporting Waldo's logic and gift.

Course if it's really that bad I could lend you the private use of the bathroom for five minutes and this extremely sharp knife which I use to cut the lime and lemon pinwheels.

Skull-soiled fuck, thought Dodge reflexively before settling in comfortably, spooning so to speak, with a little idea: suicide. Now Dodge was always at his handsomest when he was pondering, thinking hard on some concept that he genuinely believed original. He was aware, furthermore, that he cut an attractive silhouette when deep in thought, so that often, in bars, he would set himself the task of trying to come up with a radically new but fundamentally practical shape for glassware in the hope of picking up a woman. Once, when a vagrant microcloud of THC, which had been blowing around in his system for about twenty days, cloaked the event of a synapse fired, Dodge began thinking about radically new but fundamentally practical ways to utilize standardly shaped glassware. Ironically, on this particular occasion Dodge could have had his pick of any from the ranks of an over-30 female softball team lounging close to the salad bar. Had he looked over, his eyes would certainly have been shunted toward the array of grass and mud stains disproportionally located on the collective chest of the team. And had he then looked up he would surely have met at least one pair of over-made though not unalluring over-30 eyes, which would have said, essentially: I beg you to cut me from this common herd, this consensus of fright, and take me to a clean, well-lighted place (the eyes at this point would have flickered like an early 80's movie effect making sure that Dodge understood the importance of the literary allusion as an arrow to intelligence) where we might explore with surgical scrutiny the soft, slick fissures of my brain and yours. Dodge, as mentioned, missed out on his chances on this particular occasion because he was too confronted by the spectacle of his latest invention, namely: oversized, lidded beverage glasses of all types denoting the favorite cocktail or non-alcoholic refreshment of the relative whose ashes were contained therein. Toasts at Christmastime would have that all inclusive ring to them, Dodge reasoned, the dead clinking to each other's health up on the mantle, or so it would seem if the living didn't turn about too fast. Grandma in her gimlet glass would give the fleeting illusion of grandma *with* her gimlet glass, Dad with his highball, Uncle Ted with his bottle of Schwepps Tonic. At exclusionary parties there'd be no reason why *all* the men, dads and sons, cousins and brothers, friends and great grandfathers alike couldn't watch the Superbowl together while *all* the women, dead and alive, discussed compulsory heterosexuality as a political institution while sabotaging power tools in the garage. Oh, what an idea! Dodge thought, immortality through beverage association! The last deliberate thought Dodge ever gave to this idea occurred long after the last belching ballplayer veered through the correct doorway and out onto the street, and not so long after the waitstaff had put up all the chairs. He imagined Drummond Urns, some time in the touchable future, as instinctive acquisitions, like sharp kitchen knives: an eternal trend, their essential popularity unforeseen in the wildest or the most inductive of science-fiction novels. An adaptation turned enigma: *The Urn* it would be called, Drummond having dropped evolutionally from its title like a mythical fifth limb, like Sony from all brands of Walkman, which didn't bother modest, reclusive geniuses like Dodge at all.

A little to Dodge's right Waldo chortled. People had entered the Elm Street Diner unnoticed by Dodge: two men in the traditional sense and a pale, skinny youth with yellow/orange fingers, pink highliter marks on his forehead and a vaseline smear down the outside seam of his new and beltless bluejeans. I know what you are, thought Dodge, eyeing the youth surreptitiously. The newcomers had arranged themselves on either side of Dodge, forming a butt-punctuated line along which Dodge constituted point number two: the "men," you see, were friends. Faced with the unpeopled depths of the bar they had gathered around its single patron as is the custom with mid-afternoon meetings between beer drinking strangers.

Another, Dodge? called Waldo, his hand resting lightly on the draught handle like a bombardier's hand on a bombardier's button, his other hand holding an angled sleeve below the spigot, his intense eyes steady on Dodge. But you gotta pay for this one unless you're still thinking about —

Dodge's hand precipitated the pouring of the draught, though Waldo brought it over without further instruction.

Thanks. How on earth did you get me thinking about suicide, by the way? Whatever gave you the idea that I wanted to kill myself, by the way?

Dodge, you've been gainfully employed at about eighteen different addresses for a total of about two-and-a-half years out of the eleven I've known you. It's obvious you've got no taste for work. You're a smart man in sort of a well-disguised way, but you simply haven't got the tenacity to wrestle down a pension, forge dreams from the pickle jar savings; you won't dig in the dirt or scratch on the paper or cut the hair; you won't tend the bar, sell the donuts or pump the gas; you hate children and education and sports and politics; you're a lousy artist and you can't cook. You're like something sentient knitted into a sweater. The world wasn't built for you, Dodge, nor you for it. There's no solution that I can see except of course the final solution.

Waldo! Jeez, I mean jeez, whaddaya mean, asked Dodge incredulously, I'm incredulous. You're a bartender, Waldo, for God's sake. Whaddaya say to all those flunking students who flock here eight months outta the year, or to all those old, cancerous, womanless men who're here every night threatening to beat each other's brains in, or all those failed and failing poets.

I say: there's no solution that I can see.

C'mon, Waldo, isn't that a little like throwing a crippled widow —

Don't be offensive. It's not at all like that, it's often the one thing you can say that makes them realize that there is a solution.

What about problems with teen-agers, asked the "man" farthest to Dodge's right, 'cause man my kids are a pain, more trouble than I ever was to my folks I'll tell ya and a lot less willing to answer for their crappy judgement.

Ah, Toby, trust you to hit Waldo's Anomaly right off the bat. The only aberrant construct in an otherwise flawless and brilliantly simple piece of deductive logic: teenagers. Drown 'em, that's all you can do, the only solution is to drown 'em. I hate the little fuckers. As a group they're as profound as a styrofoam cup, and believe me I'm tempted to go on from there. Suffice to say that the teen ager's major problem is a total inability to find fault with self or the social genre in which s/he is enlisted, which translates into an inability to comprehend any other point of view. Teenagers are merely earless humpers of redundant simplicities; and even at that possess only a modicum of expertise.

Boy does that give me a lot more to think about, thought Dodge (Dodge had always believed adolescence to be the pivotal period in one's life, a time for experimentation, premiering experience, the fight for identity, the development of a rudimentary aesthetic, the social/individualistic dialectic, the sex, the drugs, the dogs that bowl; the development of the MAD concept in dealing with parents, teachers, anything over 21; in short, the four to five year period of trench warfare that begins just as the goddess of puberty has finished tickling a hair pattern and lust from your squeaking, hipless little mass, and all you can safely do is scream at anyone who pretends to understand what you are all about when even you yourself — running every two weeks to the dictionary because you're sure that you've finally caught up to the definition of symptomatic schizophrenia — don't have a clue what the fuck you're supposed to do with the body and mind that you're saddled with: adolescence, a time when life is so confusing that you don't have the time or the will to consider LIFE questions so you inadvertently end up laying the foundation for, obliviously determining, the LIFE you end up living. This was how Dodge had always conceived of the teen-age condition, but Waldo's Anomaly seemed to provide a more comfortable, less demanding and easily defensible intellectual position regarding teen-agers: something to think about certainly), and twisted into a position that would accommodate thinking more comfortably.

Before Dodge could fully settle in to what had been descriptively labelled on one occasion a state of sublime ponderment, and on another as reverie personified, a couple of things happened. First of all, in from the wetted daylight stepped beauty, astoundingly accumulated over a slight period of sixteen or seventeen years, haloed briefly and totally by spectral, overexposed light reflecting from the rain-shined sides of sloshing, pacing automobiles and a paperbox. After the door dipped quickly the last six inches toward closure on its pneumatic hinge the feather-light light stayed with the girl for a full, brief second. Trained the light seemed, or trapped willingly inside the water beads that rolled and ran down the smooth, pale, blue-tinged skin of her face and legs and neck to stop, quiver, then fall from one of the pouting places that covered her body like sores. She wore the water — her denim skirt, thin green V-necked sweater and shredded rain slicker were like the running makeup she might have been wearing but wasn't save the pomegranate slash of lipstick, wonderfully, enigmatically waxy, rejecting like fire the timid drops of water that nudged too near. No, the clothes detracted as afterthoughts often do; the rain was her natural suit, her everwet sublimity her natural gift: the perfected descendant of mythic water children was this girl, eyes bluer than the skies Van Gogh saw; hair — though matted and pounded — luminous, snail-stroked. Beauty as timeless as a Rolex.

The men of the Elm Street Diner stared as older men in the presence of young, stunning women often stare: tamed, stupefied, slightly sad. Except for Dodge who was frenetically fondling an empty beer mug in all sorts of ways, and staring, not at the girl but at a place just to her left and up, preferring the most auspicious of his deep-thought profiles. Wasted effort, Dodge, he thought to himself, for I am thinking too much of towelling down gently that little godette, fluffing and drying her, then, centering her gently on the azure coverlet of a large, large bed: scrubbed and perfect, a pallid mushroom ready on a blue plate for the substantiating prod of my thick, dirt-imprinted fingers, the lick and flick of my warty tongue, the vile punctuated landscape of my stubbly, bubbly skin. Now of course these latter thoughts got him into the swing of the correct facial expression, but, enwrapped as he was, he remained completely oblivious to the explicit come hitherings of the girl's hip, finger and eye movements; to the way her tongue toyed chasingly with a lip-circumscribing raindrop, which eventually came to rest, shivering gently, in the puffy cleft of her lower lip. She drew it lazily into her mouth.

The squelching of the girl's footsteps snapped Dodge from his free-flowing fantasy, but by this time the girl had begun ignoring him in favour of the sallow youth who still sat, unmoving, with his back to the door. When she was close enough she reached out a slender, steady hand — a carved or carver's hand — and rested it lightly on the boy's shoulder. Her thumb began making little, circular appeals as though she were stroking fondly the head of a small lizard. He didn't stir except to puff once on his cigarette. Dodge took in all he could from his proximate vantage: first the thumb, which his line of sight traced all the way back to an incredibly delicate and sensitive-seeming nose, rabbitlike in tone without all the distracting movement, the nostrils of which could have accommodated nothing larger or more perfectly round than a pair of fresh garden peas. He moved from jawline to neck nape to an exposed section of stretched-tight sternum to the empty cling, the bauble-like convex, of wet skirt over buttock-hollow: all this with much more determination and accelerated breathing than he had been aware of. The youth turned to stare at him, a surly, hateful stare that ran out of eyes so red they looked to be haemorrhaging. An albatross, thought Dodge, a very mean, or salt-stung, albatross.

The albatross turned away from Dodge and said, more to his own reflection than to either of the people who bracketed him, Well?

She didn't hesitate, and with a voice that rose like Auschwitz violins in the bar she said: I'm sorry, Panco, and if it happens again, I'll be sorry again.

Panco reached up to his shoulder and placed his hand affectionately over hers, gave it a squeeze that released like a sigh. His stained fingers took on the colour of sunset beside the girl's lurid skin.

Forsaking the barstool after a silent half minute Panco dug for

61

money in the loose front pockets of his jeans while the girl helped herself to one of his cigarettes. Panco placed two twos, folded lengthwise, beneath his empty mug then turned squarely to face Waldo, Dodge, the two "men." He plucked gently the lit cigarette from the girl's mouth and placed the reddened filter in his own; he dragged deeply without squinting and suddenly he wasn't the skinny, sallow youth that had entered the bar thirty minutes earlier. Suddenly he was something penultimate, something very quick and hard and at ease with intimate violence; suddenly he didn't need the richness and the essentiality of the girl to qualify his motives for he by himself personified every word in the continuing cycle of words used to describe those people riding the crest of self-fulfilment, self-sufficiency, efficacy of personality, the Jesus Christs and the Stings of the world and all the people who possess the sort of mutated confidence that everyone desires.

Panco hadn't said a word; his confrontational presence was more than enough to set the minds of the Elm Street patrons that afternoon whirling into motion. Dodge had even become marginally handsome twice during the stare down, but the threat of menace so close by had kept him duly alert and, for the most part, marginally ugly. Each of the four men present had, under the gaze of Panco, calculated, to the day, their respective ages before moving swiftly on to maudlin self-mastications of character: minor opportunities wasted, major opportunities never within the scope of feasibility to begin with. A pall had settled within the already pallish bar and the butterfly silence of reasonable fear at an unreasonable cost fluttered down around their ears. Here before them was a boy who, it was evident suddenly, was not even old enough to have been sold a beer, standing them off, without words defying and denying them, gutting all their pasts and all their presents and especially their long, long futures with his sharp, confident personality. Awareness seemed everywhere in the room and only one strain of it worth envying. Panco, not ironically, broke the tension of depression by looking to his rightful and logical partner, looking down upon the upturned regretless face of an escaped and insatiable angel, and smiling the most natural, life-loving, secret-speaking smile imaginable: a smile to impress mothers and city girls alike.

Thank you for showing us your tender and reverent side, you little prick, thought Dodge. Thank you for showing us the choir-prompting beauty of your obverse dimension. O thank you, Panco, thank you.

C'mon, Fish, said Panco, and away they strolled, slowly, arm in arm, a rumple of cool youth, out through the heavy door of the diner and into a bright noisy light that looked, from a barside perspective, like the light at the beginning and at the end of life's tunnel. The door swooned shut.

An imperceptible lack of silence hovered like a chemical cloud above the tight knot of old men defined by Waldo, Dodge, Toby and Toby's friend. There were many sounds not filling the air after Panco and Fish departed from the Elm Street Diner. Each man sat lumpenly anchored to his thoughts just as each man's right hand remained anchored to the handle of his beer mug. Thoughts and hands. The four men might as well have been curtains blowing in the same breeze.

Eventually, though it seemed suddenly to those present, movement and conversation began again. Waldo, for his part, remained silent but proceeded with somnolent, precise motions to cut up a lemon into twists. This completed he started in on the rinds or oranges and limes, disdaining pinwheels in favour of intricate, minimally abstracted ballerinas, dancing bears, racing cars and Prime Ministerial profiles. His hands worked methodically and dexterously below the light scowl of an artisan, and the figurines began dropping fast from the ugly fruits. He kept carving, the knife diving and twisting, until a pile of obsolete cocktail garnishes, the resurrected minutiae of an ancient ballroom, lay curling on the counter behind the bar.

Now it might have been a tear hovering decisively in the cradle of Waldo's left eye but more than likely he was merely juice-stabbed.

While Waldo carved memory's echoes from fruit rinds Toby and his friend sent spinning a loud, pestilential conversation. Their game was base, an obvious, vociferous effort to edify and sentimentalize a youthful exuberance that neither could remember; a myth-making process whereby a clawless, ultimately passionless past is beaten to the point where it hisses. Their conversation wound up loudly, sluggishly (it had been constantly crass) and in agreement: a mutual boyhood friend, who had hit the big time with a refrigerated storage business, had become: a pompous asshole. Both concurred with nods serious and gesticulations sanguine, and wiped with buttoned shirt cuffs their spittle speckled chins.

Dodge by this time had wandered over to a small table-for-two tucked inside one of the dark edges of the dark bar. And sat.

Chapter 559

Sure, tear down the shutters, sighed Waldo, let the spiders see their fat, ugly selves for once.

Slat by rotted slat the shutter came down and grey, overcast light stepped tentatively down onto the soft wooden floor. Dust motes corkscrewed in crazy confusion and the still-anchored main ropes of an old, old web swam dolphinlike in a minute draft. Dodge, his hands bleeding from splinters and nail gouges, returned to his chair set just to one side of the muted shaft of Speilbergian sunlight. His mug of beer looked playful and airy in its yellowish, backlit effervescence, less the ritual poison of old men and more a squat, golden god beside his bloodied, mutilated hand. The scene, captured from a southern vantage, would have made an effective photograph or painting: the pile of broken shutter slats on the floor by Dodge's feet, his distance from the other men, from the downcast, glass-wiping Waldo and, a few feet further to the right, the two chubby pals, legs akimbo on bar-stool footrests, vociferating beneath a thundercloud of cigar smoke; the enigmatic beam of dust-filled sunlight, splitting the darkly bleeding room, obtrusive yet accepted: all in all a God-raped space with, as its focal point, a blood-covered human hand.

Dodge stared out the window at the rain-hastened toings and froings of shiny pedestrians, the hapless cyclists and the phantom cars with their unseen drivers behind steamed windows. Everywhere blurred indicator lights beat an expectant rhythm, and headlights, insignificant beneath a wide grey sky, plumbed minor depths in reckless fashions. The sun resembled a tangerine seen through a dozen sheets of tracing paper.

Dodge heard footsteps falling away before finding a damp cloth in his hand. He wiped at his scratches then pulled out some matches and swiped a cigarette lit.

A minute later Dodge was thinking; schoolgirls began to gather on the pavement outside, mouths agape, umbrellas slowly descending behind them. Dodge blew smoke behind the dirty window pane, and to the girls his profile was that of a lover/guitar-hero of contemporary England and his expression betrayed thoughts divided painfully between a woman and women. Outside the Elm Street Diner it began to look, from a distance, as if a fistfight was drawing a crowd.

Carol Anne Wien

BEDROCK

Dorothy's parents flew north the Thursday after receiving the telegram. The wedding was scheduled a week from Saturday. Dorothy had spent her first year of teaching in a community of a thousand Inuit and settlers at the far end of a bush flight, and telegrammed in early June her impending marriage to Johnnie Lash. Elizabeth and Ted, in anguish, flew north from Montreal to save their cultivated daughter from a life of poverty in an unfamiliar culture.

The cramped cabin of the bush plane was noisy and smelled of fuel; it made Elizabeth nauseous. When she scanned the landscape below, the scant trees were like a two-day old beard stubble. As the plane moved up the cheek of the land, the stubble thinned, grew scarce, until the trees were isolated hairs on a smooth cheekbone. Elizabeth worried about her daughter: it was too soon for her to marry, what could she see in someone up here, her children would not speak English properly, how would she cope with the alcohol abuse, the scabies. Why throw her life away on a year's whim? (She had said teaching in the north was her project for Canada's centennial.)

"She wants us to rescue her," Ted said suddenly. His hands were coiled together tightly on his lap.

"How can you be so sure?"

"She sent the telegram before the wedding, not after."

It was the first flight of the season to land on water, a cold black chop which rocked the pontooned craft like a baby duck, and chunks and crusts of ice still littered the shoreline. The plane taxied to a rough-cut floating dock rocking dizzily on the water, and after a tricky descent from the plane hatch, there was a log ladder to climb twenty feet up to the main wharf. Elizabeth had thought the settlers would look like her and Ted and Dorothy, but from the dock all the people looked Inuit, hands cupped with cigarettes, dark bulky jackets, missing teeth. She had worn her navy blue wool coat with kid gloves and boots to match. Her gloves would be ruined climbing the ladder. How could she worry about torn leather in the face of all those missing teeth? She quickly hid the gloves in her pocket.

Dorothy had found them a room at a local settler's who took in temporary boarders. They walked up together through the old Inuit section, tiny wood houses without foundations (the corner of one house was propped on several stones) where the raw sewage lay in open ditches and a lone wire loped from house to house lighting single bulbs. Dorothy told her parents the settler's wife was in hospital in Newfoundland, having given birth to premature twins, one of whom had died. The roads were a corrugated mush, alternating strips of slushy ice and mud. At the house, they were given a basement room, walled off from the furnace with plywood. Ted was surprised the man had central heat: on the walk up he had noticed that the Inuit houses had wood stoves, in an environment where you could easily count the trees. Elizabeth carefully scraped the mud off her designer boots with moistened tissues, aching for a daughter she no longer knew.

She was already appalled by the apparent wretchedness of village life, dogs rutting along the edges of sewage, a fat couple lying on the road drunk in the middle of the day, but Dorothy could not understand. She said she loved it.

"You should have been here in the winter. It's so exhilarating going out on the hills on a *komatik*."

"On what?"

"The runner behind the snowmobile, like a sleigh. You feel so free, like you belong to the whole world and it belongs to you. And everyone is so kind, people look after each other here."

"What? Without water and sewers, drunk and poor, you tell me they look after each other?" Elizabeth was hurt by the implication; she and Ted had dropped everything in their concern for Dorothy. Dorothy could only marry once, divorce was unthinkable.

"If your hands are cold out on a trip, for instance, everyone helps you warm them up. The adults listen when a child complains.

"But I always had to make supper for the others when you came home from skating at the park with your feet so cold. I thought you were just tired."

"I didn't mean anything personal, Mother."

Elizabeth wept when she saw the inside of the schoolhouse decorated by the children for the wedding. There isn't much paper in the north; the walls were festooned with toilet paper streamers and bows, and strings of pastel-coloured marshmallows. Dorothy had a real wedding dress too, tiers of Chantilly lace from the

Sears catalogue, hanging on the back of a door next to the freezer full of arctic char. Alongside were handmade *mukluks* from her husband-to-be, stuffed with old newspapers so they would stand up straight, the Chicago *Tribune* it was. When Elizabeth asked about the newspaper, Dorothy said it was in the attache case she had bought from Teporah for three dollars.

"Who's Teporah?"

"An Inuk who harvests the dump. She works very hard."

Elizabeth tried to be broad-minded, but there was nothing in her austere Presbyterian childhood or her experience as a war-time bride to prepare her for the things that motivated her daughter.

On Saturday Dorothy's husband-to-be invited them to an island off the coast for an outdoor lunch, camping without the overnight. Elizabeth and Ted did not want to go, did not want to have anything to do with him, but Dorothy said they could not refuse his hospitality, such rudeness would be unforgivable.

Johnnie greeted them at the wharf. Although taller than Elizabeth had expected (his father was an Irish settler) and sporting wavy instead of straight black hair, he was missing several bicuspids, had nicotine-stained fingers and a nervous glitter to his eyes. Elizabeth thought he looked sneaky. Rage bubbled uncontrollably through her chest at the very notion of Dorothy, McGill educated and bilingual, throwing herself away on this poor soul who offered only the warming of hands.

Yet his hands fascinated Elizabeth. He took her hand to help her into the boat (an English, not an Inuit gesture) and his hand felt confident and welcoming and left her a little subdued. It was a fishing boat, white with dark green trim and an outboard motor, and far too small, she thought, to go out onto open ocean, but to her surprise she found it exhilarating barrelling over the open water under a whistling wind, shivering with cold, weaving in and out among the dark mountain islands rising up out of the water around them. How trusting they had been. What if this Johnnie simply decided to dump them and make off with their daughter?

Dorothy demonstrated her new finesse by cleaning the silver-gray char which Johnnie caught for lunch. Elizabeth felt a tremor of shock along her spine when her daughter calmly slit the wet fish right through the belly and scooped out the innards. Why are the young so unselective in choosing where to be competent, she thought. She watched how Dorothy and Johnnie's arms and hands mirrored each others' actions. Occasionally, Johnnie ran his palm across the tips of hair along Dorothy's shoulders. He had well-muscled thighs and forearms and Elizabeth did not understand why she felt so repelled by the attraction between them. She was momentarily overcome by a terrible bursting rage at the thought of this unknown man claiming her daughter, touching her and kissing her — how could Dorothy kiss someone who ate raw meat, it didn't feel right. She found her own intolerance unbearable: nor could she bear to lose her daughter to this man, this environment.

Later that evening Dorothy wanted to give her parents a tour of the village. Ted wouldn't go, said he had to catch up on his paperwork.

"You won't be deflected when you have a purpose, will you?" Elizabeth thought there were times when Ted's determination, his ability to focus, went too far.

"Aren't you the least bit worried, my dear, that she'll charm you into believing that she should marry him?"

The sun hung low, throwing attenuated shadows over the landscape, the air so golden from the angle of the light Elizabeth thought she could taste it. Such beauty, and then she clenched her impeccably-kept teeth with guilt that she could call the scene of so much poverty beautiful: poverty is not picturesque to live. Dorothy would be ruined in a few years.

"This is the best section. In the old part, they have to get all their water up the hill from one tap."

"For laundry, everything?"

"It's easier in the winter when they can pull it on the *komatik*."

Children gathered around them like the flies on the dried ribs of caribou hanging from trees and porches. Dorothy carried an infant for a seven year-old, the baby dressed up in a red and white embroidered dress with matching bonnet and ruffled pants.

"See this house," said a pre-teen in designer jeans, "Debbie crush here, she crawl under the house when they moves it and she die." It was so horrible Elizabeth thought the child was making it up for effect, but Dorothy continued.

"They had the house on blocks to move it to a foundation and she spotted an earring underneath. The corner of the house slipped off the block as they manoeuvred it. She was just nineteen."

"Why would anyone crawl under a house that's being moved? Don't they have any safety sense?" (*How could any mother let a young life slip away like that?*) "Don't these people take any responsibility for each other?"

Dorothy shrugged at her mother's anger. "All kinds. The kids are pulled out of school at the drop of a hat for any sort of family commitment."

"Well that's not very good, is it!"

"They put the family first, not school or job. They'll work for the family, reshingling, sealing, looking after someone who's sick. I like that."

Elizabeth bristled, her upper lip puckering, and tried to hold back. "All the effort we put into teaching you a sense of responsibility! How can you agree with that? They'll never get anywhere, will they?"

Dorothy stopped in the mud, the bedecked infant child in her arms. "Where is there to get, Mother? If they leave and go south to school or a job, then they've failed their family. If they quit school and stay close to their family, then they've failed the school system and white values. They're caught, Mother, they can't win."

So it's an atonement for the sins of white society, thought Elizabeth.

"You want to stay to help, it that it?"

"It's the sense of community, of belonging, that I like."

"But surely you don't belong, do you, as a white southerner?"

"Not yet."

Elizabeth thought if they could just get her out of the community she'd come to her senses. If they could just get her home for the summer . . .

They had reached the edge of the poorest section, the weathered houses crowded together with the odd gap between them like the broken rows of teeth in the Inuit mouths. Dorothy told her mother that the gaps were the charred remains of house fires. She beckoned up a narrow path to a clapboard house next to the little church. "Come on in, let me show you what we're doing." The mud yard was littered with construction materials, plywood and two by fours. On either side of a flagpole, four tiny black cannons poked their English snouts out of the old grass and pointed at a rakish angle toward the sea. Elizabeth thought the cannons looked helpless and silly. Dorothy took the group through a small maze of dilapidated outbuildings to the back door.

"They tried to keep a few chickens."

"Who?"

"The Moravian missionaries."

"Where are they now?"

Dorothy shrugged insolently. That was a new gesture. She had picked that up from Johnnie. Her mother didn't like it. It allowed her to evade anything, just shrug and look away.

"We come, we come, too!" The children pushed and shoved to enter the house. Dorothy unlocked the door, calling, "Don't touch anything," to the children as they surged past. They were fixing it up, this old manse abandoned for a decade, this is where we will live, she told her mother, Johnnie is so good with his hands, just look at the newel post he made. The Mission Board said they could have the house if they fixed it up.

In spite of herself, Elizabeth was caught up in the excitement of turning a discarded house into a place of life. It had real potential, real potential, she could see it herself. The front two rooms had very gracious proportions by any standard. Oh they were a mess at the moment, bits of torn linoleum flooring in ugly brown patterns, sagging window frames and cracked walls, but real plaster on the walls, not plywood or cheap panelling, and a magnificent dutch stove in the corner tiled to the ceiling in the European fashion. This wasn't so bad. Oh it was awful, positively awful, but it had potential, and it was certainly better than anything else in the settlement. Elizabeth's heart would break to see Dorothy live in one of those gray shacks with only a single light bulb in the ceiling. She beamed at her daughter.

The children all wanted to use the toilet. It struck Elizabeth that Dorothy wouldn't have to go for water with a *komatik*, this was still the civilized part of town despite its age and proximity to the poor parts. She was cheered. She could imagine Dorothy fixing this up, Dorothy with her good taste. She could send her down-filled quilts from Ogilvie's. The cluster of children argued with Dorothy, negotiating use of the toilet, all in desperate need, and Elizabeth waited in an empty storeroom. The window was cracked and boarded up, so that she could not see out. It was dark, a single forty-watt bulb dangling gracelessly from the middle of the room, but her eye was caught up and held, startled by the most beautiful hook fastening the casement. It was soft and smooth, heavy and solid, and absolutely exquisite, a rat-tail hook from a ship perhaps, with a long coiling handle. Touching it reminded her of Johnnie's palm brushing the tips of Dorothy's hair. What was she doing, almost forgetting why they had come, almost giving in to the idea of leaving Dorothy here? Ted must not find out, must not know about her back-sliding.

"Mother, why do you look so grim, I though you liked it?"

"I don't look grim, dear, I can see it has potential."

"I'm learning how to toe nail studs! But what's wrong, you look so uptight. You don't have to have perfect manners here, you can tell me."

"Manners allow me to treat others well." She thought Dorothy was already dark and sun-worn. Her skin would be a mess of wrinkles before she was thirty. "I just cannot believe you really want to spend the rest of your life with this man, as if I'm told to take the way I've lived my own life and . . . and . . . stuff it!" Elizabeth was crying, her tears for her daughter leaving her cheeks smeared with mascara.

Dorothy cried too. "You talk as if I'm out to hurt you, but I just want to choose my own life, and I love it here. People are what counts here, Mother, not changing your purse from white to black on Labour Day. And the land, the land just swallows you, you never want to go back."

Elizabeth held out her arms, hugged her. "I'm trying to understand. Don't tell your father we've been fighting."

Not far from the manse was a white hut, a sort of papier-mâché style igloo that looked more like a decapitated mushroom. Elizabeth thought it unnecessarily tacky. Inside were barrels of used clothing, a jumble of dark unpleasant clothes, discarded by the south and shipped north by the IODE. Used clothing always made Elizabeth shudder. Dorothy searched through the piles and bins for something, her mother couldn't tell what. A ratty old raccoon coat swathed a cardboard box; Elizabeth could not imagine sending ratty old fur to the Inuit, surely that was insulting.

"Dorothy, is there a piano in the community?"

"Kitura's mother has an old pump organ auctioned off by the mission but it was broken when she bought it."

Dorothy had grade ten Conservatory piano, she could be a piano teacher even if she found performance too strenuous. Her centennial project (doing something for her country, she said) would take over her life, if she wasn't careful.

"Do you remember how you used to be so nice to the winos on the benches when we went for walks to the park? You'd say 'hello' in the sweetest little sing-song voice, and I was mortified walking past in case someone thought we knew them."

"No, I don't remember." Dorothy was lifting every piece of clothing, as if there was some prize just within reach, if she searched long enough. Her gorgeous black hair dangled over the piles of fabric, grazing the clothes as she riffled through them. Suppose she got lice, Elizabeth thought, her heart wrenching again.

"Found it! Kitura said there was one!" Dorothy pulled out a neon purple sweater with raised flowers in carpet-like patterns of cerise and red across the shoulders. "There! What do you think!" She pirouetted before her mother, holding it across her chest for size. It was violently hideous. "How's that for a going-away outfit?"

Elizabeth slapped her daughter across the cheek before she could stop herself. "I didn't bring you up to be an Inuit slut, I can't stand this any more." Elizabeth's face was taut and white as she turned to flee from the squalid little hut. Dorothy's words rang after her. "To Inuit men, it's white women who're the sluts."

In the end, and with seasoned coaching on his part, Elizabeth told Ted about the sleazy sweater and the slap.

"It was such a shock, our daughter combing through second-hand clothes for something for herself! Taking me to witness it. Just because she thinks trousseau teas are stuffy and snobbish. She goes to such extremes to show how far she has fallen from decent values!"

"Elizabeth, it isn't exactly indecent to buy a second-hand sweater, is it?"

"She practically said if she didn't marry him she'd be considered a slut. Our daughter, of all people!"

"Elizabeth, let's think this through. How are we going to get her home?" She watched his hands working his papers in the briefcase. His wrists looked so slight and vulnerable for such a competent man.

"She always wants more from the world: she never liked limits, but she doesn't see the ones she's taking on."

Sunday morning Elizabeth was still so upset she did not want to see her daughter and spent too long smoothing the bed sheets with a hand like a slow iron, mitering the corners with hospital precision.

"She'll think we're angry if you don't go out with her," said Ted.

"Why don't you go." She knew he wouldn't. He sat in their basement room, his briefcase open on his lap like a shield, and she knew he would not act until they had worked out how to win Dorothy back.

Monday was a school administration day and Dorothy had paper-work. Elizabeth didn't like the idea of her sitting in that classroom, beckoned into marriage by those forlorn festoons of toilet paper: it is the sadness of everyday life which becomes the greatest burden, not the moments of drama. She walked to quell nervous energy, for she had to decide whether to stay for the wedding if they failed to prevent it. The night before she and Ted had planned what to do. Ted would talk to Dorothy alone, covering four areas, effects of isolation, cultural difference, opportunities for their children, opportunities for Dorothy herself. They thought it unfair to gang up on Dorothy, two against one.

Elizabeth was reminded of her schoolmate, Donna, a first-rate singer and athlete, who married hurriedly at seventeen, pregnant of course and briefly radiant. (She was married in a white lace dress with a thin gold belt, the belt signifying she was a touch sullied.) Ten years later her store clerk husband left her and Elizabeth heard she rummaged for clothes for her five children at the Salvation Army.

Elizabeth climbed the worn and stony path to the water source far up the hill, a single pipe sticking up out of the ground high enough to place a bucket underneath. *"I'd like to present our arguments for why you should come home with us,"* Ted would begin. Below lay the sad little town of bungalows, shacks and shanties. Along the shore was a string of fishing boats. From this distance they had the thin curve of fingernail trimmings ready to be cast off a lap. Behind her wandered a range of mountains and before her lay the sea, dark blue and choppy, and all around lay mountains of rolling bedrock, and above her rolled masses of clouds like muscular thighs breaking apart to show a flash of sky. It was too vast and barren, people meaning no more than a punctuation mark on an empty page, and Elizabeth was filled with longing.

On the way back she was accosted by a drunk couple, drunk before noon. She could not tell what they wanted, their missing teeth and patchy English mixed with the alcoholic slur. Newfoundland, she made out. No, she was not from Newfoundland. The woman slipped suddenly and fell at Elizabeth's feet. She had to step back so the woman didn't roll onto her boots. The man tried feebly to pull up his wife but she lay in the wet mud like a seal. Elizabeth left them, heaving and rolling, as the woman broke into fierce swearing. She felt frightened by what people could become.

She entered the schoolhouse and paused in the cloakroom. The walls, even the coathooks marching around them, were the same institutional green she remembered from her own childhood. She could hear Dorothy and Ted in the classroom itself, serious and engrossed, and could not bring herself to enter it.

"He has kindness, that's the most important quality in marriage, isn't it, Dad?"

"He won't give you stability."

"Stability's not very interesting."

"Marriage often isn't: it's more like bedrock, a foundation."

Elizabeth's lips compressed. It was a bit strong: she'd never felt like flooring, but she knew what he meant.

"I was hoping marriage might be fun."

"An unsuitable partner won't be fun for very long."

"He's artistic."

"What proof do you have?"

Dorothy paused, searching for something specific. "He handles wood well."

"They're a tool-oriented culture."

Elizabeth thought Dorothy would be overwhelmed; Ted should ease up or she might overreact.

"I can't explain the potential I see in him, but I could make a difference in his life." Dorothy's voice was subdued.

"What about yours? What about the alcohol problem here?"

"I think I motivate him. He hasn't been drunk since he's been with me."

Elizabeth's heart leapt and she paced the narrow corridor of the cloakroom. She tapped the tips of the hooks in a two-beat rhythm as she passed them: *he will beat her, when he's drunk, he will beat her, when he's drunk.*

"Where will you live?"

"Until we get the manse fixed up, with his parents."

"I can see there's a housing shortage. Do you think you'll be allowed to keep the manse for yourselves? What about his family?"

Silence. Elizabeth thought Dorothy must see her father's point — and how could she say no if Johnnie wanted to moved his brother's family upstairs, give his grandfather a more spacious corner of the living-room?

"It hadn't struck me before," Dorothy's voice sounded weak, "that I'd lose control over my own life: I though I was gaining it."

"You know in our family you only get one shot at marriage. It's not a monogamous culture, is it? Do you expect him to be faithful?"

"We'll certainly try but I don't believe it's so essential to marriage as it used to be — for my generation."

The gall, the gall of it, thought Elizabeth, the child knows *nothing* about fidelity, neither the costs of keeping it nor the destruction of its betrayal. How could she even *think* it doesn't matter any more. Elizabeth was so angered she found herself planted in full view in the doorway of the classroom. Ted was rising from one of the oak mission desks to stare out a window and Dorothy sat with both hands cupping her forehead. Her long hair masked her face.

"No, Dorothy," Ted spoke very softly, "fidelity is knowing basically that the other person is for you, that some things are guaranteed. It's a great freedom really, because your energy can then be given outwards to other things. It removes self-centredness, that worry for self."

Elizabeth's eyes filled uncontrollably to hear him describe it so, that gift of restraint from one person to another. She wanted to shout, "Don't marry him unless you can be faithful," but it sounded maudlin. And then Ted, in the softest and loveliest of voices, said to Dorothy, "Do you respect and love this man enough to be faithful for a lifetime?" Elizabeth felt his eyes shining on her — he had seen her in the doorway — though tears flooded her own eyes and she couldn't focus clearly. To have so much love and hope for one man, then to try to pass that on to a child, was almost unbearable. She walked slowly, blindly, down the aisle and sat in the little desk behind Dorothy. She reached out to touch her hair but Dorothy did not respond.

"Johnnie seemed the perfect way," Dorothy said hoarsely, "to take on something totally unexpected, totally my own."

They were all still for a minute, hearts on edge and the room spinning with tension, until Dorothy let out an enormous sigh.

"But Johnnie wants more from the world than — this!" Her gesture took in the flimsy streamers, the mission desks, the mud beyond the door.

"Did you send for us because you were unsure?" asked Elizabeth, afraid for the fragility of her daughter's feelings. "Couldn't you just be friends?"

"We understand the courage it takes to betray him" said Ted, "but it's better now than later."

Waiting for the Tuesday plane on the government wharf, it was the children who saddened Elizabeth, looking so forlorn and miserable like their toilet paper streamers. They shuffled in their sneakers, bands flapping over downturned faces. "Why you not stay, Miss Dorothy?" Dorothy hugged some, patted others and said maybe she'd come back some time. "Who be our teacher now?"

75

A teen-aged girl appeared on the slushy road above the wharf, her arms absurdly burdened with a rolled up bundle of lace, and *mukluks* dangling from her hand. "Dorothy, you forgot these, they were downstairs." Dorothy walked slowly toward the settler's daughter. Elizabeth watched as, moments later, the girl was trudging back up the road, the bundle of white still in her arms, and Dorothy returned to the wharf with the *mukluks*.

"You don't want to bring the dress home, dear?"

"It belongs here. Someone else can have it, it'll probably be worn for years. Mother, didn't you ever want to have a different life than the one set out for you?"

The plane rounded the rock promontory across the bay soundlessly, and Elizabeth pulled out her navy gloves, smoothing the kid skin over each finger, concentrating. "I was brought up on a code, not on options. Choice didn't enter into it."

They boarded without incident, but when the pilots were loading boxes of char into the compartment behind the cabin Dorothy suddenly leaped out of her seat and through the plane hatch, catapulting herself onto the log dock. Ted calmed his wife: "Leave her, she's not going to bolt now." Elizabeth stood at the hatch waiting and plucking helplessly at its aluminum edge with her gloved hands. Her legs shook. Dorothy stood on the ladder to the main wharf. Johnnie was leaning over the top of the ladder, his arm extended toward her. Elizabeth watched as Dorothy passed up something which he stuffed inside his zippered jacket. Then he stood up and walked away through the crowd without a wave. Dorothy returned to the plane and took her seat, Johnnie's handmade *mukluks* on her lap. "Why did you give him the newspapers?"

"He needs them for the stove."

"Doesn't he need the *mukluks*? There's a lot of work in them"

"He made them for me, they are mine." They were the colour of new butter, festive red tassels along one side. Dorothy sat the entire trip to Goose Bay with the *mukluks* cradled in her lap. Later Elizabeth saw that Ted was holding Dorothy's hand, and tears came to her eyes that she was so useless to her daughter, that her care came out as graceless, an intrusion.

Two years later Dorothy married a graduate student in Geology from McGill. After their first child was born he accepted a position at the local university in St. John's, Newfoundland. Dorothy went with pleasure at the possibility of discovering new environments, new accents, new cultures. A decade and two children later, she was less enchanted. One Christmas about that time, she sent her mother a very handsome bracelet inset with an unusual stone. When Elizabeth bent her white wrist to the light at different angles, the stone changed from gray to turquoise, gold and purple at its edges. The attached card said the colour effect was due to microscopic plates of metals formed in parallel lines, iron, copper, nickel, and described the work of Johnnie Lash, a native artist now working in Labrodorite. Elizabeth remember the butter-coloured *mukluks* on the long plane ride home, how Dorothy had kept them in her lap even on the jet from Goose Bay to Montreal. For years Dorothy displayed them at the foot of her living-room fireplace, stuffed with newspapers to hold them upright. Elizabeth always liked to think that she and Ted had done the right thing in bringing Dorothy home from the north.

GOLDFISH

I found myself on the couch downstairs in the livingroom, shivering stark naked. The light was on. The green numbers on the VCR said 4:52. A towel was on the floor. For a soothing moment, like the first waking memory or a really weird dream, it all seemed perfectly normal.

I was really cold. Beside the couch, where I lay curled up, in goosebumps, the filter in the fish tank hummed loud as a refrigerator. Air bubbles burst on the surface of the water, I could hear them even through the chattering of my teeth. I reached out and grabbed the towel, draped it around my shoulders. It was an old towel, coarse-textured, and not very warming.

I should be in bed, I thought, in bed, in bed, but I just lay there shivering. It occurred to me that I ought to have been questioning what I was doing naked in the livingroom in the middle of the night, but it seemed too challenging a problem to tackle then. I glanced at the fishtank instead. Sputnik was a large goldfish and I should have been able to see him instantly. I pulled myself closer. Blub-lub, the water plants swayed around the bubbles. There was no other sign of life in the tank, there was no fish.

Alertness entered my body like a drug I hadn't planned on taking. I must have sleep-walked. Maybe I ate my fish in my sleep, let him slither down my dreaming throat. Was that a flutter of fins I felt in my stomach? Or fear?

I peered over the arm of the couch. There he was, lying on the carpet, unmoving, opalescent orange on early-morning blue shag.

I want you to know that I'd had that fish for more than two and a half years.

Once a year, in May, the Portuguese church around the corner is transformed for its spring festival. Christmas-light crosses and flowers illuminate its facade, hundreds of winking lights trace up and down its spire. Even the surrounding streets are regaled with decorated poles joined one to the next by strings of coloured flags and streamers that riffle in the breeze. A flowered gazebo, where bands can play even in the rain, is erected on the south lawn of the church and, on the remaining grounds, a variety of tableaux are arranged. One of these tableaux consists of a man, a plow, and a shoddy replica of an ox. The man is a mannequin dressed in ill-fitting clothes. He is missing several fingers. The wounds do not heal from one year to the next, rather they get worse, like leprosy.

Behind the church, the tarmac of the school is turned into a fairground faster than seems possible. Friday afternoon the trucks roll in, gears grind, back-up beeps beep, tents unfold, and by dinner time rides are already swinging squealing kids within inches of the windows they stare from in boredom the rest of the year. Glistening weiners turn on stainless-steel rollers, stray candy floss sticks to the soles of shoes or becomes matted in hair, and carnival hucksters, the usual motley assortment of toothless youths with drug-glazed eyes, loudly offer wonky-weighted darts to passersby — hit a red star in the middle enough times and you too could win a mirror screen-printed with the logo of a popular brand of beer.

In the centre of all this action is the goldfish game. On a low, square platform small-mouthed, spherical glass bowls are neatly arranged in concentric circles. Each bowl is filled with coloured water, and, swimming or floating in each is a single tiny goldfish. For a buck, a woman who has a skin condition that allows only one side of her face to tan, gives you seven ping-pong balls. Toss one is a bowl, win a goldfish.

Frank and I decided that it was imperative we save at least one of the fish. It took eight dollars worth of ping-pong balls, but we finally bounced one into a bowl of fuschia-coloured water.

When the woman with the two-tone face handed us the bowl we'd won we questioned her about the occupant's health. She told us that she had a huge tank in her trailer, filled with hundreds of fish. She buys them from a supplier for a penny a piece. At this price, the supplier guarantees that the fish are free of disease.

"We treats them good," the woman said. "Normal water like, in the big tank." She pointed at the display bowls. "Not to say that colour there is bad of them. It's just like what they uses on birthday cakes."

Apparently she was right. Not only did Sputnik survive, he thrived. Four inches long by now, he lay stiff and sticky in my hand. His long, elegant tail was encased in cat hairs. He must have thrashed for a long time, flopping about on the blue shag rug.

Although I was sure there were little X's in his eyes, I decided to try artificial respiration anyway. I rushed him to the kitchen sink and turned on the tap to a gentle trickle and let the water run over his gills. The cat hairs slid off and disappeared down the drain. Sputnik had not been the most entertaining living companion I had ever had, but I had grown fond of him.

"Breathe," I whispered, "Breathe, goddammit." But nothing happened. His eyes remained static.

For fifteen minutes I urged him to breathe. His orange scales were so desperately beautiful that I refused to give up on him. But it was late at night and I was weary. I had sleepwalked for the first time in my life and my feet were freezing. The tiles of the floor were so cold they could have been cemented onto a block of ice.

To keep myself awake, I began planning Sputnik's burial. I would put him in a Baggie in the freezer and when spring came, when the soil would be workable again and there would be tulips and narcissi to decorate his grave, I would thaw and bury him in the back garden. Maybe on Festival Weekend. That would be fitting. I was nearing tears. The cat sidled into the kitchen and rubbed her warm fur around my legs.

For a brief instant, I believed that I saw one of Sputnik's gills flutter, but decided upon reflection that it was a simple hallucination. I stared at my fingers. They had turned into albino prunes. I thought I saw Sputnik's gill flutter again. It seemed quite impossible, but I was sure it did. And then the gill quite plainly flipped open, quivered, then closed again.

My heartbeat quickened. After several more minutes, Sputnik was breathing steadily, even when I held him an inch beyond the flow of the tap. I felt like a medic or a fireman returning someone the gift of life. It was a grand feeling. Sputnik flopped briefly in my hand. I filled a mixing bowl with water and placed him in it. He lay on his side floating on the surface, laboriously moving his gills, but he was alive.

With morning came a vague memory of tragedy. I had dreamt Sputnik had jumped from his tank and onto the livingroom floor. This I found to be true when I saw him swimming in slow circles in the mixing bowl in the kitchen. He was not quite right, still a little off keel, but much better than dead.

But I had also dreamt that Frank was seeing someone else.

Behind my back, the swine. I accused him of this. I told him my dream.

"You're mad at me because of a dream?" he asked, incredulous. "A dream?! For godssake," he said, "You've gone loopy on me." He stirred his coffee with a spoon. Frank never stirs his coffee. Frank drinks his coffee black, taking neither cream nor sugar, so why was he stirring his coffee with a spoon?

"Good thing for Sputnik you walked in your sleep last night," he said, "Guess you're psychic or something, eh?" He put the spoon down.

I tried hard not to be, but I couldn't help being affected by the dream. I still felt as if I had been betrayed, especially since I kept getting flashes of Frank's face pressed against some strange woman's. At odd moments I would even smell her perfume. But after a few days the realness of it passed, as the memories of dreams always pass, into the gauzy place dream-memories are held, until I could only remember the memory of the dream and not the dream itself.

The annual spring festival came and went. Sputnik recuperated completely and continued to grow. He leapt out of the water. After his near-death escapade, we put a piece of screening over the top of the tank so he couldn't escape. I watched him sometimes leap high enough out of the water that his dorsal fin, even his slippery back, bumped against the wire mesh. Water splashed against the wall and made blisters in the wallpaper.

It happened so frequently that I began to wonder if Sputnik were trying to commit suicide each time he thrust himself out of the water and into the air. Had it been a conscious effort to end his life the night I found him on the carpet? Or simply a cry for help? Had I been wrong to meddle? Even if he was only a fish? I became wracked with guilt over these questions and finally convinced myself that Sputnik was a terribly unhappy fish.

"Let's take him to the fishpond in Allen's Gardens," I suggested one Saturday morning. Frank was groggy. He'd come home late the night before, had had extra work to do.

"It'll be an expedition, an adventure," I said to rustle up some enthusiasm.

"Okay," he said, "in a little while. Frank seemed drained to me, sapped of energy, not quite his normal self, but a couple of coffees perked him up.

I love the way the humidity hits you when you walk into the palm tree house, and the alien pollens and smells. I was carrying Sputnik in a plastic bag filled with water from his tank.

"It's okay," I said with forced conviction, "You're going to love it here. Honest."

The goldfish pond is in the camellia and English ivy house. The air there is as humid as in the palm tree house, but cooler. Water drips onto moss-covered rocks. At the far end is the pond, small, but a charming place for a goldfish to retire. Leda holds an ewer that spills a steady stream of water into the pool. The swan's neck is bent, his beak partially open, frozen forever, in such a way that it looks as if he wants to drink of the trickle, or to snap at it if it gets out of line. That day, the spilling water reminded me of when I ran the tap water over Sputnik's gills and brought him back to life. I was suddenly confused. Was I doing the right thing? Or was this another mistake?

"Frank," I said, "could you do it?"

He took the plastic bag from me. Sputnik thrashed for a moment, then settled down. Frank squatted beside the pool.

"Okay, sport," he said, "This is it."

My throat and stomach suddenly constricted with a feeling of dread, of impending doom, as if the physical nature of the universe was about to be irreparably altered, and I alone would be responsible.

Carp mouths sucked at the surface of the water. Frank untwisted the twist-tie. The water began to spill out, but Sputnik swam against the flow, obviously not sure that he wanted to follow it out of the bag. And then out he slid. With a wet plop, he slipped from one world into another, like Alice stepping through the looking glass. For a moment he seemed disoriented, hung still just below the surface, but then he rallied and darted under an over-hanging ledge.

Frank put his arm around my shoulder and squeezed.

"Well," he said, "are you okay?"

I was impressed by the soothing tone of his voice, the sensitivity it implied. Maybe he really was the man I'd have a family with.

"Let's wait a minute," I said. I wanted to see Sputnik swimming free before we left. We stayed ten minutes or so. Nothing happened. Sputnik didn't come out of hiding, the world didn't end. We made it as far as the palm tree house before I burst into tears.

That summer, whenever we rode past Allen's Gardens on our bikes, I would always honk my horn. I'd ask Frank to ring his bell.

Maybe Sputnik would hear, maybe not. Frank thought this was completely insane, but he indulged me. I visited Sputnik, sometimes alone, sometimes with Frank. Frank, I think, was more fond of our fish than he cared to let on — you know how men are.

It was not hard to recognize our goldfish. He was the one who was completely orange except for a dime-size white spot centred in the middle of his back. Sometimes, when the light hit him just right, the spot even looked silver. Also, his tail was more extravagant than any of the others.

I would bring him dried shrimp treats. For some strange reason, the manufacturer of these things even shaped them like shrimps. They floated on the surface of the pool, flesh-coloured commas, and drew a crowd of sucking and nibbling mouths.

Frank told me that I walked in my sleep again. He heard noises downstairs in the middle of the night. At first he thought it was an intruder, then he realized I was not in bed beside him. He found me in the kitchen, running water over my cupped hand. He said that at first he thought I looked like Lady MacBeth. He was a little spooked until he heard what I was saying.

"Breathe, goddammit, breathe," I repeated over and over again.

Frank steered me back up to bed without waking me. I have no memory of this at all.

That dream I had foreshadowed the truth. Frank was seeing someone else. Too many late nights, too many wrong numbers hanging up on me, too many days he was cheerful as a lark, flushed with that look newly-pregnant women get, or people who have fallen newly in love. Sorrow, and a heavy emptiness in my stomach were my constant companions. Also, Frank was nicer to me than usual, more tolerant of my quirks, my foibles. This clinched my suspicions. I've read Ann Landers. I know the signs.

The house became smaller and smaller when Frank was not there. I used to think it was a big house. I took to sitting in restaurants and cafés writing cheerful letters to friends, hoping they would somehow sense the unhappiness I was unable to put into words. I rode my bike around the city, aimlessly, hoping that the exercise would help to release from my body the toxins caused by negative emotions. I swam through the traffic.

I saw Frank with the other woman. I don't know who the hell she was. I had never seen her before, but Frank had brought her to see Sputnik. I could not believe this audacity, this duplicity, this betrayal. Him bringing her to see our fish was a violation of all kinds of things, as bad, maybe, as inviting her to use my toothbrush, or climbing into bed with me while still redolent with her smell. This finally brought anger to me.

Seething with rage, I spied on the two of them through the camellias. My heart was pounding so furiously that my temples and the sides of my neck were pummelled by my blood. The rush of a non-existent waterfall filled my ears. I watched Frank put his arm around this woman, watched his hand squeeze her shoulder as they gazed down into the pool. I know they were looking at Sputnik through a reflection of themselves.

I snuck away before they saw me, backtracked through the palm house, past the banana trees, all the way to the cactus house where the dry hot air let me breathe more normally again. Maybe I was sleepwalking and this was just a dream. I ignored the sign that said Do Not Touch and reached down to a long-spined cactus, jabbed my palm hard into its needle-sharp points. This action didn't wake me, it drew a drop of blood from my life-line, it loosened the tears from my eyes, but it didn't wake me up.

I knew what I had to do, but I could hardly unlock my bike because the steady flow of tears was screwing up my sight. It was probably the tears too that made me blithely ride into an opening car door on my way home. My bike stopped quite suddenly but inertia insisted that I continue, now in flight. I sailed up and over the door, completely weightless, so slowly that I saw everything, so slowly that I had time to make rhythmic but futile gropings in the air before I returned to the ground.

I landed on my back on the pavement, the wind knocked neatly out of me. A streetcar rumbled by, very loudly, jostling the pavement like a mild earthquake. It was a long time before I could draw in a breath. A man was looking down at me, his lips moving, but all I could hear was a deep resonant ringing in my ears.

When I had recovered, I mounted my bike again and continued home. I picked up Sputniks's old scoop net and a plastic bag, then pedalled back to Allen's Gardens.

Frank and the woman were gone. Sputnik was swimming slow circles in the middle of the fishpond. I filled the plastic bag with water and then, with surprisingly little trouble, scooped up Sputnik with the net and wrangled him into the bag.

The pebbles on the beach down by the waterworks are multi-coloured. The wet ones, lacquered by waves at the water's edge, are so beautiful they could be polished pieces of amber or amethyst or bloodstone. I have always loved that beach. Frank and I used to go for walks there and have picnics perched on sun-bleached drift-wood. I used to imagine that we would bring our kids there and search with them for trilobites and gold.

The plastic bag Sputnik was in was opaque so I couldn't see him, could only feel the sloppy weight of the water. I had no idea if this was the right thing to do, but it felt right. Even if he only lived the summer, it would still be an adventure for him. After all, he was a carp, a survivor. I took off my shoes and socks and waded a couple of feet into the lake, carrying Sputnik in the bag.

When I released him, he didn't dash off immediately. He stayed instead in one position, confused perhaps by the alien movement of the water, the thrust towards the beach of the waves above, the swing of the undercurrent in the opposite direction. His fins flut-tered, his flamboyant tail waved. Tentatively, he swam forward a few inches, and then a few inches more. Do goldfish feel fear? I wondered. Was Sputnik as afraid as I was? And then he was gone.

Insects whispered above my head. Lake Ontario licked its shore. I sat on the dry pebble beach for a long time until imprints of the stones were left on my thighs, even through my jeans. I lay back and stared up at the clouds that were sweeping slowly east, waiting expectantly for one of them to split apart, waiting for a big net to appear, for it to scoop me up and transport me to some other place, to a place where I would be free of this anger, this throbbing sor-row, this pain. I stared at the clouds until it was me who was mov-ing and not them, until I was floating in the opposite direction, effortlessly swimming against the rotation of the earth.

Andrew Pyper

MAGNIFICENT

When they released my father from the hospital after his stroke we put him in the guest bedroom on the top floor, so he could look out the window over the fields. Through the fake lace curtains his land spread out from the line of the concession road to the VanDorsen's distant silos. According to my mother, though, he never turned his head to look. All that winter he lay beneath the blankets she would heap unnecessarily upon him, moaning when he was hungry or had to be helped to the bathroom. The first few days he tried to speak, but his lazy tongue and fallen lips could not form any of the words he wanted, and soon he gave up altogether. I drove out to visit almost every weekend, and my mother would greet me with hopeful news, some evidence of improvement: "You know, yesterday he sort of sat up on his own when I brought in his lunch," or, "When I told him you would be here for dinner he nodded his head, and I'd say he smiled. He can't talk, but he can still smile!" When he died later that March, the snow was retreating into earth-veined patches in the fields. "He didn't hang on until spring," my mother said to me when she called to tell me. "He might've been happier if we could have opened up his window for the spring."

I moved my mother to Toronto from the farm so she could be nearby, and so that she didn't have to live entirely on her own. I assumed she would be lonely, she would find it impossible to manage the affairs of the farm, and that if she stayed every corner of the old house would hold for her some minor episode or image from the past. Every April-flooded basement and crooked Christmas tree, every fight with my father which ended in slammed doors and shouted promises of divorce, all my illegal crayon wall drawings (now covered with violet wallpaper) would come out at her from the walls, voices sounding up from the red brick foundation. Maybe I'm wrong about that, though; my mother was not likely to be so haunted. Still now, when I remember her face before and after the move to the city, there is a difference. She lived in Toronto only three years before she too died, but I see her life there as impossibly extended. A grey pattern of small domestic tasks, television, long moments gazing out the apartment window at the crawling activity on the streets below. I remember, or at least I remember imagining her there for a whole other lifetime. One that went on in a chronic state of absence, without narrative, notice or event.

When she first came to Toronto my mother and I spent our mornings looking through pictures of condo projects in the real estate section. Places with important-sounding descriptions and names borrowed from old English estates told us that we would be missing a very special opportunity if we did not "explore" their "new world of living." I asked what was important to her: Was she bothered by the idea of a high-rise, or would she prefer a flat in a renovated Victorian? She said she didn't mind, they all looked very nice. I told her that some of these buildings had indoor pools, exercise rooms where they held group aerobic classes for seniors, activities- nights through the week. She said she doubted she would be in any hurry to do those kinds of things with strangers.

On the weekends and some of the evenings I would drive her around to see some of these buildings. Sometimes we would park and go in as far as their mirror-walled lobbies, to stand beneath the icicle-glass chandelier. "Well, well," my mother would say absently to the brass door handles, tuxedoed doorman or impossibly huge potted trees.

"What about this place?" I would ask her.

"I wonder who they get to come in to water all those plants," she would say.

I see my mother before the window over the kitchen sink in our old house. It is winter: outside the fields in sun-reflecting whiteness. On the sill there are blue bottles that once contained wine vinegar but now stand empty, the sunlight passing through them in watercolour shafts. She wears a red striped shirt of my father's rolled up past her elbows and open wide at her freckled neck. Her skin and clothes smell of dish detergent and cigarette smoke. She is telling me about the year she lived in Dublin when she was a girl. She was there to go to college, to learn to be a nurse.

"I was only a wee thing, I don't know, I guess I would be seventeen or eighteen. We would work all day and late into the night. At class in the morning and doing rounds with the sister the rest of the time. And afterwards we would go out to the dance halls or see the last half of a play and then be up for eight o'clock the next morning.

We were crazy then! Go, go, go! Never stopped!" She shakes her head and looks at me, as if even now she can't believe it all. But it doesn't sound like something she particularly misses, either. There is no edge of sadness in her words, or even dreamy nostalgia. Just an amused, head-shaking wonder.

"And the doctors were always asking us out. They had no other chance to meet girls, you see, they were always working in the hospital. But they were great fun, taking you here and there. In those days people just went out like that, they didn't take things so seriously. We didn't talk about marriage until we had to, until you were ready or had gotten in trouble. Then you had to, of course, but I suppose today you don't have to do anything you don't want. We never had those choices to make, so we just had as much fun as we could for the time."

She never married one of the doctors, although she always said she was asked, over and over. Sitting at the kitchen table I would ask her why she never accepted. "Oh no. No, no," she would say, her back to me and her hands in the sink. She said it as if their proposals were only ridiculous jokes. "You see, they were only having their fun with me," she'd explain. Instead, after she had gotten her nurse's certificate, she moved back to the family farm in Sligo. There she met my father at her sister's wedding. He was in the wedding party, the groom's best friend. Soon after, they too got married, and not much later moved to Canada. The reasons for their emigration, or the details of their courtship, were never made clear to me. It was as if her youth ended in that one moment, the meeting of my father at her sister's wedding. She would recall their dancing together after the band had left and been replaced by a single-speaker phonograph playing Sinatra, but that was it. The stories of Ireland, of girls' games and family characters would end there, with the two of them dancing in the front room of the town's only hotel to the tinny sound of American brass. "Chicago, New York! What did we know of those places Sinatra would sing about?" she would laugh and go no further. After that, it seemed her life stopped being so insanely full of activity. The stories of spontaneity and foolishness were replaced by episodes in my growing up, the struggle of maintaining the farm in the first years, or the minor scandals of neighbours' families.

We decided finally on one place, based on its promise of "huge terraces overlooking splendid parks". I wondered where such land existed in Toronto, but kept any questions to myself. We booked a viewing time with a sales agent named Anthony Rose. I told him over the phone that his name sounded very distinctive, but I immediately regretted it. It came to me that I had borrowed my adjective from the condo's ad: "*distinctive* residences". "Well! Thank you!" he said with an almost theatrical false modesty, delivered in a nobody's-ever-noticed-before tone. And then softer, in a confiding whisper, "But you know, let me tell you, it's not my real name. I just made it up. But I like it!"

When we arrived at the building, Anthony Rose was there to greet us. I remember he talked a lot, and he wore a beautiful, expensive-looking suit. "How are you today madam? Ready for a little tour?" he said to my mother, bending over at the waist to level his smiling head upon her. She nodded and worked up a difficult smile herself. Then he took her unnecessarily by the arm into his clean and book-less office, where he offered us coffee and doughnuts. "Actually, my mother and I prefer tea," I told Anthony Rose. "Oh you know, so do I!" he said, but did not get us any. Instead he moved us out to be taken around the main floor, to see the "lifestyle amenities" before going up to the condo itself. As we moved down the silent hallways that smelled of new carpet and varnish, Anthony Rose kept urging us to poke our faces into different rooms, each of which offered some luxury, service or ornament. By now his talking was mostly addressed to me, particularly when he spoke of money. He didn't think my mother would be able to understand the meaning of the figures, the urgency of the situation which they implied.

"So, as I told you, this unit is now priced at one-sixty-two-seven, but I can't say it'll be around for long. Not at *that* price. We have a couple other layouts available at this point, but if you don't mind my saying, I think this one best suits the needs of your Ma."

The needs of my Ma. "Needs" meant old age, fragility, the desire to be close to a hospital. "Ma" meant people from the country: ordinary, decent, a little senseless.

"This seems like her sort of place," he added after a moment of apparent thought, as if sincerely considering its suitability. I wondered, watching my mother's forced look of amusement, if he could possibly be more wrong.

I see my mother digging around in the flower bed that lay beneath the front picture window at our old house. In the summer, in the few hours after dinner and before dark, she would come out and work in that muddy square that she enlarged each spring until it crept around the other side of the house and almost out to the drive. Usually I would come out with her, sometimes to help, but mostly to sit on the brick step and talk, or just gaze out in a full-stomach fog. She never seemed to mind my being there, even if I sat in silence.

When we talked, we talked about little things. How strange and sort of sad it was that the morning glory would bloom only once, or how much the sound of the cicada was like an electric generator's hum. Once, the summer before my last year of high school, she asked me if I would ever come back here. I told her I didn't know what she meant.

"Will you ever come back here to work the farm? Like when your father gets too old to do it himself," she explained with her knees at the base of a rose bush.

"No. I don't think so," I remember answering without a thought, without even considering the potential for insult. But she went right back to the branch she was pruning without pause, without drama.

"No, you wouldn't," she said without turning her head. "What would you do if you did?"

As Anthony Rose showed her the apartment's small assets, switches and kitchen conveniences, my mother maintained a look of keen interest. Everything he said appeared to be impressing her more and more. This was a fancy showcase, an exhibition at the C.N.E. showing how we might live a century from now. But here it was being offered to her now: the food disposal, dimmer switches, the silver-doored garbage chute that, when opened, exhaled a warm, papery breath from six floors below.

All the time my mother said little except, at the moments when she felt obliged to be impressed, she used the same word over and over. "Magnificent!" she said. I had never heard her use it before. The word itself seemed to her a welcome discovery, something to hold onto. It functioned as a bridge between herself and the person she believed should be here, an accomplished woman being guided through the luxurious rewards of her work, her life. She knew she was supposed to be impressed. If my father was there, he would've been too busy pointing out all the inadequacies and useless expenses to allow my mother a chance for comment. But now she was alone. This would be hers alone.

As we moved before the bare picture windows which framed the bundle of downtown office towers, she moved her head from side to side, as if carefully checking everything out. Her lips were tight and pale from the work of maintaining a showy, unmoving smile. "Magnificent!" she said to nobody in particular as we stepped silently through the sterile rooms of off-white walls and grey carpet. The space absorbed us, leaving my mother's unlikely word to fill every vacant corner. Again and again its royal syllables were formed by her thin, colourless lips. "Magnificent!" she said. "Oh yes, magnificent!"

Al Purdy

THE IRON ROAD

Riding the boxcars out of Winnipeg in a
morning after rain so close to
the violent sway of fields it's
like running and running
naked with summer in your mouth

— from "Transient"

In 1936 I rode the freight trains west to Vancouver. It was year Six of the Great Depression, called the Hungry Thirties in a later era. The poor were poorer; the rich sometimes hesitated before buying a third Cadillac; farmers traded eggs for groceries; the mood of nearly everyone was bleak and discouraged. Jobless Canadians by the thousands were also riding the freights from town to town, searching for work desperately.

I was 17 in that dark year. An only son and much pampered by a doting mother, I had never been more than a hundred miles from home. What made me leave? Why didn't I stay in Trenton, where things were safe, comfortable and easy, going to church just often enough to silence neighbourhood criticism, pretending to look for work when I got tired of loafing? Why didn't I do that?

I don't know. Perhaps I was bored. Besides, wasn't the west coast the evergreen Chamber of Commerce country, the Vancouver Lotosland, where drunks don't freeze in winter: they just lie on green lawns and gently mildew?

At first I hitch hiked. West to Toronto, north to Sudbury where I slept in a used car lot, raped by passionate mosquitoes. Then west again on the Trans-Canada Highway to a point just north of Sault Ste. Marie. And had to stop. There was no more highway. It hadn't been built yet.

At Searchmont, a little CP Railway watering hole, I decided to ride the box cars west, despite fear of railway cops.

The train arrived at midnight, a black thing with flashing lights, groaning painfully. It drank like an animal, great sloshing gulps from the dark water tower. Brakies walked the trackside cinders, swinging bullseye lanterns. Then a sudden shudder, the couplings' iron vertebrae jerk spastically in imitation of life; the far-distant engine sends multiple explosions backward like firecrackers.

"It's gonna go, it's gonna go," I whispered to a fellow wayfarer crouching beside me. "Naw, it ain't," he said in a normal tone. "Wait for the highball. That's what tells ya —"

Moments later the engine's voice in the night went "Toot-Toot" almost timidly. We ran for it.

I clambered into what seemed half a box car, the top half removed, a gondola that had once held coal. Wearing a waterproof canvas jacket, clutching a bag containing an extra pair of shoes, shaving cream and razor, and a large hunting knife. I was equipped for adventure, but for this kind?

Overhead the stars moved crazily. Dark trees rushed past in the bordering forest. All around me, coal particles danced invisibly on the gondola's wooden floor, my own bones shuddering in sympathy. And it started to rain, a slow drizzle whose velocity was increased by the train's speed into a barrage of stinging missiles against my face. Blazing cinders from the engine flew past, often crunching in my teeth with a bitter taste. North into nowhere we plunged, while I huddled miserably wet under the forward wall of the gondola.

Hours passed. I dozed and slept in acute discomfort, then woke into an abnormal stillness. Dopey and half-conscious, I decided that the train must have stopped, leaving me feeling vulnerable, no longer a moving target. As if when trundling along at forty miles an hour I had been unnoticeable and hence secure?

In half-light and half-rain I stirred, desperate to escape that dirty coal car and the water that trickled down my neck. Clambering down the steel ladder I searched for shelter, box cars shouldering endlessly on either side. Ripping the strip of metal seal from a box car door with my hunting knife, I tried to haul it open. The thing wouldn't budge. I went back to my gondola, bewildered and miserable.

A black-slickered railway cop materialized in the rain. He climbed into the gondola, regarding me with distaste. "You broke the seal on a box car," he accused. I admitted the charge meekly, knowing he wouldn't believe a denial anyway. He locked me inside a caboose with bars on the windows and a padlocked door.

Inside this railway prison I contemplated my fate, which didn't seem too terrible. After all, breaking a piddling strip of metal couldn't be very important, could it? But what would my mother think of all this, her only child locked in a backwoods prison and now beginning to get very hungry? Or the United Church minister who had awarded me a book-prize for attending services 44 Sundays of the year?

At noon the CP Railway cop escorted me to his house nearby for lunch. Along the way people glanced curiously at the unconvicted but undoubtedly guilty criminal. And by this time I discovered that the little railway town I had landed in was called Hawk Junction, 165 miles north of Sault Ste. Marie.

I sat at table with the policeman, his wife and small daughter. He grinned at me, a little more human with his family present. Encouraged, I ventured to ask if breaking box car seals was a very serious offence. He grinned again. "You could get two years." That was serious, in fact it was appalling. My face must have showed how I felt. They looked at me, the cop inexorably, his wife with sympathy, the child without understanding. "Tomorrow I'll take you back to the Soo for trial," the blue uniform said with finality. His wife gave me some *Ladies' Home Journals* to read, and I was returned to the lock-up.

In my prison caboose I was jolted again: two years! What would my mother say? Or the neighbours think? And worse, to be shut away from sunlight for two years!

With a great deal of care I examined the car's interior again. Its windows were all broken, presumably by earlier prisoners trying to escape. But the steel bars of these windows were firmly embedded in the frame, and moved not at all when I tried to shake them. The door was wood, opening inward, secured with padlock and metal hasp on the outside. It was discouraging. Other prisoners had apparently failed to escape, despite being older and stronger than me.

Still, they might have overlooked something. The window bars were obviously much too formidable. That left only the door. It was fairly heavy, with hinge keys outside so they couldn't be removed from inside. I tried the door knob, releasing the latch enough to allow the door to move inward a quarter inch or so, hearing the padlock rattle in its hasp outside, and ran my fingers along the narrow springy opening between upper door and sill, pulling tentatively inward. My heart beat heavily and I felt breathless. The door was flexible enough at the top to permit my fingers to work around its edge and close on the outside.

I swung myself off the floor, body supported by finger grip

between upper sill and floor, feet jammed against the sill near my hands. And pulled. Yanked inward as if I were about to fall off a cliff and my fingers were holding to life itself. And scared, a scared boy, grown fully aware of the power and authority ranged against him, his own fear overcoming fear.

It seemed the door was too much for me. I hung high in the air for at least a couple of minutes, like a giant safety pin. And yet it was a kind of triumph to make this all-out effort, even if driven by fear. But stalemate. Then came a sound like ripping cloth. The door pulled inward abruptly, screws yanked from the outside hasp. The boy, who was not exactly me, plunged to the floor on his back, almost too scared to realize what had happened, lying there listening to a strange sound. My own laboured breath. Then peering outside, into an early Sunday afternoon. Into sunlight.

It was gloriously deserted, not a blue uniform or railway cop in sight. Everyone was digesting their midday meals peacefully, or snoozing on the sofa. Nothing visible but long parades of brick-coloured box cars ahead and behind. I felt almost too nervous and hyped-up to take advantage of this freedom. And it would be much worse to be caught escaping; they'd sock me away for life! At least the caboose-prison supplied a kind of safety, demanded nothing of me but the acceptance of events, passivity, destiny, and fate outside my hands.

I dropped quietly onto the cinders between cars. And started to walk south along the tracks. Mind in turmoil, nerves popping and pinging with the effort to control panic. No more freight trains for me. It occured to me that the Trans-Canada Highway, ending north of Sault Ste. Marie, continued again farther west at Port Arthur and Fort William. I'd get there somehow. In the meantime, people were to be avoided; they'd report seeing a gangling youngster with nervous eyes, wearing a blue windbreaker, to the police. There'd be something in my face that would give me away. Something criminal? I couldn't believe I was really a criminal. Just rather stupid.

Furtively, feeling very noticeable, I headed south toward Sault Ste. Marie. Slinking close to the sheltering box cars, peering back and forth. But the railway divisional point was quiet; only one sound, the crunch of cinders under my feet that sounded like small explosions. Then another patter of feet, small feet, like a child's, following me. The source of the sound was on the other side of those marching box cars. But no use stopping now; that would indicate I'd heard them.

Eyes fixed straight ahead I hiked south. The footsteps continued, more or less keeping pace with mine. Surely whoever was over there, just out of sight, was aware of me, had some kind of dangerous intention. I tried to catch a glimpse of them in the openings between cars. Nothing. Just the sound of feet on cinders.

The marching squadrons of box cars ended. I emerged into open daylight, without protection of any kind against curious eyes. It was like being naked, exposed and vulnerable. But the mystery of those pattering feet was solved. A dog rushed out from behind the last car, frisking at my heels, wagging his tail, wanting to be patted. A brown dog. Knee-high and very friendly. He liked me, migawd, he liked me! I waved him off furiously: "Get away, get the hell outa here! I hate dogs!" At that moment I certainly did hate dogs. A man or boy walking quietly and blending into the landscape is one thing; a dog racing around him like a mad dervish is another. At least he wasn't yapping, at least.

The brown pooch dashed at me playfully, crouched on front paws, ready to leap left or right if I showed any inclination for fun and games. His bright eyes said: "Let's have some action, let's be friends and enjoy life." I groaned inside. And picked up a stick from beside the tracks and threw it backwards as far as I could toward the miserable little railway town. A mistake. The dog chased it, brought it back to me, crouched again, the stick clenched between his jaws, wanting another throw. I ignored him, or tried to ignore him. That wasn't possible. He barked, not loudly but enough to attract attention if anyone happened to be watching.

Thus far I'd done all the wrong things in my reactions to the dog. Resolved to ignore him, I marched south without looking at him. The last houses ended at a railway bridge across a wide river. The dog gave up on the town-side of the bridge. With a last disappointed bark he trotted off toward the houses. I wasn't the sort of playmate he had in mind; nor was he to my liking. But his tail was wagging again on the return journey.

One hundred and sixty-five miles of walking railway ties, a distance duly noted by regularly spaced mile markers on the telegraph poles. Walking the ties is rather like having invisible chains around your ankles, permitting only a certain length of step. The ties are spaced at such short distances that stepping from one to the next is too short a step, but stepping two ahead is too long. A small thing, but if you have to walk 165 miles it becomes important. And I was afraid to return south again by freight train: they'd be looking for me.

Thick spruce and maple forest crowded in on either side of the tracks. It was late afternoon, and I was hungry again. I stopped at an isolated cottage, knowing I couldn't walk all that distance on an empty stomach. For a dollar, the housewife made me some generous sandwiches, providing also a hunk of cheese and some cold meat. My jumpy nerves were quieting down now as I considered the possibility of pursuit. Probably I'd be safe for the rest of the day, but tomorrow the hounds would be in full cry. The hounds? Migawd, they wouldn't have dogs, would they? I dismissed the thought as ridiculous, but it started my nerves jumping again.

Thinking it best to take no chances, I decided to walk along the edge of the bush, just out of sight of the tracks. Follow the railway from a distance of twenty-five or thirty feet inside the woods. Keep an eye on any possible activities along the tracks. Work crews had Sunday off, but the little two-man push-and-pull railway scooters might be abroad. Whatever. I plunged into the forest.

It was soft and spongy going. Trees and bushes had been cleared some distance from the tracks, but new growth was again springing into life. Angry little creeks occasionally sluiced from the forest and under culverts. Despite the fairly chilly temperature I was sweating, and flies buzzed around my head. After half and hour of plunging down hillocks or staggering up them, I headed back to the railway tracks. But there were no tracks.

My mind told me the railway was only a short distance to the left, since I had veered right and away from them into the forest. But I'd wandered into the trees farther than I'd intended; now everything looked the same. No landmarks, just trees. And never in my life have I been able to distinguish north from south or east from west. Other people may say casually, that's north; but I can get lost in a telephone booth.

The day had grown dark and gloomy, and without the sun to give me some small indication of direction I was tangled in a maze. I kept trying to veer left through the forest. Unless I had lost my mind completely, the railway was in that direction.

After two hours or so of aimless wandering I knew I was lost, admitted it to myself. By this time all movement of my insides had speeded up: I was pouring sweat; blood seemed to be coursing at high speed through my body; my heart thumped heavily; my face felt hot, feverish. The process of rational thinking had stopped; images of home and fear and prison flew into my brain and out. Nothing in my experience had prepared me for this different reality:

like suddenly being born, with only scattered flashes of awareness, looking around and realizing that your mother's face and the faces of doctors and nurses were something else, were trees. The world itself, nothing but trees.

I started to run. Up hill and down, slamming into trees full length and bouncing off, face whipped by stinging branches, tears pouring from eyes, panting and sobbing with fear. Fear not of being hurt, slammed by hard fists and pain, or the mental fear of being inadequate, incapable of understanding ordinary things — but fear of death. Leaving my body to rot in this brilliant green forest, mossy bones discovered years later by some woodsman or hunter. Fear of not being.

Running. I scooped handfuls of water from a creek, dashed it into mouth and over my face. And kept running. Aware of hunger, I chewed at the sandwiches crushed in my canvas bag and kept running while eating. Legs buckling, face scratched and bleeding from whiplash bushes, lungs heaving with exhaustion I reeled through the forest. And with the onset of darkness collapsed finally on a hillside, wrapping myself around a tree trunk in nearly foetal position, as if the tree were a vegetable mother.

And started to think about God. All through childhood and early adolescence I had been afraid of Him. He knew too much, comprehended all my secret thoughts, dislikes and weaknesses in the enormous cosmos of His mind. When I had attended church for 44 Sundays of the year, receiving a book for reward, the reason for doing so had been this angry all-knowing God, not the book. I resented His authority, His omniscience, but never allowed my resentment to surface in my conscious mind for fear of His vengeance.

But some of the irreverent books I'd been reading in the last few years had begun to have an effect. I was no longer very sure that God actually existed — that He hadn't been invented by men who wanted to keep other men in continued subjection and fear. This was next door to atheism. But now I needed Him, needed help badly. And threw myself on His mercy, begged and prayed, mentioning heavy transgressions against His laws and His Holy Bible. The Bible had a special significance for me: after first learning to read, I had studied certain implicitly sexual passages, and I knew that He in his blue sky conning tower knew everything I was thinking.

"Get me outa here," I prayed, "and I'll do anything at all. Go to church, return to school, obey my mother, anything." And was vaguely ashamed of myself, for the appeal seemed to come directly out of my own weakness rather than conviction about the deity's existence. Never mind, take no chances. Just in case. Cover all the angles. "Please God, Please God" — and fell asleep.

The tree was an uncomforting mother. I woke up several times in the night, having lost orientation, not knowing whether I was locked in a barred caboose, comfortably tucked in my own bed at home, or chilled and cold in the midst of a forest. I floated in some dark limbo of the mind, shrunken and foetal, withdrawn into the basic spore of myself.

When grey light filtered through the trees and realization of being lost sank in even more deeply, there seemed no reward or recourse in getting up and moving around. Conversely, staying there on the cold ground was uncomfortable. I debated the issues with myself, weighing the disadvantages of action or non-action. They cancelled each other out. And obviously now God was not going to take a hand, not just yet anyway. I was on my own.

As the light increased to a grey ambience in which there was no visible sun, needs of the body became pressing. I had to piss. But that could be managed without altering the situation: I could open my fly and piss sideways down the hill. But I was thirsty as well. And thirst could not be satisfied while lying among great trees on a hillside; lower country with a creek or pond must be found. As I thought of these things, the silence began to enter me. A silence broken only by the faint continual ringing in my head to which the brain returned occasionally with a question. As if there was a place in my mind, apart from the reasoning brain, where activities were going on that could not be fathomed, a place barred to me.

I was seized with curiosity: what could be happening in my head which I did not know about? Whatever it was seemed neither friendly nor unfriendly, just indifferent. And yet it was concerned with me, its vehicle and necessary carrying case. My thoughts roamed around in my head, searching for the location of these and other activities, a point I could come back to and ask questions. Question: *Who are you?* Question: *What do you want?* No answer. Only that soft ringing sound, denoting the other was still there. Perhaps everywhere, co-existing and omnipresent?

The forest was not dark and gloomy but pervaded with luminous grey light, surrounding green branches and, pooled below, shadowing tree trunks. The ground was spongy with dead leaves and rotting branches, tall trees interspersed with moss-grown stumps where loggers had been working years ago. I chewed on the last of my sandwiches and drank at a clear stream. There was a heavy, depressed feeling in my stomach and chest, as I trudged in any direction where I could push a thought through an opening between trees and hope to find it again later.

Despairing, I wandered through the woods, not rushing around madly but wandering slowly through a leafy maze in which everything looked the same. Then a shape I couldn't identify from a distance, which turned out to be an old hunting camp, built of mossy logs with the roof fallen in. About ten feet square. And so ancient there was no hope the hunters or loggers would ever return.

Having found my continual leftward turning futile, I tried to straighten out the curve in my progress by sighting on a tree ahead of me to the right and heading for that. Then repeating the process. Reaching a hilltop, I climbed another tree to search for some landmark. But at a height of thirty feet or so I could see nothing but greyness, nothing.

Twice more I returned to that hunting camp, the woods myth of anyone lost in a forest tending to circle back to the same place thus being verified. It occured to me that perhaps the circular route I was taking would get smaller and smaller and finally become the circumference of my own head, causing me to reel and stumble from tree to imaginary tree. One possible plan: to close my eyes and stand perfectly still, fall down and not rise again.

In a greyness like sleep but not sleep, I heard an alien sound, muffled by mist and distance. Engines snorting softly, box cars shuffling backward and forward, steel couplings jolting together. It came from the railway yards at Hawk Junction only a few miles away, but it might as well have come from the moon. Entirely directionless, the sound was sometimes behind me, sometimes in front.

"Goddamn the trains!" I whispered in the greyness. Then "Goddamn God!" But that last was sobering, using His name to blaspheme Him. And it was contrary to my unstated philosophy: Take no chances. I shuddered at the possibilities being raised. Vengeance is mine, saith the Lord. The thundering preacher at King Street United in Trenton upreared from his varnished pulpit like an angry spectre and pointed a bony finger at me and shouted: *Sin*.

I walked tired, rested on my feet tired, walked in a dream — listening for any possible sounds besides the shunting trains at Hawk Junction. And ate my last cheese and meat when hungry, drinking at clear streams in the forest. The junk in my dufflebag was abandoned the third time I hit that hunting camp. An extra pair of running shoes, a tube of shaving cream with razor (I shaved only once a week), and other unnecessary items. They were extra weight to carry, useless when you might be dead soon.

Discovering old logging roads with renewed hope, I followed them until they tailed off into nothing or joined other old tracks that were equally ambiguous. A dozen years at least must have gone by since this area was logged over.

The passage of time could only be estimated. I had no watch, and the sun was invisible. My second night in the woods arrived as only a slow thickening of the greyness, which seemed more and more a prelude to rain. But there was no shelter, not even a stone overhang. Yet for some reason I can't explain, the bugs scarcely bothered me at all. No animals either, except the odd rabbit and a few squirrels.

A darker knot of consciousness inside the darkness, I chose the side of a hill again for sleeping site. Low-lying ground I thought a vulnerable area. Which wasn't conscious thinking at all; perhaps that different part of my brain which I called the Other was responsible. Perhaps also when I slept the Other was in command, as some kind of guardian and warder. If I awoke suddenly and came to full control of my thought processes quickly enough, would it be possible to find out more about this Other, whom I was now convinced existed and functioned inside myself?

Night passed as a succession of uneasy dozings, stirrings into incomplete consciousness, a condition in which it was impossible to distinguish between shadowy night figures and the blurred images of my own night thoughts. That barred caboose-prison with broken windows flashed into my head. The moment when the caboose door exploded inward recurred, and I was again too surprised at freedom to be elated.

Rain whispering on leaves awoke me, a light drizzle that increased as morning wore on. My waterproof jacket ensured I stayed mostly dry above the waist, but did nothing for legs and feet. I was half-drowned in less than an hour, plunging through undergrowth and ferny clearings. I was hungry, and kept trying to catch a glimpse of the sun, which I hadn't seen for two days.

A passage in the Bible occurred to me. Something like the text that runs: *Shall a man by taking thought add one cubit to his stature?* Something bright flashed and glimmered in my mind, beyond all the greyness: that bright green river. The one I had crossed on a bridge from Hawk Junction, followed by a frisking unfaithful mongrel when I first headed south.

The river. The bridge. They formed two sides of a geographic triangle in my mind. The third part was this dripping forest.

Half-drowned, miserable and hungry as I was, a blessed euphoric bloom of hope: the odds two against one, and favoring me, that I could stumble on either the river or railway tracks that continued south after crossing the bridge. And paid myself the first compliment possible in several days, ego and hope reviving together.

A single glimpse of the sun was all I needed, even a bright spot where the fiery ball was burning a hole in thick clouds. I climbed a hill, then shinnied up a tree with low-growing branches. Slid back down the horny trunk, trying to keep sighted on one silver-grey spot amid its surrounding dark-grey sky; sighted from one slightly more prominent tree to another, staying on high ground, heading north, glorious north, glorious sun. Running again. That was a mistake. Panting. Dizzy. A gamut of emotions, fizzing and alcoholic in racing brain and heart.

Keep thinking. Don't forget to think, the way you did before. But the mind wanders; it won't stay fastened to one thing or place for very long. The thudding rhythm of my feet paces my brain. Clementine occurs to me. "In a cabin, in a canyon, excavating for a mine/Lived a miner, a forty-niner, and his daughter, Clementine."

Singing. Not even feeling foolish about it; rushing through wet undergrowth, roaring the chorus of Clementine: "Oh my darling, oh my darling . . . ." What was the rest of it? "Took her ducklings to the river, ever morning just at nine/Stubbed her toe upon a sliver, and went down in the foaming brine." Why was it brine, how could the river be salt?

Squelching breathless through thick wet undergrowth on marshy ground, I nearly fell into a strange river. And still felt crazy from two days lost. What's your name, river? Tell me your name.

It was a fast-flowing green river, and it was there, it was actually and blessedly there. I followed its banks to the right, and the right had to be more or less east, and *right*. Rain stopped, the sun beamed down. There was a bridge, *the* bridge. My bridge, not Hart Crane's or anybody else's.

Soberly now, I walked south again on the CPR main line, careless of possible observers. My nose snuffling a little, body chilled in damp clothes. But they dried quickly in the reappearing sun. East of the railway tracks some fishermen , taking down their tent and breaking camp. I asked them if they knew when there were any trains going south. They said there was a passenger train just a few minutes from now on which they were returning to the Soo. They said I could ride behind the coal car if I wanted to take a chance. I did want to. They were Americans, one of them gave me a US dollar without my asking for it. He took me for a bum. I was. And grateful for warmth of any kind.

When the highball toot-tooted, the box cars and passenger cars hitched on behind stirred their steel bones, moving a foot or two indecisively. Then chuffed south. In the nearby bushes a dirty hobo tensed his muscles and dashed for a ladder behind the coal car.

And the rain of cinders began, stinging my skin, watering eyes, blackening everything like the Biblical rain of locusts. Feet braced against shuddering couplings, I endured. I was still euphoric at having rediscovered the world. I was stung with cinders, hungry as an adolescent wolf, snuffling with incipient pneumonia, and damn glad to be alive.

We stopped a couple of times on our progress south. Not for cities or towns — there were none — but at small clusters of houses, perhaps for hunters or fishermen who had made appointments to be picked up, as had my own personal Americans. When the blurred mileposts slowed and a few houses appeared beside the tracks, indicating the Soo was just ahead, my nerves started to prickle. Had the CPR cop wired ahead that an escapee was on the loose? How much time would be added to the two-year sentence because of my jail-break? And would my mother be able to visit me in prison?

Jumping off the train before reaching the station would be the best plan. But its speed was such that I'd be sure to break my neck and need a new skeleton after hitting the cinders. Courage and bravery were silly dictionary words not applicable to me, and I knew, I knew with certainty that I didn't have the nerve to jump.

The train steamed and roared past brick-coloured sheds, slower now, but still fast enough to render people mere snapshots. Each brief glimpse between the cars left them standing stockstill, like storewindow dummies . . . .

A wooden platform, then the dull red station, drifting past slowly and ever more slowly . . . . When the train stopped, my body climbed down. It stood on the platform as if it belonged there, legally, like the real passengers.

And deceived no one. The inevitable cop materialized beside me. He was sausage-shaped, blue-coated and silver-buttoned. Pointing a schoolteacherish finger at me, he said, "Stay right here! I'll be back to deal with you after I've looked over the train."

Frozen stiff as a codfish on that railway platform, I stayed there for several moments while the well-dressed paying passengers looked at me as if I were an unwelcome foreigner. Then the voice of that Other, so knowledgeable about mathematics and triangles, spoke to me. And I felt a deep and abiding affection for him. He said, "Tarry not upon the order of thy going. Depart forthwith. Fuck off!"

And I did.

Reviews

Kate Sterns, *Thinking About Magritte.*
HarperCollins, 1992

Surreal and lyrical, *Thinking about Magritte* draws images from both the real city of Kingston and the dream city of Kate Sterns's imagination. For Kingstonian readers, this book is an odd but interesting experience. We can't help but search through the array of characters and settings, looking for the street people we've seen and the places we've been to.

Not that this is anything like a *roman à clef.* The book is made of memory inflated and quickened by graceful fantasy and caustic humor. The real enjoyment, for a non-Kingstonian, is in watching Kate Sterns spin out a wild notion and then bring it up short with a comic remark. Even though I harbor vague suspicions about the sources of certain characters, the individuals in the novel are strictly themselves, living their own fictional lives and meeting their separate fates.

Not counting flashbacks and digressions, the story covers one night. In the center of the ageing city of Limestone, somewhere in North America, we follow the nocturnal adventures of a group of tenants from a run-down house that was chopped up into apartments years ago. The troupe includes Cowboy (a thirty year old hydrocephalic child/man), Frank (a middle-aged former mental patient who believes he is pregnant), Maxine, Old River, Doris and others. A tireless family of acrobats, who may or may not be angels, watches over them all while swinging from the spires and gables of the city's fanciful 19th century architecture.

The clearest narrative thread in the book is provided by Maxine, Cowboy and Old River. Maxine and Old River are the two halves of a drunken, chaotic and often violent marriage. When Cowboy is sent out to find the delinquent Old River, he does it partly out of his innocent desire to please Maxine and partly because he's wary of her anger and intensity. Poor Cowboy is immature for his age and easily manipulated. He wants to please and wants to be helpful, but his obvious deformity makes him the occasional target of local goons and his only constant companion is loneliness.

As he makes his way to the Plaza Hotel, where Old River is most likely to be, Cowboy meets Ernie, Savage and Frank, Fastboy, Doris, and the ghost of Mrs. Munscher, who was killed by a faulty hairdryer in 1969. The characters are picaresque and the events are surreal. Temporarily forgetting his quest, Cowboy devotes part of the night to finding his late mother, the long dead and almost saintly Lily, once a hairdresser in a salon called The Rainbow House of Beauty.

Like the acrobats in her book, Kate Sterns takes a lot of chances and she has to be admired for her daring. Small flaws, however, crop up and detract from the dreamy bravado. For instance, Sterns's humor is flip, wise, and more than a little sophisticated; but sometimes she can't resist putting a really good line into the mouth of someone who isn't smart enough or sane enough to actually say such a thing. Most of her people are half mad or deluded and have to step out of character on occasion to say things that are brilliantly funny.

Of course when it works, her comic touch is wonderful. Her narrator's voice has some delightfully nasty things to say about a tacky all-night restaurant:

> Waitresses with connect-the-dot eyebrows, lacquered hair and orthopaedic shoes performed a dance peculiar to Libra's. One hand went up, balancing a tray, while the other removed an unwanted arm from around the waist. The bottom swung around to avoid being pinched while the feet skillfully stomped on the cockroaches scuttling brazenly across the floor. Patrons called it the Libra shuffle.

By the way, most residents of downtown Kingston can direct you to the place, should you wish to go there.

Thinking About Magritte is an enjoyable and effervescent book. Considering that this is a first novel, it is a considerable achievement. There are flaws in the book, and they are hard to distinguish from the quirks, of which there are many. Some should have been caught by an alert editor, one who would have know for instance that *la rêve* should be *le rêve*. These quibbles will no doubt be cleaned up and forgotten in Kate Sterns's later works, which I and many other Limestone inhabitants look forward to reading.

Eric Folsom

Ingrid MacDonald, *Catherine, Catherine.*
Women's Press, 1991

Ingrid MacDonald is a writer and broadcaster for feminist and lesbian and gay media. Her story "Travelling West" was a winner in the 1990 PRISM *international* Fiction Contest and is included in her short story collection, *Catherine, Catherine.*

While these are identified as lesbian short stores, the characters are not exclusively sexual beings. The first section, "Overwintering", uses conventional seasonal motifs to describe the waning of one relationship and the waxing of a new love. The last four stories are in first person, and range in mood from tempestuous to childlike. "In a Second Language", with its evocation of school and church coercion, recalls the confident, apocalyptic language of Jeannette Winterson's novel of an evangelical childhood and coming out, "Oranges Are Not the Only Fruit".

The strongest section is the middle third, entitled "Catherine, Catherine". In three parts, it presents testimony about a woman accused of "sodomy" in Prussia in 1721.

Catherine Margareth Linck escapes poverty and oppression by donning men's clothes and joining the army of King Frederick William. She leads a checkered career, deserting, and escaping execution twice when her "true nature", her female gender, earns her a pardon. She discovers the temptations of the flesh and of drink, marries, endures the death of her mother and grave illness of her wife, then is accused by her mother-in-law, tortured and confesses to sodomy.

Three versions of her story are provided in testimony by Catherine herself, who also goes by the names Cornelius, Peter, Anastatius; by her interrogators; and by Catherine Muhlhahn, her wife.

MacDonald convincingly replicates the biblical rhythms of oral histories of this period. Clearly our sympathies are with the lesbian Catherines who are martyred. In presenting the historical social realities, MacDonald implies that their fates were shared by most women, indeed most of the lower class, throughout history:

> From my birth I have rebelled against my flesh and wanted to live as a man, for a woman is forever spoken to by life and forever forbidden to respond, but the magistrate has no sympathy for me . . . [I] watch[ed] my beloved mother carry stones and grow crops, humiliated by the

107

dryness of the unyielding earth. I saw how my life would emulate hers with its meagre harvest and how sorrow would echo through my face into the faces of my children.

Soldier Catherine, by taking another woman as her wife, donning men's attire and even a mechanical penis, is an obvious threat to the established order. In wearing this disguise she is claiming social and geographical mobility.

As Marina Warner writes, one of Joan of Arc's greatest offences and threat to the established order was her transvestism. While wearing men's clothes offered women practical protection from assault, and mobility, it also has mystical and magical overtones. It is a kind of usurpation and renunciation of the world — and of womanhood, with its associations with beauty, luxury and pleasure.

St. Catherine was the patron of unmarried women — she represented courage, autonomy, book learning, culture. For MacDonald, both Catherines are tortured and suffer for their independence — and for that of all women.

In this collection, MacDonald shows she is able to write in many voices. In tackling historical themes about the repression of lesbians and women in general, she seems to have found a career's worth of themes.

Cheryl Sutherland

M.G. Vassanji, *Uhuru Street*.
McClelland & Stewart, 1992

This collection of 16 stories is Vassanji's third book. His first, *The Gunny Sack* (1989), which straddles geographical, cultural and literary boundaries to evoke the complex history of East Africa through four generations of an Asian family living in Tanzania's Dar es Salaam, won a Commonwealth Literary Prize for a first novel. *No New Land*, published two years later, is set in Toronto and takes a searching and ironic look at Canadians through the eyes of a family of newly-arrived Asian immigrants.

Uhuru Street returns to the multicultural community of Dar and to many of the same characters and episodes of *The Gunny Sack*. It covers roughly the same chronology — "Uhuru" means independence, the author explains in his preface, and the stories follow the inhabitants of Uhuru Street (formerly Kichwele Street) during the years just preceding and following the nationalist movement. Thematically, there are parallels as well. Both books are coming-of-age stories in which nations and individuals (and less obviously the author Vassanji himself) struggle to realize their identity and secure their place in the world. Many of the stories were written around the same time as the novel; that may explain the similarities.

Stylistically, however, *The Gunny Sack* and *Uhuru Street* are very different. Vassanji's first novel is an ambitious undertaking: complex, colourful, dynamic, a panorama of East African life. Most striking is Vassanji's ability to evoke history, to re-create human action and emotion in a specific setting through tradition, folklore, dialect and detail. He uses a kind of shorthand of description to reveal the psychology of his characters, to bring forth gradually in the reader's imagination a complete and multifarious world, vivid right down to the most minute detail.

The Gunny Sack traces the evolution of character and incidents, demonstrating that each human life has an influence on history, and that the development of individuals through childhood to maturity is inextricably bound with social and political events. As characters change, so do they change others around them, until, imperceptibly, the whole historical framework of their nation has changed. At the same time, however, characters individuate history and carry it with them: the continuation of the past into the present is an inevitable shaping force, Vassanji suggests, which may be denied but never escaped.

Uhuru Street follows the same pattern, reiterates many of the same themes, contains some of the same characters, but the form Vassanji chooses here, the modernist short story, necessarily limits the scope of his achievement. What we get in *Uhuru Street* is a series of portraits, and while each is a slice of Tanzanian life, together they do little more than suggest the vastness and complexity of the human condition that Vassanji evokes in his first novel.

Nevertheless, there is much to enjoy in the short stories. Vassanji is above all a storyteller: his tales are skilfully executed, evoke a vivid sense of place, and are peopled with engaging and fascinating characters. Through characters such as Roshan Mattress, the neighbour named both for her shop and her voluptuous body; the family of five orphans — three of them mutes who cannot speak but make soft, melodious sounds when they are content and let out terrifying howls when they are angry; the mad Goan, *Tembo-mbili-potea*; and

Mzee Pipa, "the fat Indian shopkeeper . . . who would gyp you of a penny if he could," Vassanji reconstructs the Asian community of Uhuru Street and examines the forces which shape these people's lives.

Several of the stories are narrated by a boy of Indian descent living in Dar and growing up near Uhuru Street with his siblings and widowed mother. The stories follow the narrator from boyhood and the final colonial years of the 1950s to adulthood in the 1980s. In the final story of the collection, "All Worlds Are Possible Now," the narrator returns to post-colonial Tanzania (poorer since liberation, corrupt, and more hostile to Asians) after being educated overseas. The Dar of his childhood and the modern world he discovered abroad are "contrary as the ends of a cross," but the narrator feels compelled to try to reconcile them, at least within himself.

Vassanji is now a Canadian citizen living in Toronto. But it is a measure of the responsibility he feels towards his homeland, and a testimony to his profound humanist vision, that he has his narrator stay in Tanzania to reclaim and reaffirm a life there, despite tremendous cost to himself.

Tara Kainer

Contributors

Eric Breddam lives and writes in Winnipeg. "Sally" is his second published story.

Lewis DeSoto immigrated to Canada in 1967 and now lives in Vancouver. He has been active for the past ten years as a painter, and is currently working on a novel.

Vaughan Dickson lives in Toronto. "Chapters 558 and 559 in the Life of Dodge Drummond" is his first published story.

Eric Folsom edits the Kingston literary magazine *Next Exit*, and is an associate editor of *Quarry*.

Bobbie Jean Huff has published stories in *Event*, *Queen's Quarterly*, and *Quarry*. She lives in Perth, Ontario.

Tara Kainer is an associate editor of *Quarry Magazine*.

Don Maynard is a Kingston artist who has had many shows in Toronto, Montreal, and Kingston.

Al Purdy still rides the rails, each spring and fall, between his summer home in the country north of Belleville and his winter place in Sidney, B.C. A collection of his correspondence with Margaret Laurence will be published by McClelland & Stewart next year.

Andrew Pyper lives in Montréal, where he is finishing a Master of Arts in English Literature at McGill and writing short stories.

Diane Schoemperlen's most recent collection of short stories, *The Man of My Dreams* (Macmillan, 1991), was shortlisted for the Governor General's Award.

Cheryl Sutherland recently came to Kingston from Saskatoon and is now an associate editor of *Quarry* and a columnist for the *Kingston Whig-Standard*.

Jan Thornhill writes and illustrates books for children as well as for adults. Her most recent children's book is *A Tree in a Forest* (Greey de Pencier, 1991).

Carol Anne Wien is an occasional teacher of creative writing at St. Mary's University in Halifax. Several of her stories appeared in the 1988 edition of Oberon's *Coming Attractions*.

•

Quarry Magazine apologizes to Tricia McCallum, whose last name was misspelled "McCalham" in Quarry 41/2.

FICTION

$5.95

Quarry

FICTION • POETRY • ESSAYS

HARVOR • STENSON • WISEMAN

WINTER SOLSTICE

It took the snow all day
To bury the shadow
Of a white birch tree.

— Leonard Gasparini

Quarry Magazine

VOLUME 41 NUMBER 4 FALL 1992

GENERAL ISSUE

ISSN 0033-5266 ISBN 1-55082-032-X

This issue of *Quarry Magazine* was published with the financial assistance of The Canada Council and the Ontario Arts Council. *Quarry* is listed in the Canadian Periodical Index, Canadian Literature Index, Canadian Magazine Index, Canadian Business and Current Affairs Database, American Humanities Index, and Index of American Periodical Verse. Back issues are available in the original from the editor and in microform from Micromedia Limited, 20 Victoria Street, Toronto, Ontario M5C 2N8.

Manuscript submissions and subscription requests should be mailed to:

Quarry Magazine
P.O. Box 1061
Kingston, Ontario
K7L 4Y5

Manuscripts must include a SASE with Canadian postage or International Reply Coupons. Subscription rates are $20.33 for 1 year (4 issues) or $36.38 for 2 years (8 issues), GST included.

Distributed by the Canadian Magazine Publishers Association, 2 Stewart Street, Toronto, Ontario M5V 1H6.

Cover art: Kanangianak Pootoogook, *Umingmak* (1973, stonecut print).
Typesetting by Susan Hannah, Quarry Press.
Published by Quarry Press, Inc., P.O. Box 1061, Kingston, Ontario K7L 4Y5.

Publications Mail Registration Number 7293. Issued December 1992.

Contents

Elisabeth Harvor

ALWAYS THE NOISE THE NIGHTS I AM ALONE

Always the noise the nights
I am alone — the swish of a long
dress or a rodent —
comes when some much more sane sound
chooses this same moment to compete with it:
on the heels of a stopped

rustle behind the sofa a
flutter in the heart of the refrigerator motor
so that I listen and listen,
longing for it to repeat itself so
I can name it, willing to
trade frenzied stillness for a name, a name,
longing for absolute silence for diagnosis,
silence in which

there is no bird
in a brief panic beneath the cold white door's
louvered motor, no discreet click on linoleum, no click
with the ghost of a claw in it — no clock's
tick and topple in the small white plastic sack
stuffed with eggshells and peelings.

For what is a wrong rustling
in the too oddly populated silence but
a thoughtful, frightful sifting
too carefully calibrated to
dovetail to how little you were
expecting to hear it? Or a promise
broken? And the terror on both sides of the
wainscoting (for you, for the rustler), so that
you have no choice but to pray you could

peel the fear from fear
with a paring knife,
peel your way down to the
pure core of what's safe, what might be
relied on, now and forever,
world without end, amen, but no,
 it's not that simple —

for what is my life on a
night like tonight but a history of
bargains? Years and years of
trying to impress God
by showing affection to the children of others as a
way to guarantee safe passage through all of
life for my own children, a thousand and one
grudges given up for the guarded journey of a
husband on his way back from the city
on one of the rain-slicked nights of my
children's childhood — the car taking a quick
skip to the left down one of the wet evening's
highways, but then the world

wrenched right
by a tired man in a raincoat,
to say nothing of the years and years of
safe passage for certain chosen
friends and relations

in exchange for prayers
that were nothing more than
held breath or cringing. But these were always the
real prayers, the prayers of the body — only the
marketplace of the big bed by the night window,
sheets blotched with red poppies and the
damp poppies of love
used to hold them at bay for an
hour or two. All those fine old trades and
bargains of night, all of them
behind me now:

whose turn to plunder
whose turn to be tender

    You miss all that?
    I miss it.
    All the same, you like living alone?
    I do. I do like it. My books, my sunlight. My
    life. To do as I will with it.
    But you're afraid of something?
    A noise in the night.
    Why does this frighten you so?
    It means I can't always be safe.
    Why does this bother you?
    I don't want to die.
    Are you afraid you'll die in pain?
    In pain, yes, in the middle of the night.
    What else?
    The old story.
    Which is?
    No one to turn to.

Judith Cowan

THAT SORT OF THING DOESN'T BOTHER ME

It was a bright, bloated day in June, and there was a hot wind blowing the greenery around as we drove up the long approach to the Pont Laviolette, on our way south across the St. Lawrence River. For a few minutes, at the top of the big bridge, the air was cooler. Through the girders I had glimpses of miniature blue waves sparkling far below, although the real estate man, talking, never looked down. He was a man with purpose. When I'd told him that I was interested in a house in the old town, he'd glanced up from his desk, studied me briefly, and simply said no.

"What you want," he said, "is a country house, an old country house. *Une maison ancestrale.* We'll go this afternoon."

It had been hot even in the morning, and the historic centre of Trois-Rivières was silent and empty. Probably he knew that there would be no customers that day, or maybe he simply wanted a chance to get out of town. Anyway, he had a reassuring authority, this man, so here we were, on our way. He was a wonderful driver, seeming to inhabit and possess his little car like an alter ego. He was also a wonderful talker.

"*Appelez-moi Gérald,*" he said. Not Gérard, not Gerald. Gérald. As he talked, and as the summer wind blew through the car, his large blond head seemed to take up all the space inside it, and his thick hands on the wheel and his quick reflexes made him seem like part of it, and all the while his voice went on, bland and patient and unrelenting. He was sure of himself, in control, and it was easy to relax and be carried along. At the same time I wondered about taking up his time. This was a thirty-mile drive.

It was past two o'clock when we came up alongside the village church in Saint-Pierre-les-Becquets and had to stop for a diesel tractor wheeling back and forth in front of the *dépanneur*. In a cloud of black smoke and heat shimmer, there were men standing around a hole in the road. It seemed too hot to be working, and also too hot to be looking at a house for winter, too hot to be making decisions of any kind, or even to be trying to understand what other people were saying. Yet this persuasive man was still talking in a gentle, hypnotic monologue, telling me that he knew exactly what I wanted, although of course he didn't.

"*Et ça vous engage à rien . . .*" Just have a look at it, you don't have to buy, but you never know.

In the soporific heat, it was pleasant to let him talk. In time with the cadence of his sentences, his hands rose from the steering wheel, then fell back with a thump.

And as we waited to let the backhoe wheel and turn, he had a chance to show me that the thirty miles were nothing, that we were still in his territory. Through the heat ripples, he recognized one of the men standing by the excavation. He leaned out of the car and bellowed.

"*François, hé, François!*"

François turned around, slowly. In the yellow sun and the noisy smoke he wobbled in our vision, looking back at us, first at me and then at Gérald.

"*Salut François, comment ça va?*"

At first François didn't seem to recognize him. Then, through the shimmer, he moved towards us slowly, with his hands hanging at his sides. He let the diesel engine fill in some time before he spoke.

"*Salut, Gérald,* " he said, "*ça va, comme ci, comme ça.*"

He said he wasn't working this summer and he stood there, not looking into the car, staring away from us over its roof and down the road.

He didn't look like a construction worker, it was plain that he was a spectator at the hole in the road, but it was difficult to see what he might be. He was just a hard-bodied man with an alert diffident look, averting his eyes so that it wasn't easy to look back at him. From the way he said hello, it was impossible to know whether he and Gérald had last seen each other days or years before. For a moment it looked as if Gérald didn't know what to say to him either, because there was a pause.

"Yeah, well," said Gérald, "I'm just showing this lady a house, but maybe I'll look you up later, if you think you'll be at home."

Then François did look at us, for a moment. He looked from one to the other of us and then he turned to look back at the men working.

"Yes," he said, "I'm sure to be home."

And he turned around and walked back to the excavation.

"Friend of mine," said Gérald, twitching the car past the hole and under the jaws of the backhoe. "We used to work together. Not sure if he's still at the same job though."

The house for sale was a disappointment. It was over a mile from the river, it had no trees, it was a blistering frame-built hovel, and there were cows in the field next door, with flies everywhere, so I told Gérald that no, I didn't want it. Even now in June I could imagine how the winter winds would blow right through the place and besides, I said, this was no house for a woman to live in alone. No, he conceded, perhaps it wasn't, and we turned around and went back to the village. The tractor was parked now, and the hole in the road was deserted. Driving this way we were facing into the sun and Gérald, frowning into the glare, sweating, slowed his car in front of the village tavern. He looked sidelong at me. I saw him look hesitant for the first time. What now?

Did I drink beer, he asked, tentatively.

I said yes I certainly did.

"*Parfait*," he said, and parked his car.

In the dim, empty, air-conditioned beverage room, he bought me a beer and left me under the Molson's clock while he went away to telephone. The waiter was plump and tough-looking, with a tiny gold horse-shoe dangling from one ear. He wouldn't talk to me, so I sat staring out the window at the lush trees moving in the hot wind, glad to be in the cool and out of the sun, even though there was this nice man trying to do his job and sell me a house that we both knew I wasn't going to buy.

Then he came back and sat down. He said no more about the house and instead started to talk about himself. He did this in a detached way, slowly and precisely, as if with some purpose. Sitting across from him in the tavern, I could look at him more directly. His big face was almost perfectly round but with high cheek-bones and a reddish-blond skin that had been out in the sun too much. It was cross-hatched with thousands of tiny wrinkles. When he held his beer glass in his meaty hand and looked down into it, the wrinkles focussed and brought his expression to a concentrated point. Under the roundness and the redness there was nothing blunt, nothing obtuse about him at all — in fact there was a counterpoint and a keenness there. He seemed unselfconscious about being watched and he went on talking. But he was also watching me. Did he expect me to start confiding in my turn? He told me that he had grown up in this village and he informed me that his father had in fact used to run this very tavern when it was a real hotel. In those days there was a ferry across the St. Lawrence, he said, and people used to come over from the north shore for the evening.

"And friends would come, you know," he said, "like François."

He shifted in his chair and laid both his heavy hands on the table. For a flash the keen wrinkles were pointed right at me. He looked at my glass, saw that I hadn't finished, and ordered another for himself.

"Those were really the good times," he said, "a lot of fun. Everyone just walked up from the dock, no cars, and left when the last ferry left. Anyone who missed it stayed over right here. And it's here, maybe even right here at this table, that I've drunk with so many friends. I met my wife here too, I think, and we're still together. That's not so easy these days."

And after he'd said that he looked away. The last bit hadn't come out as smoothly as the rest, I suppose because he'd had to make an effort to fit it in. He must have had to say it because he wanted to let me know that he wasn't courting me. And I felt that familiar, unreasoning disappointment that a woman feels when a man makes a point of mentioning his wife. Did I look so predatory? What was it that he did have in mind? He swallowed his second beer and looked at his watch. He was waiting for me to finish mine, so I drank it and stood up. He paid and we stepped out into the heat and the glare and started back towards town.

But about a mile out of the village, he turned off the highway and pulled into the driveway of a mobile home, a long glossy one on a cement-block foundation, with shrubs planted around it, sharing its driveway with a ranch bungalow next door. Again he was looking sideways at me, wiping the sweat off his forehead with a paper napkin from the tavern. This time he didn't ask, though. He simply said, "This is my friend François, I told him we'd be stopping in for a beer."

The sun-wrinkles looked away as he waited to see if I minded. But we were here now. The beer I had already drunk had made everything golden in the heat. And I did like him, so we went in.

François *chez lui* turned out to be a middle-sized sun-tanned man in a very white T-shirt and extremely well-scrubbed jeans, a man whose body wasn't just hard-looking, but had something tight about it, something tense in the way he held himself and walked. And again he stood looking at us, seeming uncertain what to say. But again it was cooler inside than outside. This time I looked back at him. He had big biceps and very clean fingernails and he was barefoot. His feet looked scrubbed too, as did everything else in his trailer. It was all utterly, gleamingly neat. He must have spent hours wiping it all down and setting pots of plastic flowers in the exact centres of all flat surfaces.

He averted his eyes again as he led us into his antiseptic kitchen, gave us each a bottle of beer — to me he gave a glass as well — and invited us to sit at the table. So we sat in the gleam reflected off its formica surface and looked out the window rather than look at each other. Gérald's elbows made damp patches on the table around his beer bottle. He still didn't seem to know what to say to François and it was François who suddenly made an effort to ask the right questions.

"How's your wife," he said, "how's business?"

"Fine, okay," said Gérald.

We looked down at the table and we drank. Then we all looked out at the perfect back lawn, which gave François a subject. He stared out at it.

"Hard to keep that mowed," he said, "hard to keep this place clean. I used to have some ducks and geese, but no more. What a mess they made. I had to get rid of them."

All the while he kept his hand on his beer bottle as if he were preventing it from escaping.

"I hate mess," he said, "and it's hard, it's hard to keep things decent when you're alone."

Gérald turned his beer bottle between his hands. He traced a little trail of condensation along the edge of the table.

"You still in the *Sûreté*?" he asked.

"Yeah but, well . . . yeah," said François, "I'm still a cop."

Gérald explained.

"We were both divers," he said. "We worked together doing underwater jobs for the police. And then François actually went into the *Sûreté du Québec*. And I . . . well, I don't do that much diving any more, except sometimes just for fun. I started doing this instead. But we worked together for quite a while."

At that I took another look at both of them, at François's big arms and at Gérald's thick-bodied toughness. It would certainly take him a long time to get cold in the water.

But François was still talking, and not about their diving days. Suddenly he was saying that he was divorced. He was bitter about that. He said that he'd lost contact with his children. That he was on sick leave from his job because he'd had an accident to his hand. He'd been off work for six months and he was lonely.

"I'm not even sure I'd recognize my own daughter," he said. "She's eighteen now and I haven't seen her for two years. You know they sent me out to the Magdalen Islands? It's not like here. The people there are good people and I liked them, but they all know each other. And they don't accept strangers. And there were no women. You know what I mean? No women."

He didn't look at me when he said that but he looked hard at Gerald.

"*Il n'y avait pas de femmes là-bas.*"

Gerald gave him a searching, puckered look.

"There must have been women," he said, "there are women everywhere."

"No," François said, "not that you could get away from their families."

It seemed that his wife had refused to go to the islands with him.

"That was really how the split happened," he said. "She had a job here and she didn't want to leave it. And anyway, by that time, the marriage was pretty well over. I did like it in the islands after a while, I was getting along with the people by the time I left. And there wasn't much crime, just a little breaking and entering and ordinary theft."

François shrugged at his beer bottle.

"*On les pognait toujours,*" he said, "we always got them, it's an island, they had nowhere to go."

"And something happened to your hand," said Gerald, slowly, "and that was why you came back?"

"No," said François, "that was afterwards, after the divorce came through. I haven't seen my wife now for more than two years. But the divorce took time."

He looked out the window and then he got up and went to wipe a few drops of water off the counter. As he walked past me,

I could smell the soap and the ozone in his T-shirt. Then he came back and sat down and looked at us again. By this time I'd had enough beer to look straight into his eyes. His irises were a clear brown but they were going to blue around the edges. He wasn't as young as his body looked. He was holding his left hand on his knee, under the table, keeping it out of sight.

"It was an accident," he said." I mean, I told them it was an accident with the lawn-mower and they accepted that. But it was an accident with my gun."

And Gérald said "*Ah bon.*"

"Yes," said François. "Yes." He looked down at his knees and at his hand under the table and he set his jaw. "I shot myself in the hand."

He pulled his left hand out from under the table and held it up, then laid it on the table. The sun-tanned skin had healed over a strange lump on the back of it. It wasn't very noticeable but we looked at it, at him, and back at his hand. Neither of us wanted to ask him how an officer of the *Sûreté* could just shoot himself in the hand.

Still not looking at me he said, "Why is it so hard . . . why is it so hard to meet women? And when you do, why do they expect so much? I don't expect anything any more. Just to go out to dinner maybe, and talk a little bit and be polite and say thank you very much and go back home again. That's all. Why isn't it simple?"

He was looking at Gérald.

And Gérald, steady, expressionless, was looking back at him.

"*C'est toujours ben compliqué,*" he said.

François decided that he wanted to smoke.

"Complicated, yes," he said, "it certainly is."

He stood up again, opened a kitchen cupboard and took out a pristine ashtray. Then he took a packet of cigarettes from one of the drawers under the counter and he sat down and he smoked, turning away from us and waving at the smoke.

"You saw the house here beside the *roulotte,*" he said.

"Yes," said Gérald.

"Well it's mine. I don't know what to do with it. That's where I lived when I was married. Now I don't need it, it's too big. I want to sell it."

Gérald said nothing.

"What am I supposed to do, all alone in a big house like that? Can you tell me that? What am I supposed to do?"

He dragged on his cigarette, then held it under the table. He turned to me.

"You came out here looking for a house?"

"She wants an old house," said Gérald, "not like that one."

François shifted his ground immediately.

"Everyone thinks they want a house," he said. "They think if only they can get a place of their own, then they'll be happy. What's so wonderful about a house? The truth is I ought to get out of here completely. I never thought things would end up like this. Maybe I should get myself a bike."

He put his left hand out of sight under the table again.

"Remember," he said to Gérald, "remember the time we found that guy's Harley under the bridge?"

"Yeah," said Gérald.

"It'd only been in the water three weeks, it was still okay. It was a nice bike. And he'd already collected on the insurance."

"Well," said Gérald, "I guess he sold it after that."

"Of course he did," said François. "And remember the time we got that little girl out from under the ice?"

"Yeah, yeah, I do," said Gérald, swallowing beer.

"How long was she under there?" I wanted to know. "Wasn't she brain-damaged?"

They both looked at me, policemen.

"She'd been dead for a week," said François.

There was something about the way he said it that made any distinction between life and death seem pointless, a detail of such small importance that it was foolish to mention it. Now he leaned on the table, forgetting to hide his hand, smoking and hunching his shoulders.

"In the Magdalens," he said, "I found an old guy who'd committed suicide. The family really wanted the body and their divers there couldn't find it. I knew why. They didn't want to find it. They were scared. They went too far out on purpose. I knew. He jumped off the dock, right? And there were an awful lot of fish around that dock, too many. That's not normal for fish. So I told them, they were all standing there, I said, I'll find him for you, and I suited up and jumped in. This was only spring, you know, there was a lot of ice floating in the water, you couldn't see much, but he

17

was right there. And he was already just a skeleton because the fish had been at him. So I put a line on him and came back up right away. And they said what's the matter? They thought I was the one who was scared. They thought I was giving up before I'd even started. But I just said, right, I've found him. And they didn't believe me. They said, what do you mean, you've found him? You haven't even gone out there yet. So I told them I didn't have to go out that far. He was right there all the time. I told them just haul on this rope and you'll see. And they didn't want to believe me and then when they did believe me, they didn't want to pull him up. After all, he was their father. And he was just a skeleton, mostly. But that sort of thing doesn't bother me. And anyway, he wanted to die."

François finished his cigarette and wiped the ends of his fingers as if it had polluted them. He went immediately to rinse the ashtray under the tap. He stopped for a moment in the middle of his kitchen, staring out into the light.

"Yeah, I liked it in the islands," he said as he dried the ashtray with a paper towel and put it away. He put the cigarettes back into their drawer too. "Except that there were no women."

And he put the paper towel into a plastic-lined garbage bin in a special compartment under the sink.

"Remember that kid who jumped off the Pont Laviolette?" asked Gérald. "Remember in the spring when we found him . . .? He was under the ice too, that was dangerous. The current was strong. And my line got snagged, remember?"

His hands fell to the table again. Thump. And there was a silence.

"Yes," said François, sitting down again, "I do remember that." He turned to me.

"That kid was dead too," he said, with a tight smile. "They were always dead."

Then he and Gérald both laughed down at the table, into their beer.

"But those were the good times," said François. "Don't you remember, oh, all the cars . . ."

Gérald suddenly sat back from the table.

"Your hand going to be all right?" he asked.

"I guess so," said François. "It still hurts. And it's not finished yet. Next week I have to go back into hospital. They're going to take some bone from my leg and graft it into my hand. I messed up some bones in there."

He looked straight at me with his clear and clouded blue-ringed eyes.

"That's when you realize how much you need someone else around," he said. "I'll be coming back here with one hand out of commission again and a leg cut up as well. Alone."

I didn't answer that and there was silence again. Suddenly the heat seemed to have got into the cool little kitchen and I was aware of a drop of sweat tickling its way down my back, under my shirt. François looked over at Gérald and Gérald looked at his watch. François sighed and stood up.

"I forgot," he said to Gérald. "It's a working day for you."

"Well," Gérald said, "it's true I would like to get back to the office before five."

"I understand" said François. "It's just that when you're not working, you forget."

He gathered up the beer bottles, then put them down again as he saw that we were actually walking to the door. He followed us out to the driveway and stood with his back turned to the bungalow, frowning at the sunlight. He laid his good hand on the roof of Gérald's car. It must have been burning hot but he didn't seem to feel it. When Gérald started the engine he lifted it with a sort of delicacy, as if he had been holding the car back, and stepped away from it.

"*Bon*," he said, "*salut*." He seemed to be going back to his trailer but as we turned out onto the highway, I looked over my shoulder and saw him still standing there. He was watching us leave, his hands hanging emptily, just as when we first saw him stepping out of the smoke.

On the way back into town, I waited for Gérald to say something about his friend. Instead he drove fast and neatly, letting the sunlit air that sucked and buffeted through the open back windows provide a cover for his silence. On both sides of the road, the blowing grass seemed a deeper, thicker green than before. François hung between us in the lowering afternoon. Neither of us knew what to say. Instead I studied Gérald as he gripped the wheel, contemplated his solidity, his reassuring steadiness and the way he was now giving his entire attention to what was, for him, the exceedingly simple task of driving a car. His sales pitch had evaporated. It was easy to see why François would value his friendship, but it was no longer possible to return to the casual friendliness that had been so easy and pleasant a couple of hours before. As we attacked the long upward slope of the bridge he suddenly reached over the seat behind him and, still driving, rolled up both rear windows. It wasn't until we were actually at the top of the bridge, high over the river, that he said something. Looking straight ahead, he told me that François was his best and oldest friend.

"But somehow he never got his life together, there were ways he just couldn't grow up . . . *il essaie toujours, mais il se débrouille mal, c'est pas de sa faute . . .*"

We were directly above the glitter of the waves again, last resort of suicides, better known to police divers than to the rest of us. And Gerald appeared to be struggling with something he wasn't sure he wanted to tell me. Was he apologizing for his friend or what? There was more silence as we came down off the bridge and turned to the right into the suburbs of Trois-Rivières. As we pulled up at the stoplights across from the shopping centre, he seemed to decide to speak, shouting above the roar of a big tractor-trailer that was revving and shuddering beside us, trying to choose a gear.

"But there's more to him than that, François I mean, because what he didn't say, wouldn't know how to say was, well, about the time when I was caught under the ice . . . you heard us talking about it . . . "

The light changed and he thrust his car out ahead of the truck before it could heave itself forward.

". . . but what he didn't say was that he saved my life. Really. And maybe you don't know what that's like, but it's something that's hard to accept, it'd be easier just to forget about it . . ."

I wasn't sure of what I'd heard because the truck was catching up with us, its huge wheels towering beside the car, its valves clattering and clunking.

"What . . .?"

"He just came down and got me out," Gérald shouted. "And it would be so easy for me to forget that, to say, well, I was in a tight spot all right but I got myself out. I'd rather have got myself out, sure. I'd rather be able to say afterwards that it wasn't really that bad, you know, because I survived. No one else ever had to know about it. But it was bad. It was critical. I was as good as dead. And he just came back down and took the time to untangle my line. He could have drowned too. But it's true that he's never scared, not of things like that."

I looked at Gérald gripping the wheel, not thumping it now. He had turned his face away from me, out the window and off towards the statue of the Virgin Mary in the centre of the traffic circle. Then he said something into the traffic and the hot greasy wind that I really couldn't catch. So I seized the moment to ask the question that had been hanging between us all the way back.

"Do you think he shot himself in the hand on purpose?"

But now the transport truck was almost on top of us, gearing down again, drowning everything out. It was swinging over into our lane too. Deftly, in the turn by the port, Gérald found a way between potholes on one side and giant wheels on the other. And he chose that moment, through the roar and the smoke, to say something else, something about being a cop, then stopped. The big truck had drowned him out. But it had veered over because it was making a turn, and now it rumbled off towards the grain elevators at the port, while we came into the straightaway down the Rue Notre-Dame. Gérald clenched the steering wheel at the top and seemed to be sighting down his arms between his fists.

"I guess being a cop is tough enough," he said, "and I certainly never wanted to do it, but . . ."

"But what?" I asked.

The sunlight was shining into the car sideways, catching in the reddish hairs on his arms and making them sparkle.

". . . but I suppose being a cop's wife is even harder."

After that I didn't dare ask about François's hand again, but I waited and the question continued to hang between us for the few minutes it still took to traverse the downtown core of the little city. It wasn't until Gérald had pulled up by the sidewalk in front of my apartment that he finally spoke again, and then all he said was what he'd already said to François:

"*C'est toujours ben compliqué.*"

And that was his last word on François. There was no further mention of the house we had visited and I realized that we had both forgotten it the moment we turned our backs on it. Now Gérald said goodbye rather formally and drove away, leaving me on the sidewalk, looking after him. I was still trying to understand what had really happened, and wishing I didn't have to let him go. At least I had that much in common with François. But he turned the corner without looking back and vanished into the heat haze — a loyal, hardworking man on his way home to have supper with his wife, and to tell her that he'd put in another whole day without making a sale.

Matthew Remski

GOOD FRIDAY

I am alive on the planet with nothing
to show for it except a little blood
collecting at the feet. My lips
form the strange words *I love you* in my sleep:
nothing has been more practised than this.
I love you, I am poor.

You return the word — earth becomes
water, water becomes air, air becomes fire.
I am bitten from inside, a madman, running
from dirge to dirge, collecting tears.

The mold a body makes on the ground
is as distinct as three November trees
against the march sky. I want to be
with you, settling perfectly into the earth,
each vertebra a bulb in a dark garden.
I don't want to be noticed apart from the field
I have married. I want to be
lain upon, as one more young man fuses wrists
to his lover's shoulder blades.

Do you know the number of children on the planet?
They are all mine, I am calling their names now,
and I love you, and I am poor. I love you
for nothing, with no more of a reason
than one hand reaching for another.

DEDUCANT TE ANGELI

for Luciano, in memory of his father

Spring is changing its mind in our heads,
my jaw is locked open on the white sky, while
your hair dries in the wind, you woman of my eyes:
the landscape is an older brother
rolling up a sleeve to show a scar, or some writing.
A man dies in the morning, his last meal in hand,

his heart exploding like an angel entering a room
with her mouth set against the goodbye
of a long conversation.

I want to move to a city
where immigrants don't hock their language
at the border, where creole flowers on main street
in the moment after the birth of the first
generation, the children who will understand
a dying wish, when medicine and english fail.

I want a third floor apartment in a two-story
town, I want to converse with pigeons
lodged behind plaster. A city

where my hands will balcony the river, and gather in
every starving woman swimming with the tide.
I will bow before the dark ships of death,
spewing cremation from the portholes.
 I will announce every wedding skiff as it tows the sky
with great darkening roses spinning in its vortices.
All this, while I dream of my son,

my son, whose voice dolphins the air.

Kathyrn Morris

GALA

I am a thin woman dressed up,
my bones laid in satin
like a gift of jewellery.

This is my party.

I tell them:
we dance for new wheelchairs.

But I tell you:
it is not the means
and it is not the end.

It is the pictures the next day.
Of my bones, my perfect bones.

1. Bacon names a meal.
   If there is bacon,
   it is breakfast.

2. Bacon does not
   sneak up on you.
   It makes the sounds and smells
   of preparation.

3. When I wake up
   and there are signs of bacon
   I think someone
   might be making bacon for me.
   I think who
   is making bacon for me.

4. When we eat our
   big bacon breakfast
   I pretend that I am preparing
   for a hard day
   of working new earth.
   I am almost a pioneer.

After the last meal,
it is still such a long time
to an excusable rest.

My neighbours and I eat early
and take to our plastic chairs.

We listen carefully.
We appreciate it all.

A leaf moves, and I remember it
from a long-ago sickness.

In this daylight,
my waiting is the closest
I can have to sleep.

WATERING BAN

The neighbourhood slowly turns brown.

Green lawns are the well-fed children
of this famine. We point our fingers
and wait for them to be turned in.

The wiser among us let the front lawns
wither. After dark
carry buckets to the most precious
of our backyard flowers.

FUGITIVE

If you committed a crime
there would be questions.
Your picture.
Something to talk about
in the streets and on the radio.

Out of my room,
out of the drawers you curl up in.
Your name, blinking in the light.

I don't know much,
besides what he told me.

Kept to himself, really.

Knew his wines, though,
and didn't need much sleep.

Linda Manning

She dreamed the prairie
rolled it out
a wheat-filled bolt of cloth
across Toronto twelve lane
all-night traffic
down the winding Don
over city stacks,
skyscrapers
to the lake-bound skyline
where she stitched the edge
a flatlock seam
horizon over wheat
flung it east
darkened rolling
glacial hills,
blanketed the proper
towns and hamlets
polite sixth
generation smugness
rolled it north to
forests holding lakes
stern rock faces
sentries on the giant
Northern Shield
pegged it to their
stony boots
then lovingly
reached back
selecting threads
embroidered
bluffs and sloughs
small stark towns
with houses clustered
close against their
Wheat Pool elevators,

grass sighing
against wooden boards
wind canopies above
her needle followed
into cities'
wide treed streets
pungent caragana hedges
slow brown rivers
dark blood red
knots of tough chokecherry
a silent fabric lifeline

she lugged this bolt of cloth
everywhere she went

Fred Stenson

HITTING THE MONKEY

Sixteen minutes and seven seconds are gone in the third period of this hockey game. We are behind 4-3. In tomorrow's newspaper it will look like a close game but the small crowd on hand here in the Dairydome know better. For most of this period play has been in our end, as if the game was a party and we were the hosts.

The other team's goalie is making an exhibition of himself, doing a sort of dramatic pantomime about how little work he's getting. He takes his water bottle down off the top of his net every minute or so, either sprays some in his mouth or all over his face with his mask tipped up. Sometimes, he does the Ken Dryden thing and leans on the knob of his goalie stick. Other times, he puts his arms out over the top of his net, crucifixion style, and rests in that position. It really makes you want to pound one past him but, on the rare occasions when the coach calls for my line, the fourth line, we promptly get as bottled up in our own end as everybody else.

I know what I used to do at times like this. I used to dream. In my head I would rove all over my life, trying to make sense of it. I can't deny the need for such life-roving, such sense-making, still, for here I am seven games into an NHL comeback and I really have no idea why.

I may not know why I've come back to professional hockey but I certainly know when the urge came upon me. It was an evening in late June this year. I was home alone in my apartment and the solstice light had begun to get on my nerves. I didn't want a day to go on that long so I closed both sets of blinds over it. In the false darkness I turned on my only friend: the provincial educational channel on my TV set.

What I was trying to avoid besides the light was the feeling that I should move cities again. During my retirement from hockey I had succumbed to a chronic itchy-footedness that had taken me all over the map of North America. I didn't move in order to move again. I moved in search of a place to stick. But I never seemed to.

This time I had landed back in Canada, back in Bison-town where I had had my National Hockey League career. I was finding it uncomfortably full of memories and strangely empty of people I knew. Even my old friend and cornerman Smitty Smith had moved away. He had taken his wife and child back to our old hometown of Beaver Creek, Alberta.

Anyway, there I was, watching the educational TV channel and trying not to think about anything except what was coming out of the box. In the past year, a colony of white supremacists had bought a local farm. They'd been wearing swastikas, brandishing guns and burning a lot of good crosses. The affair had gained national attention and the sub-text of things written and broadcast in the Eastern media was, isn't it just what you'd expect, out there on the red-neck prairie?

To counter this, the provincial government had given its educational TV channel an anti-racism hot-foot. The channel had scoured the world for documentaries on non-white people and a lot of these were about rain forest tribesfolk threatened by lumber cartels. I wasn't sure how this related to cross-burning Nazis but it was sure making me mad at the wood industry.

The show I was watching that particular night was set in the Amazon Basin. It focused on a father-son monkey-hunting team. The father was a barrel-chested man who was said to be near the end of a great career as a hunter. His son was just short of puberty, a thin and wiry boy. They took up their blow guns and hacked their way into the steaming jungle. I was liking the show so much I popped my VCR onto Record.

All that really happened through the rest of the show was that the father set the son up for a shot and he missed. Then the father spotted another monkey, followed him through the trees for a while, and knocked him out of the high canopy right at their feet. They took the monkey home and the father presented it to his wife. She went off to get it ready for dinner—or at least that's what I imagine happened. The show was over by then.

Back in the Dairydome, the game is down to its final minute. The score hasn't changed. We have a rare face-off inside the other team's blue line and Clement, our coach, has called a timeout.

We all crowd around Clement and his notepad, a huge thing on which he is drawing a diagram so increasingly complex it could be the formula for nuclear fission. Clement has decided to pull the goalie and, if I'm reading this thing right, he has decided to use me, the old power play specialist, as his extra attacker. At least, in the maze of curves and arrows, I see the letter combination F-1(B). B stands for Burns.

Surveying the circle of faces and finding mine the blankest, Clement asks, "Burns, who are you?"

"F-1(B), Coach."

"Correct. What are your coordinates if we get the draw?"

"Red-3?"

"Wrong. F-1(M)?"

F-1(M) is a thirty-year-old Russian rookie named Muktov. Muktov lunges forward and studies the page. "Red-6," he says.

"Correct. And if we don't get the draw?"

"Red-3."

"Correct again. Burns, sit this one out."

In order to participate in the time-out scrum, I climbed over the boards. Now I climb back, slide to the end and sit. I have been retired from hockey for only five years and yet I often feel like Rip Van Winkle. I can remember when there were no time-outs in hockey. I can remember when coaches called you by your last name or your nickname, or "Shithead" or "Lard Ass," as suited the occasion. I remember when pep-talks consisted mainly of people screaming "Skate!" and "Fight!"

I'm not saying those were the good old days; I'm just saying that, in so short a time, everything seems changed.

The monkey hunting show had a powerful effect on me. I was hugely moved by it. Tears were actually running down my face at the end, a bothersome situation if you don't know why.

All I knew was what I must do next. I jumped up and ejected the tape. I dug in the pile of other tapes under the TV stand until I found the one I wanted: an old Montreal Canadiens highlight tape. Except for some black-and-white stuff about Boom Boom, Jacques Plante and the Richards, it mostly celebrated the incredible team the Canadiens built around Guy Lafleur in the 1970s. I fast-forwarded until I was watching Lafleur do some of the incredible things it seemed at the time only he would ever be able to do.

It had just been announced somewhere that, after his first comeback year with the New York Rangers, Guy Lafleur was going to play one final season with the Quebec Nordiques. That is, he was going to play the last season of his career in his home city.

I'm just stating a bunch of facts here; I'm not yet aspiring to explain my own comeback. The facts are:

1) I watched a show about monkey hunting and wept;

2) I watched a Guy Lafleur highlight tape and felt aftershocks of the same emotion;

3) when finally I shut the TV off, I went directly to the phone and tracked down my old agent Bernie, Bernie who had recently been released on parole after doing white-collar time in the slammer for dealing cocaine.

Clement hasn't finished drawing when the referee whistles for the teams to come back and face off. The referee drops the puck and our centre pulls it across, right onto Muktov's stick. Muktov moves it forward into Red-5.

I won't bother you with the rest of the code names and coordinates but I'll tell you that the whole thing up to this point is going like clockwork. Muktov's pass into the slot hits the pinching defenceman right on the tape. From there on it's not quite so pretty. D-2's slap-shot misses the net by a yard. It has tremendous velocity, though, and rebounds off the end boards all the way past everyone up the ice.

Possibly because of the unfinished state of Clement's diagram, no one is covering D-2's place on defence. An opposing winger catches up to the puck and deposits it casually into our empty net. 5-3. Toast.

Clement's face appears over my shoulder, a little tightness to the lips.

"Coordinates, Burns, coordinates," he says.

"Right, Coach. Coordinates."

"Complete Interactive before you go home tonight."

"Right, Coach. Interactive."

When I finally got ahold of Bernie that night in spring, my first discovery was that he was no longer in the agent business. That's what he told me over the phone from Toronto. He was selling software for a young, government-subsidized high-tech company.

"Strictly legitimate," Bernie stressed to me. "Entirely on the up and up. And I'm clean. Really."

There was so much paranoia coming through the telephone cable that I got a case of it myself.

"I beat the booze thing too," I told Bernie.

"You? You never drank."

"Not as a player, no. But I got the habit at a rest ranch after my nervous breakdown."

"Nervous breakdown! Holy cow!"

"But I'm sober now, you betcha. And quite sane, really."

We talked like this awhile longer, about how new and improved we both were. Then I sprang it on him.

"Bernie, I want to make a comeback and I want you to fix it for me."

The silence that followed was heavy. I suppose Bernie had an imaginary tablespoon piled high with white stuff hovering near his nose. I broke in with some very carefully chosen words.

"It doesn't have to be a comeback for both of us, Bernie. You wouldn't need to quit your day job, or any of your new good habits. All you have to do is give Mr. Topworth a call. Fix this one contract, line your pocket a little bit, and go on exactly as you are. What do you say?"

"Why do you want to do it?"

"I don't know, I just do."

"Are you in shape?"

"No, but I'll start tomorrow."

"You been out a long time, Dougie."

"I know that."

"All right. I'll give it a shot. But keep your expectations really low. Absolutely as low as you can."

It is quiet and empty here in the Educational Centre, one of our team rooms below ice level in the bowels of the new Dairydome. The Ed Centre is lined with personal computers and it is Clement's pride and joy.

I am sitting at one of the terminals about to begin Interactive, a program Clement created. Interactive contains 800 game situations which, by Clement's calculation, represent 80% of all situations in hockey. The players have nicknamed the software "Biff" and, right now, Biff wants to know who I am.

"F-1(B)," I type in. Biff is "player specific," meaning that when

I type B for Burns, it presents a different speed and play selection than if I had typed F-1(M) for Muktov.

I push Enter and the game begins: a series of dots with letter-number combinations on them zooming around at near game speed all over the bloody screen. Suddenly it freezes and Biff asks, "Where to F-1(B)?"

Now hackers out there may be saying, beauty, where do I get one, but consider this: if I can't make up my mind, I take a penalty which is added to my total time. I'm likewise penalized for pushing wrong coordinates. If, when I finish, my total time is over the "current acceptable threshold for F-1(B)," I have to start over. I could be here for hours.

And it's no good typing in "F-U, Biff." All that happens is Biff types back, "F-U-2, F-1(B). Start over."

Bisons' team owner Mr. Angus Topworth has always had a mysterious affection for me, ever since he drafted me about four rounds too soon leading up to my rookie season. This affection, unexplainable by mere human logic, was Bernie's and my only hope.

While Bernie talked to Topworth, and Topworth to his General Manager, and Bernie to the General Manager and Coach, I stayed well clear. I worked out. I will spare you a description of the exercise program by which I brought myself back into playing shape. Suffice to say it involved weights, a running track, a rink — and a great deal of throwing up.

Anyway, it wasn't long until Bernie was back on the phone. His success was telegraphed immediately by his tone. The wheeling and dealing sound had returned.

"I got the call, Dougie boy. It's thumbs up."

"You got me a contract with the Bisons?"

"Hey, hey. Beam back to the Enterprise, fella. Of course I didn't get you a contract. Beelzebub couldn't have got you a contract. What I got you is a try-out."

"Oh."

"Don't you sound let down, you schmuck. Have you any idea how hard it was to get you that much?"

"You're right. I'm sorry."

"It's in your hands now, Bucko. If you prove yourself at rookie camp . . ."

"Rookie camp! Not even regular training camp?"

"You heard me, rookie camp. Thing is, Doug, Bisons management wants proof you've got the guts for a comeback."

"Oh."

"You got to admit they have reason to doubt. So, that's me outa here, Doug. My only advice is keep your head up. Call me if you make the grade."

It's the day after my night with Biff. I had to start over four times and then I got too lucky: Biff assigned me a new acceptable threshold which I doubt I'll ever reach again.

Right now, we are in the midst of practice and I am skating hard through every exercise and drill. After about an hour of this, Clement comes off the bench. He slips and slides over to me. Clement can't skate. He has played about five minutes of hockey in his whole life.

"Burns, I've got to complement you. I've never seen you work so hard."

"Do you want to know where I am, Coach?"

"Pardon me?"

"F-1(B) is in Blue-8."

Clement looks around in befuddlement, then grins. "That's right, Burns. That's absolutely right."

"If it's okay I'd like to complete Interactive again after practice. I'm going for a higher threshold."

"Good, Burns, good." Clement's smile begins to lose something. "Do you mind my asking, Burns, why . . . why you're putting out so today?"

"Nordiques in two days, Coach. I have a personal thing about the Nordiques."

"I'm very happy to see you so inspired, Burns. And, if I may say so, seeing a veteran on the comeback trail working his, his tail off is a real inspiration for the kids."

"Thank you. I hope so. Could I ask you a favour, Coach?"

"Why, of course, Burns. Ask away."

"Could I play opposite Guy Lafleur Saturday night?"

Clement plays a little Interactive in his head, bites his lip hard. "I had a different assignment in mind, Doug." He sees my disappointment, goes through a life-changing experience of some sort.

"Oh, what the hell, though, Burns? Hockey isn't all coordinates and science, is it?"

"With all due respect, Coach, no, it isn't."

"Yes, Burns, you can play opposite Lafleur. What's more, I intend to tell the team and the press that you're going to. How's that?"

"That's good of you, Coach. Can I get back to work now?"

"Of course, Burns. Off you go."

Clement slips and slides away. He is so jaunty that he falls down.

Rookie camp was hell, a kind of designer hell modelled after my deepest fears: a potent and toxic distillation of everything about the male sex that will have to be bred out of the human race if life on this planet is to continue. The forty or so crazy youths I shared the camp with specialized in hitting people from behind in close proximity to the boards, as if their best chance of progressing was to turn another young hopeful into a quadriplegic.

And Bernie was right: the old codger of slightly more than thirty on the comeback trail was the stone on which the young warriors lined up to grind their sabres smooth. I wore the longest plastic face shield money could buy; I found an elaborate mouth guard apparatus with a rubber toggle that I clutched in my teeth. I wore so much extra padding around my kidneys, I had to strip down in front of the coaches twice to convince them I hadn't arrived at camp overweight.

But such was the violence of rookie camp, mere armour wasn't enough. By about the second day, I had run out of cheeks to turn. It was time for counter-aggression and I dipped deep into my veteran's bag of tricks for a chestnut called "playing with your head down."

Whenever hockey sportscasters want to explain why someone is suddenly lying senseless on the ice, they invariably say, "He had his head down." They imply that, if he were lying on the ice like that after having had his head up, it would be a serious matter; but, since he had his head down, it is entirely appropriate that he be lying unconscious.

My version of this is that I will at times *appear to be skating with my head down.* What this causes is an automatic response in most of the players on the ice. They feel a stimulus in the reptilian cortex of their brains and, powerless to do otherwise, they go for you. Because I am only pretending to skate with my head down, I am ready when they come. At the last possible second, I leap away. If I am by the boards at the time, the in-coming freight strikes the boards with enormous force, sometimes breaking ribs, at the very least driving every molecule of air from its lungs. One way or another someone is left lying on the ice, rolling helplessly forth and back, and it isn't me.

Of course I didn't avoid all the hits. I absorbed my share. After each, I would force myself up and back into the play. What's more, I made damn sure the SS bastards who ran the camp saw me doing it. I also put the puck in the net often enough that they couldn't keep me from moving on to the real camp where the real jobs were on the line.

"Why do you want to play opposite Lafleur?"

It is the morning of game day. We are having a team breakfast after a light skate. Clement often insists on these team meals, at which we are all supposed to bond in new and meaningful ways. He usually brings an overhead so he can toss a few new squiggles on the wall. Today is different, though, and it is my fault. With a slight glisten in his eyes, Clement is telling us why he has always loved hockey.

As a little boy he couldn't play because of some problem with his feet. All the pairs of skates his lockey-loving father bought him tormented his feet with pain. So Clement worked as a stick boy, and watched and learned a great deal about the game.

When he lists off the hockey greats who were his heroes — Beliveau, Ratelle, Orr — all the statuesque and graceful players — he is starting to sound a tad gay. Not that I mind such a preference but, when he asks why I want to play opposite Lafleur tonight, the question somehow aspires to include me in his special passion, whatever that might be. With the whole team staring, I reply, "Because he's a legend."

"Exactly!" cries Clement and something dribbles out the corner of his eye. "He is a legend of the game that we love, and that's why we have to go out there tonight and beat the, the CRAP out of the Nordiques! Isn't that right, Burns?"

Though the logic of what he has said escapes me, I feel compelled to agree. "Right, Coach. The crap, right out of them."

"Let's hear it for Dougie," Clement yells. "I know Dougie's going to play his heart out tonight. Let's hear it!"

A silence, and a long one. Livesay, one of our assistant captains, raises his hands and holds them palm-opposite. He fakes them together while jerking his head at team captain Smollet. Smollet gets the message and starts clapping. The others join in.

As the applause dies I hear Muktov say to the fellow next to him, "I no get. Is Burns' birthday?"

The fundamental oddity about all this is that I was never clear on why I was doing it — not during rookie camp and not during the team training camp that followed. And I asked myself continually. Every time I took a hit or a slash, or needed to puke after a long shift, I asked myself but got no answer.

You may say that it was obviously the money, but that's not right. The comeback represented a highly insecure minimum salary for less than a year. What I was leaving to get it was a quite secure and not unlucrative practice as the good salesman in the used car sales gambit of good salesman/bad salesman.

In all my years outside hockey, I had been the smiling guy who met you in the car lot and took a sincere interest in your quest for the ideal automobile, the one who suggested you could get more for your old car than you had even dared to ask. After the bad salesman was introduced, the one who did the actual appraisal on your old car and found all the rust and hail dents, I was the guy who took you aside and fed you a cup of coffee. I was the one who called the bad salesman a real bastard and, rousing myself to believable anger, took him one last counteroffer. I was the guy who talked the asshole into throwing in the free tape deck.

No, it wasn't the money, a point that became clear to Bernie at last when I survived the final cuts and he negotiated my contract. The lowliness of that contract astounded him, left him shocked and bitter. What's more, he blamed me; as if I were the devil and he'd traded me his soul for a vegetable slicer.

But, whatever the reasons, my comeback did occur. I got my old number back and, before our first home game, there was a little ceremony at centre ice to welcome me back. Children in the crowd looked at one another with perplexed lack of understanding. A few of the older fans remembered me well enough to boo. I had a terrible game and was relegated to the press box for games two and three.

In the dressing room before the Nordiques game, Clement gives us yet another inspirational speech about his tormented feet and his mother. He confesses to a torrid lust for the Stanley Cup. He speaks with dewy eyes of retiring the number of a player named Moose Ochsenbach. Darting glances all round illustrate that none of us have heard of the guy. Clement explains that Moose was a gritty stay-at-home defenceman who played for the team at its old franchise address in Louisiana. Moose did not wear a helmet and a head-first slide to block a slapshot catapulted him into early retirement. Moose is still alive, Clement tells us, in a Regina nursing home. Ironically, he does wear a kind of helmet now, on the inside of his head.

Clement carries on so long in this vein that we are late getting on the ice. The Nordiques are already out there skating circles, not just in their end but, owing to our absence, all over the ice surface. In dog terms, they are marking all over our territory. To make matters worse, every single fan is chanting, "Guy! Guy! Guy!" But why not? This being the only Nordiques appearance on Dairydome ice this year, it is very likely the last chance any of them have to see The Flower play the game he used to own. I am rather proud of them for this.

Lafleur's line starts the game for the Nordiques so I line up opposite. My first career happened during his first retirement so I have never seen him up close before. His hair is still long and he still doesn't wear a helmet. We're an odd combo considering I wear every piece of protective hockey equipment money can by. Lafleur doesn't look at me at all, has all his attention focused on the puck in the ref's hand. When the puck drops, something like electric current leaps through him, ignites him into action. So begins an evening where much of what I see is the blades of his skates churning up sprays of ice that hit me in the face.

Still in the first period, Lafleur gives me the slip at centre ice, takes a long cross-ice pass at our blueline, and unloads a slap shot that hits the post behind our goalie bang on. I've seen that shot a thousand times and this one appeared to have much of the old zip on it.

"Lovely shot," I tell him next time we face off. Team captain Smollet hears this and gives me a snarling look. Lafleur's expression is more on the puzzled side.

With a minute left in the first, I'm going for a loose puck in their end and Lafleur skates me off. The play turns quickly up-ice and all the officials turn with it. This is what I've been waiting for. I put my forearm around Lafleur's chest and, gently as possible, mug him to the ice.

"Sorry about that, Guy, but I was just wondering if you remembered me at all."

"Get off me."

"Doug Burns? The guy a reporter said could go into the corners with eggs in his hockey pants and never break a one?"

"I remember the line. I don't remember you."

"Well, no matter. I was just wondering . . ."

"Get off!"

Remarkably, when the ref sees Lafleur wrestling to get away from me, he thinks we are fighting. He gives us both two minute minors for roughing. Skating near Lafleur toward the penalty box, I say, "Hope that doesn't scotch the Lady Byng for you."

"You're nuts," he says. "Stay away from me."

In between periods—we're behind 1-0, by the way — Clement tries to makes something of the roughing incident, claiming my chippy play should be viewed as inspirational. Smollet grumps aloud that he'd be more inspired if I scored a goal.

Smollet's insult turns out to be a prophecy of a kind. With about five minutes left to go in the second, I swerve onto my wrong wing and nobody picks me up. I am allowed to stand off the corner of the Nordiques' crease for several unchecked seconds. A rebound comes right to my stick and I stuff it under the diving goalie. 1-1. By the look on Lafleur's face I'd say I'm really getting on his nerves.

Between the second and third periods, there's another bad moment with Clement. "He wants us all to kneel down and pray. No one moves. Still feeling that I'm to blame, I say, "You probably didn't know this, Coach, but I'm a Muslim. I couldn't in all conscience say a Christian prayer." Clement is persistent. "There must be some prayer we can all say."

Muktov to the rescue. "I no believe God. He dead."

Clement looks crushed.

"A little suggestion, Coach?"

"Yes, Burns?"

"What's a prayer after all but a common wish expressed?"

"Yes?"

"So couldn't we all just commonly wish to beat the crap out of the Nordiques?"

"I suppose . . ."

"Good. All together now . . ."

During the third period, I begin to understand that this game which seemed very long when it started is now very short and soon to be finished. As the sportscasters never tire of saying: time has become my enemy. I try and try to get close to Guy Lafleur but he keeps skating away from me. My younger legs are tiring while his, if anything, seem to be getting stronger. I must do something now, I tell myself. I must instigate!

Instigate is probably the longest word you'll commonly find in a hockey player's vocabulary. What's more, we all know what it means: it means to start a fight.

Given that I have spent my whole career avoiding fights, starting them isn't my specialty; and yet I know what to do. The surest way is to rough up a small player, a goalie, a good player, or a player who doesn't fight. In short, it means I must rough up Guy Lafleur.

The next time Lafleur and I are near a corner, I run him. I don't run him very hard; in fact, I make sure that most of the impact is me hitting the boards beside him. Then I give him a little shove on the shoulder. He gives me a little shove back and we're in business.

A giant enraged meathead whose job is to protect Lafleur steams over, flinging off his gloves. He is all spit and obscenity. Now comes the hard part: I must let him hit me. He winds one hand into my sweater, cocks the other fist back and moves it around, deciding where exactly to let me have it. On my part, split-second timing is required. When the fist does come, I jerk my face down. There's a sundering impact of knuckles on plastic as he nails me on the top of the helmet.

After this blow is struck, a new page in hockey's book of etiquette has turned. I am now the victim of a bigger, meaner opponent, which means that one of the meat-axes on my team should race in to defend me. But, look out, the Nordiques goon is winding up again: an uppercut to get around my helmet defence. What's going on here? No one's defending me. Before the second blow can land, I collapse, an unexpected manoeuvre that jerks my jersey free. Our goon, who has apparently decided to let me absorb a few before intervening, finally does arrive and the donnybrook is on.

Meanwhile, I am on the ice, on hands and knees, threading my way toward daylight through a forest of equipment-thickened legs. This is as planned.

When I'm finally out, Guy Lafleur is easily found. He is leaning against the boards with his chin resting on the knob of his stick, looking peacefully bored. I skate very slowly in his direction, making no eye contact, trying to look as if I intend to skate by toward our bench.

"Get lost," he tells me mildly when I get too close.

"Pardon me, Guy," I say and, with that, I whip off my gloves and grab his sweater.

"What is wrong with you?" he asks, dumping his gloves and grabbing my sweater.

"I have a question to ask you."

As I had hoped, everyone else is fighting and there is no one free to come to Lafleur's aid.

"Why did you do it?" I ask.

"Do what?"

"Come back?"

"It's none of your business."

"I realize that. But it's important to me all the same. I'm making a comeback too, you see, and I'm not really sure why. Is it the money? Is it vanity? Do I still think that hockey will attract me a wife better than I deserve? Or is it even remotely possible that I like hockey?"

Lafleur is looking almost interested. "You going to make it?"

"The goal tonight helps. My agent thinks if I score between fifteen and twenty and keep my minus down, I'll last the season. But, come on. Tell me. Why?"

A linesman jumps between us. "All right, you guys, break it up. Lafleur, get to your bench. You . . ." He glances at the back of my sweater. "Burns, you're done for tonight. Go take a shower."

"Would you just relax? We're having an interesting talk here."

"One more word, asshole."

Just as the linesman is pushing me out the gate, Lafleur comes up beside. He shrugs and smiles. "I missed it, that's all. I really like to play."

As I pass through behind our bench on the way to the dressing room, Clement slaps me on the rump. "Good boy, Dougie. Highly inspirational. Good boy!"

Lafleur slices past a Boston defenceman, feathers a pass to Shutt in the high slot. He one times it. Goal. Lafleur goes end to end, pops the puck through a Detroit defenceman's feet, ducks round him, fires. Goal. Pete Mahovlich carries the puck straight down the middle, is sandwiched by the New York Rangers defence. Lafleur picks up the loose puck, fakes the goalie down and drops it back to Mahovlich with the whole right side gaping.

The screen goes blizzard grey, then black. There is a flipping sound inside the VCR. But I can't seem to move. I keep seeing things there: Lafleur setting up pretty goals; the aging Amazonian hunter, blow pipe to his lips; and me, I see me too, stuffing that goal under the sprawling Nordiques goalie.

Then, for some reason, it's old Smitty Smith I'm seeing, my old cornerman. Smitty, who so seldom scored, is shooting from centre ice at an empty net. He nicks it off the post, completing the only hat trick he ever got as a pro. I remember how, in his excitement, he lost all control of his legs, how he slid all the way past the goal into the end boards and had to crawl back to retrieve the puck.

Good lord. That's it, isn't it? I've come back to hockey because I enjoy hitting the monkey.

A Nassau team does high fives as the Space Shuttle lifts off; research scientists hug each other because a diseased rat is displaying an increased immunity to infection; I give a motivational lecture to a huge crowd on the virtues of hitting the monkey. Wait a minute — I'll have to change that: on "sinking the putt that is yours to sink." Something more new age and sensitive like that.

I suppose that I understand that my highlight tape is broken, that I should get myself up and go to bed. I imagine myself doing that but I don't think I have. Meanwhile, the images continue to swarm: monkeys skating with arrows in their chests; hockey players trading dentist cards; a rocky waste transformed into a painted desert by the simple and very human means of thought. Still feeling slightly wise, I suppose I am asleep.

David Alder

WINTERING

We sit here in the garden
Trying to turn logic into flowers,
Making no headway.

Watching the hours harden
Into winter like this dream of ours
We let the thread play
Out, unravelling
The season, its careful rows of leaves.

Between conjectures
The grass is travelling
Back underground, stranding us in thin sleeves
And summer deck-chairs.

NO SIGN OF SPRING

A cold made of stars
Crisps candescent grass as it grows
Tomorrow's frost. Water's
Lap slows:
Ice is so near.
Out in the reeds
 The apocryphal ferryman lights his lamp.
A madonna-faced ewe on the shore
Intercedes
Her bleat for the lost lamb.

Eleonore Schönmaier

TREADING FAST RIVERS

1

Birth

Babies bundled
in Isolettes, waiting
for lessons.
You were born an hour ahead,
our mothers friends in the hospital.

My mother thought I was twins
but I came out alone.
Your mother hoped for a boy, after
eight girls, her oldest already
having babies.

2

Third Grade

I was drawing stories about my minnow
in its jar, turning it into a goldfish
in a store bought aquarium.

You were kissing boys
at the water fountain, casting
real nets.

3

Sixth Grade

You danced with the boys and tried
to show me how, your beauty
and your breasts already exotic
blossoms pressed against
my flat chest.

Health class we learned about our eggs
slipping down narrow rivers.
You calculated sperm travel rates,
the pluses and minuses of pregnancy
while I gave the boys mathematical answers.

4

Grade Seven

You played games at night after my curfew
where you were the loser and had to eat
sperm swimming on baby biscuits,
told me vague lessons of tops, bottoms
and all the way, as though you were
the sum of your fractions.

I had my flashlight
and my books
under the covers,
knew only the anatomy
of arms and legs.

5

Grade eight

Your party room in blue light
while I was eating birthday cake
in the yard and you treading
fast rivers under the Ping-Pong
table, measuring returns and serves.

The day after the boy laughing
at you, and my mother instructed me
I was lucky I had braces,
wouldn't get caught
in kisses.

6

High School

You gave me words to help me
fathom depths, and a dictionary
for my fourteen birthday
which provided no definitions. I gave you

a maternity dress and watched your belly
swell as I formed the sounds
of spermatozoa and ovum in biology class
touching their surfaces to my lips.

7

University

I came back in summer, a nursing student
and again you were my first
lesson. At twenty-one

you had your third baby, sucking milk from your chest,
your abdomen held together
with stitches, tubes tied.

8

At thirty-five

Nights in REM sleep you visit me,
ask me how I'm doing.
You're a grandmother and I

still haven't given birth
to my first child,
have strayed so far from your front steps
to find my own definitions:

9

Penis to you is a blade tearing
with words — fucking
under an eighth grade table — men,
the three fathers of your three children.
Cocks which entered and then
exited.

Penis to me is a root entering
soil, sent by a man's warmth
in my bedroom's light.
The planting of a salt water
garden together
where kisses float sweet and wet.

Janet Madsen

THE ROOM OF FALLING MAPS

(for my brother)

Eerie arm of flashlight brilliance,
round glass face rolled up to nylon tent
casting a beacon for bugs.
They flutter and gather in the light.

By day you abandoned me to the sun,
ran half-naked-wild with other boys,
while I had to wear shirts
and leave you alone.
I collected smooth stones
to make paths in the sandbox,
built houses with empty
cottage cheese buckets,
and vowed I'd never forgive you.
But at night when we were sent out
to sleep in the summer air
we'd lie shoulder to shoulder,
chins propped on hands,
and tell each other stories
as the bugs gathered round the flashlight.

We hunted back creek salamanders,
turning rotten logs in the search,
sometimes ankle deep in fir needles,
our faces slapped by wet leaves.
A salamander body fit in one hand.
We held their tiny hips in two fingers
to ensure gentle capture, their
back legs beat the skin of our palms

and taught us the temper of delicacy.
Translucent stomachs, hearts
beat in the wide open forest,
echoing our own fear.

Your bedroom was coated in maps, like shields
covering the little car wallpaper
you grouched you'd grown out of.
We planned journeys, and favourite
places became grease spots
trailing tails from a Vancouver source.
I was so sure you would travel
to your imagined worlds,
return triumphant and new-alive
after battles you waged
in some wild Interior.
I created countries for myself
so I too might run
shirtless and free.
My fingertips on your face followed
the new stubble's path.
Like a creek, I followed you
into whiskey sipped from jars
still smelling of the olives
we popped on our tongues.
After dinner we'd sneak out to drink,
then find ourselves waking
on foreign rec-room floors,
bodies empty as tents.

And where should I travel
but a place never imagined,
a province full of winter,
foreign tongue rattling frozen in my mouth,
refuge made home.
Not wanting to be away from you,
yet wanting to be hidden from the man
whose hands and body had entered
and marked me like a territory.

Returning by train, now
four years since we drove
to the station,
where you bought coffee and recalled
the room of falling maps;
how now and then the dormers drooped
to show cars rolling surely underneath.
The stories we imagined we'd tell!
I will tell you now
of the hands that held my hips
to make the capture sure,
how he so surely watched
my heart beating fear.

I don't know if that sound is water or wind
in the trees bending green
boughs that drip to the surface
of what you promised
would be beautiful. Here, you imagined
the honesty of trees would overcome me,
their gentle fingers touching light
the purpose in my back
as I rinsed my face in the bottomless lake.

Morning has come
and gone, but night
remains, thick wet cloud in my eyes.
You wait with hope for me to change
all I decided this overwhelming week.
But I won't change.

To my eyes the town
strains at its corners, places
where we've been together split
like a log alive with termites.
There's no magic to camping
here, nothing will shift
just because we're away.
Tender trees
won't make a difference, I swear
I know the feeling I want
to hang onto —
    sharp   clear —
morning soothes that cut
the lake's flawless image
of the fragile tent
whose pegs you pounded motionless.

Though you may try
through night to find me,
you won't overcome me
with your light naked hands.

I'll be here at the edge
of unknown water, back turned
to you and your belief in magic.
Still in the dark
throwing stone after stone away.

Christina Michelle Pease

HOWARD'S PLAY

1

9: 02 — Howard wipes sweat covered palms on his pant leg before picking up his briefcase. Sweat, rapid heartbeat, quivery stomach — after 23 years Howard still has the same symptoms every quarter. Why do I let them intimidate me? he asks himself.

Year after year, always the same — I walk in . . . 50 eyes staring at me. God. I hate being on a stage ! But they're not really looking at Howard. No. They only see a fat stomach in tight sweaty yellow armpit stained shirt. They see buttons straining, belly hanging out over stretched pants, fat pulling the pants in obscene wrinkles from groin outward. They see the soft fleshy underside of his chin hanging down, bobbing with each syllable. They see the glistening bead of sweat that slowly drips down his forehead and dangles distractingly at the end of his nose when it gets hot in the high school building in August. Even now they stare from classrooms as he passes, looking up at the heavy wump wump sound of his heels on tile.

Walking into the classroom the first time is the hardest. Why can't I look at them? he thinks. Howard knows they're disappointed that he's not one of those cute little part-timers, or at least a teacher who looks like he knows something. Maybe he doesn't look at them because after two decades he's seen enough of their sideways smirks and handcovered whispers to their neighbors.

Set briefcase down on desk, class roll in hand, turn around . . . and the shock of first eye contact. Howard peers at them through fleshy eyelids. How many blond shiny-haired cheerleader bitches this semester? They hate fat me the most. How many muscled, suntanned boy-men in tight jeans? Today, they are a nameless mass of faces. In eight weeks, they will still be strangers but Howard will recognize them. He will know the names of the smart-alecks, he will have evaluated their worth on a scale of five letters, and they will still hate him.

"I'm Mr. Felmann (squeaky scratching of chalk on board) I'm handing out your syllabus now. Please turn to the second page and blah blah blah . . ." Howard knows that's all they hear . . . blah blah blah. He tells them the same damn date fifteen thousand times, circles it, underlines it, flashes neon lights, and they still miss it on the test.

You didn't tell us you wanted us to know tha-at! whiney, complaining, accusing voices, pointing fingers at him. Carbon copies of the year before, and the year before and the year before. Brains screaming at him, accusing. Who told you that you know how to teach? If you were a good teacher we would've remembered that date. Howard's audience silently boos and hisses at him.

Howard hides behind his material. After 23 years he can spout it off flawlessly, while his brain is inside his kitchen at home probing through the cupboards looking for dinner. Blah blah blah and read Chapter 1 for tomorrow. Goodbye. The bell rings, shuffling feet and folders and books and Howard is alone again. He has to go through this hell again four more times before he can go home.

A young boy approaches his desk. Howard notices his faded jeans — not too tight, red Adidas shirt — stylishly big brand new hurt-the-eye white Nikes — probably bought them on sale at K-mart just for school, good complexion — olive, and curly black hair. But the eyes, Howard thinks, deep ocean blue eyes with those long up-curling lashes that the mothers always lament over because sister got born with short stubby ones.

Howard averts his eyes, self-conscious of this first personal encounter, when his class is no longer a bunch of strangers.

"Excuse me . . . Mr. Felmann?" the boy says. "Here. You didn't call my name." He timidly offers a green sheet of paper.

Howard takes the paper. *Adam Balsamo*, it says. Howard writes the name in his roll book.

"Thanks." Adam smiles as Howard hands back the paper. Howard notices Adam's white teeth. They never smile at me, most of them. He considers smiling back, just for a second. But instead he only nods in acknowledgement. And the Eyelash Boy walks out of the room. Adam . . . the Eyelash Boy, Howard thinks. I will remember that name.

Howard thinks about Adam as he sits in his living room drinking kamikazes after work. Blue eyes and white teeth. His students usually don' t smile.

The clear liquid burns his throat as he drinks it down. Liquid

fire burning away school, burning away 50 eyes . . . burning.
Adam is the Eyelash Boy.

Oh damn Adam! Howard thinks. Damn the others. He shoves
his glass down on the table. Howard hates these stupid dreams. He
knows that fat people aren't supposed to dream. Why do I keep
forgetting that? he asks himself. Just ask the cheerleaders. They'll
tell you. Hell, they'll probably sing-song it to you in one of their
cheers:

Fat People! Fat People!

They Can't Dream,

They Can't Do

Anything!! . . . YAAAAYYY!

Gimme an F!

Gimme an A!

Gimme a T!

Whadda Ya See?

FAT ! FAT ! FAT !

Squeezing through the doorways

Huffing up the stairs.

FAT ! FAT ! FAT ! ! !

Waving their purple pom poms . . . bouncing their shiny hair.
Shiny blond hair. Like Theresa had. Combing her long blond
shiny hair in the bathroom mirror. Little fat Howard reaching out
to touch. "Howard Felmann, don't you touch my hair! Auntie.
make fat Howey leave me alone!" Little Howard just wanted to
touch your hair, Sister. Little Howard just wanted you to love
him, Sister. He wanted something better than . . . but you were too
busy looking at yourself in the damn mirror to ever see Little
Howard, Fat Howard. He wanted to tell you about his dreams.
Sister, he's not fat in his dreams. Resa, don't you see, inside his
head he's one of those letter jacket football boys taking you away

in big cars after dinner. Running his stubby hand through your shiny blond hair. But it ends there, Resa. Nothing . . . wrong. He just wanted you to love him Sister, enough to listen to him, enough to believe him, enough to make Uncle leave him alone. But you didn't. And now the shiny blond hair disappears and Howard sees long hippy hair instead, hanging in grinning Uncle's face. *Don't tell anyone, Howie, this is our secret.* No, god, no. Howard remembers hot liquor breath on his young fat neck. But no. It is only Howard's breath now. Heavy and labored. And the grinning face becomes the Eyelash Boy with white teeth.

Damn it. Quit dreaming. He opens his eyes and notices his empty glass. He grunts as he pushes himself up from the old brown velour chair. Fat legs and stomach wiggle up and down as he walks over the worn orange shag carpet to the kitchen. Fat wiggles, shaking quickly back and forth with each step blobbing up and down like it wants to escape out from under his tight stretched skin. "Oh don't be deceived, my dear fat" — he likes to imagine himself as a skinny Howard standing on a stage, Fat Howard only some other character standing next to him looking stupid while the audience wildly applauds the skinny Howard. "Oh don't be deceived, my dear fat. I would loose you from your disgusting sweaty cage in a second," he recites to the fat Howard. "I would slice open this huge belly and scoop you out with a spoon — inch by yellow inch — till you lay in putrid steaming mounds on this dirty kitchen floor." Howard watches as the audience madly cheers.

Howard makes another kamikaze and grabs a bag of peanut butter cookies from the cupboard. He shoves a cookie in his mouth and washes it down with the burning liquid. Howard knows that he will gorge himself with cookies tonight until his stomach aches. Cram himself so full of them that his feces smell like peanut butter and he often wishes he could just crap out all his insides including his bleeding heart and be through with it.

II

Four weeks of the quarter are gone. Same as all the pitiful ones before. Hell at school, waiting for the bells to ring. Endless courses of food and liquor at home. Watching skinny big-booby girls strut around on TV. And godforsaken dreams that stab at his heart like gas cramps. He can feel his mind warring with his heart and he dreams those dreams that feed the cramps and fill him up with bitter acid every time. Dream, drink, eat. My god, Howard thinks, this could last for twenty more years.

Howard knows he must do something.

But for now he sits in his old velour chair so old that the velour is rubbed off in the fat shape of his body. He sits with naked feet propped up on a milk crate staring at the TV over his crooked toes. Some local commercial where a guy blows up his recliner in the middle of a field. Here comes this little bitch in a bikini; local commercials always use sex to sell their wares. They aren't smart enough to come up with anything original. Of course the bitch has long blond hair, my god, it's like these buffoons just run to embrace the stereotype. Stereotype Resa with long shiny blond hair and long legs running to meet her letter jacket white teeth stereotype at the front door.

Dreams of Adam consume Howard now. He smiles at Howard at school with his white teeth. Howard still can't smile back, just can't. But he waits for Adam's smiles, every day. "Every day, Adam," Howard thinks, "smile at me, please. With your white teeth and long eyelashes." Howard whispers Adam's name in the mornings when he shaves his fat face. "Adam is the Eyelash Boy." He doesn't even think about Sister so much anymore, doesn't even think about Uncle. Just blue-eyed dreams of Adam staying after class to talk to him again. Adam calling him at home. Dreaming Adam's voice: "Mr. Felmann, I'm sorry to bother you at home but . . . I need to talk to you. I know you will understand."

"Boy, please see through this fat," Howard begs, "don't you see that I am capable of love too?"

But if he ever did call, Howard knows it would probably just be, "Mr. Felmann, I need to know if I can turn my paper in on Friday . . . . Will that be okay?"

"Fine, just put it in my mailbox." Click. Twist that cramp in a little deeper.

Howard waits and waits. The longer he waits the more he hurts. The more he dreams the more he hurts. "My god, boy," Howard says to the blue eyed boy in the audience, "Don't you see that underneath all of this flesh-covered jello is a beating heart spewing out hot red blood just like yours? Suck out our beating knobs of flesh, Adam, and no one could tell them apart lying side by side on a blood smeared table." As the audience cheers, Howard looks down and sees with horror that he is standing naked on the stage. For one moment, he thinks that fat belly is his own.

Howard must do something.
He thinks he knows what it must be.

Howard grunts up out of the chair and wiggles to the bathroom. He reaches down to the shower knobs, turns on the water steaming hot and wiggles right in there. The hot water washes over his sweaty body, reddening all his miles of skin like he's some kind of obscene pink monster baby. Ah shower — the only place left where it is okay to be fat, okay to be naked. The steaming liquid surrounds his body, pulsating like mother's heartbeat, surrounding him with water, heat, and steam like a womb where he is innocent, ignorant, and content. He turns around and puts his fat round head under the water, letting the pulsing throb of the spray work into his mind, vibrating, soothing. He takes the green soap bar in hand and rubs it on his body, between the fat folds on his sides, down the fronts of his legs, hanging onto the shower door with one hand so he won't fall over. The steam rises up and he breathes it in deeply. Yes, Howard thinks he knows what it must be.

He turns off the water and opens the shower door and cool air rushes to meet his pink steaming flesh. He wiggles out of the shower, dripping on the floor. The towel is embarrassingly small against him. It won't even go halfway around. He rubs his steaming skin with the yellow stained towel and walks, wiggling, into the bedroom.

Howard puts on his biggest shirt — knit short sleeve with collar, dirt brown with green horizontal stripes. He pulls up his pants — brown denim, not so tight that they give the obscene crotch wrinkle effect. Shoes — half inch worn off bottom of the soles brown earth shoes. He combs his thin-on-top brown hair sideways. He is ready.

He tries to remember a name . . . *Stars*? The name of a bar he heard about . . . overheard about, really, from the other teachers in the lounge. They were laughing about it. "Full of queens," they said, "Fairyboys." Howard had wondered if they had meant for him to hear. Flipping through the phonebook, he finds it. Yes, he thinks, *Stars* is the name. He sees the address. I can find that, Howard thinks. Yes, it's not too far. This is what he must do.

He walks to the kitchen and his fat stubby fingers pick up his jangling keys. His fat hand reaches out to the front door. Reach for the stars, he thinks. But then he remembers "Fat Howey, leave Sister's hair alone!" And greasy Uncle reaching out to touch. No. Curly headed Eyelash Boy offering green paper — an offering of love, a name. Fat hand around doorknob turning. "I can do this, anyway."

But the same damn symptoms — rapid heartbeat, quivery stomach, sweaty palms. Okay, sit down. Howard thinks, this I can't do. But twenty more years of kamikazes? My god, thinks Howard, I've got to do something.

But this I can't do and the stars are falling. Fifty staring eyes every quarter are enough. So Howard gets up, grunts, wiggle wiggles to the cabinet and makes a kamikaze. He sits back down in the kitchen. The hot liquid burns as he sits with the jangling keys in his fat hand. He sits and waits. Waits for courage from somewhere he doesn't know where. He certainly never had any before, courage like the fat cowardly lion. But he must do something. So he waits. Waits, drinks, and dreams of long Curling Eyelashes and white teeth waiting for him at *Stars*.

III

9:00 — Last day of the quarter, finally. The students have no idea that Howard looks forward to it even more than they do. There is only one pain today, one regret, Eyelash Boy. Talk to me, Howard thinks. Smile at me, something, please. I won't be able to see you again.

Briefcase in hand, Howard wump wumps down the hall to class. Goodbye 50 eyes. Blah blah blah till the bell. Adam sits with white teeth and long eyelashes, third row back in the middle. Howard watches him.

Howard's audience is louder than usual today, with fevered excitement of the last day. Long-haired Dave Swingle in Levis and fist in air, singing one of those rock 'n' roll songs they listen to. Jenny Krismer, makeup and hairspray squeezed into short shorts, laughing seductively at Dave. Skinny little Keith Borman yelling at a friend in the hallway. But Howard doesn't care about them. They hate him. Only Eyelash Boy smiles.

Blah blah blah. Loud bell ringing and black curly hair looking down at folder closing on desk. Howard watches as Adam's faded jeans walk out the door forever. But there was something, yes, Howard thinks. Something. A glimmer of a promise, Howard thinks. Yes. An unspoken agreement.

Blah blah for four more hours until time to go home and once again Howard is sitting in velourless old chair drinking kamikazes. Waiting for the time to shower, dress, and sit in the kitchen by the door. Now it is a ritual, every night. Sitting by the door, jangling keys in fat hand, waiting. At first Howard thought he would really go. Sometimes he still thinks so. But sometimes just waiting is enough to keep the cramps from twisting, waiting for the courage, dreaming of unspoken promises, dreaming of Adam at *Stars*. Every night for eight weeks, waiting, drinking, eating, dreaming. Promises of Eyelash Boy waiting for him at the bar. "My dreams, Adam," Howard thinks, "I'm not fat in my dreams. Like me. Listen to my dreams. Smile at me, white teeth." Yes, sometimes just waiting is enough but now school is over and the cramps are twisting again. Howard must do something.

So he gets up, grunts, wiggle wiggles through his shower-womb routine. The rapid heartbeat starts early this time. Tonight is different, for the saving of the dreams. Howard knows what he must do. His dreams are calling louder than ever tonight. Calling him to *Stars*. Fat wiggles to the kitchen, jangles keys, and fat hand turns doorknob, really.

Fresh night air meets still steaming pink skin. The door is really open and Howard is walking outside. His heart is beating so furiously, creating this strange breathless feeling in his stomach. Outside, the road is blurry. A strange orange light covers everything. I'm really doing this, Howard thinks. Eyelash Boy, help me, give me courage.

Howard sees that tonight there is no one in the audience except Adam. Adam is smiling at him. "Look through this fat, boy," Howard dramatically gestures as he recites. "See this heart beating furiously in my chest. It is alive. It is human. It is capable of love. Eyelash Boy, put your hand around this throbbing heart and pull it next to your ear." Howard looks down and sees that he is still naked. He is almost sure now that the fat belly is his own. But he sees that in the audience Adam is smiling and so he continues. "Listen to my heart beating its mad song, spewing out hot blood throughout this fat body, floods of it covering the floor, staining your white-toothed curly head." Howard bows as Adam erupts with applause.

Then Howard sees it. So this is *Stars*, a small curbside bar, a crude handpainted sign with no lights, a neon Miller beer sign flickering timidly in the dark window. Two men are standing by the door, one tall with back hunched over, talking wildly with hands to short fat-bellied other.

Howard hears the Eyelash Boy calling him and he opens the car door. He wiggle wiggles out, and slowly walks wump wumping across the street. The tall hand-talking man stops and looks up. Howard nods once in acknowledgement. But Adam is waiting for him inside and the Fat Belly man steps aside as Howard opens the graffitied, gum covered, pissed-on wooden door.

Loud music and smoke surround Howard. He walks in, eyes adjusting to the dimness. He hasn't been in a bar in many years. But this is different. He searches the bar for blue eyes and curly black hair. He searches the smoky bitter faces that look up as he passes and then quickly resume conversation with lover or stranger. Men are sitting at tables, drinking, talking, touching each other. Some are kissing passionately and caressing. There is a small creaky dance floor on the opposite side with several male couples swaying in time to some loud rock song. *Ohh, love to love you babyyy. . . .* One short man with black hair greased back and a smiling face dances alone, swaying his hips back and forth to the music and flailing his arms around his body. He sways over to a young skinny man watching him and kisses him on the mouth.

Some men are sitting at the bar and there is Adam! Bobbing his curly black head up and down as he talks to a man sitting next to him. Howard quickly walks toward him, wump wump and wiggling between tables. Howard is breathing hard. Adam is here for me, he thinks. Eyelash Boy is really here!

But as Howard reaches Adam, he sees only a wrinkled old face with a cigarette dangling from thin lips. Howard stops, staring. The man sneers at Howard. "Hey there, Pudgeyboy, you lookin' for me?" he says over the loud music. Howard stands and stares, his fleshy eyelids wide and confused, heart thumping slower and failing. Sneerface gets bigger. Howard thinks this man must be trying to smile. "Hey, c'mere and let me sit on yer lap," Sneer yells over the drum beat of the music.

Howard backs away and Sneerface returns to his drink. Howard frantically searches the smoky air around him. He thinks everyone must be watching him but they are not. And he sits down at an empty table which is covered with sticky puddles of some spilled drink.

So Howard sits. Around him they talk and laugh and dance. And Howard sits alone. Adam is not here. Howard watches all of them laugh and touch and kiss. He realizes that he does not belong here. The booming music surrounds Howard but it does not touch him. It does not make his body sway like the smiling man on the dance floor. This is not how Howard imagined it would be. This is not like his dreams. It looks strange to see men kissing men.

A hand on Howard's shoulder and hot alcohol breath in his ear makes him jump, startled. "You wanna' drink?" It is Sneerface. He puts something in a tall glass in front of Howard on the table. Little bubbles shoot up from the bottom of the glass through the murky liquid like stars falling backwards. He scoots a chair next to Howard and sits down. "I'm Danny," he says and sneers bigger. His wrinkled hand with dirty fingernails flicks cigarette ashes onto the sticky table. "You smoke?" he offers his pack. Howard shakes his head no.

Danny Sneerface watches Howard. He doesn't look like Adam at all now. Skinny and wrinkled but not that old — middle forties probably. Faded blue jeans, worn tee shirt — too tight, with "Get Down at Helen's Lounge" written across the nipples. He leans closer. "Hey, Pudgeboy, I thought you looked lonely over here." Howard watches him but cannot say anything. "You gotta name?" Danny sneer-smiles bigger. His hand moves up Howard's leg very slowly.

Green disgust creeps up from Howard's stomach and fills his mouth with bitter spit. Sneerface turns into hippy Uncle's leering face with long greasy hair hanging down. Hand reaching out. *This is our secret, Howie.* And then Howard remembers. He remembers Resa's face that day when she found them. Her screeching pink mouth telling everyone. "Howard Felmann, you disgust me," spat her pink stereotype lips. Resa blamed him. How could she blame me? Sister, you could have saved me. But you hated me too. I do not forgive you, Sister.

Dirty fingernails creep up. "What's wrong?" Danny asks, "Can't you talk?"

What *is* wrong? Howard wonders. Isn't this what I wanted? What I always dreamed about? No. This is not the same. And Adam is not here. Adam is not waiting for me. Danny's hand is creeping up and green disgust threatens to vomit out of Howard's mouth all over Danny's sneering face. "It's okay," Danny says, "Fat boys are my favorite." He leans his face toward Howard.

Howard stands up quickly and Danny's sneer is replaced by a surprised "O" mouth. "I've got to go," Howard mumbles and wiggle wiggles quickly to the door and out into the fresh night air. "O" mouth stares stupidly after him.

The slimy wooden door slams on the beating music behind him and Howard breathes in the cool air. The retching feeling pushes up the bottom of his stomach. His hand reaches out to the wall and he leans over to drool on the sidewalk. Drool runs into a weedy crack and here come the peanut butter cookies. Cookie chunks erupt out of his lips and splatter onto the sidewalk and his earth shoes. The stink rises to Howard's burning face.

Howard rises, slowly. The Fat Belly man and Hunchback are gone now and the street is empty and silent. Howard slowly walks to his car and gets in. His heart is calm now, and quiet. His mind feels strangely clear and he drives down the road thinking, driving with no destination, just thinking.

Adam was not there. I will never see him again, Howard thinks. He grips the steering wheel tightly and forces himself to say out loud, "Adam will never be waiting for me at *Stars*." He looks at himself in the rearview mirror and silently adds, nobody ever will be. He looks out and sees that his theatre is empty now. And the something Howard must do is not what he thought it was.

Bruce Bond

BACH'S IDIOT SON

He plunks the fat string
on his father's gamba
and watches the sound
blur like a bee's wing:

how lucky to be alive,
to have slipped out somewhere
between stillbirth
and genius, to arrive

here in stubborn wonder
and neglect by a dry pot
in the winter-light.
In a near room, his father

plays the virginal — a ground
bass for the glory of God.
The music says that heaven exists.
The boy hears his own sound

vanish into his father's.
So too, the father's music
vanishes into the boy's:
his spoon and platter.

The clattering says that stars
listen: take me to the house
of doors and colors, lift me
over the carriage stair.

Lord give me talented sons,
the father thinks,
but then this is God's child,
the art of faith comes

easily to him. The father buries
himself in a broad chorale.
And all across Leipzig, the idiot
children are glad and needy.

MESSIAEN

The day he arrived at the stalag, he stood for hours
naked in the heat. Above him, the birds
braided their paths in a Moebius strip.

He'd never known such hunger. Keeping his watch,
the guards gave back his bag of scores: Schumann,
Bach — the dead, he thought, made flesh in song.

He told himself hunger would be his blessing. It vivified the world:
the night the aurora borealis unfurled, he saw the music he'd been
hearing. By flashlight, he bored

a hole through the core of night conceiving
a quartet for the end of time. Each note perched
on the fence of its clef, anxious to assume

the air. This was his dream. That he would pass
like sound through barbed gates into an abyss of birds.
As he wrote, the bones of his hand floated to the surface.

Edith Van Beek

WANTING THE LIGHT

If yellow is the colour
of madness
then bring on the flowers,
that rough cut flip-flop
yarn of the brush
yearning to the last seed
in a trial by flower
modeled on sun in swollen joy.

If yellow is the colour of madness
Van Gogh begs for light.
Tearing the sky down
he yells his years
in the burning blaze
of a yellowed star.

Thomas Kretz

QUMRAN COMMUNITY

Were ostracized, did not care;
lived alone in pottery jars
below a decent level of sea;

sneaked out like squirrels
to stretch and gather dates,
darting eyes, no woman dare

show her softness or sense;
backing down to their lair
awaiting the Righteous One

to trample down liberal sects
and elevate Essenes to where
aridity a preserving virtue.

One by one they suffocated
in their crockery leaving
scrolls of long grey hair.

Tatiana Tonks

(FROM "A STRANGER HOME")

27

What's left to say about mountains?
You know how they feel
misty cool and bluish in a morning
despite the sun flashing off snow caps
that never cease to startle.
There they are. You know the ones I mean.

Maybe I'll tell you instead about the glory
of clotheslines intersecting them everywhere from this angle
workshirts, old housedresses, grey t-shirts
wrinkled from wringing and flapping somewhat
desperately against their pins.

Or about square patchwork
hovels, corners sinking into mud
and women who trudge the paths between
cracked hands kneading the smalls
of their thick-set backs in anticipation
of still more time at the laundry tub
or perhaps waving impatient from his ragball gang
a skinny kid whose ready smile
converges in overlapping front teeth.

You may never have heard
remarked against a backdrop of mountains,
Was a good dog, that one, but got the rabies so l shot it.
Right here. Through the head.

You must know the mountains I mean, now.

Lawrence Mathews

WHY I HATE HER

Sometimes I almost forget why I hate her. Sometimes I think I really *have* forgotten. Then it all comes back. Mostly it has to do with the Lord.

Of course with her just about everything had to do with the Lord. I remember one time we were in a restaurant, and the waitress was really friendly and cheerful? So Cora says, "She's so happy, I bet she must know the Lord." As though there couldn't be any other reason to be happy? "You can see it in her eyes," Cora says. Then she looks at me and sort of nods sadly. I guess I still didn't have it in *my* eyes.

OK, I'll admit that doesn't sound like much of a reason to hate anyone. But it's symptomatic.

And she lied. Said Yes with her mouth and No with her actions. Like when I asked her to marry me, she said Yes, but I knew she meant No. Even though she let me kiss her on the lips, something the Lord usually didn't approve of. Even then, I knew.

Oh, and here's something else I just remembered. I haven't thought of this in years. She idolized Suzanne Pleshette. This was years ago, when Suzanne Pleshette was on the Bob Newhart show, the old Newhart show, and she'd watch every week, Cora would. She'd never laugh at anything Bob Newhart said, she'd just watch Suzanne Pleshette like she was in a trance. Not only that. Not only that. She'd *also* — and this really sickens me — she'd also check all the talk show schedules to see if Suzanne Pleshette was going to be on Johnny Carson or whatever, and then she'd stay up to watch, even though the Lord usually wanted her in bed by eleven.

For some reason it didn't matter that Suzanne Pleshette didn't seem to know the Lord particularly well. Cora got all uptight when I asked her about that.

Maybe she liked Suzanne Pleshette because they're both small and dark.

I myself have a sort of mild loathing for Suzanne Pleshette. But I'm getting off the point, which is why I hate Cora.

"If only you'd give your life to the Lord," she'd say. "Earl, please try it. It's not for me, it's for you. It's for your eternal salvation." And then we'd go through the whole business, the prayer and everything. I really tried, but it just never took somehow. Whatever was supposed to happen, it just never did.

Oh and speaking of prayer, here's another reason I hate her. She was into TM before she gave her life to the Lord, before I met her and everything. Once she was telling me about mantras, and how everybody has their own or whatever, and I asked her what hers was, and she told me, I've even forgotten what it was now, but anyways she told me, her point being that using a mantra was the same as praying to Satan. And then months later we were talking about TM again, and I happened to mention her mantra again, the word she'd told me, and she goes, "Oh, that was what I said my mantra was, but that wasn't it, really. I've never told you what the real word was, that's private."

Do you see why I hate her? Am I making myself clear? What she pretended to give, she wasn't really giving. She was that way about everything.

But I really did love her. Even now, sometimes when I'm alone I'll say her name out loud without meaning to. That's how bad it was.

Maybe she thought that if she agreed to marry me, I'd somehow automatically come to know the Lord. Maybe there was some sort of good intention somewhere in the back of her mind like that. I believe there was. As long as I kept going to her church, which I did regularly, she probably thought there was some kind of hope.

Anyway, we met in the spring, and by about July maybe she'd agreed to marry me, and then we started to fight about when. I said why not right away, and then she'd say that she knew it wasn't the Lord's plan or it wasn't in the Lord's will or some such. She said she felt the Lord was leading her to remain single for the time being. I said, when will the Lord be likely to stop leading her to be that way, and she said, Three years, probably.

And of course the Lord didn't want us to have sex before the wedding. That went without saying. I didn't mind that, though. That's how bad it was. All the Lord was up for was an occasional kiss, mouths closed of course. I'd say, "Couldn't the Lord cut the time down to two years or maybe a year and a half?" She'd get all upset. She'd go, "Maybe if you sincerely gave your life to the Lord, he'd reduce the time."

So I kept going with her to church, every Sunday evening. I

73

guess she was hoping it might infect me with whatever she had. We'd go out there with her roommate, Karen, who had a car. I haven't said anything about Karen, a gross pig of a woman. She and Cora did everything together. She was always going on about how wonderful Cora was while Cora sat there looking down modestly. It's amazing that this never pissed me off at the time.

Anyway, Cora and Karen and I would go to their church, a Pentecostal assembly in the south end. It was a nice new building that the Lord had given them, Cora said. Everybody out there looked happy, maybe a bit *too* happy. They all said "Praise the Lord" a lot, and they all looked kind of shiny. Even Cora looked shiny when she was with them.

So we'd go in and there'd be singing, and people would stand up and speak in tongues, and then someone else would interpret what the first person said, at least that's how Cora would explain it, but how would you know. The messages all seemed to be fairly standard stuff about how Jesus loved us and wanted us to draw closer to him and that sort of thing. And there'd be preaching — they had a woman preacher most of the time, but sometimes there'd be a guest speaker. And at the end there'd be an altar call, like Billy Graham does it on TV.

Cora never actually *told* me to go down front for the altar call, but I knew she wanted me to. I'm sure she believed it was for my own good and everything, but she was a bit too pointed in remarking about how many souls were being saved each week. "But we're all on different timetables," she'd say. "The Lord's time isn't our time."

But then she'd look at me kind of funny, as if to tell me that I was about three days late coming in on track twelve.

But that's not why I hate her. I hate her because I was ready to give my life to *her*, never mind Jesus. And she spat on it.

One Sunday that summer there was this Australian guest preacher, bouncing around all over the place. He thought pretty highly of himself, you could tell. He told us about his own conversion experience, what a sinner he'd been and so forth, and how dramatically his life had changed. People didn't have such powerful experiences anymore, he said. Then he told us that after that he'd given everything to the Lord, studied for the ministry, gave what little money he had to the church, and so on. "I didn't even have a car," he said. "I had to depend on my girlfriend for transportation." Lucky for him *she* wasn't moved to give everything to the Lord, I guess. Then he got into the sermon. I can't for the life of me remember a single thing he said in it.

But after the sermon — that was when the real action started. This guy was famous for his charismatic abilities. He wanted to give us all the opportunity to be slain in the Spirit, he said. What he did was walk up the aisles and put his hand on people's foreheads and say some kind of prayer, I guess, and they'd fall over backwards. Cora explained that they were so overcome by the power of the Holy Spirit that they passed out for a few seconds. Apparently this sort of thing happens a lot at other Pentecostal churches, but it was something of a novelty at Cora's.

Finally the Australian starts moving up our aisle, knocking people over left and right. Karen jumps up immediately and gets in line, but Cora just sits there. The Australian gets closer and closer, and I can tell Cora's getting a bit nervous. I would've laid odds she'd never been slain in the Spirit herself.

"This is probably too heavy for you," she says. I can tell she's looking for an excuse not to have to do it. Meanwhile Karen goes down for the count, all two tons of her, the people around her moaning softly and saying "Praise God" and mumbling away in tongues.

What the hell, I'm thinking. If she can do it, I can do it.

"I think I'll give it a try," I say, knowing it will piss Cora off and impress her at the same time.

"I'll wait in the foyer," she says and takes off.

So I get in line. The Australian has a sort of assembly line going. A couple of ushers stand behind the people he touches, to catch them and let them down gently to the floor. After a minute or two they get up again and walk away like nothing's happened. While this is going on, other people keep coming up to him and stuffing money in his pockets, which he ignores, apparently concentrating totally on knocking the next person over.

When he finally comes to me, I can tell it's not going to work. He's about three inches shorter than I am, and he's got really bad breath, which I get a full shot of as he lunges up at me, muttering something, probably in tongues. When he puts his hand on my forehead, I do feel something — a tingle, like a small electrical charge — in my forehead, just between my eyes. But that's it. I'm the first one who doesn't keel over. He looks at me suspiciously.

"You'll have to try harder," he says, and moves on. Just call me Avis, I guess.

Meanwhile Karen is charging back up the aisle grinning from ear to ear as though she'd just dived off the high board for the first time in her life. She'd want to tell Cora exactly what it was like before I could join them.

Later I say to Cora, "It didn't work."

And she goes, "I knew you weren't ready for it, Earl. But I didn't want to say anything."

One more reason to hate her in retrospect. At the time I thought maybe she really did know what she was talking about.

Then she went on to explain that it didn't work for me because you had to be born-again first, before any of the fancier charismatic stuff would kick in. And really, you needed to have a certain spiritual maturity along with it.

So I went, "How come you didn't try it then?" knowing full well it was because she didn't have the guts for one thing, and, two, she'd be as embarrassed as hell if she *did* fall over like her shiny friends. Beneath her dignity, and everything.

But you know what she says? She says, "Oh, Earl, you wouldn't understand. My relationship with the Lord is more — meditative. I don't need that sort of experience."

She had blue eyes, Cora did. There was poison in those eyes — strychnine, arsenic, cyanide, you name it, that's what those eyes were made of. Look at them and you'd disintegrate.

But I knew I'd impressed her with my willingness to be knocked over by the Australian. Maybe she thought I was on the brink of giving my life to the Lord. The next day she says, "I think it's time you met my parents."

Her parents live in this remote small town on the west coast of the Island. We could borrow Karen's car, she said, and leave Friday morning — neither of us was working at the time, so that was no problem — get the ferry to Nanaimo, and drive across the Island in the afternoon. We'd be there in time for dinner. We could come back on Sunday. We'd even be in time for church.

I was really excited. I thought this would be a big step in the right direction.

Friday didn't start off that well. Ten minutes after we get out of the harbour, she asks me to go and get some coffee. It takes me a while because the lineup is so long. When I get back to our seats, she's gone. My jacket is still on *my* seat, so I know I've found the right place, but all her stuff has vanished.

So I sit there for a while, thinking maybe she's gone to the washroom or something, but then enough time has gone by that it can't be that, so I get up and walk around, looking in all the different passenger areas, and out on the deck, and so on. No Cora.

I'm a bit worried at first, thinking of her falling overboard or whatever, mugged on the way to the washroom, but I know in my heart that whatever happened was her own doing. So I sit back down and read my book.

Just when they announce that we're five minutes from Nanaimo, Cora materializes, with a big smile. She'd been inspired to share the Lord with another woman, she said, a woman she'd met in the washroom. They'd gone back to the car for complete privacy, even though you're supposed to stay off the car deck during the trip — they'd managed to do it without anyone noticing, because it was the Lord's will.

"It's such a joy to witness," Cora says.

I believed her then. Today I think she probably spent the whole trip in the washroom, or maybe in the car. I don't know why she would've done this, but I think that's what she did. But then I believed her. I tried to sound as though I understood.

But she must have sensed something. She said, "You're not angry, are you, Earl?"

"Of course not," I said, lying through my teeth.

That's what love does to you.

After a while we're driving up the highway toward Campbell River, listening to a tape of Pastor Edith, the woman who preaches at Cora's church. The title of the sermon on the tape is "Married or Single?" When Cora puts it in, she says, "I think we should listen to this, Earl. The Lord might use it to speak to us."

Pastor Edith begins by saying that she's never been married herself, in fact at fifty-two she's still a virgin, so she can be pretty objective about the whole idea of marriage. She's searched the Scriptures pretty carefully on this topic, and her conclusion is that while marriage is good, being single, in the eyes of the Lord, is even better.

Marriage, Pastor Edith goes on, is for those whose love of the Lord is not quite as strong as it should be. The early believers, of course, expected the world to end at any moment, and saw no need for it. By the time of Paul, though, it looked as though the world was going to be around for a while, and somebody had to do the dirty work of producing children to keep the human race going until God decided to wipe out the planet for keeps. Which, of course, he might decide to do at any time. Didn't we all share the conviction that even now we're living in the last days?

"Amen," Cora goes, almost under her breath.

"We are?" I say. This was news to me.

She stops the tape.

"Don't be naive, Earl," she says. "You've heard Pastor Edith preach on this topic. Haven't the children of Israel returned to the Holy Land? Aren't the superpowers getting ready for nuclear wars, which has to be the battle of Armageddon? You know nothing of prophecy, Earl," she goes on. "There's the Book of Ezekiel, for example. The bear from the north will descend on Jerusalem. Bear, get it, the symbol of Russia, and how did Ezekiel know that back when he was writing unless the Lord told him? It's all there in the Bible, Earl, if only you'd allow it to speak to you."

So I say, "Where does that leave us as far as marriage is concerned?"

She smiles her little I-know-more-than-you-do smile and says, "Let's keep listening to Pastor Edith."

There are so many reasons to hate her.

Then Pastor Edith is explaining that marriage has its place, even in these last days when we're in all probability the last generation to inhabit the earth. "Better marry than burn," the apostle Paul said, and he knew what he was talking about. Burn in the fires of lust, which would soon enough become the fires of hell.

"Isn't this great?" Cora says, glancing over at me, blue eyes sparkling behind the glasses. "Pastor Edith is right on."

The sermon lasts quite a while, several tapes' worth. By the time Pastor Edith is finished, we're off the main highway and bouncing along one of the worst gravel roads I've ever seen. I offer to drive, but Cora won't let me. I think maybe she thinks that because it's Karen's car, I wouldn't mind damaging it, which, now that I think of it, isn't totally untrue.

And I can sense that she's sort of showing off for me, wanting to impress me with her driving skill, and I love her for that as I sit there, thinking how wonderful our life together is going to be, staring straight ahead, or pretending to, while actually peeking at her out of the corner of my eye, because I know how pissed off she'll get if I stare at her openly.

78

"Wake up, Earl," she goes. "We're here."

We're driving down a hill overlooking the town. Actually, the town is mostly the mill itself, as far as I can tell, with some houses on the hillside opposite to where we are. It's like a valley, with the mill at the bottom, and beyond the mill there's the ocean, or at least a sort of inlet which they call a chuck, Cora is explaining.

As we pass the baseball diamond she tells me that sometimes a bear would come down out of the woods, right behind the fence in centre field. She's getting really excited, showing the place off like this. The balloons attached to the wires over the water are there so that the planes won't hit the wires when they come down to land in the chuck. "We do have regularly scheduled flights," she says, very serious.

In about two minutes we're in the residential section — the place isn't very big at all — with the bigger places for management people down closer to the water, and the ordinary houses, as Cora calls them, for the working people, farther up the hill. These ordinary houses look pretty shacky to me, gray and weatherbeaten, and I ask her why these people don't keep their houses in decent shape, and she says, "I don't know," and then here we are at her parents' house, as gray and beaten-up as they come.

Neither of us says anything.

We go inside to meet her parents. Cora sort of shrugs as she introduces us, as if she's saying, "Well, here he is, here they are, it's the best I could do, take it or leave it." Her parents are small, like her, and older than I thought they'd be, in their mid-to-late fifties by the looks of things. Cora must've come along pretty late. It turns out her father is named Earl, too, something she hasn't mentioned before, and we all laugh about the coincidence, and after that her father shuts up and hardly says anything. But her mother never stops talking. She keeps firing questions at me, but she seems friendly enough. Cora just sits back and lets her go to it. In fact, she's acting a bit bored, staring out the window or down at the floor. Her dad is just sitting there, smiling, not saying a word.

After a while, two things dawn on me. One, Cora is a bit ashamed of her parents, maybe concerned that I'll think they're hicks or something, which is pretty rotten of her, but it makes me feel good anyway, to think that she cares what my opinion is. The second thing is that not once has the Lord crept into her mother's conversation. And Cora hasn't mentioned him since we got inside either. I'm wondering, can it be that her parents are normal? Maybe her mother and I can form some kind of alliance. Things are looking up.

At some point during dinner, Cora gets back into the conversation, and she and her mother start in on local gossip. I try to get Earl talking, but it doesn't work. When I ask him what his job at the mill is like, he says, "It's not too bad." "But what do you actually *do*?" I ask him. He looks at me as though I'm from another planet. "I work at the mill," he says, digging back into his mashed potatoes. After that we just sort of beam at each other while Cora finishes catching up on the news.

When it's over, Cora says, "Let's check out the nightlife," and we say goodnight to her parents and head out into the unknown. I have no idea what's coming. At first I don't say anything, and neither does she. Usually in situations like that she could always outwait me, so that I'd have to be the first to speak, and then she'd have the advantage. Now that I think of it, that *is* one of the reasons I hate her. She could sit forever without saying a word, must've inherited the ability from her father. Once I even timed us: twenty solid minutes staring at our coffee cups before I finally broke down and said, "Isn't this silly?" And she said, "What?" — pretending not to understand, and I knew I'd lost again.

So that's one of the reasons I hate her, but this time, this specific time leaving her parents' house, she's the first one to speak.

"Not what you expected?" she goes, and I feel a surge of love for her, of love and pity combined, and I want to say something that'll make her feel good but I can't think of the words, and all I say is, "I wasn't expecting anything in particular." But that seems to be OK.

"I want to show you what the Lord has delivered me from," she says. "We'll go to the tavern first, and then maybe the Legion. Just don't ever say a word about this to Karen."

At the tavern, she tells me they've had to replace the doors three times in the last five years, getting stronger ones each time, because of people kicking them down after closing time. If there's a fight, it'll almost certainly be millworkers versus fishermen. "We hope for the guys from the mill." When she's telling me this sort of thing, she keeps flashing her slightly lopsided grin that was one of the minor reasons I loved her, together with others so numerous it would make me sick to list them.

Then she orders four draft.

"I didn't know you did this sort of thing," I say.

She says, "There's a verse in Timothy about taking a little wine for your stomach. It's basically the same thing." And she flashes the grin again.

So we're sitting there not saying much, and then she says, "What do you think of the clientele?"

I look around. They look pretty ordinary — guys in their twenties and thirties mostly, the kind of guys who wear Caterpillar caps and work clothes.

"They seem like an ordinary bunch of guys who work in a mill," I say.

"Have you noticed how many of them keep looking over here?"

"No. Why? Do I look funny to them or something?"

"No, Earl, it's not you — it's *me*. Look around. Do you see another woman in here?"

I don't.

"Imagine what it was like growing up here. Unattached men outnumber unattached women about a hundred and fifty to one. And most of those hundred and fifty are sunk deeply into habits of serious daily sin. And here I was, almost the only girl in town."

I try to say something that sounds sympathetic.

"This town is Sodom and Gomorrah rolled into one," she says.

So I ask her how she got through it, what it was like for her, and then — I can hardly believe it — she *is* telling me about it. To go through childhood with a few close friends, and when you hit adolescence, to watch them start turning bad, one by one, and then to be sucked into it yourself. The worst, the most hurtful, was her friend Rick, the one she'd been closest to, closer even than boyfriend and girlfriend — Rick, who'd been the first one to discover drugs and now, she knows, is deeply into Satanism, though she prays for him daily. And Rick's mother, Velma, her high school English teacher, who was Cora's role model for a while, she too has turned out to be a disappointment, irredeemably hardened into worldliness.

"She'll probably show up here sooner or later," Cora says, starting her second draft.

And then Cora tells me more about growing up in this godforsaken place, and after a while Velma does show up, bringing a few of the guys along with her. Her husband, Jim, is too old to have a so-called good time, Cora will explain later, but Velma, a reasonably well-preserved forty-nine, is still a marketable commodity, if I know what she means.

Velma seems cheerful enough to me, even if she is hardened and worldly, and so do the guys she brings with her, guys who delight in telling outsiders stories of the mill, mostly involving mangled or severed limbs.

"So," Velma says at one point, "it's not true about you joining a convent."

"No," Cora says, as though she's not surprised to have the subject brought up.

"That's what we heard," Velma says. "Nobody would ask your parents about it, but that was the word, that you'd got religion and you were going into a convent."

"No," Cora says —and I'm expecting her to give Velma the *real* story, but she doesn't, she just says, "No, I'm going back to school in the fall. I'm going to be a teacher, like you."

"Like me," Velma says with some bitterness, and downs the rest of her draft. Then she excuses herself.

One of the guys is finishing a story. "Backed his goddamn pick-up right into the chuck," he's saying, and then everybody laughs, and Cora grins at me like we're spies or something, with our own secret ways of understanding things.

She leans over to me and says in a low voice, "How does it feel to be in Sodom and Gomorrah?"

None of this has anything to do with why I hate her.

Later we go back to her parents' house, and she makes coffee, and we talk for a long time, or she talks and I listen mainly. She tells me what it was like to go out on her first date when she was twelve with a guy from the mill who was twenty-six, and what it was like when she was fifteen to have another guy call from a pay phone saying he'd just slashed his wrists with a broken bottle because she'd refused to go to bed with him, and it turned out to be true, and how the first time she'd done acid, she and Rick had a vision of the whole mountainside going up in flame, and how she thought it was really happening no matter what he said to try to calm her down, and how later Rick wanted to get her involved in black magic, wanted to kill his own father as a sort of experiment with magic, and she knew it was wrong, and this was what had started her off in her search which ended with finding the Lord (or the Lord finding *her*, she says, is what it really was, not that he'd *lost* her exactly, but maybe one day I'll know what she means).

And the more she tells me, the more I feel this overpowering love for her, and we talk all night until the sun come up over the mountain, and we stand at the window together and watch the world start to get light. And then we kiss solemnly, and I feel completely peaceful.

That's why I hate her most of all.

R2847

TELEPHONE:
GERRARD 3251 (2 LINES)

TELEGRAPHIC ADDRESS:
FOYLIBRA, WESTCENT, LONDON.

W. & G. FOYLE LTD.,

DIRECTORS: W.A.FOYLE, G.S.FOYLE.

Books Purchased—
A single volume
to a Library.

Booksellers,
Second Hand and New.

Over a million
Volumes always in
stock.

121-125 CHARING CROSS ROAD,
LONDON, W.C.2.

Cheques and Postal Orders should be crossed and made payable to W. & G. FOYLE, Ltd.

29/9/-   1926

To The Rev C. Rigby   Ganton Vicarage
                                    Scarborough.

Hamslaw Social & Polit Ideas etc (7/6)		6	3
Postage			6
		6	9

Christopher Wiseman

GRANDFATHER, THE SOMME, AN INVOICE

1.

Machine-guns were the worst,
Sweeping the bare mud in arcs,
Though marching forward from the trenches,
Bayonets fixed, attracted everything
Else they had too. One massacre. Another
Massacre. Noise enough to kill.
And you there. But before the subaltern's
Whistle sent everyone over the top again,
A shell exploded in the trench, blowing
You like paper against the boards,
Ending the war for you.
And other things.

2.

I hold an invoice sent to you
Ten years after that, the date, everything,
Hand-written, copperplate, in pen.
I only found it recently in a book
Your daughter gave me.
An impressive heading:
29/9/26. W & G. Foyle, Limited.
Booksellers, second-hand and new.
121-5 Charing Cross Road.
Over a million volumes always in stock.
Telephone Gerrard 3251 (2 lines).
It looks good. Has kept its life well.
Survived.

3.

I try to understand this.
In five months starting July 1, 1916,
415,000 "British and Empire" soldiers were killed
At the Somme. More than 20,000 on the first day
Alone. Around 600,000 Germans. More than
Half a million others wounded. Over and over
They marched towards the wire and died
From trenches often knee-deep in mud and water.
A few tree-stumps, leafless.
Bodies floating in pools of old craters.
The dead laid in rows or buried where they were.
Only later the precise enormous cemeteries.
Five months, the Somme. A million dead.

4.

Men in their nineties on TV, remembering.
The screams, one said. Men screaming
And nobody could get to them.
Collecting the discs and paybooks of the dead,
Another remembered, carrying them in emptied sandbags.
Men crying like children, said the oldest.
Terrified, clawing at their faces, gone mad.
And they remembered writing home
On wet and muddy scraps of paper,
Singing "Wait Till the Sun Shines Nellie"
Before they went over the top again.
His friend's head blown off next to him
In the trench, said one, still grieving,
75 year old tears in his eyes.

5.

You comforted the dying, prayed
Over the dead and closed their eyes
Before that shell got you.
Your hands on all those faces. Blood. Dirt.
You held services before the battles

From your Communion set, silver vessels
In a battered carrying box. Wine. Wafers.
An old wooden folding table for an altar.
Rough bass voices roaring hymns
In the desolation of the mud-fields,
Trying to drown the guns.
The last time many of them would sing,
Would ever hear music.
"O God of Battles" was one prayer.
The broken landscape. Open mouths.
Screaming shells. Screaming men. Screams.
Wide desperate eyes. These never left you,
Gentle man.

6.

After all that, you hid deep
In the Yorkshire countryside, buried
Yourself in the small old peace of villages.
The country vicar. Safe now.
The Rev. E. Rigby, Ganton vicarage,
Ganton, nr. Scarborough, it says. Tells us
The book you sent for — *Hearnshaw,*
Social and Political Ideas.
Six and Threepence, postage sixpence.
Total Six and Ninepence. Clean dry paper.
Not cheap then, and I wonder
What ideas you were hoping to find,
To quiet your mind with, in that dark house
In the trees — oh yes, I've been to see it —
In the burble of pigeons, the song of thrushes.
Did living with that wound make you
Want to find out why people fight?
Did reading and thinking drown the screaming?
Find out what is just and politic?

7.

And one remembered a 17 year old
Wandering, sobbing, away from his trench.
They led him back then shot him.
(300 shot for desertion at the Somme.)
Did you have to be there at executions
To pray and comfort? Please not.
Most cracked up in the bombardments,
Day and night shelling up to a week.
Screamed. Went quiet. Wandered off like toddlers.
"Lack of Moral Fibre," the military called it.
Abnormal behaviour for a soldier.

8.

Telegraphic address Foylibra,
Westcent, London. Technology
Humanized by the Latin, not like those
Telegraphs in the killing fields.
And that huge shop a family concern —
Directors W. A. Foyle, G. S. Foyle —
Offering personal attention to customers,
As to a dying man in mud, reaching
For help, for anyone, for you.
Books purchased — a single volume
To a Library. One man in a shell-hole
Or scores of bodies laid in rows together.
Sorting bags full of paybooks.
Over a Million Volumes Always in Stock.
No invoice from the Somme, but you paid
With interest, on the installment plan.
It took years.

9.

I imagine you in Ganton vicarage,
All the bright birds whistling like bullets,
And you with this book, looking past the pages.
I imagine a shotgun blast by some local,
Blazing away at rooks, and you shaking.
I doubt if you told anyone the things you'd seen.
You lived quietly, your daughters say.

10.

Blood. Water. Screaming. Shell-holes. Gas. Death-sounds.
Five months of "the great offensive" underground
Or seeking cover. Five months. A million dead.
And at the end they'd won five miles of mud.

11.

Birds and bullets singing in your head,
Shells in trenches, in old village trees,
Bodies lying, uniformed or feathered,
Twitching in mud or soft grass,
And you trying to clear your dreams with Hearnshaw's
Social and Political Ideas,
Your dreams where living things kept falling
Down and calling for you. All the time,
In Ganton village or the Somme, calling for you.
Home, for months you wouldn't close the bedroom
Windows. Wouldn't be shut in.
Sometimes your wife had to sleep in her overcoat.
Your daughters remember.

12.

My Foyle's invoice this year is small, two colours,
Fashionably unpunctuated. Headline —
The World's Greatest Bookshop — less stylish
Than yours. A different world.
*This Bill Must Be Produced In The Event
Of Any Query Regarding Purchase.*
And the address is not the same now.
113-119 Charing Cross Road.
But they've multiplied, built up their strength.
Now it's a *Stock of Over Five Million Volumes*.
I paid nearly seven pounds for a paperback.
I was there, by chance, on the 75th anniversary
Of the second day of the Somme offensive,
The day they realised with disbelief
That fewer than half the 120,000 had returned
Unharmed to their trenches, the day they picked up
20,000 books.

13.

I hope the dying learned something from you,
If that is ever possible. I hope
You learned something from this dull red book,
Because each year, at your quiet gravestone,
Swept by a vicious wind straight from Europe,
I learn nothing. I reach out. Nothing.
Just the loss. Just the silent scream of loss.
A shell, a book, a long-dead wounded grandfather
Who never knew me.
Invoice number R2847.

Michael Holmes

AURAL HALLUCINATIONS/VIRAL FICTIONS

Clubbiness and nostalgia have sunk the avant-garde as
surely as bad writing, self-indulgence and the fear of
engaging content. Sanctimoniousness hasn't helped
either. The fact of "no party after the reading" — or at
least, none worth attending — is a symptom of decay.
Then there is writing for *effect*, affected writing. The
most common methods of cheating (cheapening) . . . are
inflation of the material and/or rendering the material
more violent than it deserves to be. Next down the line
comes the device of being winning, e.g., naughty, sensitive, cute or deliciously urbane. Add a hobby horse or
two and a generous helping of pieties, new and used;
shake briskly to the sound of axes grinding, and let stand
overnight. Come morning — *voilà!* Finally, and perhaps
most revolting, is the correct sentiment. When read aloud
with just the right timbre and rubato, preferably with
moist eyes, the effect can be similar to nerve gas.
 — August Kleinzahler, "The Skinny"

***

1 *(Dis-ease/Koodies)*

Words like a chemical assault. The *affect* has become all too familiar. It's beyond boredom or embarrassment. Beyond, even, frustration or chagrin. And telling it like it is means calling it a physical
response: the restlessness that stirs in your haunches and ties up
your shoulders and bowels. It's the gaping, sucking wound that
opens in your chest now, in this café, listening to this damned
interminable logorrhea. And you don't know how or when it
began. But the buzz and drone of this guy spilling his guts about
his divorce, his dead parents, his pets, his lover, or how the
Canadian landscape (mountains, prairies, rivers, cottage country,
etc.) is in essence a pathway to a true conversion experience, has

caused a blood clot to begin its long but inexorable migration from your sleeping buttocks. And it's there deep inside your brain now, pounding and tearing up the place, though you're much too young and polite to have a stroke here in public. So you smile into your drink and maybe smoke yourself through it. You let your mind wander over next year's Leafs roster. Or try to remember the name of the women in that show the big foreign company put on. The one about the guy who gets it in the end because he messed with the girl played by the director's sister. (You know, she was in that film you saw last week with what's his name.) Maybe even imagine the possibilities of all this boy-and-girl flesh. Better still, think about your own work, your own acumen. That's safe enough. (Times being what they are.) Hell, you can get as high and far away on the blue stench of meretriciousness as the next guy. Yeah, that's right, *your* prose is the good stuff: uncut, clean, and healthy. (See the suit? They'll get you that council grant for just a little shmooz.) So wait it out: every story's got a beginning, a middle, and an end.

The problem is that it's still not over. You've gathered all the wool you can to try and chase away the pain. But the last paragraph took just about a week off your life — at least a carton of Player's Filters worth of time. And there's no comfort in the fact that if this was a case of having ingested a little bad verse you'd know that it would likely be a mercifully short lyric flu. 'Cause at least when a poet senses the crowd's restlessness she can get out quick. There's a kind of artful dignity in escaping with a little spontaneous editing. So what if it's opaque? It's poetry ain't it? This here, however, is a creeping paroxysm: terminal prose.

Doc, you gotta help me. I've been exposed to the first chapter of Chester's new novel.

Mr. Smith, I'm afraid the X-ray tells no lies; you have the shadow of a malignant short story on your lung. I'm sorry. But there's nothing I can do. If only you had come to me sooner . . .

Prose worse than ptomaine. Worse than rotten verse. Kleinzahler is correct in his diagnosis:

> Variety and quality are not merely disappearing in the production and dissemination of poetry but throughout all of the arts and society. *Rambo V* and chickens pumped full of hormones and antibiotics are closely related to

Waldenbooks and the Iowa Workshop [and you can sub-
stitute any number of Canadian publishers and CW
encounter groups here]. They are symptoms of the same
disease, a disease resulting from profit's disconnectedness
from real production.

And though I don't want to conflate the specific maladies of
Canadian prose and poetry the escalation of the incidence of infection make a virtue of necessity. (Really, I reject the theory-driven
cop-out of talking about prose in terms of poetics because it's a
backhanded ploy to reduce poetry to a kinder and gentler form of
writing — one that is, like straightforward prose, easier to understand or "deal" with.) The reports from the pathologists and
researchers are perfectly clear: most prose carries an even more
insidious strain of the virus, a more deadly toxin, than poetry. It's
worse because the disease is better camouflaged. There's more room
to hide in a story or novel. Cheap language and clunky rhythms give
away a poem every time, but prose has a tendency to lull you into
letting down your guard: making the illusion of safe sense.
    A typical ploy of the infected story is to render the reader/vic-
tim insensate (usually with language, rhythms, ideas, and senti-
ments that are both innocuous and "easy on the ear") and then to
strike the central nervous system while the poor fool is defence-
less. Students in the *Megadeath* school of pyrotechnical prose,
however, favour a different but related approach. Using a dazzling array of $100 words, phrases, and effects to dizzying and
powerful extremes, these viral vortices blind you to all the smoke
and mirrors, leaving you incapable of understanding that in effect
you have read nothing at all. Then there are the "feel-good" psy-
che-killers, the ones that push all the right buttons: with the winning opening line and just a hint of "twist" to finish it all off.
They are usually cross-generational and tragically human. Only
the calf will survive the birth, or a good kid will buy it on the
backroads. ("It was late. And the tree came out of nowhere . . . ."
*Yeah, right. You put it there just so's he'd kick. C'mon, who do ya
think yer dealin' with?*) Some texts of this ilk have been known
to seduce perfectly sane and rational individuals. (*"Gee honey, I
wish you were as sensitive as the narrator in this book".*) Don't be
fooled. This kind of prose actually tries to convince you that its
good for you, like riboflavin. It plays on the mechanisms of fond

reminiscence, producing the same chemicals in the brain. But it's as addictive as crack, and might leave you just as obtuse. (Please, just say NO!)

What's clear is that the disease of bad writing, in its several strains, uses variations on the same formula to disseminate itself, preying on our general weakness, our lack of immunity.

And we're suckers for this virus.

Bad writing thrives because we let it. Bad prose especially.

Diseased poetry, at least, is sometimes publicly ridiculed. Poets get away with less in the dark.

Prose writers have got something akin to *carte blanche* with respect to our sensibilities. Why?

Ezra Pound's *ABC of Reading* gives you an out if you want it: "It is a waste of time to listen to people talking of things they have not understood sufficiently to perform . . . Had I written a dozen good novels I might presume . . ." (Ezra, you'd figure, was not a presumptuous man.) But resist the temptation: accept your responsibility as a reader, don't let it slide. So what if you haven't written anything better. And don't let their-finger pointing and Beckettian cries of "CRITIC" faze you; let 'em shake in their boots with rage or whatever — at least *that* might be original. As Wordsworth almost said: prose ain't that different from poetry, so don't treat it like a lonely, wandering sacred cow. Finally, when it makes you so ill that your hair hurts then fight back: and don't pull your punches. (Booing and hissing may not be polite but it sure is good for the ego.)

Still, all this harping on about a visceral response to *writing* seems a bit too canny. (Pause for a moment before taking the leap of faith that means calling this stuff literature.) But what else is (a) reading? The oral/aural phenomenon: putting words into your mouth, ears, or any other orifice that will accommodate them:

> *Junior! What in God's name are you doing?! You don't know where that's been! Filthy! Filthy! Filthy! You bad little boy! GERMS! BAD! BLECH!*
>
> *Grab a life, mum. Take a valium, pop. It's only an honourable mention in the X "Postcard Fiction Contest." A little reading won't kill me. Geesh! You'd think I'd just horked down some money or used gum or something.*

(Listen to yer parents kid. They'll save you miles of aggravation. Not to mention a visit or two to that psycho G. I. man; you know, the specialist with the eyes like Charles Manson, the one who enjoys looking into folks' guts for a living.)

So why not reinscribe the body from the start? Why not acknowledge desire in the physical engagement with the text? Reading ain't metaphysical — it's a bodily function, one that should be enjoyed. (Reading is very erotic.) *Jouissance*: "The pleasure of the text is that moment when my body pursues its own ideas — for my body does not have the same ideas I do" (Roland Barthes). It's your body that's becoming dis-eased, reading or listening to this crap.

Of course, something near the opposite should be said about relatively healthy prose: about how it too elicits a physical response. But not anything corny or vulgar like "It makes me feel happy" or "special" or "stimulated." 'Cause all good writing can do is kick you in the gut a little harder: like its diseased counterpart it should make you uncomfortable. Only instead of feeling sick you should be punch drunk with envy. It's like Jaromir Jagr and Juan Guzman. Or Charlie Sexton and Amanda Marshall. All youthful life and potential. It's the hollow throb inside that makes you wish you'd written *the Word*: that you were the one who embodied a little Being in language. (Yes, even Tom Stoppard: "Words. Words. They're all we have to go on.") We read to do someone, or something— at least ourselves — one better. Writing is about making the body . . . move . . . or feel . . . or do.

And remember, above all else, this is no fiction. What you're being subjected to is not semantics or make-believe. Your pleasure is *on the line*. (See Phyllis Webb's essay, "On the Line".) Reader/Writer: heal thyself.

Hey pal ! Listen! You, yeah you. The guy doubled over and turning blue. Or you, the woman choking to death on second-hand sentiment. You know this short story is killing you, so what're you going to do about it?

(They should put warning labels on these things. CANADIAN FICTION IS HAZARDOUS TO YOUR HEALTH. CANADIAN FICTION IS A MAJOR CAUSE OF HEART DISEASE. CANADIAN FICTION REDUCES LIFE EXPECTANCY.)

And if you're not doing it for you, think of Timmy. What about his poor little pink lungs?

Choose pleasure. (Make love, not prose.) And fer Christ's sake, try, like the lady says, to "X-press yer-self". You've got a body. And a voice. Use 'em.

2 *(Dis-embodied Voices)*

Apart from normal human language there is also a kind of *nerve-language* of which, as a rule, the healthy human being is not aware. In my opinion this is best understood when one thinks of the processes by which a person tries to imprint certain words in his memory in a definite order, as for instance a child learning a poem by heart which he is going to recite at school, or a priest a sermon he is going to deliver in Church. The words are *repeated silently* (as in a *silent prayer* to which the congregation is called from the pulpit), that is to say a human being causes his "nerves" to vibrate in the way which corresponds to the use of the words concerned, but the organs of speech (lips, tongue, teeth, etc.) are either not set in motion at all or only coincidentally.
— Daniel Paul Schreber, *Memoirs of My Nervous Illness*

Schreber, Freud's "gifted paranoiac," suffered from aural hallucinations. (He also believed that God was turning him into a woman, and that as a woman — after being raped by God — he would be impregnated by "divine rays to the end that a new race of men might be created.") He heard voices (is it that surprising that Schreber was a doctor of jurisprudence?) and most of them spoke in God's "basic language": "a somewhat antiquated but nevertheless powerful German, characterized particularly by a wealth of euphemisms (for instance, reward in the reverse sense for punishment, poison for food, juice for venom, unholy for holy, etc.)." Some were "nerves" or "*remnants of souls of human beings who had become blessed*" that "appeared . . . in the shape of *birds created by miracle*": they spouted "senseless phrases learnt by rote" and expressed "*in human sounds* the *genuine* feeling of wellbeing in the soul-voluptuousness of [his] body." As agents of either the Upper or Lower God, Ormuzd and Ariman, the "nerves" had a whale of a time.

But God's attraction to Schreber was also a threat to the world as we know it:

A *fundamental misunderstanding* obtained however, which has since run like a red thread through my entire life. It is based upon the fact *that, within the Order of the World, God did not really understand the living human being* and had no need to understand him, because, according to the Order of the World, He dealt only with corpses . . . . Thus began the *policy of vacillation* in which attempts to cure my nervous illness alternated with efforts to annihilate me as a human being who, because of his ever-increasing nervousness [and thus desirability], had become a danger to God Himself.

To combat this danger, God manifested another of His many "miracles" (for Schreber, everything from "bellowing" to "shitting" was a "miracle"). Through the "miracle" of the "writing-down-system" He hoped to be able to "withdraw" from "the power" of Schreber's "over-excited nerves": He would get "creatures" to write down everything His "nerves" or "rays" might desire to know about Schreber (everything about the essence of Schreber's being) so that Schreber himself would no longer be "necessary" or desirable. God's "absurd" mistake, however, was in believing that Schreber's "store of thoughts could be exhausted"; in his struggle to explain, through the very occurrence of language itself, the doctor demonstrates God's error:

That [the writing-down-system] exists is overwhelmingly proved to me day after day; yet it belongs even for me to the realm of the unfathomable because the objective it pursues must be recognized by all who know human nature as something in itself unattainable. It is obviously a stop-gap measure and it is difficult to decide whether it arises from a wrong (that is contrary to the Order of the World) intent or from faulty reasoning.

Books or other notes are kept in which for years have been *written-down* all my thoughts, all my phrases, all my necessaries, all the articles in my possession or around me, all persons with whom I come into contact, etc. I cannot say with certainty who does the writing down. As I cannot imagine God's omnipotence lacks all intelligence, I presume the writing down is done by creatures given human shape on distant celestial bodies after the manner of the fleeting-improvised-men, but lacking all intelligence; their hands are led automatically, as it were, by passing rays for the purpose of making them write down, so that later rays can again look at what has been written.

This passage, as language that is "written down," makes it clear that writing itself is always already an embodying of thought; in Schreber's terms, God does not recognize that writing is a self-perpetuating representation of the fact that "human thinking is inexhaustible ."

And thus, ironically, it's this "miracle" that's responsible for Schreber's *Memoirs of My Nervous Illness*: a more concretely textual kind of virgin Birth. God's "writing-down-system" fosters / fathers a phenomenological analogue: Schreber's text. The prose itself defies generic description (as in any good Sacred Book), but Schreber's "fiction" seems to be the perfect model for anyone with enough guts to write *through* the body, to make the(ir) word(s) flesh. (It's your body that *reads*, so why not let it *write* itself?) In fact, his *Memoirs* serve as a defence against the psychical *and* physical assault (launched by God and joined *in medias res* by Psychoanalysis) of being subjected to a "reading." That both God and Freud found it necessary to erase Schreber's body illustrates, again, its necessarily problematic status in the discourse of textuality, epistemology and ontology.

So, do you remember the haunting refrain from Terry Gilliam's *Brazil*?

"What have you done with his body."

Hey God! Hey Sigmund! Hey pal! You, the "author"! What have you done with Schreber's body?

To his body? *To* my body? *To* her body? *To* your own body? It's the question every writer should echo.

Yeah, OK. I know. What's this got to do with the future of rutabagas, right?

Why ask what happened to Schreber's body?

Well, there is a reason. It stems from a fascination with Freud as a writer. (He didn't win the Goethe Prize for nothing.) In particular with the curious simile he borrows to figure the essential "question" of what's called "The Schreber Case":

> In Schreber's system the two principle elements of his delusions (transformation into a woman and his favoured relation to God) are *linked* in his assumption of a feminine attitude towards God. It will be an unavoidable part of our task to show that there is an essential *genetic* relation between these two elements. Otherwise our attempts at elucidating Schreber's delusions will leave us in the absurd position described in Kant's famous simile in the *Critique of Pure Reason* — *we shall be like a man holding a sieve under a he-goat while some one else milks it* .

Hunh? What? Do *you* get it?

Freud the empiricist tells us that a failure to make the "genetic" connection which *will* shed light upon Schreber's "delusions" *will* leave him (and note the certainty here — he doesn't say "might"), the analyst, in an "absurd position". And yes, the position Freud the writer describes with Kant's simile *is* absurd. But why is it absurd? Well, of course, because you can't milk a he-goat. Still, something else is going on.

Why is the writerly flourish, the simile, not only necessary, but in fact central to, an analytical case study? Why resort to metaphor in what should be pure science?

Is it just me? Or does Freud seem afraid of being discovered in the even more ridiculous position of the milker's accomplice? I mean, trying to get blood from a stone is one thing, but helping someone else do it?

And what about the new heights of absurdity that are reached with the introduction of the assistant's milking "prop" — the sieve? I, at any rate, wonder what this ludicrous toady hopes to filter out of the imaginary milk. (Meaning perhaps?)

Finally, who the hell would Freud be working with on the Schreber case anyway? Who is he helping?

Not Jung. Not Rank.

What about Schreber?

Yes. Daniel Paul Schreber. *Der Fall Schreber*. Doctor Schreber, the writer.

It can only be Schreber, the "gifted paranoic" whose "details of delusional structure" sound remarkably like the "endopsychic perceptions of the processes whose existence" Freud "*assumed* . . . as the *basis* of [the] explanation of paranoia."

If Freud fails to prove "an essential genetic relation" between Schreber's "transformation into a woman and his favoured relation to God" (if his analytical *assumptions* are unfounded and the hallucinations are not "linked in [an] assumption of a feminine attitude towards God"), then he becomes as absurd, as delusioned, as "crazy," as Schreber.

This way madness lies.

In his "Otherwise" we discover what Freud and psychoanalysis has *invested* (as always, note the *economics* of writing through the body; Lyotard: "to work out the code of signs *for power* . . . the important thing is the *final return*") in the diagnosis and explanation of paranoia: the definition of sanity itself. By safely defining the other as paranoid we can be comfortable in our own mental "health". There is but a fine line, a fragile rubric, a *scarlet thread*, between Schreber and his accomplices — Freud, Lacan . . . etc.

What have you done with his body?

Well, we put the damned he-goat milking nutbar as far out of sight and mind as possible. And we did it because we don't like to be reminded that he isn't so different, that he really is human — the same, in effect, as us . . . As Freud himself writes at the end of his (somewhat paranoid?) attempt to establish the analytic priority (or originality) of his theory of the "processes" of paranoia: "It remains for the future to decide whether there is more delusion in my theory than I should like to admit, or whether there is more truth in Schreber's delusion than other people are as yet to believe."

The fact is, to write the body you have to be as deluded as Schreber. Crazy? Like a fox. At least you should be. (Most writers deserve the reprobation of Mike Muir from *Suicidal Tendencies*: "You wouldn't know what crazy was if Charles Manson was eating fruit loops on your front porch.")

Schreber "heard things" and translated them viscerally. His writing was an em-body-ing of the voices; their words would "sound" in his "mind's ear" just as with his "mind's eye" he would "see the rays . . . as long drawn out filaments approaching [his] head from some vast distant spot on the horizon."

Everything, again, is *on the line*.

And yes, the filaments and voices are made both linear and physical in the synaesthesia of the "writing-down-system." All senses become one in the translation of perception (through the body) into writing. It's like the voices told Schreber: *All nonsense cancels itself out*:

> There is no subject in the claws of desire,
> but God's eye a period,
> this watching, listening
> to the sentence closing.
> The damned automatic closing.
> Those voluptuous clause closing.
>
> (Chris D'Iorio, "Scriptorium")

3 *(Dear John: Anonymity)*

"the piano's voice is such a happy horse"
— John Barlow, "Blessing"

***

He writes: "Maybe you're having some sort of spiritual baby." And I wonder. (Asking myself: what have I done with my body?)

It's a letter from Barlow, the physicality of his paraph actually, that makes me recognize the implications of Schreber's deconstruction, his self performing exegesis upon the textual body. The flourish of John's signature, always shattering the lie of presence. (It's the writing, not him. I've got his words, but he is *not* here.) His *now*, in Vancouver, is almost three hours ago Toronto time. And every word of every poem, story and missive he sends my way attacks the illusion of comfort, flux, and health. John, like Benjamin's "angel of history": "Where we perceive a chain of events, he sees one single catastrophe which keeps piling wreckage upon wreckage." And he puts his body in the thick of it.

He doesn't just look at it. He sees it. He doesn't just hear it. He listens to it: "when i am sleeping it is this pragmatic sound / of mystery / that unravels my forty lips . . . and / sets my ears / to speaking" ("Blessing").

Barlow's language is taut, sinewy. Every verb pulses. Each word kicks at time. And the written page is a bloodsheet. It's what Kleinzahler calls "honest writing." A writing that engages "the matter at hand in all of its nuance and complexity, or plainness," writing that never "bails out until the last possible instant." His is the voice that emerges from the white noise, clear and menacing: "From this machine to your one reality, I am the jackknife in the box . . ." (John Barlow, "Nearbottom"). But again, it's the writing, not him.

In this letter John returns to our ongoing exploration of the limits of language writing. (*To boldly go*: like Data and Worf.) But the point of the debate is lost in my fascination with the words: "To relinquish objectivity, logic, order, presumption, in favour of kaos, the undermining of language, the refinding of the old self of no self at all, animal mind, alien language systems, alien politics, alien world, that is our world, never to be trusted again, tv, hegemony, you know the gig, mind-stretching." And still I wonder. What have I done with my body? How did John discover Schreber's insight? Mind-stretching. A language writing the body.

What do I write? How does the body respond? Hearing things.

***

Dearest John: I have just finished reading the "Congratulations" page (page 7) of the winter 1991 issue of *Grain*. It's purpose is to congratulate the "winners" of the "Short Grain Contest."

It was very well written, for the most part. But what is "short grain"?

(I'm afraid I won't get past this page.)

Tell me: how does one get to judge the merits of "short grain?" Is there a school? Are there field trips? Can I go? And exactly what will it cost me? I am, needless to say, flummoxed: busting with questions. My belly hurts.

So you can imagine my consternation when I stumbled upon the third paragraph: "As in previous years, *all entries were judged anonymously*. Both judges remarked on the high quality of the entries."

What does this mean? Judged anonymously? When is an entry anything else? Unless "short grain" is a euphemism for some kind of archaic beauty pageant, then the entry has to be anonymous.

And if this contest is about judging fiction then are they trying to tell me that the author is "present" in the entry? I ask you: Is the writer standing there, saying, "Hi! It's me!"? How *does* one fit into an envelope that gets mailed to Saskatchewan? And wouldn't it be a hell of a lot of postage? I'm sorry, but I just can't figure out the purpose of this disclaimer. Are they afraid that the "judges" will be swayed if they are able to attach a name to the writing? Am I my paraph? Does the fiction change if you can decode or authenticate the signature? Really? If this is true then the judges are incompetent. (Impeach them, no?)

Is this kind of paranoia healthy?

Or is it that the *judges* are anonymous? This possibility makes a little more sense. Maybe you're not allowed to submit your "short grain" if you know them. Still, how would the fact of knowing them change what they thought of your writing? Is it necessary to legislate critical honesty?

It shouldn't be, at any rate. But we've all heard the stories . . . .

A judge, it seems, has an identity that might require anonymity. The same cannot be said for a piece of fiction: it can run, but it can't hide. The whole point of writing is that it can't be anonymous: it is what it is, not who you are. It's just there, in all its complexity or whatever. Buck naked. And loving it. But still the ambiguity plagues me. What have myths like origin and presence got to do with "short grain"?

Contests are a symptom of decay.

Contest rules are what happens when cousins marry.

That writers are following these rules is a sure sign of imminent apocalypse.

Derrida: "(. . . Such a missive therefore had to be signed. Which I did, and counterfeit here. Where? There. J.D.)"

Yer servant.

Micaleh (signature Event Context).

***

Fiction: feigning, imagining. And hallucinations. Aural and visual. (Perceiving what's not there at a glance.) Paranoia: writing the logic of fiction, writing all of the fiction at hand. Discovering what "healthy" folks won't see or feel or hear.

Bad writing won't accept this. Bad writers don't go far enough into the hallucination. They "bail out" too soon. They try to create a fiction to fill up the spaces where they don't perceive anything.

Putting your body *on the line* is always a terrifying prospect. If you don't lose everything then you have nothing at all.

A few writers come right out and tell you this, they dare you to see it. Writers like Barlow. And Alice Munro. Consider what she writes about Almeda Joynt Roth: "The countryside that she has written about in her poems actually takes diligence and determination to see" ("Meneseteung"). Putting your body on the line is risky, one hell of an investment .

No one said it was going to be easy.

It took Thom Gunn almost 15 years to write his poem "Saturday Night." 15 years before its forty or so lines sounded "right." (It works out to about 25 words a year, check and you'll see.)

OK, for some this must seem a bit extreme. But isn't it good advice? I mean, doesn't it seem fair that a prose writer at least take an extra week or so before calling it quits? Ask yourself, at least once, about the language. Is this the way things were? Is this honestly how the delusion went? Can I live with this?

What will the fiction do with the body?

If it's good, almost anything.

4 (Body Language: A Sixth Sense)

It should be lke Armundo's whistle. Always cutting its own tune.

In the west end of Toronto, Armundo is the guy next door with the bandsaw that never sleeps. He's somewhere between 50 and 100 with a house of his own and a 40 by 25 slab of lead-salted terra firma. He's got a garden, but no English.

Broken hockey sticks, the old waterbed mattress, the pipe the city dug up: nothing goes to waste. The wheezing doesn't stop him: neither does an ungodly hour. He's all smiles and single-mindedness, waiting for a break in the heavy weather. For Armundo it's about one vision: making something grow. And come fall he's got enough wine to get him through a mind full of February nights.

Armundo is language like Mark Richard's fiction: the thick stew of a Cajun-Creole-French descent. Richard's words like a knock-out blow, always searching out something to eviscerate:

In Indian, this place is called Where Lightning Takes Tall Walks. I figure that to be about right. What happens here is this is the first landfall those water-heavy thunder-heads make when they quick-boil up from across the bay. Long-legged stretches of bonewhite light come kicking through the treetops of the tallest shortleaf pines, ripping limbs and splitting crowns. When they leave past, your ears are ringing from the thundershots and there is the smell about of electric-seared sap. It is a heart-racer to have happen around you in the day, and at night you still have coming to you the cracking hiss and branching swish in the whole dark of crowns falling so heavy unseen and so close they push air past your face and the ground bounces you up on your toes.

— Mark Richard, "Her Favourite story"

No, it isn't easy. What might be the stuff of fiction — in a storm, for example — is hard to see: the language of *the story* is born in a hallucination. And it's not about the delusion that's not there, just the one that is: you've got to look hard to separate the wheat from the chaff, to find the right words to make it so.

For Richard it's the words that make the lightning walk. And not the other way around.

A body can sense this. Sniff it out.

One of the best examples of this kind of remarkably acute perception can be found in Michael Ondaatje's *The Collected Works of Billy The Kid*. Billy, in the "Mistuh . . . Patrick . . . Garrett! ! !" story, puts the Chisums' cat out of its snake-bitten misery. But this, for both the reader and Garrett alike, is simply the circumstance of an occasion of greater significance: the important thing is not the killing, but the way Billy does it. Billy writes, reads and kills through the body, using all of his senses:

He stood up and took off his boots and socks, went to his room, returned, he had washed his hands. He asked us to go into the living room and sit still. Then he changed his mind and asked us to go out of the house and onto the verandah and keep still and quiet, not to talk. He began to walk over the kitchen floor, the living room area, almost bent in two, his face about a foot from the pine floorboards. He had his gun out now. And for about half an hour he walked around like this, *sniffing* away it seemed to me. Twice he stopped in the same place but continued on. He went all over the house. Finally he came back to a spot near the sofa in the living room. We could see him through the window, all of us. Billy bent quietly onto his knees and *sniffed* carefully at the two square feet of floor. He *listened* for a while, then *sniffed* again. Then he fired twice into the floorboards. Jumped up and walked out to us. He's dead now Sallie, don't worry.

— Ondaatje, *Billy The Kid* (emphasis mine)

Patiently and methodically stalking his prey, Billy is the consummate writer: never giving up until he's reached the heart of the matter. He removes all distractions and then zeroes in for the kill. Again, this can never be easy. And yes, Ondaatje makes sure that we recognize the horribly brutal aspect of Billy's skill: the threat of sexual violence that hangs over the end of the story is both disgusting and arresting. That Billy's ability is at the same time both attractive and repulsive is the point that Garrett *almost* makes; and it's what Billy's girlfriend, Angie, obviously knows: he's able to kill the cat because he *sniffs* it out. His senses are so keen that he can *smell* a silently cowering *pussy* through the floor-boards. Clearly, Angie understands that Billy will always be able to sniff her out too; he'll never forget, or lose, *her* scent:

> Our faces must have been interesting to see then. John and Sallie were thankful, almost proud of him. I had a look I suppose of incredible admiration for him too. But when I looked at Angie, leaning against the rail of the verandah, her face was terrified. Simply terrified.

What he has done with the body is sublime: both beautiful and terrifying.

And the fact is we can all find ourselves capable of something just as sinister: there's a very fine line between having a vegetarian *for dinner* and *having a vegetarian* for dinner.

It's what your body can write if you're willing.

You can find it there (the story), in the hallucination (in the fiction of fiction), if you've got enough guts to both look and listen *and also* to see and hear. It's what August Kleinzahler describes in his poem

"Disappointment," the "voice you had let yourself believe was dead." And it whispers to you, always:

close now by your ear, intimate and sweet:

Well, well, well,
look what we have here.

— Kleinzahler, "Disappointment"

Reviews

Don McKay, *Night Field*
McClelland & Stewart, 1991.

The nature poetry that was for so long associated with Canadian writing is not really gone. In spite of the ridicule it once drew from Modernists, the blissful vision of Lampman and company is still with us, only now it is filtered through our own politically charged and highly urban atmosphere. Such zen-like East Coast writers as Allan Cooper and Leigh Faulkner have obvious links to the old 19th century writers who haunted the Tantramar Marsh, but it's also possible to look at someone like Christopher Dewdney as a nature poet. In his case, nature quite comfortably includes cosmology, fossils, and human consciousness.

We're talking about attitude really, not form or style. There is an understanding shared by all such poets that what matters is our relationship to the real or natural world, and that this relationship is endlessly exciting and complex. If we hadn't already had such a tradition, someone would have called this eco-poetry and proclaimed its importance in saving the world. As it is, it's what we do and what we've always done.

All of which is a roundabout way of introducing Don McKay, a poet who writes sophisticated poems about birdwatching, hiking, his dog Luke, and a lot of other things. His poetry approaches the world sensitively and casually, "tipped to the oblique." His frame of reference is wide, his ideas are deep, but what he seems to enjoy most is seeing — really seeing.

A walk through McKay's latest book, *Night Field*, is like a walk through the forest with an experienced woodsman, someone who can read every sign and misses nothing, someone who can tell you about every flower and every cloud. He doesn't rub it in of course, although sometimes you get the feeling that he could if he wanted to. Instead he's a thoroughly human companion, his muscles complaining under the canoe's weight, his manner sometimes revealing a sad knowledge of life's mistakes.

The book contains poems like "Meditation On A Geode", a

geode being the kind of hollow rock you see in gift stores, cut in half with purple crystals winking from the inside. McKay takes some delight in explaining how these strange stones are formed and I enjoyed the tale. He also brings ovaries, halos, the void and potato salad into the poem, making lots of energy and stretching the reader considerably. A nice bang for your buck.

Then there are other poems where the tension is flattened and stretched like a canvas ready for painting. Those are the more sombre poems where pain and mortality intrude, then refuse to leave. In the title poem there is a painting of a field at night and, in a corner, what the author perceives as a bit of straw. His mother, who is seriously ill with heart disease, sees instead a monster, a death's head. The painting itself doesn't look different to McKay after that, but whenever he sees it he can't help thinking about what others see.

Night Field is a strong and evocative book. It's not as dramatic and different as *Sanding Down This Rocking Chair on a Windy Night*. In fact the newer book is a kind of lyrical extension of the previous one. Nevertheless the poems show McKay at the top of his craft and his book is far more engaging than many others that have been published. He is not always interesting, nor always profound, but he combines the two often enough to make his poetry lively and rewarding.

Eric Folsom

Clarity Between Clouds, Susan Ioannou
Goose Lane Editions, 1991.

Beyond the Lighthouse, Winona Baker
Oolichan Books, 1992.

Clarity Between Clouds is subtitled "Poems of Midlife," and *Beyond the Lighthouse*, too, is written from the perspective of middle age. But there the similarity ends. Whereas Ioannou's poems are as amorphous as the clouds invoked in her title, Baker's are terse and concise, shaped by her numerous allusions and sharpened by her satiric wit.

Ioannou's third book of poetry is written in three parts. Many of the poems of Part I, "Rimming the Dark," are set abroad where scenes are observed from a distance, often from behind closed windows. In "Pink & Indigo," the poet/speaker and her companion are momentarily secure in the unfamiliarity of their café surroundings, "watch the world pass" and "love the darkness for that reason." Similarly, in "Across the Piazza" and "Dusk, Highway Seventeen," the poet is characteristically cloistered and detached.

Throughout Part I the poet is insulated by a sort of buffer zone, like the fog which envelops her literally in the final poem of the first section, "Boardwalk, Early Morning":

Walking through heavy fog
we see no forward
no back
only now, here
immobilized in a white dream.

Characters consequently wander aimlessly, devoid of purpose and direction. Children depart and leave mothers at home to ponder their futile existence, husbands abandon their wives to feelings of loneliness and longing. The landscape of these poems is colourless, or at best monochromatic; the mood is meditative and melancholy. Poems are characterized by boredom and indecision, and they embody unacknowledged or inarticulate suffering, if they enunciate anything at all.

In this first section the clouds of the book's title are omnipresent. But unfortunately the collection never gives way to the clarity that the title also promises. The argument is obscure, and connections between sections are difficult to ascertain. Nevertheless, there is some movement. From the fear and uncertainty of "Rimming the Dark," there is a gesture towards peace and acceptance in Parts II and III.

This shift is manifested in the colour and grace of "Domestic Artistry," as well as in the domestic images of the following dramatic monologue:

"Now silence glows in this space between flowers,
the pull of trees leafing
the empty whiteness of plates.

Orange juice is my sun in a little glass
the blue napkin's silver ring
a piston that moves the sky to spread
across the lazy horizon's lap."

("Convalescent")

Overall, however, the poems of the final two sections — "The
Black Speck" (which is death, and momentarily we think that
Ioannou is sounding the depths and finding her bearings), and
"Dawn Snow" — are marred by clichés and diminished by tired
phrases. The image, "Poised on a poinsettia point, / our spirits twin-
kle", for example, and the similes, "happy as slop pails" and
"plump as an organ pipe David gurgles" are so uninspired and
imprecise as to jar on at least this reader's poetic sensibility.

While *Clarity Between Clouds* suggests that we are blinded by
choices and should instead accept what comes our way, Ioannou's
poetic rendering of that idea is neither particularly elegant nor clear.

Winona Baker's third volume of poetry, *Beyond the Lighthouse*, is
loosely organized around the west coast landscape which has been
her home for over forty years. It is an eclectic collection, incorpo-
rating haiku (for which Baker has won international acclaim), feminist, traditional and humorous poems.

The poems both surprise and delight, imbued as many of them are
with a rebellious spirit akin to that of the fifteenth-century English
poet John Skelton, whom Baker quotes in an epigraph to her collection. Baker's irreverence travels far afield but focuses particularly on
romance and tradition. (After all, there is so much to counteract in
the mythology of love, the tyranny of the masters.) In her sonnet
"Listen Willy" she challenges Wordsworth: "You say nuns fret not,
but of course they do," Baker retorts; she criticizes da Vinci in "On
Mona's Smile":

I know what brought
that expression to her face
during one of her sittings
Leo said, "You know Mona
you're very intelligent
for a woman"

Baker's biting humour is just as likely to be turned against herself, however, as it is in "When I'm Perfect" and "Getting the Picture": "If he took my picture / he might / cut my head off / It appears / I haven't been using it," the poet notes wryly.

The love lyric comes under particular scrutiny. Baker ponders whether there is a place for it, since romantic love, as she presents it in "Swimming Toward an Island," "Considering Yeats," and "Young Girls Dream of Love," no longer seems possible. Nevertheless, in "Time for Roses," Baker considers salvaging the love song and transplanting it into her own poetic landscape.

Several poems record the brutality of modern existence; others trace the vicissitudes of life and caution us to enjoy ourselves while we can because "You know / you can't stay forever".

Even in poems as complex and difficult as "Woman in Winter," Baker assures accessibility through her concrete imagery, through her use of the ordinary and everyday. Yet the commonplace is elevated and transformed through her carefully crafted forms, her meticulous language. In addition, the many allusions (to poets and painters, astronauts and friends, TV shows and current events) resonate through Baker's poems to create a multiplicity of meaning.

In one of several poems on poetry, Baker says,

> I would like to write a poem the way
> swimmers who've
> tied a rope beneath the bridge
> swing over the river and
> at just the right time
> let go

I, for one, don't doubt that she has succeeded.

Tara Kainer

Cousins, Paulette Jiles
Alfred A. Knopf, 1992.

Property, Marc Diamond
Coach House, 1992.

So what's a poet who makes her home in Nelson, B.C. — with gusts up to the Arctic Circle — doing wandering around Texas, Missouri, Tennessee and points south in an RV vehicle? Well, the simple answer is that she's looking for her first cousins, hence the title. There are some twenty-eight of them, radiating out from the ancestral home base of Poplar Bluff, a town in the southeast corner of Missouri. And, of course, Jiles, as an expatriate, is also looking for her own roots, i.e. herself. But don't write this off as just another "searching-for-myself-as-the-sensitive poet" piece — or even another *Roots*.

There are at least four separate yet intertwined overlays to *Cousins*: the basic interviews with the cousins and aunts and uncles; Jiles' own rocky romance with a married Texas cattleman who accompanies her on the odyssey; the attempt to come to terms with the lack of love she feels for her dead father; and the meta-fictional dialogue she sets up with the reader.

Jiles' balancing act among these overlays gives the book much of its unique focus — and its driving force. We don't so much learn second-hand about the Jiles family as find ourselves right in the middle of the discovery — with all the struggle and pain that entails. It's as if, rather than being handed some dogfaded portraits, we were magically transported to the moment when they were being taken. And, because of this, we're given a multiple viewpoint: the key personalities as seen from various generational perspectives.

For example, the book starts with Jiles' memories of her father after he returned from World War Two. Jiles remembers him as always being in a state of rage, much of it fuelled by alcohol, as a man who wanted things done his way — or no way. Yet, during the interviews with some of her cousin, Jiles discovers another side of her father: a man who always had a joke to tell, debonair, witty, self-assured and attractive.

Of course, this isn't always the case. There are times when the interviews start to take on a sameness — how many times, for example, does one have to be told about Grandpa Jiles' phenomenal ability with numbers? But Jiles manages more often than not to keep the caravan moving — if not with memories of her own childhood then with descriptions of life on the road with Jim Johnson, her cowboy-Vietnam-War-vet lover.

The descriptions — of the past, of the trip, of the cousins — are extrememly vivid, full of precision (as befits a poet), and with the resonance of a truth that goes beyond the mere facts (as befits a storyteller). And, when she's not doing any of these things, Jiles raises the entire project onto a different level: she talks to the reader about how difficult it was to put the book together and how some of the people felt about the prospect of seeing their lives in print.

Cousins is the kind of work that marks a watershed in an author's life. There's a definite sense of one thing ending and another beginning. From this point of view, it'll be interesting to see what Jiles' next book will be like. I'm betting that she won't be able to return to writing the kind of poems she herself says are "about walking on seashores and how I look down at my slim white feet and have Big Thoughts."

That's the price you pay when you decide to dig so thoroughly into the past. That past may make you more solid and fixed, may show you the steps you took to get where you are now. But the future suddenly becomes murky and uncertain.

Marc Diamond's *Property* isn t so much a novel as a book-long diatribe on the twin evils of family and ownership. It's both an attack and a cry from the heart, both a meditation and a plea for individuals everywhere to stand their ground in the face of technology and its all-pervasive intrusions into privacy. It equates family with death, disease and decay; and property with stagnation, containment and the inability to escape from the chains of mortgages and upkeep. Diamond also makes the linkage between family and madness, the self-destructive, suicidal tendencies that these types of relationships engender.

Now, there's little that's obviously new in all this. Attacks on the perils of family and property have made the rounds in literature since at least the time of *Oedipus*. They probably reached their greatest expression in Dostoevski. What makes *Property* intriguing is the monologue form Diamond uses to get his message across. It is sharp, witty, funny, and in places startling, what used to be called a tour de force. It catches your breath after the first sentence and then holds it at that level all the way to the end.

It all starts with a letter that arrives at the Vancouver home of the main character with "the sound of a gloved hand striking a face." It's a letter from his hometown of London, Ontario, the place from which he hopes to escape, the place where the rest of his family still lives — at least those who haven't committed suicide or been run over by cars. More specifically, it's a letter from the next-door neighbor of the house where his mother should be living — although she isn't. The main character has "lost her" in one of the many psychiatric hospitals in London, Ontario. The letter requests that the main character clean up the grounds of the house (which house actually belongs to the main character).

Diamond uses the monologue to weave in many of the ills of modern society: from the intrusiveness of phones to the blandness of the mass media; from the repression of women (and their retreat into madness at least in his mother's case) to the choking, all-embracing tentacles of business (in the shape of his "brilliant cousin" who tries to swindle him). In the midst of it all, Diamond manages to give us some extremely sharp character sketches: the monologist himself as a neurotic paranoid who has trouble dealing with both animate and inanimate objects; his mother who manipulates others around her and uses them until they're no longer useful; the "brilliant cousin" who could have been a nuclear physicist but instead chose to go into jewelry and real estate.

What Diamond does best, however, is to force the reader to make the connection between family, property and evil. For most, this is hard to swallow. We usually tend to remember family with nostalgia and the memories grow fonder as the years go by. But Diamond isn't attacking particular families: it's the concept of family in the late 20th century that disturbs him. And, when seen in that light, the family can be insidious. Diamond is particularly nasty when the main character describes the family at his brother s funeral:

"I looked at them and realized that they were all fat, some were obscenely fat, so fat that they could barely waddle out of their cars after the service, they were so fat as a group that their bodies threatened to burst out of their clothes spill over the folding chairs and spread great globules of puddled fat over the entire funeral home."

If there's one problem — or uncertainty — hanging over *Property*, it's the ending. In it, Diamond re-asserts the rights and dreams and strengths of the individual, what he calls the "I will go on" powers granted to every human being. That's fine. The trouble, however, is that it may have been this very set of assertions that led us to the dilemma in which we find ourselves. We have here the age-old battle between individual and collective rights, the same battle that has vitiated so much of modern life. Of course, Diamond makes it all very funny — and it is, in a blackly "ha ha" way.

But that doesn't answer the question. By siding so strongly with the individual, Diamond misses part of the point: in order for humans to have any chance of survival, some form of re-integration is needed; a new definition of family-property must be found. Diamond's hilarious monologue goes a long way towards making us see the fundamental flaws; it doesn't go far enough to bring us a new vision.

Michael Mirolla

Contributors

David Alder has worked as a gardener, a journalist, and in the book trade, and has published poetry in various British magazines. He lives in Manchester, England.

Bruce Bond now lives in Texas, after a year-long stint teaching at Wilfred Laurier University in Waterloo. He has published three books of poetry, most recently *The Anteroom of Paradise*, which won the Colladay Award from the *Quarterly Review of Literature.*

Judith Cowan is a writer and translator living in Trois-Riviéres, Québec. Her translation of Gérald Godin's *L'ange exterminé* has recently appeared under the title *Exterminated Angel* (Guernica), and her story "By the Big River", published in *Quarry* 40/3, was republished in *The Journey Prize Anthology 4.*

Eric Folsom is an associate editor of *Quarry* and editor of the Kingston literary magazine *Next Exit.*

Leonard Gasparini recently moved to New Orleans from Vancouver. He writes poetry for children as well as for adults.

Elisabeth Harvor is a sessional lecturer with the Division of Humanities at York University in Toronto. *Fortress of Chairs*, her first poetry collection, was published recently by Véhicule.

Michael Holmes is co-editor of the Toronto literary magazine *Sin Over Tan*. His first collection of poetry, *got no flag at all*, has just been published by ECW Press.

Tara Kainer is an associate editor of *Quarry*. She has written reviews and essays for various Kingston and Ottawa publications, including *Between the Lines.*

Thomas Kretz, SJ, currently lives in Rome, writing poetry, fiction, essays, and book reviews, and working on a major historical study of the Jesuit Brothers. His most recent poetry collection was *Sifting Every Spadeful* (Gregorian Press, Rome, 1989).

Janet Madsen is the box office manager of the Grand Theatre in Kingston. Her poems have appeared in various Canadian magazines, including *Poetry Canada* and *Proem.*

Linda Manning lives in Cobourg, Ontario, and makes annual pilgrimages back to her prairie birthplace. Her popular children's book *Animal Hours* (Oxford, 1990) will be followed in 1993 by *Dinosaur Days* (Stoddart).

Lawrence Mathews is a St. John's writer whose fiction has appeared most recently in *Grain* and *The Fiddlehead*.

Michael Mirolla lives in Guelph, Ontario. He has published one collection of short stories, *The Formal Logic of Emotion*; a story from his recently-finished second collection was published in *The Journey Prize Anthology 4*.

Kathryn Morris is studying Philosophy at King's College in Halifax. Last year she was Assistant Captain and leading goal-scorer for the Dalhousie University Women's Ice-Hockey team, but plans this year to devote herself to her poetry.

Christina Michelle Pease lives and writes in Cape Girardeau, Missouri.

Matthew Remski lives in Toronto, studies Theology, and hosts and produces the poetry radio program "Invoking the Muse" on CIUT 89.5 fm.

Eleonore Schönmaier lives in Ketch Harbour, Nova Scotia. Her fiction and poetry have appeared recently, or are forthcoming, in *The New Quarterly*, *Prairie Fire*, *Pottersfield Portfolio*, and *The Antigonish Review*.

Fred Stenson is a Calgary writer. His books include the novels *Last One Home* and *Lonesome Hero* and the 1990 short story collection *Working Without a Laugh Track*.

Tatiana Tonks was born in Chile but has lived in Canada since 1974. Since her recent graduation from the University of Toronto she has been working part-time and writing — for children as well as adults.

Edith Van Beek is the author of two books of poetry, *My Side of Fruit* and *Points of White*. She lives in Orangeville, Ontario.

Christopher Wiseman teaches English Literature and Creative Writing at the University of Calgary. He has published six books of poetry, the most recent being *Postcards Home: Poems New and Selected* and *Missing Persons*, both of which won the Alberta Poetry Prize.

Quarry

is pleased to congratulate

Judith Cowan

author of

By the Big River

and

L. Rex Kay

author of

Travelling

who were chosen for the 1992 edition of

The Journey Prize Anthology
The Best Short Fiction from Canada's Literary Journals

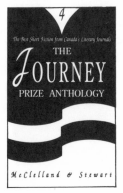

Published by
McClelland
& Stewart

Available in
fine bookstores
everywhere

POETRY

David Alder	Linda Manning
Bruce Bond	Kathryn Morris
Leonard Gasparini	Matthew Remski
Elisabeth Harvor	Eleonore Schönmaier
Thomas Kretz	Tatiana Tonks
Janet Madsen	Edith Van Beek
Christopher Wiseman	

FICTION

Judith Cowan	Christina Michelle Pease
Lawrence Mathews	Fred Stenson

ESSAY

Michael Holmes

REVIEWS

$5.95

17002

04

7 72006 17002 4

19293